# CONT

## MISCELLANEOUS HELPS

***Messages on the Lord's Supper***

# PREFACE

During my service of ordination to the ministry, Dr. Cal Guy quoted the words of Jesus to Peter: "Feed my lambs"; "Feed my sheep"; "Feed my sheep." He then summarized by saying that this does not mean "warmed-over mutton three times a day." He emphasized that one must not only study the Bible and pray, but also love and know the needs of the sheep if he is to feed them.

As a seminary student, I was introduced to the books of Andrew W. Blackwood, professor of homiletics at Princeton. His book *Planning a Year's Pulpit Work* made a significant impact on my thinking as I began to give serious consideration to the task of being a "feeder of the sheep" over which the Good Shepherd had made me an undershepherd.

It dawned upon my mind that the Holy Spirit did not have to wait until Friday night or even Saturday night to impress upon my heart what the Lord intended for the sheep to receive on Sunday. As this truth became a conviction, I became convinced that the sheep would probably receive a greater variety and much better quality of messages if the "shepherd" did some looking ahead rather than just waiting for the agonizing "inspiration of the hour" that might not come on Saturday night.

A prayerfully prepared program of preaching helped to organize my study habits and made significant some events, articles, or truths that otherwise would have escaped my notice. It is easier to accumulate fresh illustrations when one has a good idea of what he or she will be speaking on for the next few weeks.

With a planned program of preaching, it is possible to have greater assurance that the specific spiritual needs of the congregation are being met. Dr. J. B. Weatherspoon taught that every sermon should have one central aim and that the aim is determined after a need has been discovered and defined. As pastors get better acquainted with their congregations by personal visitation and counseling, and as they study the conditions in their communities with an awareness of the world conditions that affect us all, there is no limit to the spiritual and moral needs that they should seek to meet. As good mothers work to provide balanced diets for their families, good pastors should give careful attention to the spiritual diets they are "dishing out" to their congregations Sunday after Sunday.

Each sermon a pastor preaches should be born out of a personal experience with God as he or she seeks to meet the needs of the congregation. These abbreviated manuscripts and outlines are only to be used as a guide. If the manuscripts in this volume can be of assistance, we will thank the Father and rejoice in each pastor being a better undershepherd of the Great Shepherd who encouraged us to feed his sheep.

*—T. T. Crabtree*
*Springfield, Missouri*

## SUGGESTED PREACHING PROGRAM FOR

# JANUARY

### ■ Sunday Mornings

Four of the seven sayings of the suffering Savior provide the texts for this month's messages. The messages are intended to help listeners better understand and appreciate what God has done for us through the death of Christ on the cross for our sins.

### ■ Sunday Evenings

The Ten Commandments are the topics of the Sunday evening sermons this month.

### ■ Wednesday Evenings

"Prayers That We Sing" is our theme for Wednesday evenings. Some of our finest hymns are prayers in poetic form. Four hymns have been selected for use during the month. The hymn that a sermon is based on should be sung at both the beginning and conclusion of the message.

---

## SUNDAY MORNING, JANUARY 4

***Title:*** The Suffering Savior's Concern for Sinners

***Text:*** "Father, forgive them; for they know not what they do" **(Luke 23:34)**.

***Scripture Reading:*** Luke 23:32–38

***Hymns:*** "Wonderful, Wonderful Jesus," Russell

"Christ Receiveth Sinful Men," Neumeister

"Though Your Sins Be as Scarlet," Crosby

***Offertory Prayer:*** Heavenly Father, we pray that you would open our eyes and help us to see the grace and the graciousness of your gift to us through Jesus Christ. As you have given your best for us, even so today we offer our best to you. Help us to bring the firstfruits of both our love and our labor to the altar of worship. May your blessing be on these tithes and offerings. Bless not only the gifts but the givers. Through Jesus Christ our Lord. Amen.

#### Introduction

Luke records one of the turning points in Jesus' life: "When the time was come that he should be received up, he stedfastly set his face to go to Jerusalem" (9:51). We should steadfastly set our faces toward the cross that we might appreciate what Christ accomplished and what God offers to those who trust in his salvation. Charles Spurgeon said, "A view of Christ on Calvary is always beneficial to a Christian."

Repeatedly, we need to go to Calvary where God so loved the world that he gave his only begotten Son. We need to go to Calvary where Christ was wounded for our transgressions and bruised for our iniquities. We need to go to Calvary and by inspired imagination behold him bearing our own sins in his body on the cross. We need to go to Calvary to be overwhelmed with the tremendous truth that God has commended his love toward us in that while we were yet sinners Christ died for the ungodly.

There were great crowds on Calvary that day when the sinless, stainless, spotless Lamb of God was crucified. Some of the onlookers were indifferent, but also in the crowd were the triumphant, self-righteous Jewish leaders who bitterly resented Jesus because he did not fit into their plans for a nationalistic and materialistic messiah. The brutal Roman soldiers were there as well, unconcerned about the sufferings of him whose agony of soul for sin far exceeded the physical anguish of death by crucifixion. Further back were the distressed and desolate loved ones of Jesus whose hearts were indescribably crushed by this shameful catastrophe.

If we had been there that day on Calvary, we would have seen and heard many things that needed interpretation if we were to relate ourselves properly to him who died on the center cross. For example, listening sympathetically to the cries of those who were dying on the crosses would help us to learn more about Jesus. He had said on one occasion, "Out of the overflow of the heart the mouth speaks" (Matt. 12:34 NIV). The words that fall from our lips are photographs, to some extent, of the mind from which they come. The words of Jesus spoken from the cross present to us a photograph of his heart's concern for sinners.

It is highly possible that Jesus' plea for forgiveness for those who were in charge of the crucifixion helped bring about the change in attitude of one of the thieves who was also being crucified. Matthew's gospel records that at first both of the thieves railed upon him and mocked him (Matt. 27:38–44). Something happened to cause one of them to acknowledge that he was receiving the due reward of his deeds, and there arose from his heart a plea for merciful consideration once Jesus entered his kingdom (Luke 23:40–42). Possibly his curses and insults were changed into a prayer for mercy as he heard Christ pray, "Father, forgive them; for they know not what they do" (Luke 23:34).

### I. The desperate need for forgiveness.

"Father, forgive them." It was beyond the power of those who had a hand in Jesus' crucifixion to comprehend fully the enormity of their sin. They could not possibly recognize, at this time, how greatly they needed the forgiveness of God.

A. *Judas, the betrayer, needed forgiveness.*

B. *The Jewish leaders, who in proud, prejudiced self-righteousness were gloating in success over Christ's death, needed forgiveness.*

C. *Herod, the puppet king who considered Jesus as a worker of magic and who requested the performance of a miracle, was in need of forgiveness.*

D. *Pilate, the conniving, cowardly politician who had delivered an innocent man into the hands of a malicious mob needed forgiveness.*

E. *The cruel Roman soldiers who, in total indifference to his sufferings, gambled for his robe while he suffered indescribable agony needed forgiveness.*

F. *The milling mob who came by to curse and revile and taunt the suffering Savior was greatly in need of forgiveness.*

G. *The disciples who, in fear for their lives, had fled during the night because of their personal peril needed forgiveness.*

H. *All of us stand in need of forgiveness, for all of us are sinners.* We have broken God's holy law. We have fallen short not only of the divine standard but of our own human standard and ideal. Honesty would require of each of us that we admit, "I am a sinner and in need of forgiveness."

## II. The meaning of forgiveness.

A. *Perhaps Jesus was interceding to hold back the wrath of God upon those who were unjustly crucifying an innocent man.*

B. *Perhaps Jesus was praying for them to have a full opportunity to repent and to experience the cleansing of forgiveness.*

C. *To experience forgiveness is to have an indictment based on personal guilt removed and canceled.*

D. *To be forgiven is to have a warm relationship restored that has been broken because of sin.*

E. *In the parable of the prodigal son, which in reality is the parable of the waiting father, Jesus exhibits the meaning of forgiveness.* It is to receive the wayward son home with a welcome. It is to hold his sin against him no longer. It is to restore a warm relationship.

Jesus was concerned about sin to the extent that he was eager to forgive those who had driven the spikes into his hands and feet.

## III. The consequences of forgiveness.

In the midst of his indescribable sufferings, the Savior was expressing the hope and the prayer that his crucifiers might experience the joy of forgiveness.

A. *To be forgiven is to enjoy the love of the Father's heart and home (Luke 15:20).* The father in Jesus' parable had eagerly awaited the day with loving compassion when his wayward son would come to his senses and forsake the way of life that disappoints and brings destruction.

B. *To be forgiven is to experience the prestige of divine sonship.* "But the father said to his servants, Bring forth the best robe, and put it on him; and put a ring on his hand, and shoes on his feet" (Luke 15:22).

To recognize the consequences of divine forgiveness is to understand why David rejoiced and praised God for the assurance of forgiveness following his confession of sin (Ps. 103:1–3).

### IV. Conditions for receiving forgiveness.

Luke's gospel, which alone records this prayer of intercession for forgiveness, majors on the offer of forgiveness through repentance toward God and faith toward the Lord Jesus Christ.

A. *Repentance is necessary for one to enjoy the blessings of forgiveness.* God is eager for people to receive forgiveness, as the Savior's prayer on the cross indicates. Jesus insisted, as had John the Baptist, that people must repent or perish (Luke 13:3, 5). Before people will repent, they must recognize that they are sinners in need of forgiveness. The scribes and Pharisees were guilty of believing that they had already received the favor of God and had no need of repentance. In irony Jesus had said to them, "I came not to call the righteous, but sinners to repentance" (5:32). In the parable of the waiting father, Jesus emphasizes that there is more rejoicing in heaven over one sinner who repents than over ninety-nine righteous persons who feel no need for forgiveness (15:7, 10).

B. *Faith is necessary for one to receive the consequences of forgiveness.* When four friends brought a paralyzed man through the crowd to the Great Healer, his first reaction when he saw the combined faith of the five was to say, "Friend, your sins are forgiven" (Luke 5:20 NIV). The faith of their hearts, which he detected in their eyes and which they had proven by their efforts, made it possible for him to bestow the blessing of forgiveness on the man who was looking to him alone in his time of need.

   It was the faith of the prostitute in the forgiving grace of God through Jesus Christ that made it possible for her to receive the gift of forgiveness (Luke 7:50). Because of the blessed benefits of forgiveness, she had within her heart an immeasurable love for the Savior that manifested itself in a lavish display of gratitude (Luke 7:44–47).

C. *Genuine repentance and saving faith are two inseparable sides of one coin.* They are so inseparable that at times the call to conversion comes in the form of a challenge to repent. In other instances, it is an invitation to trust. Genuine repentance and saving faith—the two parts of the human response to the good news of God's love—are as inseparable as a man and his shadow in the brightness of the sun at noon.

### Conclusion

In the midst of his awful agony on the cross, the suffering Savior manifested God's concern for sinners by praying for his crucifiers. Do you qualify to be included among those who receive the benefits of forgiveness? Have you sinned? Are you willing to admit it? Are you sorry for it? Listen to this prayer from the cross, believe that he loves you in spite of your sin, and come for forgiveness now.

## SUNDAY EVENING, JANUARY 4

***Title:*** First Place Belongs to God

***Text:*** "I am the LORD thy God, which hath brought thee out of the land of Egypt, out of the house of bondage. Thou shalt have no other gods before me" **(Exod. 20:2–3)**.

### Introduction

The Ten Commandments are the cornerstone upon which Western civilization has built its house. When men ignore or defy these ten principles, the house begins to totter. The Ten Commandments are not ten statements from an arbitrary and capricious God; they are a revelation of the religious and moral attitudes and practices that are absolutely necessary if life is to be worthwhile.

The law of gravity is basic to life on the earth. There is no way by which humankind can do away with this law. So it is with the Ten Commandments. They are as necessary for a wholesome society as the law of gravity is to our physical universe.

The Ten Commandments are divided into two sections: The first four have to do with a person's relationship and duty to God, and the remaining six have to do with a person's attitude toward and relationship to fellow humans.

Duty to God stands first and lays the needful foundations for the right discharge of our duties to others. The love of God is the foundation of all love to our fellows. Neglect the duties of piety, and you will soon neglect your duties to your neighbors.

### I. The first commandment declares the authority of God.

A. *People have a tendency to reject the authority of God.* People are inclined to substitute the authority of their own personal whims or the authority of tradition or the authority of fleeting fads and fashions for the authority of God.

B. *God's authority is based on three great principles:*

1. The principle of creation (Ps. 19). We are his property: he owes us nothing, and we owe him all. He has the right to rule. No loyalty that conflicts with one's loyalty to God can ever be legitimate.
2. The principle of redemption. In the Old Testament, God redeemed his people from bondage in Israel. In the New Testament, he sent his Son Jesus Christ to redeem people of all ages from their sin.
3. The principle of providence. As the children of Israel journeyed through the wilderness toward the Promised Land, God adequately provided for their needs, even supernaturally supplying manna every morning. Today the God who feeds the sparrows and clothes the lilies of the field continues to provide for those who both work and put their faith in him (Matt. 6:26–30). Our loyalty to our God should be absolutely unmixed and unshared.

**II. The first commandment reveals God's purpose of grace.**

A. *This commandment is not the demand of a cruel, divine tyrant who is insistent upon having his selfish way in the world.*

B. *In this unequivocal demand for first place in people's love and loyalty, God is revealing the most fundamental truth of the universe: all false gods disappoint.* To worship a false god is to bring disaster into one's life that is not only self-destructive but destructive to others. God is here saying that to permit any other god to have first place is to experience disappointment in the end.

C. *If life is to have maximum meaning and fullness of joy, it must be lived according to the instructions of its Creator.* For a person to buy a product and neglect to read the instructions concerning how to assemble it would be foolish. Very likely the product wouldn't function properly if at all. For a person to buy a cake mix and then ignore the package instructions would most likely result in a kitchen catastrophe. In the first commandment, God is laying claim to the fact that he is our Creator, and therefore our lives should be lived in relation to him and to his will.

**III. The first and greatest commandment recognizes a person's spiritual capacity.**

A. *People were made to be worshiping creatures.* People are made in the image of God.

B. *Every person has a shrine where he or she worships.*

C. *A false god may be at the center of life.* False gods rush into the heart when a vacuum is created by shutting out the true God.

D. *When a man or woman dethrones the true God, that person often deifies self.* He gives first place to his own whims and wants. Lust replaces love. Greed supplants generosity. Time becomes all important and eternity of no significance.

If people lack a constant awareness of the true God, they are in danger of sinking into subhumanity, for if they do not see life as belonging to the true God, they will live as if they belong to a false god.

**Conclusion**

We can have the true God only as we let lesser gods go. First place belongs to God. God will not play second fiddle to a false god. For him to do so is to deceive us and to destroy us, because when any lesser god is substituted for the true God, everything gets out of proper perspective and balance, and nothing will come out right in the end.

Are you willing to give God first place in your heart and head and hand? Are you willing to let him have the place that belongs to him in your home? Are you willing to let him help you in your business?

God has demonstrated his love for us in the coming of Jesus Christ, who died for our sins that there might be nothing to prevent us from having fellowship with the eternal God. Be wise and give God first place in your life.

## WEDNESDAY EVENING, JANUARY 7

***Title:*** "Savior, Like a Shepherd Lead Us"

***Text:*** John 10:27

### Introduction

One of the most meaningful prayers that has ever been spoken by the lips of a believer is one ascribed to Dorothy A. Thrupp. This prayer has been put to music, and congregations around the world have joined in singing it with both delight and profit. Let us join together in singing the beautiful prayer hymn "Savior, Like a Shepherd Lead Us."

Did you sing it as a song, or did you sing it as a prayer from a needy heart? Let us examine some of the petitions contained in this prayer.

### I. Petitions in stanza 1.

A. *"Savior, like a shepherd lead us" (Ps. 23:2).*
B. *"In your pleasant pastures feed us" (Ps. 23:2).*

### II. Petitions in stanza 2.

A. *"We are Thine: do Thou befriend us" (John 15:14–16).*
B. *"Be the guardian of our way" (Matt. 28:20).*
C. *"Keep Thy flock from sin, defend us" (Luke 11:4).*
D. *"Seek us when we go astray" (Ps. 23:3).*
E. *"Hear, O hear us when we pray" (1 Peter 3:12).*

### III. Petitions in stanza 4.

A. *"Early let us seek Thy favor" (Ps. 27:4).*
B. *"Early let us do Thy will" (Eccl. 12:1).*
C. *"With Thy love our bosoms fill" (Rom. 5:5).*

### Conclusion

Again let us join together to sing this prayer hymn. Let us sing it as a prayer rather than just a hymn.

## SUNDAY MORNING, JANUARY 11

***Title:*** The Suffering Savior's Agonizing Thirst

***Text:*** "After this, Jesus knowing that all things were now accomplished, that the scripture might be fulfilled, saith, I thirst" **(John 19:28)**.

***Scripture Reading:*** John 19:16–30

***Hymns:*** "Alas! and Did My Savior Bleed," Watts
"Blessed Redeemer," Christiansen
"The Old Rugged Cross," Bennard

***Offertory Prayer:*** Holy Father, today we rejoice in your generosity. We are thankful that you deal with us on the basis of the riches of your grace rather than on the basis of our personal merit. We thank you for every blessing of life—in the realm of the material as well as of the spiritual. With tangible material gifts we come to express our faith, our gratitude, and our recognition of our obligation to love others. Help each of us to discover the blessedness and happiness that comes to the unselfish giver. Through Jesus Christ our Lord. Amen.

**Introduction**

John's gospel gives a description of the graciousness of our Savior who was both God and man. He was God to the extent that at his word water would blush into wine (John 2:7–10). He was human to the extent that he became weary and suffered the pangs of hunger and the torment of thirst. His thirst provided an appropriate point of contact with a Samaritan woman whose life had been a failure and was filled with frustration and emptiness.

While waiting for the return of his disciples, who had gone into the city to buy food, Jesus sat resting by the well. To this woman whose soul was thirsty for the Water of Life, the divine but human Savior made a request: "Give me to drink" (John 4:7). The woman was shocked that Jesus would request a favor of her, for not only was she a woman but she was a sinful one and a Samaritan at that. Her question provided the occasion for Jesus to tell her about the living water that can quench the deepest thirst of the human soul (John 4:13–14).

Both the humanity and deity of Christ were manifested on another occasion when he was suffering from an unsatisfied thirst. One of the cries that fell from his lips while he was undergoing the unutterable agony of the cross was "I thirst." It would take a volume of words to describe the agony and the deep personal need expressed in those words.

With our face toward Calvary and by means of inspired imagination, let us seek to behold him. With reverent awe let us tarry close enough to hear his prayer of intercession for those who crucified him: "Father, forgive them; for they know not what they do" (Luke 23:34). With gratitude for a Savior whose concern for sinners was so great, let us listen to his promise made in reply to the plea for pardon from the penitent thief: "Today shalt thou be with me in paradise" (v. 43). Let us recognize Jesus' concern for the welfare of others as we hear him bestow the responsibility for the care of his mother upon "the disciple standing by, whom he loved," as he said to his mother, "Woman, behold thy son!" and to John, "Behold thy mother!" (John 19:26–27). Shortly before Jesus' death he gave voice to a cry that revealed his deep personal need and the intense desire of his soul.

**I. "I thirst" for water because of physical sufferings.**

The night before the crucifixion was a horrible ordeal for Jesus from every possible viewpoint.

A. *From the Passover supper, at which time Judas departed to accomplish his vile deed of betrayal, and following the institution of the Lord's Supper, the Savior went out with his disciples into the night (Matt. 26:19–30).*

B. *In the garden of Gethsemane, Jesus prayed in great agony of soul for victory as he faced the ordeal of taking upon his spotless soul the sin of the world (Luke 22:39–46).*

C. *Jesus experienced the cruel and hypocritical kiss of the betrayer (Luke 22:47–48).*

D. *Jesus was taken to the house of the coldhearted high priest Caiaphas, where he was detained until daybreak by the Jewish authorities (Luke 22:52–54).*

E. *At the earliest possible time in the morning, Jesus was officially condemned (Luke 22:66–71).*

F. *Jesus was taken to Pilate's judgment hall where he was found innocent by the Roman governor.* From there he was sent to Herod, the Galilean puppet king, who was in Jerusalem for the Passover. After refusing to perform a miracle for Herod, he was mocked and returned to Pilate (Luke 23:1–11).

G. *The cowardly Pilate granted the wishes of the howling mob, who cried for his crucifixion even though he knew him to be innocent of the charges that were brought against him (Luke 23:13–25).*

H. *He was ordered to bear his own cross and did so until he collapsed in exhaustion (Luke 23:26).* The indescribable physical agony and the intense fever associated with his suffering created a great thirst for water.

He who could have called down twelve legions of angels to his rescue and, had he so willed, commanded rivers of water to quench his burning thirst, cried out in agony, "I thirst."

## II. "I thirst" for the full restoration of fellowship with the Father.

A. *In coming into the world, Jesus gave up the glory that he had enjoyed with the Father from the beginning.* In taking upon himself the form of a man by clothing himself in human flesh, the Savior, for the period of his incarnation, laid aside his eternal glory (Phil. 2:5–7).

B. *In his great high-priestly prayer recorded in John 17, the Redeemer declares and prays, "I brought you glory on earth by completing the work you gave me to do.* And now, Father, glorify me in your presence with the glory I had with you before the world began" (John 17:4–5 NIV).

With an intense thirst, the divine Son, who had come to minister rather than to be ministered unto, was thirsty for the approval of the heavenly Father. Three times during his earthly ministry he had received an expression of divine approval and satisfaction (cf. Luke 3:22; 9:35; John 12:28–29). In this moment of supreme agony, the heart of the Redeemer was thirsty for his Father's approval.

### III. "I thirst" for the salvation of a lost world.

A. *An intense thirst to redeem wayward humans brought Jesus from heaven to earth (John 12:27).*

B. *Jesus' intense thirst for the salvation of lost souls kept him faithful to the task when Satan tempted him by offering to give him the kingdoms of this world in return for his worship (Matt. 4:9–10).*

C. *Jesus' intense thirst for the salvation of the lost kept him faithful to the task when he was misunderstood by the people of his home town (Luke 4:28–30).*

D. *Jesus' intense thirst for the salvation of the lost caused him to decide to leave the safety of Galilee and to turn his face toward Jerusalem and to the cross that awaited him there (Luke 9:51).*

E. *Jesus' intense thirst for the salvation of the lost held him firm to his purpose even when his disciples sought to persuade him to do otherwise (John 11:8).*

F. *It was Jesus' thirst to see people come to know God as a loving Father that kept him on the cross when the malicious mob taunted him and challenged him to come down from the cross and prove that he was the Christ (Luke 23:35).*

### IV. "I thirst" for fellowship.

A. *For at least a moment the suffering Savior had felt utterly forsaken by all, including God: "My God, my God, why hast thou forsaken me?" (Matt. 27:46).* In every other instance, Jesus had addressed the eternal God as Father. Their fellowship had been unhindered. While he was on the cross, a mystery took place in which God "made him to be sin for us, who knew no sin; that we might be made the righteousness of God in him" (2 Cor. 5:21).

B. *The Christ had been forsaken by the apostles.* They had scattered like bewildered sheep when he was betrayed by Judas and arrested in the garden. For fear of their lives, with the exception of the disciple whom Jesus loved, they had remained at a distance during the terrifying hours that Jesus was on the cross.

C. *As Jesus thirsted for the assurance of the divine favor and the fellowship of his chosen apostles, he has a thirst for the fellowship of his disciples today.* He promised, "Where two or three are gathered together in my name, there am I in the midst of them" (Matt. 18:20). Could it be that even as we rejoice in our high and holy moments of communion with God that he also rejoices in fellowship with those who trust him?

### Conclusion

The Savior, who had an intense thirst on the cross, continues to have an intense desire to come into your heart as Savior, Redeemer, Teacher, and Friend. He wants to bring the blessings of God to you personally. Listen to him as he says, "Behold, I stand at the door, and knock: if any man hear my voice, and open the door, I will come in to him, and will sup with him, and he with me" (Rev. 3:20). The thirsty Savior stands at the door of your life. Your faith and trust and love are the cup of cold water that can quench his thirst. Let him come in today.

## SUNDAY EVENING, JANUARY 11

***Title:*** Gods Made with Human Hands

***Text:*** "Thou shalt not make unto thee any graven image, or any likeness of any thing that is in heaven above, or that is in the earth beneath, or that is in the water under the earth" (**Exod. 20:4**).

### Introduction

Jesus summed up the Ten Commandments on one occasion when someone asked him which one was the greatest. He said, "Thou shalt love the Lord thy God with all thy heart, and with all thy soul, and with all thy mind, and with all thy strength: ... Thou shalt love thy neighbour as thyself" (Mark 12:30–31).

If we love God with all our heart, soul, mind, and strength, we will certainly try to keep the first four commandments, which have to do with our attitude toward him and our worship of him. If we love our neighbor as we do ourselves—that is, if we have an unbreakable spirit of goodwill toward our neighbor as we do toward our own private interests, we will certainly try to keep the remaining six commandments, which have to do with our relationship with our fellow humans.

As God gave the commandments having to do with our relationship to our Maker, he issued:

### I. A warning against the dangers of idolatry.

A. *Specifically, he forbade the use of images as an aid to worship.* He strictly required that people should not bow down before physical objects.

B. *Down through the ages people have asked, "To whom then will ye liken God? or what likeness will ye compare unto him?" (Isa. 40:18).* This has particularly been true when a person's spiritual awareness of God has grown dim or when a person was at a distance from God because of sin.

C. *Eventually the image becomes a snare.*

1. Such was Aaron's golden calf (Exod. 32:1–4).
2. Such have been the images that were brought into the church immediately following the conversion of the Roman emperor Constantine. The idols of the Mideastern and heathen religions were brought into the Christian church and used as symbols of the true God.
3. The use of the crucifix was unknown in Christian worship until the sixth century. Some have made an idol of the cross.
4. The use of images of Mary and of other great people of the faith is strictly forbidden by the second commandment.
5. Inevitably, superstitious sentiments gradually cluster about the image. The image begins to be treated as a sacred object due special reverence, and the worship of the true God is transferred to the image.

### II. The second commandment forbids the misrepresentation of God.

A. *The use of images presents a false conception of God.*

B. *The use of images presents a limited conception of God.*

C. *"God is a Spirit: and they that worship him must worship him in spirit and in truth" (John 4:24).* By this commandment God was seeking to reveal his unique spirituality. He was seeking to protect his people from limited, inadequate understandings of the nature of their God.

## III. Modern idolatry.

An idol has been defined as anything that comes between the soul of a person and the true God. That which persons put first in their lives is their object of worship, and when the true God does not have first place, we are left with the inescapable truth that one is an idol worshiper. Modern idol worshipers do not bow down before stone images. They are too refined for that.

A. *All people are tempted to worship the god of success.* Instead of desiring to be saints, we hunger for the privilege of being a success so that we can enjoy all of the gadgets our society has to offer. We want to save ourselves by the work of our own hands.

B. *Some of us let society occupy the place of God in our lives.* To some people acceptance and the approval of peers is of supreme importance. Decisions are made, not on the basis of the will of God or on the basis of the ultimate outcome, but on the basis of what the crowd wants to do in the present.

C. *Some worship at the shrine of science.* Only ignorant and lazy people, they say, look to God for help. Independent modern people can solve all of their own problems, answer all of their own questions, and lift themselves to an antiseptic heaven by their own bootstraps.

## IV. The inevitable consequence of idolatry.

God speaks of being a jealous God. God is not envious, but he is grieved when we are disloyal. He insists on being recognized for what he is as our Lord, our God, and our Creator.

When people reject God's authority, the inevitable consequence is judgment—judgment that affects one's family and associates. No one lives to oneself and no one dies to oneself. A person cannot go to hell without at the same time blocking someone else's road toward heaven. When a person fails to be what God calls him or her to be, others suffer.

## Conclusion

People continue to ask, "To whom then will we liken God?" As Christians we believe that in the person of Jesus Christ the eternal God became man to reveal himself to people. "In the beginning was the Word, and the Word was with God, and the Word was God" (John 1:1). "And the Word was made flesh, and dwelt among us, (and we beheld his glory, the glory as of the only begotten of the Father,) full of grace and truth" (v. 14). "No man hath seen God at any time; the only begotten Son, which is in the bosom of the Father, he hath declared him" (v. 18). "He that hath seen me hath seen the Father" (14:9).

Jesus brought to us a revelation of the Creator as the heavenly Father who loves the sinner to the extent that he came to show his love and mercy on the cross. He demonstrated his power by rising victorious over death and the grave. In his ascension back to the Father, Jesus stepped back behind the curtain of indivisibility to be worshiped in spirit and in truth.

---

## WEDNESDAY EVENING, JANUARY 14

***Title:*** "Teach Me to Pray"

***Text:*** Luke 11:1

### Introduction

It is interesting to note that following a time spent in prayer, one of Jesus' disciples requested that he teach them to pray as John the Baptist had taught his disciples to pray. Jesus replied by giving to them and to us a model prayer, often times called the Lord's Prayer. In reality, it is a pattern for the disciples to follow as they offer their prayers. Are you guilty of neglecting the closet of prayer?

*Ere you left your room this morning*
*Did you think to pray?*
*In the name of Christ, our Savior,*
*Did you sue for loving favor,*
*As a shield today?*

—*Mrs. M. A. Kidder*

Is it not true that all of us need to join with Albert S. Reitz, who placed in poetic form his prayer "Teach Me to Pray"? Let us join in singing this prayer hymn.

### I. Petitions in stanza 1.

A. *"Teach me to pray, Lord, teach me to pray" (Luke 11:1).*
B. *"I long to know Thy will and Thy way" (Rom. 12:1).*

### II. Petition in stanza 2: "O give me power, power in prayer!" (Phil. 4:13).

### III. Petitions in stanza 3.

A. *"Renew my weakened will" (Rom. 7:25).*
B. *"Subdue my sinful nature" (1 Cor. 9:27).*
C. *"Fill me just now with power anew" (Acts 1:8).*

### IV. Petition in stanza 4: "Teach me to pray, Lord; teach me to pray" (Luke 11:1).

### Conclusion

As a united expression of our need and in the assurance that our request is in harmony with the will of God for us, let us conclude our service by singing together our prayer, "Teach Me to Pray."

## SUNDAY MORNING, JANUARY 18

*Title:* The Suffering Savior's Lonely Cry

*Text:* "My God, my God why hast thou forsaken me?" **(Matt. 27:46)**.

*Scripture Reading:* Matthew 27:29–50

*Hymns:* "O Sacred Head, Now Wounded," Alexander

"At the Cross," Watts

"In the Cross of Christ I Glory," Bowring

*Offertory Prayer:* Gracious Father, today we thank you for giving us the challenging task of proclaiming the gospel to the uttermost parts of the earth. May your richest blessings be upon the missionaries who serve on spiritual frontiers far from home and loved ones. Give them the strength and the courage that come from you alone. Grant them the faith and the understanding they need for living in these days. Grant them the power of your Spirit that they may serve effectively. Bless these tithes and offerings that make it possible for them to dedicate their days to a ministry of teaching, preaching, and healing. In Christ's name. Amen.

### Introduction

The casual reader of the Word of God will notice a recurring refrain as God called people to cooperate with him in redemptive activity. He always promised to bless them with his abiding presence.

When God called Abraham from the Ur of Chaldees, he promised him prosperity and protection (Gen. 12:1–3). The biography of Abraham is a record of God's faithfulness to that promise.

When God called Moses to lead the children of Israel out of Egyptian bondage, he was encouraged by a promise from God: "Certainly I will be with thee" (Exod. 3:12). If it had not been for the faithfulness of God to that promise, Israel never would have become a nation and the sons of Jacob would have been swallowed up in the bleak, barren waste of the desert.

Following the death of Moses, Joshua was chosen to lead the children of Israel across the Jordan in a conquest of Canaan. To encourage Joshua, God said, "There shall not any man be able to stand before thee all the days of thy life: as I was with Moses, so I will be with thee: I will not fail thee, nor forsake thee" (Josh. 1:5). In battle after battle, God gave the Israelites victory. As long as they trusted him and obeyed him, God more than kept his promise to always bless them with his presence.

When the voice of God came to Jeremiah, the son of Hilkiah the priest, calling him to be a messenger to the nation, he was encouraged by the promise of God's abiding presence. "Be not afraid of their faces: for I am with thee to deliver thee, saith the LORD" (Jer. 1:8).

As we read the New Testament, we cannot miss the fact that on three different occasions an audible voice from heaven spoke words of divine approval concerning Jesus Christ who had come to do the will of God (Matt. 3:17; 17:5; John 12:28).

God was well pleased with everything about Jesus. As readers come to the account of the crucifixion, questions are bound to arise as to why such a horrible fate should befall one who was so innocent, gentle, and merciful toward others. Why should he be treated so cruelly that he would give utterance to this lonely cry of distress: "My God, my God, why hast thou forsaken me?"

Jesus found it impossible to convince his apostles that he should die on the cross. Though he spoke of this repeatedly during the last six months of his ministry, it was only after his death on the cross and his victory over the grave that they were able to understand why he came to die. It is interesting to note that Jesus "explained to them what was said in all the Scriptures concerning himself" (Luke 24:27 NIV) and "opened their minds so they could understand the Scriptures" (v. 45 NIV) before they discovered the real purpose for his coming and his dying.

Today let us pray that the living Lord will open our understanding that we might more fully understand and more deeply appreciate his substitutionary death on the cross. In sympathetic imagination, let us attempt to travel back through time to that day when Christ Jesus died on Calvary's cross.

What is your reaction when you hear the Christ cry out in agony, "My God, My God, why hast thou forsaken me?" Had the God who had proven so faithful to Abraham, to Moses, to Joshua, and to Jeremiah, forsaken his sinless Son on the cross?

### I. Listen to this lonely cry.

"My God, my God, why hast thou forsaken me?" It is impossible for anyone even to begin to understand these words, much less appreciate them, if he has no awareness of the nature and purpose of Christ's unique death on the cross. His death on the cross was not an accident in the divine program of redemption. Christ was not dying as the apostle of a lost cause. Neither did this cry fall from the lips of an unbalanced religious fanatic who was dying a martyr's death.

A. *The Savior's lonely cry is an expression of appalling woe.* Job had cried out of a feeling of utter desolation, "Oh that I knew where I might find him! that I might come even to his seat!" (Job 23:3). Job felt forsaken and unable to find God. Christ had shared an intimate relationship in which he had been assured of the divine approval all along the way. This was changed while he was on the cross. He felt utterly alone and forsaken.

B. *The Savior's lonely cry expresses the deep pathos of his soul.* This cry marks the apex of his sufferings.
   1. Jesus had suffered misunderstanding by his friends.
   2. Jesus had been forsaken by his own family and especially by those who lived in his own home town (Luke 4:29).
   3. Jesus had suffered betrayal by one of the chosen Twelve.

4. Jesus had experienced denial by one within the inner circle of the Twelve.
5. Jesus had been utterly forsaken by the eleven remaining apostles.
6. Jesus had been completely rejected by his nation.
7. Jesus was suffering indescribable physical agony from the wounds that would bring about his death.
8. Jesus was suffering the insult of the most despised form of death that could be inflicted on the lowest class of criminals.
9. Jesus experienced the apex of his agony when it seemed as if he had been forsaken by God.

C. *The Savior's lonely cry gave voice to words of deepest solemnity.* The mystery behind the meaning of these words is beyond human comprehension. Only by the aid of God's Spirit can we even begin to understand why he should feel forsaken by God.

## II. Why did Jesus give voice to this lonely cry?

A. *With reverence we would ask, "Was Jesus really forsaken while he was suspended between heaven and earth as the Lamb of God who takes away the sins of the world?"* Perhaps the only correct answer to that question is contradictory at first glance. The answer is, "Yes, he was forsaken," and yet at the same time, "No, he was not forsaken."

B. *There was never a time when God was so close as when Jesus Christ was dying on the cross.* Paul says, "God was in Christ, reconciling the world unto himself, not imputing their trespasses unto them; and hath committed to us the word of reconciliation" (2 Cor. 5:19). Someone has said that there was a cross in the heart of God long before there was ever a cross on Calvary's hill. If we are to see the supreme exhibition of God's love for sinners, we will find it in the suffering and death of the saving Redeemer as he died on the cross.

C. *In contrast, there was never a time when Jesus Christ was so far away from God as when he was suffering on the cross.* In awe-striking words, Paul tells how that on the cross God "made [Jesus] to be sin for us, who knew no sin; that we might be made the righteousness of God in him" (2 Cor. 5:21). It was on the cross that he who was so rich became poor in order that we, who are so very poor, might be made rich in the things of God (8:9).

Jesus' cry of utter loneliness can help us to begin to understand what Isaiah the prophet was saying: "Surely he hath borne our griefs, and carried our sorrows; yet we did esteem him stricken, smitten of God and afflicted" (Isa. 53:4). Isaiah continues, "Yet it pleased the Lord to bruise him; he hath put him to grief: He shall see of the travail of his soul, and shall be satisfied: for he shall bear their iniquities" (vv. 10–11).

Christ's suffering on the cross was spiritual as well as physical. At Calvary we see the sinless, incarnate Son of God taking upon himself the sins and guilt of a lost world and dying in their stead. He was dying for our sins. The Father was as close to Jesus as his breath, yet he was as far away as the east is from the west, because Christ had the sin of the world upon him as he died on the cross.

### III. This lonely cry helps us to measure the price of our redemption.

A. *These words reveal the awfulness of sin.* Sin not only separates people from God, people from their better selves, and people from their neighbors, but it caused Christ Jesus to feel separated from God as he died on the cross. If we are to recognize the awfulness of sin, we must go to Calvary: "He was wounded for our transgressions, he was bruised for our iniquities: the chastisement of our peace was upon him; and with his stripes we are healed" (Isa. 53:5). Peter described his sufferings in terms of substitution. He declares that Jesus suffered for us and that he "bore our sins in his own body on the tree, that we, being dead to sins, should live unto righteousness: by whose stripes ye were healed" (1 Peter 2:24).

B. *These words reveal the character of the wages of sin (Rom. 6:23).* The death that sin brings is spiritual death, separation of the soul from God. Because Jesus had taken our sins upon himself, he was suffering as a sinner as well as the divine Son. This cry of loneliness from the cross is the only instance recorded in the Scriptures in which Jesus did not address God as Father. Although Jesus' cry claims God as "My God," because he was suffering for our sin, he did not feel the closeness and the intimacy of that relationship as had been the case in the past.

C. *These words reveal the great love of God.* "But God commendeth his love toward us, in that, while we were yet sinners, Christ died for us" (Rom. 5:8). Poets have tried to describe this love and have found words inadequate to fully measure the length, breadth, height, and depth of it. Charles Gabriel wrote:

*I stand amazed in the presence*
*Of Jesus the Nazarene,*
*And wonder how He could love me,*
*A sinner, condemned, unclean.*

*He took my sins and my sorrows,*
*He made them His very own;*
*He bore the burden to Calv'ry,*
*And suffered and died alone.*

*When with the ransomed in glory*
*His face I at last shall see,*
*'Twill be my joy thro' the ages*
*To sing of His love for me.*

D. *These words help us to measure the degree of God's concern for us (Rom. 8:32).* By sending his only begotten Son into the world on a redemptive mission that would involve a crown of thorns and a cross, God demonstrated his divine concern for us. For you to recognize the value of your soul in the eyes of God, you must visit Calvary and hear the Christ utter this bitter cry of loneliness as he suffered to remove the curse of sin for you. God loves you and wants to save you.

### Conclusion

Jesus' lonely cry causes us to believe that he is the only way of salvation. Had there been some other way than the cross, God surely would have used it, and the Bible would have revealed it.

Your only hope of full, free, and eternal forgiveness is through faith in this Christ who died for your sin and who rose again that he might be your Savior. Some of you have delayed making a decision to let his death be your death for sin. To reject his death for your sin is also to reject the life that he revealed following his resurrection. He died to save you. He lives again to offer you an eternal life of victory over the sin that destroys everything that is worthwhile. Respond to God's invitation today.

## SUNDAY EVENING, JANUARY 18

***Title:*** Four Kinds of Profanity

***Text:*** "Thou shalt not take the name of the LORD thy God in vain; for the LORD will not hold him guiltless that taketh his name in vain" **(Exod. 20:7)**.

### Introduction

The first commandment tells us to worship God and no other. The second commandment tells us to worship God directly and to have no idols. The third commandment tells us to worship him sincerely and not falsely. People not only break this commandment, but they think it is a law of no consequence. God does not consider profanity a light matter, for the only foundation for a sound character and safe society is a sincere reverence for God (Prov. 9:10).

The moral foundations of society begin to crack and crumble away when people lose their sense of reverence and begin to think lightly of him who is holy and sacred. People cannot drag the holy name of God into the mud of profane and dirty discourse without undermining the foundation upon which life itself rests.

To many people the third commandment means "Thou shalt not cuss"—no more, no less. Hence, it seems hardly on a level of importance with an injunction such as "Thou shalt not kill" or "Thou shalt not steal." Those who think in this limited way miss the deeper meaning of the commandment, for this commandment not only safeguards the foundation of society, which is reverence for God, but at the same time insures the integrity of a person's word. It seeks to preserve truth as the principle by which people live. This commandment seeks to eliminate falsehood.

Why is the name of the Lord important? Names do more than distinguish one person from another. Bible names are especially significant. In Bible times the

names of Hebrew people were intended in most cases as a prayer or a prophecy and were based on parental hope. In some instances, a name was an expression of praise. For instance, Elijah meant "Jehovah is God," and Elisha meant "salvation is of God." Jeremiah meant "God hurls," and Israel meant "prince of God."

Something of the same principle holds true of the names of God. The names by which God chose to make himself known to his people are part of the self-revelation by which, at sundry times and in diverse manners, he led his people into the knowledge of himself. Each name was a fresh and lasting revelation of his nature, character, or purpose.

By his name Jehovah, God reveals himself to be eternal. By his name El Shaddai, he reveals himself to be God Almighty. By his name Jehovah-Shalom, he reveals himself as the Lord of peace. God's name stands for God himself, and to take his name in vain is to use his name for a selfish purpose or to misrepresent his nature and character. To take his name in vain is an insult to his divine majesty and power. This commandment tells us that God will not treat a person as clean or innocent if that person is guilty of taking his name in vain—that is, of misrepresenting his character and calling upon him to do that which is out of harmony with his character.

There are many ways in which this commandment is broken:

### I. The most common way is by the use of profane language.

A. *Profanity is one of the most common sins of the day.*

B. *There is absolutely no reward for profanity.*

C. *A person's speech is an index to his or her character.* Someone has said that when a man has to resort to profanity, he is using a rather strong method to give expression to a weak mind. He confesses his inadequacy to deal with what is for him a perplexing situation.

D. *Profanity not only corrupts the guilty one, but it corrupts others also.*

### II. People break the third commandment by frivolous joking about God and sacred things.

A. *People joke about God.*

B. *People joke about prayer.*

C. *People joke about holy things and undermine the attitude of reverence toward God.*

### III. People break this commandment by spiritual forgery.

Jesus said, "And whatsoever ye shall ask in my name, that will I do, that the Father may be glorified in the Son. If ye shall ask anything in my name, I will do it" (John 14:13–14).

A. *Many give to the name of Jesus a magical significance.* They would not think of closing a prayer without ending it with the phrase "and this we pray in Jesus' name." It is possible for such a habit to be a transgression of the third commandment.

B. *To pray "in the name of Jesus" is to pray in line with his character and his purpose.* To pray in the name of Jesus means to pray the prayer that he would pray if he stood in your shoes and wore your coat. One needs to know the mind of Jesus Christ to be able to pray in his name (John 15:7).

C. To attach the name of Jesus to the end of a selfish prayer is to commit spiritual forgery, and thus the third commandment is broken.

## IV. A fourth kind of profanity is that of hypocrisy.

For a person to wear the name of Christ without being Christian in spirit and conduct is to be guilty of breaking the third commandment. The term *Christian* is a term that has been cheapened by common usage. To believe that one is a Christian merely because she has high moral standards, has a vague belief in God, and holds nominal membership in some congregation is to be fearfully deceived.

If we were to interpret the term *Christian* literally, we would think of a person characterized by Christlikeness. Some people seriously question whether a believer should ever say, "I am a Christian." These people would contend that the believer should say, "I am a disciple, I am a believer, I am a follower," and then let the title "Christian" be conferred by others who see the evidence of genuine Christianity in his or her life.

A. *There is a difference between a spiritual failure and a religious hypocrite.* A great host of people fail sadly to live up to the implications of the title Christian, but they are failures rather than hypocrites.

A hypocrite is one who wears a false face and deliberately seeks to deceive others into believing that he is something that he is not. There are very few hypocrites in the modern-day church as compared with the number of those who are spiritual failures.

B. *The implications of being numbered among God's people are weighty indeed.* If we profess to be Christian and then deliberately refuse to practice what we profess to be, we take the name of Christ in vain.

## Conclusion

When we measure ourselves by the third commandment, we must all bow our heads and confess that we have sinned. Each of us has been guilty in many ways of taking the name of the Lord our God in vain. James said, "For whosoever shall keep the whole law, and yet offend in one point, he is guilty of all" (James 2:10).

All of us have broken God's law and stand guilty before him. Our only hope of salvation is through faith in him who fulfilled the law (Matt. 5:17). Christ the Savior twice met the demands of the law. He met its requirements perfectly so far as his own record was concerned. He met the requirements of the law in the second place for us, in that he died to pay the penalty of sin, which is death. He offers us forgiveness on condition that we receive him as Lord and Savior.

## WEDNESDAY EVENING, JANUARY 21

*Title:* "Breathe on Me, Breath of God"

*Text:* John 20:21–23

### Introduction

Among the good gifts that the heavenly Father bestows upon his children, there is none greater than the Holy Spirit (Acts 11:15). Jesus told his disciples to expect the Holy Spirit to render unto them the personal ministries he had given while he was visibly present with them (John 14:16–18).

Edwin Hatch felt a deep inward need for the ministries that the Holy Spirit is able to render in the heart of the believer, and he put his prayer in poetic form. Let us join together in singing of the many gifts of the Holy Spirit that we find listed in his prayer hymn "Breathe on Me, Breath of God." (The hymn "Holy Ghost, with Light Divine" by Andrew Reed could also be used appropriately for this service.)

### I. "Breathe on me, breath of God" (stanza 1).

A. *"Fill me with life anew" (Luke 24:49).*
B. *"That I may love what you dost love" (Gal. 5:22).*
C. *"And do what you wouldst do" (Gal. 5:16).*

### II. "Breathe on me, breath of God" (stanza 2).

A. *"Until my heart is pure" (Matt. 5:8).*
B. *"Until with Thee I will Thy will" (Rom. 12:1).*
C. *"To do and to endure" (Gal. 5:17–18).*

### III. "Breathe on me, breath of God" (stanza 3).

A. *"Till I am wholly Thine" (1 Cor. 6:19).*
B. *"Till all this earthly part of me" (1 Cor. 6:20).*
C. *"Glows with Thy fire divine" (Acts 7:55).*

### Conclusion

The prayer of Edwin Hatch for the ministry of the Holy Spirit glows with an expression of joy and praise as he anticipates the perfect harmony and holiness of living with God throughout eternity. By responding in faith and obedience to the leadership of the Holy Spirit, we can know the joy of eternal life in the present. Let us all join together in giving voice to the prayer that was first uttered by Edwin Hatch. Let us ask the heavenly Father to bestow upon us these gracious ministries of the Holy Spirit.

## SUNDAY MORNING, JANUARY 25

***Title:*** The Suffering Savior's Shout of Triumph

***Text:*** "When Jesus therefore had received the vinegar, he said, It is finished: and he bowed his head and gave up the ghost" **(John 19:30)**.

***Scripture Reading:*** John 19:25–30

***Hymns:*** "When I Survey the Wondrous Cross," Watts
"Jesus, Keep Me Near the Cross," Crosby
"Must Jesus Bear the Cross Alone?" Shepherd

***Offertory Prayer:*** Holy Father, because you have freely given us the rich gifts of heaven, we bring to you the gifts of the earth. Because you have given us gifts of eternal significance, we bring to you temporal gifts with a prayer that you will bless them with eternal significance. Bless the use of these tithes and offerings for the preaching of the gospel and the teaching of your truths. Help each of us to recognize that you are interested in our economic life as well as our spiritual well-being, and help us to recognize that there is a relationship between the two. Through Jesus Christ our Lord. Amen.

### Introduction

Today, with the help of the Holy Spirit, I want to lead you back through time to Calvary: "Calvary—where we see man at his worst and God at his best. Calvary—where we see the awful depths of human sin and the tremendous heights of divine love. Calvary—where the Lamb of God was slain and where the Son of God gave up his life for you and me. Calvary—where every man must come if he expects to be saved. Calvary—where all of our hopes are centered, both for this world and the next" (W. Herschel Ford).

Hymnist Isaac Watts made such a visit to Calvary and sought to describe the response of his soul and the reaction of his heart:

*When I survey the wondrous cross*
*On which the Prince of Glory died.*
*My richest gain I count but loss,*
*And pour contempt on all my pride.*

*Forbid it, Lord, that I should boast,*
*Save in the death of Christ my God;*
*All the vain things that charm me most,*
*I sacrifice them to His blood.*

*See, from His head, His hands, His feet,*
*Sorrow and love flow mingled down:*
*Did e'er such love and sorrow meet,*
*Or thorns compose so rich a crown?*

As he contemplated the extent of Christ's humiliation and the greatness of God's love for sinners, he responded by writing:

*Were the whole realm of nature mine,*
*That were a present far too small;*
*Love so amazing, so divine,*
*Demands my soul, my life, my all.*

With ears that hear, let us listen to the words that fell from the lips of the suffering Savior as he died to reveal God's love and determination to save sinners from sin.

He spoke a word of forgiveness: "Father, forgive them; for they know not what they do" (Luke 23:34).

He spoke a word of salvation: "Today shalt thou be with me in paradise" (Luke 23:43).

He spoke a word of affection: "Woman, behold thy son! . . . Behold thy mother" (John 19:26–27).

He spoke a word of anguish: "My God, My God, why hast thou forsaken me?" (Matt. 27:46).

He spoke a word of suffering: "I thirst" (John 19:28).

He spoke a word of victory: "It is finished" (John 19:28).

He spoke a word of contentment: "Father, into thy hands I commend my Spirit" (Luke 23:46).

Before his last word, the suffering Savior gave voice to a shout of triumph: "It is finished." These three words are all contained in one word in the original language. While the sentence is brief in length, it is immeasurable in its significance. This was not the last despairing cry of a helpless martyr. Neither was it the last gasp of a worn-out life or a mere expression of facts concerning the termination of the Savior's physical suffering.

At the tender age of twelve, Jesus revealed an awareness of his unique mission in the service of God. He said to Mary and Joseph when they found him in the temple, "How is it that you sought me? wist ye not that I must be about my Father's business?" (Luke 2:49).

In his great high-priestly prayer just preceding his crucifixion, the Savior prayed in anticipation of what he was to accomplish on the cross: "I have glorified thee on the earth: I have finished the work which thou gavest me to do" (John 17:4).

A few moments before he was to commit his spirit into the hands of God, we hear the divine Redeemer rejoicing over the completion of the work for which his Father sent him into the world.

With reverence we would lift the veil and view in detail what the Savior had finished:

**I. "It is finished" meant that all the prophecies connected with his life and death had been fulfilled.**

A. *We think of Isaiah primarily as the prophet who foretold the birth of the Savior (Isa. 7:14–16; 9:6–7).*

B. *The prophet Micah had prophesied concerning the place of his birth (Mic. 5:2).*

C. *The sufferings of the Savior had been prophesied by the inspired psalmist (Ps. 22:1–31) as well as by Isaiah (52:13–53:12).*

D. *During the last six months of our Savior's ministry, he concentrated on teaching his apostles.* One of the major, recurring themes concerned his suffering and death on the cross (Matt. 16:21; 17:22–23; 20:18).

## II. "It is finished" meant that Christ's sufferings were over.

Words are not adequate even to begin to attempt to describe what our suffering Savior endured on the cross. He suffered in many, many ways.

A. *Jesus had suffered the pain of rejection by the people of his own home town (Luke 4:16–30).*

B. *Jesus had suffered misunderstanding by his family and friends (Matt. 13:53–57).*

C. *Jesus had suffered at the hands of Satan.* All of the satanic forces that could be brought to bear upon Jesus during his temptation experiences had been inflicted upon him. It was Satan who had used Peter to try to persuade Jesus to turn from his redemptive mission (Matt. 16:21–23). Satan also used Judas to betray Jesus into the hands of the Jewish authorities (Luke 22:3).

D. *Jesus had suffered the justice of a holy God upon sin.* Here we stand in the midst of mystery as well as miracle. We stand in the presence of man as he commits the vilest deed of human history, and at the same time we see disclosed the indescribable and immeasurable love of God.

## III. "It is finished" meant that Christ's sacrificial work of redemption was completed.

A. *We are not saved from the penalty of sin by the remarkable life that Jesus lived, as important as the perfection of that life was.*

B. *We are not saved from the penalty of sin by the matchless teachings that fell from his lips, as excellent as they are and as relevant as we should make them for the living of life.*

C. *We obtain our salvation through Jesus Christ by virtue of the fact that he died in our place.* First, he met the demands of God's holy law with a perfect life. In no instance had he broken the law of God. Second, he met the demands of the holy law of God by dying as a substitute for sinners. By his death he redeemed us from the curse of the law. "Christ hath redeemed us from the curse of the law, being made a curse for us: for it is written, Cursed is every one that hangeth on a tree" (Gal. 3:13).

Peter speaks of Christ dying in our place because of the condemnation of sin in order that he might return us to God. "For Christ also hath once suffered for sins, the just for the unjust, that he might bring us to God, being put to death in the flesh, but quickened by the Spirit" (1 Peter 3:18).

## IV. "It is finished" meant that the power of the Evil One was destroyed.

The entire Bible is a record of God's conflict with evil and of his continuous efforts to deliver people from the penalty and the power of sin. The first hint, or prophecy, of this conflict is recorded in Genesis 3:15: "And I will put enmity between thee and the woman, and between thy seed and her seed; it shall bruise thy head, and thou shalt bruise his heel."

This verse is the first verse in the Bible that contains a messianic promise declaring that the seed of woman would bruise the head of the serpent and by so doing destroy his power. At first glance, it would appear that the serpent would destroy the seed of the woman by his death on the cross. However, death was not the end of the story for Jesus Christ. He was to come forth triumphant and victorious over death and the grave. In his conquest of death, he demonstrated his sovereignty over both Satan and death in order that he "might destroy him that had the power of death, that is, the devil; and deliver them who through fear of death were all their lifetime subject to bondage" (Heb. 2:14–15).

The Christian still has to deal with the Tempter, but we can have complete victory over him through faith in Jesus Christ because he is a defeated foe. The resurrection affirmed Satan's defeat, and the second coming of Jesus will demonstrate it forever.

### V. "It is finished" meant that a way to heaven had been provided.

Because of sin, humans were cast out of the garden of Eden, and cherubim with flaming swords were placed as guards at the entrance (Gen. 3:24).

The Bible is a record of God's continued efforts to call people to lives of faith and obedience that will make it possible for them to reenter the paradise of God. Jesus died on the cross to remove that which separated humans from their Creator. There is absolutely nothing to prevent people from having fellowship with God in the present and spending eternity with God in the future if they will receive Jesus Christ as their Savior and Redeemer.

### Conclusion

God does not coerce our faith, our love, and our obedience. God, in grace, provides salvation for us. As Jesus came to his last moment of earthly life, he cried out, "It is finished." His death will have been in vain if you neglect or refuse to trust him as your Lord and Savior.

## SUNDAY EVENING, JANUARY 25

***Title:*** The Sabbath Was Made for Man

***Text:*** "Remember the sabbath day, to keep it holy" **(Exod. 20:8)**.

### Introduction

The fourth commandment calls upon us to remember. In a scientific sense, we never forget anything. In everyday life, we are very forgetful. We forget our opportunities and responsibilities. We forget the vows we have made. We forget names and faces. We forget our friends and loved ones. In some instances, forgetfulness is deliberate, but in most instances, it is due to preoccupation with some other matter.

The fourth commandment, "Remember the sabbath day to keep it holy," deals with the peril of people forgetting that they are the crown of God's creation and as such should properly relate themselves by faith and surrender to the will of our loving heavenly Father.

### I. We are to remember that the Sabbath is God's gift to humankind.

"The sabbath was made for man, and not man for the sabbath" (Mark 2:27). The Sabbath belongs to God, and yet it was made for man. This commandment was not given for the benefit of God, but for us. In this respect, the fourth commandment is like all of these other nine rules for abundant living. To fail to keep any of them is to suffer.

### II. God gave the Sabbath as a day of rest.

A. *Man was intended to be a worker.*

B. *Idleness is a curse.*

C. *In the plan of God, man is not to work all of the time.*

D. *Man needs to be recharged.* Just as a battery can run down and needs to be recharged, so can a person. Two parties of gold seekers traveled toward the West Coast during the gold rush of 1849. One traveled every day while the other spent one day in seven resting. The latter arrived first.

Some Americans who were enjoying a safari in Africa enlisted the aid of some natives to bear their burdens. The natives labored hard for six full days, but on the seventh day they refused to bear their burdens. When inquiry was made concerning their refusal, they insisted that they must stop for the day to let their souls catch up with their bodies. Modern people could take a lesson from them, for when they disregard this truth and break the fourth commandment, they experience lowered vitality and efficiency. They reap frayed nerves, broken bodies, and premature death.

A miner who used mules to pull coal from where it was being mined to the shaft would bring his mules up out of the mine on Sunday to keep them from going blind from working in the darkness. He who never lifts his eyes to the light of God's love may become blind to the very existence of God as well as to his own unique nature as a human being.

### III. God gave the Sabbath as a day of worship.

A. *Many look upon Sunday merely as the day on which they do not go to work.* People are more than bodies; they have spirits.

B. *Sunday is to be a day of worship (Heb. 10:25).*

C. *The Sabbath became the Lord's Day in the church.*

1. Jesus appeared five times after his resurrection on the first day of the week.

2. The Holy Spirit descended on the day of Pentecost—the first day of the week.
3. The Lord's Supper was observed on the first day of the week (Acts 20:7).
4. Paul said that we are to bring our offerings to the Lord's storehouse on the first day of the week (1 Cor. 16:2).
5. John was "in the Spirit on the Lord's day" (Rev. 1:10).

D. *A secularized Sabbath will produce a materialistic society.*

E. *The Sabbath gives us an opportunity to "Be still, and know that [God is] God" (Ps. 46:10).*

1. People need time for thoughtful meditation.
2. People need to keep their hearts in tune with God.
3. People need to be made clean by cleansing and confession.
4. In private and corporate worship, we become true worshipers and rededicate ourselves to our Christian mission.

### IV. God gave the Sabbath so that worthwhile service could be rendered.

A. *Jesus would encourage us to do all of the good that we can do for our fellow humans, not just on the Sabbath day, but every day.* Especially on the Sabbath day we should seek to minister to the needs of others.

B. *When we render ministries of mercy to those in need, we are ministering to our Lord (Matt. 25:40).*

### Conclusion

The reverent observance of the Lord's Day is a constant reminder of our Lord's victory over sin, Satan, and death on our behalf. He arose triumphant and victorious "as it began to dawn toward the first day of the week" (Matt. 28:1). We celebrate his triumph not just on Easter Sunday but on every seventh day, as we come together in his name to enjoy and to respond to his living presence. One of his most thrilling promises is "Where two or three are gathered together in my name, there am I in the midst of them" (Matt. 18:20).

Consistent regular worship habits on the Lord's Day will make it much more likely that you will meet this living Lord and enjoy his transforming presence during the other six days of the week.

## WEDNESDAY EVENING, JANUARY 28

***Title:*** "Have Thine Own Way, Lord"

***Text:*** Acts 9:6

### Introduction

At the beginning of his Christian pilgrimage, Saul, who was to become Paul, asked, "Lord, what wilt you have me to do?" This question was the expression of the surrender of his heart to the complete sovereignty of Jesus Christ. He came to the end of his journey with the great consciousness that he had let the Lord have his way in his life (2 Tim. 4:6–8).

Adelaide A. Pollard expressed the sentiments of the apostle Paul in a poetic prayer that has been set to music and sung by thousands of congregations. Let us join together in singing "Have Thine Own Way, Lord," a prayer hymn that is loved by millions.

**I. "Have Thine own way, Lord! Have Thine own way!" (stanza 1).**

A. *"Mold me" (Jer. 18:3).*
B. *"Make me" (Jer. 18:4).*

**II. "Have Thine own way, Lord! Have Thine own way!" (stanza 2).**

A. *"Search me and try me" (Ps. 139:23–24).*
B. *"Whiter than snow, Lord, wash me just now" (Isa. 1:18).*

**III. "Have Thine own way, Lord! Have Thine own way!" (stanza 3).**

A. *"Wounded and weary, help me, I pray" (Luke 4:18).*
B. *"Touch me and heal me" (Mark 1:40–41).*

**IV. "Have Thine own way, Lord! Have Thine own way!" (stanza 4).**

A. *"Hold o'er my being absolute sway" (Phil. 2:9–11).*
B. *"Fill with Thy Spirit till all shall see Christ only, always, living in me" (Gal. 5:22–24).*

### Conclusion

When the vessel was marred in the hand of the potter, Jeremiah saw him crush it and make "another vessel, as seemed good to the potter to make it" (Jer. 18:4). If you have failed to cooperate with the divine Potter, it is not too late for you to be made into a useful vessel if you will yield to him now and let his will be your will in all ways always. Let us again join together in praying the prayer of surrender by singing "Have Thine Own Way, Lord!"

## SUGGESTED PREACHING PROGRAM FOR

# FEBRUARY

### ■ Sunday Mornings

Every believer needs genuine worship, and the improvement of worship should be the constant concern of each congregation. The suggested theme for the morning messages is "Worshiping in Spirit and in Truth" with John 4:12–24 as the guiding text.

### ■ Sunday Evenings

Continue the series on the Ten Commandments.

### ■ Wednesday Evenings

Selected parables of Jesus from the Gospel of Luke serve as vehicles to guide listeners toward making a positive response to God.

---

## SUNDAY MORNING, FEBRUARY 1

***Title:*** The Need for Meaningful Worship

***Text:*** "Thou shalt worship the Lord thy God, and him only shalt thou serve" **(Matt. 4:10)**.

***Scripture Reading:*** John 4:20–24

***Hymns:*** "O Worship the King," Grant

"All Hail the Power," Perronet

"O for a Thousand Tongues to Sing," Wesley

***Offertory Prayer:*** Our heavenly Father, we worship you in spirit and in truth. We approach you with an offering of love and gratitude. We invoke your blessings on these tithes and offerings to the end that others might enthrone the Christ in their hearts and give you their love and loyalty. Today we thank you for both spiritual and material blessings. Help us to be more worthy of your gracious generosity. In Christ's name. Amen.

### Introduction

Meaningful worship is one of the deepest needs of life. Individually and collectively we need to discover the importance of worship and give it the vital place it deserves.

The weakest point in the life of most of us is our worship. The absence of spiritual power, the lack of inward peace, and the failure to be genuinely Christian can be traced to failure to worship.

During the Second World War, Japan had a special division of pilots who flew suicide missions. They were called kamikaze pilots. The Allied forces considered them to be fanatics, and some even said that they were drugged. Those who are acquainted with Japanese history and customs recognize that these suicide missions were an expression of a combination of the highest patriotism and the deepest religious devotion.

The story behind the kamikaze began in 1281 when a huge armada of Mongolians landed at Hakata Bay determined to seize that portion of the empire of Japan. Before they were able to deploy their full forces ashore, a typhoon descended on the fleet and destroyed it, bringing the invasion to a disastrous conclusion. To the Japanese the typhoon was the kamikaze, or the divine wind, protecting the land of the gods from the invasion of foreigners. So, during World War II, pilots volunteered to become kamikaze—that is, the wind of God—to destroy the enemy and to protect their homeland. Their action illustrates the truth that intense dedication to a god (albeit a false god in their case) results in a special kind of people.

Is our failure to be a distinctive and unique people to be traced to the inadequacy of our worship? Is it possible we have been fooling ourselves into believing we are worshiping when in reality we are not?

**I. We must understand the meaning of true worship if we are to become the special people God desires us to be.**

A. *In some parts of the world, various forms of idolatrous worship involving body painting, native dances and rituals, and even witch doctors and voodoo are practiced.*

B. *From time to time accounts appear in the newspapers reporting that in places even in today's world people seek to worship by offering human sacrifices.*

C. *Some people think that just by going to church they are worshiping.* They listen to the pastor preach and hear the choir sing; then they go home thinking that they have worshiped.

D. *We must recognize that true worship is both an attitude and an activity.* It is a response of the soul to God's act of revealing himself. True worship is an experience in which people receive what God has to give and simultaneously give what they are and have to God.

E. *True worship is the adoration and appreciation of God by the grateful worshiper.*

F. *True worship is an experience of meditative communion with God in which the soul is in dialogue with the Eternal.* Worship is an inner posture of the soul rather than an action or posture of the body.

G. *True worship is the most dynamic and creative experience of which man is capable.*

**II. We must recognize the value of true worship.**

Vital worship relates people to God, who is the source of wisdom and inward power.

A. *True worship brings a consciousness of sin that leads to confession and to the joy of cleansing (Isa. 6:5–7).* To behold the holiness of God is to be deeply convinced of the uncleanness of sin. Confession from the heart brings the forgiveness and cleansing of divine love. This we all need, and this we can have.

B. *Real worship brings a person's soul into harmony with the will of God.* To bring the mind into conformity with the mind and will of God brings an inward peace, because destructive tension and friction have been removed.

C. *True worship gives the worshiper a sense of security.* God becomes very real and very near in love, grace, and power. The worship experience makes possible a faith that God will be present triumphantly in whatever the present or the future might bring.

D. *True worship helps the worshiper to rise above the temporal and the transitory.* The world is so much with us that we are inclined to view it from the worm's eye view rather than from the angel's perspective. As we worship, it becomes possible to set our affections on eternal things instead of being lured by the promises of material things.

E. *Real worship aids in problem solving.* As a pastor stood in the vestibule greeting the departing worshipers, a woman said, "Pastor, your sermon cured my headache this morning." She explained that she had arrived at church suffering the torments of inward turmoil and uncertainty. With a mind and heart searching for fellowship and for certainty, she went into the house of God with a hungry heart and an empty cup. God did not disappoint her. She departed with a testimony similar to that of the psalmist: "My cup runneth over."

F. *True worship always brings a new sense of responsibility toward God and others.* After Isaiah had seen God, confessed his sin, and experienced cleansing, he heard the voice of God calling. He volunteered.

If you have no sense of personal responsibility for those about you, and if you have not volunteered to help God in his ministry of mercy, then probably it has been a long, long time since you have really worshiped.

## III. We must understand the conditions of meaningful worship.

If we are to be a distinctive people of God, called out and separated from the world, then we need to understand the conditions that lead to fruitful worship experiences.

A. *Adequate preparation must be made if worship is to be beneficial.* We need to prepare our hearts and minds before arriving at church if we are to experience the greatest possible blessing. One does not automatically enter God's presence by walking through the door of a church.

While a warm, friendly spirit is of great value in a church, many people are so concerned about seeing and greeting their friends that they give little thought to the fact that they have come to the house of the Lord to see him and both receive from him and give to him.

Perhaps the most important part of preparing for public worship is private worship. How often do you pray for the worship services of your church? When did you last pray for the pastor? For the choir? For specific individuals in the congregation?

B. *Wholesome participation in worship is essential.* One can attend a football game and be a fairly inactive spectator. To enjoy the game fully, he must participate by identifying either with individual players or with a team.

When the Word of God is read, do you let God speak to your heart? When someone leads in prayer, do you also pray? Do you sing with the congregation?

## IV. The inspiration of worship must be carried into life.

In Jesus' temptation experience, the Devil did not say anything to Jesus about service when he made an appeal for his worship, but in Jesus' reply, he declared that worship and service are never to be separated. Service is as inseparable from real worship as a person is from his or her shadow in the brightness of the noonday sun.

A. *Our worship should lead us to service.* To have a life-transforming experience with the Eternal brings such a joy into the hearts of worshipers that they will desire to share this joy with others. To genuinely worship produces a joy within the heart that cannot be concealed. It has to express itself in service of one sort or another.

B. *Our service should lead us to worship.* Jesus told his disciples, "He that abideth in me, and I in him, the same bringeth forth much fruit: for without me ye can do nothing" (John 15:5).

We live in a world of vast spiritual need. Within our individual selves, we are inadequate for the task of ministering. Only as we worship and receive the wisdom, the guidance, and the power of God can we serve in an acceptable and productive way.

## Conclusion

Dr. Gaines S. Dobbins has said that "worship is the human soul in search of that which is supremely worthful." Have you recognized the supreme worth of Jesus Christ to your own heart and life? If you have not, decide to make him the Lord of your life. You would be wise to make him the object of your worship and to follow him and please him in every area of your life. Decide to do so today.

---

# SUNDAY EVENING, FEBRUARY 1

***Title:*** "Thou Shalt Not Kill"

***Text:*** "Thou shalt not kill" **(Exod. 20:13)**.

***Scripture Reading:*** Matthew 5:21–22

## Introduction

The sixth commandment is the commandment most easily accepted by people in our society today. We all suppose we understand it and that it is so clear that it requires no explanation or elaboration. Any discussion of it might appear to be a waste of effort and time inasmuch as no one doubts it and everyone accepts it, and no one would uphold wanton and unjustified killing.

In this commandment God seeks to impress upon us the infinite value of human beings. This commandment assumes that people are made in the image of God and that they are special creatures of infinite value in God's sight. That such is the case is revealed throughout the Bible. The Scriptures reveal that man's physical body sprang from the dust and that his spirit sprang from God. Thus, in the very beginning, humans were religious beings. The human body is the shrine of God's Spirit. It is the sanctuary of sanctuaries, in which the divine Spirit is enshrined. Murder is therefore not only a crime against humankind; it is also a crime against God in whose image humans are made.

The Ten Commandments are rules for abundant living. God laid down six that govern our relationships with our fellow humans. The first of these is "Thou shalt not kill."

## I. This commandment applies to ourselves: "Thou shalt not kill ... thyself."

A. *Let us speak gently, for it is doubtless true that suicide often is a consequence of some form of insanity—permanent or temporary.* Nevertheless, let us not be too sentimental here, for what is called "insanity" is often a moral madness rather than a mental disease, for which the sufferer is to blame. Suicide, when committed by a sane person, is murder, a violation of God's law.

B. *One can commit suicide by violating the laws of health.*

C. *One can commit suicide by exposing oneself to needless physical risk.*

D. *One can be guilty of suicide by exposing oneself to needless moral or spiritual risk.*

E. *Harmful pleasures are a form of suicide.*

1. Smoking causes lung cancer and other diseases that shorten life.
2. Alcohol shortens life and takes the lives of others.

## II. This commandment prohibits murder.

Some people have interpreted this commandment to prohibit the killing of anything in any circumstance, including all animal life. Some have even included vegetable life. Specifically, the commandment prohibits murder. There is a difference between killing and murder. Murder applies to the taking of a human life only and is a deliberate act of the will because of envy, covetousness, malice, or hatred.

A. *Human life is sacred.* Life is a precious gift from God and must be treated as such.

B. *Humans belong to their Maker.* To murder is to destroy that which belongs to God, and God strictly prohibits such.

C. *We should look upon each person as one for whom Christ died.*

D. *This life is the tiny beginning of an endless existence.*

## III. There are many refined methods of murder.

Some of us are guilty of murder and do not realize it.

A. *A husband can murder his wife by cruelty, selfishness, and unfaithfulness.*

B. *A wife can murder her husband by an insatiable greed for things and by a nagging, domineering spirit.*

C. *Children can murder their parents by ingratitude, irreverence, irreligion, disobedience, or a sinful life.*

## IV. Positively, this commandment means to live and help live.

A. *Do not pass by the wounded brother who is in need (Luke 10:30–32).*

B. *Look at all people from God's viewpoint, for people look different when the light of God's grace shines upon their faces.*

C. *Live by the Golden Rule: "Do unto others as you would have them do unto you" (Matt. 7:12).*

### Conclusion

We would not be stretching the meaning of this commandment if we were to interpret it as a prohibition against a person committing spiritual suicide by refusing to respond to God's grace through faith. It is the will of God that all people have life and have it more abundantly through faith in Jesus Christ. God is a loving Father, and through the gift of his Son Jesus Christ and through the continued efforts of the Holy Spirit, he is seeking to bring eternal life into every heart. God cannot and will not force us to trust him so as to escape spiritual death. When persons refuse to receive Christ, they deprive themselves of the eternal life that Christ is so eager to bestow upon them.

---

## WEDNESDAY EVENING, FEBRUARY 4

***Title:*** The Parable of the Barren Fig Tree

***Scripture Reading:*** Luke 13:6–9

### Introduction

The great prophet Isaiah told the people of Israel a parable about a vineyard (Isa. 5:1–7). The owner of the vineyard did everything he could to make the vineyard productive. He built a fence around it to protect it from marauding enemies. He removed the stones from the soil so that they could not interfere with the growth of the vines, and he planted only the finest vines. He built a tower in the midst of the vineyard and also constructed a wine press. He had every right to expect an abundance of delicious grapes, but instead the vineyard produced grapes that were bitter and repulsive.

In Isaiah's parable Israel is the vineyard. Instead of producing a harvest for the glory of God, the people had drifted into spiritual degeneracy and moral bankruptcy. Because of Israel's refusal to bring forth fruit, God spoke through Isaiah concerning the removal of the hedge that protected them. He announced that he would command the clouds to rain no more upon it (Isa. 5:5). This sentence was pronounced because, instead of justice, the people had produced oppression, and instead of righteousness, they lived crooked, selfish, sinful lives.

In the parable of the barren fig tree, Jesus spoke a similar message to the Israel of his day. He spoke of the owner of a vineyard who had for three years sought fruit on a certain fig tree during harvesttime only to find it barren. He decided that the fig tree should be destroyed because it was nonproductive. He asked the man who was in charge of caring for the vineyard a question that has an application for us today. After issuing an order to cut the tree down, he asked, "Why should it use up the soil?" (Luke 13:7 NIV). The vinedresser still had hopes for figs and suggested that it be given one more year of opportunity in which to be productive.

This parable has both a national and a personal application. Through this parable Jesus was saying that the nation of Israel had one more opportunity to bear fruit for the glory of God.

### I. This parable speaks of God's absolute ownership.

A. *Individuals forget that only God is absolute owner.* The Bible tells us that God created the heavens and the earth. He placed humans on the earth to subdue and develop it, but he did not give the earth to them. The world still belongs to God. The psalmist said, "The earth is the LORD's, and the fulness thereof; the world, and they that dwell therein" (Ps. 24:1).

B. *Governments and economic systems forget or ignore that God is owner.* In the world of today, two economic systems are contending for supremacy. The capitalistic system emphasizes that the individual has a right to own, utilize, and control property. In the socialistic economic system, individual property rights are denied and ownership is vested in the state. Both of these systems are in error, for neither the individual nor the state has the right of sole ownership: ownership belongs to God.

### II. This parable speaks of God's right to expect fruit.

A. *After the fig tree had been planted a sufficient length of time to bear fruit, the owner came expecting to find fruit in three successive years only to be disappointed repeatedly.* Not only was he disappointed, but he decided that the tree had no right to continue to survive if it was going to be nonproductive.

B. *God has a right to expect fruit from his vineyard.* He is the vine and his disciples are the branches. "He that abideth in me, and I in him, the same bringeth forth much fruit: for without me ye can do nothing" (John 15:5). Our heavenly Father is glorified as we bring forth much fruit (v. 8). "Ye have not chosen me, but I have chosen you, and ordained you, that ye should go and bring forth fruit, and that your fruit should remain" (v. 16).

### III. This parable speaks of the patience of God.

A. *In three different years, he came to the vineyard expecting fruit from the fig tree before deciding to have it cut down.*

B. *Because of the intercession of the vinedresser, the owner consented to give the fig tree one more year of opportunity.*

C. *Jesus was saying that God is patient both with the nation and with the individual, and that he would give them another chance.*

### IV. This parable speaks of the firmness of God.

A. *He who bears no fruit is a parasite.* God is patient, but there is a limit to that patience. The fig tree was given another chance.

B. *The owner of the vineyard said, "Cut it down."* God's judgments are rooted in righteousness.

### Conclusion

The unsaved about us are a total loss to God. They bear no fruit to his glory. They are in peril of experiencing his judgment. Because the mercy of God is still available to them and because of our concern for them, we should seek to persuade them to respond to the love of God that they might experience the joy of bearing fruit.

---

## SUNDAY MORNING, FEBRUARY 8

8-23-09

***Title:*** The Elements of Worship

***Text:*** "In the year that king Uzziah died I saw also the Lord sitting upon a throne, high and lifted up, and his train filled the temple" **(Isa. 6:1)**.

***Scripture Reading:*** Isaiah 6:1–8

***Hymns:*** "Praise to the Lord, the Almighty," Neander

"Take Time to Be Holy," Longstaff

"Brethren, We Have Met to Worship," Atkins

***Offertory Prayer:*** Our heavenly Father, we are mindful of your bountiful goodness toward us. We thank you for every gift of your mercy. As we bring tithes and offerings of the fruit of our labors, we thank you for the opportunity to work and the power to get wealth. Help us never to forget that you are the giver of every good and perfect gift. Help us to give to you as you have given to us. Amen.

### Introduction

Psychologist William James observed that worship is universal and said, "Men worship because they must." Anthropologists have yet to find a group of people who do not have some form of worship. People seek after the eternal because, as the supreme creation of God, they have planted within them a capacity and hunger for God that cannot be satisfied by anything but God.

Throughout the Bible we find instructions concerning worship. More often we find examples of either true or false worship. The Bible also contains many indictments concerning the use of empty, meaningless rituals that people tried to pass off as worship.

One of the greatest needs of our day is for the people of God to engage in genuine worship. Unchanged lives glaringly illustrate the neglect of true worship, for true worship always produces an inward transformation that leaves a mark on a person's conduct.

An examination of the motives that lead one to attend public worship can be either embarrassing or encouraging. Do you attend public worship simply because you desire the respect of those in your community? Do you go to please some particular person, be it husband, wife, parent, or child? Do you go because you want to see or be seen by some individual? Are you motivated only by a sense of duty or habit? Are you regular in attendance because of a fear of the consequences if you do not attend?

Perhaps some of you are present today because of a heart hunger for Jesus Christ as your own personal Savior. Could it be that some of you are present because of an intense desire for divine guidance as you face the problems and duties of life? No doubt some of you are here with a desire to impart a blessing to someone else by a lesson, by a song, or by the fellowship that you are able to extend to others.

Could it be that you are here because of a deep inward need for encouragement and the strength that comes only from God? Many are here out of a desire to express love and gratitude to God. Are you present today because of a great dissatisfaction with your life as it has been, combined with a desire for your life to be as God meant for it to be?

Many sincere people do not receive the blessing of God during public worship because they either neglect or fail to worship even though they are present. Genuine worship calls for an active response of participation rather than just a passive attendance at the place of prayer.

Genuine worship is basically an experience with God. It is the response of the human soul to the truth of God as that truth is made known to the individual. One can sing and not worship. One can read the Bible and never hear the voice of God speaking to the heart. One can attend public worship services and go away unblessed and unchanged.

The experience of Isaiah in the temple provides us with a dramatic demonstration of the elements that constitute a life-changing worship experience.

**I. The first element is contemplation.**

A. *The scene opens with Isaiah in the temple.* It is quite possible that Isaiah was there because of a regular habit of going to the temple for worship. It is most likely that the death of Uzziah was the immediate occasion for his visit to the temple. Uzziah had been a strong and successful ruler, and the nation had enjoyed great prosperity during his reign. As Uzziah achieved great success and as the nation enjoyed great prosperity, he became proud and haughty. Not being content with regal power, he snatched at the power that was reserved for the priests and went into the Holy of Holies to offer sacrifice. Because of this act of impiety, he was smitten with leprosy (2 Chron. 26:16–20). He spent the balance of his life in quarantine.

Many have supposed that Isaiah, a young nobleman of Jerusalem, had been a hero worshiper during his youth. The object of his adoration was none other than the proud king of Judah. It was with sudden swiftness that the idol of his youth was smitten by God. As Isaiah mulled over the seriousness of Uzziah's offense, it began to dawn upon him that the king's easy familiarity with God had been his downfall.

B. *Isaiah entered the temple with a sense of fear and uncertainty concerning the future.* While his mind was disturbed and on a search for certainty, he had the strangest experience of his lifetime.

C. *The vision of God.* In dramatic language, Isaiah relates how, in this mysterious experience in the temple, his inward eye was opened and he saw God in all of his holiness and majesty. While contemplating the fact that Israel's king was dead and the throne was empty, he received a revelation of the divine King seated on the throne of the universe.

Isaiah's contribution to this experience was an attitude of deep reverence and a mind concentrated on God and on his plans for the future. The earthly temple faded away, and Isaiah was permitted to look into the heavenly throne room. He was made to realize that although the throne room of Judah was vacant, the throne of the universe was still occupied by the sovereign Creator.

Isaiah did not spend his time in the temple chatting with his neighbor or taking a delightful snooze. With a reverent, meditative spirit, he came seeking God, and he was not disappointed.

### II. The second element is confession.

A. *Conviction of sin.* While Isaiah looked on entranced, he saw angels hovering about the Lord of the world to do his bidding (Isa. 6:2). He saw the fire of the heavenly altar and heard the seraphim's song of adoration and praise to God (v. 3). As the sound of the united voices pealed through the expanse, the pillars of the door shook to their foundations and the house was filled with smoke as the reaction of God's holy nature against sin.

Isaiah's response to this august revelation of God was an attitude of holy awe. No doubt he shared the belief of the Hebrews that no one could look upon the face of God and live. Even the seraphim covered their faces before him.

As Isaiah took in this vision of the holy God, he was made vividly conscious of his own sinfulness and of that of his people. Isaiah suddenly realized that he and the faithless, rebellious people of Israel were like the faithless and rebellious king who had died under the curse of God.

B. *An honest confession.* As Isaiah worshiped, he became aware of his unworthiness to stand in God's presence. He feared the worst as a result of this personal encounter with God. Had Uzziah not died because of his intrusion into the Holy Place? As Isaiah was convicted of his sin, he hastily confessed his spiritual uncleanness: "Then said I, Woe is me! for I am undone; because I am a man of unclean lips, and I dwell in the midst of a people of unclean lips: for mine eyes have seen the King, the LORD of hosts" (Isa. 6:5).

C. *The need for confession.* Unresolved guilt can be a most disruptive force in a person's life. There is no greater need than the need for confession and the forgiveness that follows. Each of us needs to confess our sins before God, for sin can destroy us and harm others. Until we are willing to recognize, confess, and forsake sin, there is not much hope for our spiritual betterment.

**III. A third element of worship is cleansing.**

A. *God is eager to forgive.* Jesus affirmed that "God sent not his Son into the world to condemn the world, but that the world through him might be saved" (John 3:17). God takes no delight in condemning the sins and the moral uncleanness of his people. Nor does he delight in our suffering the agony of a guilty conscience. God wants to forgive and cleanse us.

B. *The agony of uncleanness.* Isaiah was in an awful agony as he recognized the depths of his uncleanness. A sense of guilt is always an embarrassing experience. A sense of guilt can be very destructive if one simply condemns himself instead of confessing his sin so as to experience cleansing and the joy of forgiveness.

God reveals himself to us in his holiness and moral perfection—not to make us miserable, but to reveal to us the awfulness of our sin so that we might abhor it as the destructive thing that it is and forsake it. Those who can tolerate sin in their lives without being disturbed reveal that they have never had a vision of the holiness and purity of God. Peter had an awareness of the holiness of God while on a fishing trip. When he saw the miraculous catch of fish, "he fell down at Jesus' knees, saying, Depart from me; for I am a sinful man, O Lord" (Luke 5:8).

C. *The joy of being clean.* Instead of being driven from the presence of God because of his sinfulness, Isaiah found that the vision that had intensified his consciousness of sin was also to assure him of the removal of his sin. He records, "Then flew one of the seraphim unto me, having a live coal in his hand, which he had taken with the tongs from off the altar: And he laid it upon my mouth, and said, Lo, this hath touched thy lips; and thine iniquity is taken away, and thy sin purged" (Isa. 6:6–7). Following his confession of sin, Isaiah experienced cleansing that was immediate and complete. This cleansing was free, full, and forever.

When God forgives, God forgets. If God does forgive, then we need to forgive ourselves and face the future with the gratitude of the forgiven and with the joy of the redeemed. Every experience of worship should contain within it the joy of the assurance of sins confessed, forgiven, and forsaken.

**IV. A fourth element in worship is consecration.**

Following Isaiah's wonderful experience of cleansing from the defilement of sin, he heard the voice of God. His lips having been cleansed, he was now prepared for personal conversation with God. He heard the question of the Lord, "Whom shall I send, and who will go for us?" (Isa. 6:8). Mingled trembling and elation filled his soul as a response to this invitation came to his lips: "Here am I; send me" (v. 8).

Isaiah made no effort to escape the call. Nor did he make excuses or try to stall. His experience of worship issued in a decision of complete consecration to God's will.

### Conclusion

If we are to worship in spirit and in truth, we must bring our minds and hearts to bear upon the truth of God and upon his will for our lives. As we become aware of our sins and moral uncleanness, we would honestly confess them and pray for the power to forsake every sinful attitude and act. Following confession will come the joy of cleansing and forgiveness. Then and then only will we be equipped to bear a winsome and winning witness to our world.

---

## SUNDAY EVENING, FEBRUARY 8

***Title:*** The Preservation of Purity

***Text:*** "Thou shalt not commit adultery" **(Exod. 20:14)**.

***Scripture Reading:*** Matthew 19:3–12

### Introduction

The state of matrimony is earth's most sacred relationship. It is a divine institution and is to take precedence over every other human relationship. It carries us back to the garden of Eden where the Maker of heaven and earth joined together the parents of the human race.

There are at least five principles that characterize the marriage relationship from a biblical standpoint: *monogamy*, *permanency*, *fidelity*, *mutuality*, and *love*.

Someone has said that the seventh commandment is "the divine law-giver's ordinance guarding the chastity of marriage, the sanctity of the home, the blessedness of the household, the preservation of society, and the up-building of mankind." A theology professor has said, "About 50 percent of all human misery is caused by the violation of this commandment." This commandment safeguards the highest earthly relationship.

**I. What is adultery?**

A. *Sex outside of marriage.*

B. *Violation of the marriage vows.*

C. *Lust in the heart (Matt. 5:27–28).*

## II. Why is adultery wrong?

A. *God says so.*

B. *It hurts people.*

1. It degrades man, destroying his self-respect and causing his respect for others to decline.
2. It destroys pure womanhood by injuring the mind and leaving a scar on the soul.

C. *It destroys marriage.*

D. *It deprives children of the peace and the affection to which birth gives them a right.*

E. *It is a frustration of God's purpose and will for man.*

F. *It is a crime against God.* Adultery defiles what God has created to be holy. It makes sordid what God has made sacred.

In wrecking one home, the adulterer weakens all homes, for the keystone of society is the home of the good man and the good wife living faithfully together and keeping the vows of love and fidelity they made at the marriage altar.

Sexual corruption is one of the chief symptoms of a decaying society. The exaggerated emphasis on sex in our land today is a symptom of a rotting and decadent society. "The wicked shall be turned into hell, and all the nations that forget God" (Ps. 9:17).

## III. Can anything be done about this sin?

A. *The Christian should determine to live a life of perfect purity.* To do so a person must avoid circumstances that would encourage immorality and commit oneself to a life of moral purity, sitting in judgment on any evil impulse and dealing drastically with it as Jesus commanded (Matt. 5:29–30).

The Christian needs to strive to make Jesus Christ master of every area of life. Imagination and thoughts must be brought under his loving control.

B. *There is forgiveness for those who repent of adultery.* God is able to forgive this sin even as he is able to forgive others. Even though God forgives, he cannot remove the consequences of breaking this commandment.

C. *Jesus dealt with the woman who was accused of adultery in terms of mercy, forgiveness, and instruction for the future.* "Jesus straightened up and asked her, 'Woman, where are they? Has no one condemned you?' 'No one, sir,' she said. 'Then neither do I condemn you,' Jesus declared. 'Go now and leave your life of sin'" (John 8:10–11 NIV).

## Conclusion

God is a God of mercy and grace who is eager to forgive and to cleanse. He deals in mercy with those who come to him in repentance and in confession of breaking the seventh commandment.

If God forgives those who sin against him, we would be wise to forgive those who sin against us. To forgive is often difficult, but not to forgive is much more difficult in the long run. Trust God for grace and guidance if you need help forgiving.

James said, "For whosoever shall keep the whole law, and yet offend in one point, he is guilty of all" (James 2:10). While not all of us have sinned alike, all of us are sinners and are in need of God's forgiveness and cleansing grace. Let us come to Christ continually for purity.

## WEDNESDAY EVENING, FEBRUARY 11

***Title:*** The Parable of the Good Samaritan

***Scripture Reading:*** Luke 10:25–37

### Introduction

All of us are guilty of committing many types of sin—sins of omission and sins of commission, sins of the flesh and sins of the spirit, open sins and secret sins, shameful sins and so-called respectable sins. It was a respectable sin that Jesus graphically pointed out in the parable of the good Samaritan so as to bring conviction to the soul of the hard-hearted lawyer.

Christ still speaks through the parable of the good Samaritan to people of the twenty-first century. He indicts us for our indifference toward the ills of a suffering, lost humanity. At the same time, he challenges us to realize life's greatest joy and to experience life's highest possibilities.

Let us examine this parable for a message that speaks to our hearts in this present day.

### I. The occasion for the parable.

As Jesus approached the climax of his earthly ministry, the scribes and Pharisees developed great hostility toward him. They found his teachings of universal love for all contradictory to their customs and traditions. They resented him because he associated with sinners and because he demonstrated mercy on the Sabbath. They plotted to bring about his downfall by either disgrace or death. One from this group, a lawyer, or scribe, who was an interpreter and teacher of both the law of Moses and the traditions of the rabbis, came to him with a question: "Master what shall I do to inherit eternal life?" (Luke 10:25).

Jesus answered on a basis with which the lawyer was very familiar. He encouraged the man to carry out to the fullest the implications of the second great commandment. The lawyer, insisting on a rigid observance of both the commandments of Moses and of the traditions of their fathers, then asked a question that indicated a deep desire to place limitations on the social obligations of that second great commandment.

A. *His question indicated a desire to limit the circle of his concern.* Are we not all somewhat guilty of the same thing? We limit our concern to our own group, be it family, friends, fellow employees, social group, or church members.

B. *The lawyer's question indicated a desire to place limits on efforts spent in the service of others.*

**II. The parable illustrates the needy world in which we live.**

A. *The man wounded by thieves still suffers and is in danger of death.*

B. *Many are wounded and dying by the highway of life.*

1. Some have been robbed and almost destroyed by parental failure.
2. Others have been left half dead as a result of their own folly and choice of evil.
3. Others have been degraded by their own enslaving habits.
4. Some have been damaged severely by false teachings concerning God and life.
5. Some have been wounded by the bad influence of some so-called Christians.
6. There are great crowds in nearly every community who, far more than is realized, suffer because of prejudice.
7. Tomorrow will not go by without your meeting someone who is ready to cave in because of the fear of what the future holds.

**III. The parable illustrates the indifference of coldheartedness.**

A. *The priest passed by on the other side of the road.* Perhaps he was on his way to the temple, or perhaps he had been to the temple and was now on his way home. His refusal to provide assistance indicated a coldhearted selfishness.

B. *The Levite came by and looked at the wounded man and passed by on the other side.* His inhuman behavior indicated a calculated selfishness. Both the priest and the Levite indicated the lack of reality in their worship by not manifesting love toward the needy.

C. *Are we passing by on the other side without realizing it?*

1. When we neglect to show concern for the unsaved, we are passing by on the other side.
2. When we live an unworthy life that does not attract others to Christ, we are passing by on the other side.
3. When we neglect to train for effective service to God and others, we are passing by on the other side.
4. When we refuse to support God's work financially, we are passing by on the other side.
5. When we refuse to actively serve God, we are passing by on the other side.

**IV. The parable illustrates compassion.**

A. *The Samaritan had seeing eyes and hearing ears.* He heard the suffering man's cries of distress, and with his eyes he surveyed the victim's need.

B. *The Samaritan had a compassionate heart that was in command of both his energies and resources.*
C. *The Samaritan had willing hands that were at the command of his compassion.*
   1. Because of the man's need, he chose to be inconvenienced that day.
   2. Because of the man's need, he chose to make an expenditure of his resources.
   3. To meet the man's needs, he chose the way that was not considered popular by the priest and the Levite.
   4. He chose the way that was to bring joy to his own heart and relief to others.

   Following this story and the lawyer's admission that the Samaritan alone had demonstrated compassion, Jesus said, "Go, and do thou likewise" (Luke 10:37).

### Conclusion

Are you following the examples of the priest and Levite or the example of the Good Samaritan? It is not always popular or convenient or cheap to follow the example of the Good Samaritan, but his is the right way. His is the way of joy. His is the way to success, both now and forever.

---

## SUNDAY MORNING, FEBRUARY 15

***Title:*** Hindrances to Worship

***Text:*** "God is a Spirit: and they that worship him must worship him in spirit and in truth" (**John 4:24**).

***Scripture Reading:*** Psalm 100

***Hymns:*** "Breathe on Me," Hatch

"Nothing Between," Tindley

"Yield Not to Temptation," Palmer

***Offertory Prayer:*** Heavenly Father, today our hearts thank you for the abundance of your grace toward us. We praise you with our lips and glorify you with our lives. We proclaim your salvation to all peoples throughout the world. As an indication of our desire that others might know of your grace, we bring our tithes and offerings for the advancement of the work of your kingdom. Bless these offerings to that purpose. In Jesus' name. Amen.

### Introduction

One could read the Bible and see in it a continuous series of calls to worship. The eternal Father God seeks the worship of our hearts, for in truth he alone is worthy of the undivided worship of the human heart. For people to worship something less than the true and living God is to worship that which will disappoint them and downgrade them from their highest possible destiny.

Many of us recognize that worship is as essential to the spiritual life as bread is to the physical life. We have experienced some of the beneficent results of worship in our own life and have seen the results in the lives of others. While recognizing the invaluable results of worship, many of us would confess that we are sadly deficient in experiencing these results. Perhaps if we will stop and evaluate some of the hindrances to worship, it will help us to participate more meaningfully in worship.

**I. There are hindrances to worship within ourselves.**

A. *The lack of physical rest.* One popular joke concerns the fellow who went to sleep during a worship service and made some foolish remark when he awoke suddenly without an awareness of his surroundings. The truth is that it is almost impossible to have a creative worship experience when we are totally exhausted in mind and body. When we work hard during the week or deprive ourselves of sleep on Saturday night, we find it easy to snooze a bit when we relax during a worship service.

B. *The lack of mental preparation.* It is foolish to believe that a person can forget God during the week, watch a movie on Saturday night, arise late the next morning, rush to church, and then suddenly have a tremendous experience with God without having prepared his or her mind and heart to do so. Repeatedly Jesus spoke about the necessity of using our eyes to see and our ears to hear. We must do more than bring our bodies to church to worship. We must also bring our minds.

How much more wonderful it would be if everyone would make a careful inventory of his or her personal and family needs before going to the house of prayer and worship. If with the thoughtfulness of a wife who prepares a grocery list before going to the grocery store each of us would consider our spiritual needs, we would be much more likely to receive the needed blessings that God can so generously give.

C. *An immature, incomplete, or faulty concept of God.* The Devil has been misrepresenting God from the very beginning of history (Gen. 3:4–5). He is a slanderer and a liar. He has so misrepresented the nature and character of God that some people hate God instead of loving him. They refuse to believe in him when in reality he is worthy of their complete trust. God is no cruel tyrant or brutal bully. We need to quit listening to what the Devil says about God.

Jesus came to reveal and to demonstrate that God is a God of love and mercy and grace. He spoke of him as the heavenly Father who is more eager to bestow good gifts upon his children than even a loving earthly father is. He would lead us to put our faith in this heavenly Father and challenge us to recognize that divine love is behind every prohibition or commandment of God.

If we will listen to Jesus instead of to the Devil concerning the nature and purpose of God, we will overcome some of the hindrances within ourselves that prevent us from worshiping in spirit and in truth.

D. *Unconfessed and unforsaken sin.* Only fools treat sin lightly. God is against sin because of its evil, destructive nature. He cannot condone or tolerate sin because of his great love for us. With a persistent determination, he purposes to deliver us from that which is going to destroy us if we do not forsake it in our heart.

For the child of God to knowingly tolerate sin in his life is to break fellowship with God and to create a sense of guilt that will prevent him from coming into the Father's presence. This may explain why you have not enjoyed the warmth and love of God's presence for a long time.

E. *A lack of an attitude of expectancy.* Jesus promised his disciples, "For where two or three are gathered together in my name, there am I in the midst of them" (Matt. 18:20). With a heart of faith we should expect Jesus Christ to be present in every service when God's people come together in his name. Many of us do not receive a blessing during the hour of worship because we did not come expecting to receive one.

## II. There are hindrances to worship in those about us.

A. *Those about us often distract us from worship.* Have you ever found it difficult to concentrate because someone was whispering? Have you ever become annoyed by the person sipping coffee or a bottled drink in front of you? As a parent have you permitted an uncomfortable child who wiggled a bit to deprive you of an experience with God? If we can be distracted, we will be. We need to recognize these distractions and then determine not to permit them to deprive us of God's blessings.

B. *Those about us often discourage and disappoint us.* Human beings are habitual faultfinders. This can be a deadly pastime when one comes to church. To have the habit of finding fault in others and consequently being disappointed by them can rob us of the blessings that God has for us. Search your own heart and be honest. Is it not true that in the moment you begin to criticize your neighbor, you cease to worship? You cannot be critical of your neighbor and at the same time receive the blessings that God has for you.

If you are a faultfinder, you can always find something wrong with the minister or with the choir or with the congregation. While you are criticizing your neighbor you are actually focusing the spotlight away from God and on yourself. Instead of being critical of your neighbor, it would be much more profitable for you to let the X-ray of God's holiness search your own heart and mind for that which is deserving of your critical appraisal.

Remember the Pharisee who prayed in the temple, complimenting himself and congratulating God on how fortunate he was to have a Pharisee such as himself attending the temple services on that Sabbath. His prayer was a waste of breath and his attendance nothing but a pious pretense. The publican who was present did not spend his time criticizing his neighbor. He did not even lift his face up toward God, yet he saw God.

He also saw himself. His cry for mercy was heard, and he went home with peace in his heart and with new power to face the future.

### III. There are hindrances to worship in the world about us.

A. *The claims of false gods clamor for our worship.*

1. Some worship a person other than God. Hundreds of men allow their wives to be the supreme object of their affection. Many wives let their husbands be the lord of their existence. Many parents make slaves out of themselves for their children. Some of us are guilty of giving to another person the supreme love and loyalty of our heart that should be given only to God.
2. Some worship pleasure. Never has the world offered the promise of more pleasure than it does today. People are strongly pressured to live for that which brings pleasure in the moment rather than recognizing the eternal dimension of life.
3. Some worship a variety of different pursuits. In an age that emphasizes the need for planning ahead, many are doing so to the extent that they have accepted a goal for life that does not include worshiping the true God. They are unreservedly giving themselves to the pursuit of an educational, economic, or political goal in life.

B. *The current spirit of the world does not encourage true worship.*

1. We live in a scientific age where the scientific method is applied in every area of life. Scientists have discovered the laws of God and his world and have developed these to the extent that many have forgotten the Creator of us all. We have become fascinated with people and their discoveries and inventions and with the potential for future discoveries to the extent that many would consider the church and the Bible as something obsolete that belonged to a bygone age.
2. The pressure to succeed in the present is so great that many are neglecting to take the long look. Many have forgotten to look inside and also to look up. When people neglect to worship or refuse to worship, life becomes meaningless and empty.

### Conclusion

What is the main thing that hinders you from worshiping the true and living God? Pray that God will lead and assist you as you seek to worship in spirit and in truth. Invite the Holy Spirit of God to be your Guide and Teacher and Helper that you might worship God acceptably and that your life might glorify God so that others might see in you the results of a life of worship and service. Poet Andrew Reed recognized the need for the Holy Spirit's help in worship and prayed thus:

*Holy Ghost, with light divine,*
*Shine upon this heart of mine;*
*Chase the shades of night away;*
*Turn my darkness into day.*

*Holy Ghost, with power divine,*
*Cleanse this guilty heart of mine;*
*Long has sin, without control,*
*Held dominion o'er my soul.*

*Holy Ghost, with joy divine,*
*Cheer this saddened heart of mine;*
*Bid my many woes depart,*
*Heal my wounded, bleeding heart.*

*Holy Spirit, all divine,*
*Dwell within this heart of mine;*
*Cast down every idol throne;*
*Reign supreme, and reign alone.*

## SUNDAY EVENING, FEBRUARY 15

***Title:*** Thieves: Plain and Fancy

***Text:*** "Thou shalt not steal" **(Exod. 20:15)**.

### Introduction

The eighth commandment recognizes a person's right to property. In God's original commission to humans, they were instructed to have "dominion over the fish of the sea, and over the fowl of the air, and over the cattle, and over all the earth, and over every creeping thing that creepeth upon the earth. So God created man in his own image, in the image of God created he him; male and female created he them. And God blessed them, and God said unto them, Be fruitful, and multiply, and replenish the earth, and subdue it" (Gen. 1:26–28).

History is the record of humankind's execution of this original commission. We should recognize property as a divine institution and the right of property as a sacred trust.

Today we will look at a person's right to possess property, not from the view of the economist or sociologist, but from the teachings of the Bible.

There are four means by which people may come into the possession of property—by inheritance, by toil, by theft, or by gift.

### I. Plain thieves.

The eighth commandment forbids a man to be a plain thief. By a plain thief we refer to a blackmailer, a burglar, a forger, a kidnapper, a pickpocket, a robber, a shoplifter, a smuggler, or a swindler.

### II. All men are tempted to break the eighth commandment.

The temptation to steal springs from various sources.

A. *The temptation to steal often springs from the sense of necessity.*

B. *The temptation to steal springs from laziness.*
C. *The temptation to steal springs from fast living.*
D. *The temptation to steal springs from the love of display.*
E. *The temptation to steal springs from the haste to become rich.* How true it is that the love of money is a root of all kinds of evil. The poor may love money just as much as the rich. It is at this point that people most often break the eighth commandment.

Because this temptation is so universal and powerful, we need to beware of the peril of becoming a fancy thief.

**III. The peril of becoming a fancy thief.**

Most of us would not dream of stealing the spare tire from our neighbor's car, yet if we place our conscience squarely under the searchlight of God's Spirit and the teachings of the Holy Scripture, it is possible that we will find ourselves to be guilty of something just as serious.

Perhaps it would be better to call it "fancy" stealing instead of just plain stealing. One can be guilty of stealing things that are far more valuable than material property. It is possible that our intangible possessions are of greater value than our material property. By one means or another, we salve our consciences and justify our doing what we want to do and getting what we want to get.

A. *People justify a false income tax return by saying, "Nobody tells the truth to Uncle Sam.* Why should I?"
B. *False advertising is a form of fancy stealing.* The excuse "Business is business—they all do it" is offered.
C. *To turn back the speedometer of your car before selling it is fancy stealing.*
D. *The mother who misrepresents the age of her child so as to pay only half fare is doing some fancy stealing.*
E. *The refusal to pay an adequate salary for a day's work is a form of fancy stealing.*
F. *To refuse to give a full day's labor for a day's wage is a form of fancy stealing.*
G. *Wasting other people's time is a form of fancy stealing.*
H. *To degrade one's reputation by derogatory remarks is a form of stealing.* Shakespeare said, "Who steals my purse steals trash, but he who filches from me my good name robs me of that which not enriches him but makes me poor indeed." A gossiper is indeed a thief. Do you know a choice morsel of gossip about someone? Then swallow it.
I. *The failure to pay our just debts is a vile form of fancy stealing.* Years ago a great spiritual revival swept through a certain city. A skeptical and ungodly merchant said, "There is nothing to this revival." But soon his old customers came in and began paying their overdue bills; consequently, he changed his mind, went to church, and found Christ as his own personal Savior.
J. *Immorality is a form of fancy thievery.* He who would seduce an innocent girl or steal the affections of another man's wife is a thief of the basest sort.
K. *The refusal to bring tithes to the Lord is a form of fancy stealing (Mal. 3:8–10).*

### IV. Irreligion is a violation of the eighth commandment.

A. *All of the earth belongs to God (Ps. 24:1).*
B. *All people belong to God.*
C. *The ungodly person denies that the earth and its inhabitants are the Lord's.*
D. *The conversion experience is a deep inward personal acknowledgment of God as owner and Lord and of Jesus Christ as Savior and Redeemer.*

### Conclusion

We are our own worst enemies. We are thieves when it comes to robbing ourselves of the estate that God has provided for us.

Have you robbed yourself of the privilege of sonship to God through refusing or neglecting to receive Jesus Christ into your heart? Have you robbed yourself of the joy of forgiveness by a refusal to repent and to confess your sins to God?

---

## WEDNESDAY EVENING, FEBRUARY 18

***Title:*** The Parable of God's Sorrow

***Scripture Reading:*** Luke 15

### Introduction

Some people say that Luke 15 is the best-known chapter in the New Testament. It is called the parable of the prodigal son. I prefer to think of it as the parable of the waiting father who experienced great sorrow because of the attitudes of his sons.

Some see in this chapter one parable, while others see three parables, and still others see four parables. Is it possible that in our concentration on the prodigal son we have missed the point concerning which son was actually lost?

### I. God is like a good shepherd seeking a lost sheep (Luke 15:4–7).

Jesus tells about the good shepherd who had one hundred sheep. As they entered the fold late in the evening, the shepherd counted them to make sure all were present. He was greatly disturbed to find that only ninety-nine of the hundred were present. He felt a sense of loss because one of the sheep was lost. He went into the darkness and dangers of the night determined to find the lost sheep. God is like that today. He is seeking those who have drifted away no matter what the reason might be. God will not be fully happy until all of the sheep are in the fold. He suffers loss as long as you are away in the darkness of unbelief.

### II. God is like a woman seeking a lost coin (Luke 15:8–10).

Jesus tells the story of a woman whose fortune was concentrated in ten silver coins. One day she became terribly upset when she discovered that one of her coins was missing. With great haste she began diligently seeking throughout all of the house until she had found it. If for some reason you have slipped away, you can be sure that the eternal God, with the concern of the woman who was seeking her lost coin, is seeking you by every means at his command.

### III. God is like a father with a son gone astray (Luke 15:11–24).

In our concentration upon the son who demanded his inheritance and who departed to seek his fortune in a foreign country, it may be that we have overlooked the agony of the brokenhearted father who remained at home. The father had granted to his son the freedom of choice even if that freedom meant his destruction. The father had bestowed upon this self-centered immature son not only freedom but an abundance of earthly goods. It was a sad day for the father when this son demanded the privilege of leaving home for the far country. The father was lonely and concerned about the welfare of the wayward boy. In agony he yearned for the day when the boy would come to his senses and return.

The parable presents to us a vivid picture of the feeling of loss in the heart of God because of our waywardness and our lack of faith.

If you are dwelling in the far country, which may be only one step away from God, you can be absolutely sure that his heart grieves because of your refusal to come home.

### IV. God continues to experience sorrow (Luke 15:25–32).

The point of the parable is to illustrate the sorrow that God experiences when people refuse his grace and mercy.

When the younger son returned filled with remorse and repentance, he was welcomed by the father. He was welcomed and restored, and immediately preparations were made for a great feast.

The elder son returned from the fields and was surprised to hear the music and rejoicing. He was resentful when he heard about the return of his wayward brother. He not only rejected his brother but his father as well, for he refused to come in for the feast. His comments revealed that at heart he was a slave instead of a son. He neither admired nor approved of his father's forgiveness and restoration of his brother.

### Conclusion

Jesus spoke this parable to the scribes and Pharisees who refused to understand God's joy over retrieving lost sinners from their ways. They refused to believe that God is like a good shepherd who feels a great loss when one of the sheep has gone astray. They refused to believe that God is like a woman seeking her lost coin. They refused to believe that God is like the waiting father who wants to prepare a feast for the repentant son.

Let us rejoice in and respond to this God who suffers loss when we go astray.

## SUNDAY MORNING, FEBRUARY 22

***Title:*** The Response of the Worshiper

***Text:*** "I heard the voice of the LORD, saying, Whom shall I send, and who will go for us? Then said I, Here am I; send me" **(Isa. 6:8)**.

***Scripture Reading:*** Isaiah 6:1–9

***Hymns:*** "Holy, Holy, Holy," Heber

"Though Your Sins Be as Scarlet," Crosby

"Serve the Lord with Gladness," McKinney

***Offertory Prayer:*** Holy and loving Father, we approach your throne of grace with our best. We would not come before you with anything cheap or shoddy. Out of genuine love and gratitude we offer you the fruit of our labors as an expression of the worship of our hearts. Accept these tithes and offerings as we seek to give ourselves completely to you. In Jesus' name. Amen.

### Introduction

Isaiah's experience in the temple is perhaps the most stimulating illustration of genuine worship to be found in the Bible. King Uzziah had died after a lengthy and successful reign as the king of Israel. The throne of Israel was vacant. With disturbed thoughts concerning the fate of the king and with a fear of the future, Isaiah entered the temple.

Before the eye of Isaiah's soul, God revealed himself occupying the throne of the universe. Isaiah saw God high and holy, sovereign and supreme. As he heard the seraphim sing of the thrice holy God, he was overwhelmed with an awareness of his moral and spiritual uncleanness and of the sinfulness of his nation. There arose from his heart a sincere confession that was really a plea for cleansing and purification. By the goodness of God he experienced complete forgiveness and immediate cleansing. Then he heard the voice of God.

### I. The perplexity of God: "Whom shall I send, and who will go for us?" (Isa. 6:8).

A. *The God of Isaiah continues to be burdened and concerned for our sinful, lost world.*

B. *The divine concern for the salvation of man brought Jesus Christ to earth and carried him to Calvary.*

C. *The divine call for laborers continues now (Matt. 9:36–38).*

D. *God would and could do mighty things through us today if we had the faith to hear and the love and concern that would cause us to help him seek the lost.*

### II. The possibility of a partnership: "Who will go for us?"

A. *The kingdom of God has never had an oversupply of workers.* The labor market of God has never been overcrowded. This tragic condition continues to exist to the present.

B. *Our God is seeking you.*
   1. God is. He is the Creator and Sustainer of our universe. He loves each of us, and he also loves unbelievers.
   2. God calls. By his Spirit, by the Scriptures, and by the needs of others, God calls each of us to invest our lives in redemptive activities.
   3. God calls you. He calls you where you are. He calls you because of what you are. He calls you because of what you can become and because of what you can do if you will cooperate with him.

C. *God calls us.* He calls each one to know Christ, to accept Christ, to love Christ, to obey Christ, and to serve Christ.

## III. The plea of a volunteer: "Here am I; send me."

Isaiah was a volunteer. Although he had an inward constraint to do the will of God, he volunteered. Isaiah was no conscript or draftee who was forced to respond, but when God called, Isaiah immediately said, "Here am I; send me."

A. *The gratitude of the redeemed required this response.* God had revealed the holiness of his nature to Isaiah, and the future prophet had been overwhelmed with his own sinfulness and unworthiness. Following his confession of sin, Isaiah experienced cleansing and knew the joy of forgiveness. Because of his gratitude for being redeemed and of his joy for being forgiven, he volunteered.

B. *Isaiah's compassion for the people of his nation rose up to make up this response.* Compassion for the suffering and for those who have been deceived by sin motivates one to respond to the call to serve. This was the natural and normal response of one whose heart God had made clean.

C. *Wisdom demanded this voluntary response on the part of Isaiah.* If we would seriously consider the benefits that come to those who respond to God's invitation, there would be a line of volunteers waiting before every opportunity for service in the church. We would see these opportunities and go out into our own personal world in response to the call of God.

D. *Eternity alone will reveal the rewards of this decision.* Instead of laboring for the meat that perishes, each of us should respond to God and labor for that which endures unto everlasting life (John 6:27).

## Conclusion

Have you seen God? Have you seen your own sinfulness and unworthiness apart from God? Have you experienced the joy of forgiveness after confessing your sins? Have you heard the call of God to serve? Respond to him as a volunteer rather than turning a deaf ear or delaying until you are drafted.

## SUNDAY EVENING, FEBRUARY 22

***Title:*** Lying: Direct and Indirect

***Text:*** "Thou shalt not bear false witness against thy neighbour" **(Exod. 20:16)**.

***Scripture Reading:*** James 3:1–10

### Introduction

Someone has said, "Of the Ten Commandments, the one we break the most is the ninth—'Thou shalt not bear false witness against thy neighbor.'"

This commandment is not to be restricted to false testimony given in courts of justice. It prohibits gossip, libel, slander, and misrepresentation at any time under any circumstance. We will miss the moral significance of this commandment if we consider it as a mere prohibition of lying in general.

### I. The purpose of this commandment: "Thou shalt not bear false witness against thy neighbor."

A. *This commandment demands truth in the statements made directly or indirectly, person to person, concerning another person.*

B. *The fundamental fabric of our society is based on the truth of testimony that one person bears to another.* Such must be the case if righteousness and justice are to be achieved.

1. To lie brings harm to the person who believes the lie, for it misleads that person.
2. Lying will eventually bring harm to the liar, for the liar's untruthfulness will eventually be discovered.

### II. The importance of words—the privilege and power of speech.

Jesus said, "Out of the abundance of the heart the mouth speaketh" (Matt. 12:34). Your words reveal what you are on the inside.

A. *Speech can be used to gladden the heart.* "Pleasant words are as an honeycomb, sweet to the soul, and health to the bones" (Prov. 16:24).

B. *Speech can be used to sadden the heart.* "Deliver my soul, O Lord, from lying lips, and from a deceitful tongue" (Ps. 120:2).

C. *Children of God should watch their speech.* "Wherefore putting away lying, speak every man truth with his neighbour: for we are members one of another" (Eph. 4:25).

### III. The violation of this commandment.

A. *Direct lying.*

1. False testimony in trials of justice. Perjury has been made a criminal offense because it results in the miscarriage of justice.
2. The ninth commandment is broken by plain lying—both black and white.

B. *Indirect lying.*

1. By means of a false sympathy.
2. By means of an insinuating question.
3. By means of listening. A noise has no effect unless there is an ear to hear it. Just as the law holds the receiver of stolen goods to be as guilty as the thief, this commandment holds the eager receiver of a lie to be as guilty as the one who bears it.
4. Indirect lying can be done by merely being silent.
5. Gushing flattery is a form of indirect lying.
6. This commandment is broken by faultfinding and unjust criticism.

## IV. For a Christian to break this commandment is for him or her to be guilty of hypocrisy.

Jesus described the Devil as a liar who does not abide in the truth. He is said to be the source of lies. For the child of God to be guilty of lying is to conduct himself as if he belonged to Satan rather than to God. "You belong to your father, the devil, and you want to carry out your father's desire. He was a murderer from the beginning, not holding to the truth, for there is no truth in him. When he lies, he speaks his native language, for he is a liar and the father of lies" (John 8:44 NIV).

## V. Dealing with the problem of false witnessing.

James, whose epistle emphasizes and recommends the practice of pure religion, has a word that is most appropriate for us at this point: "Let every man be swift to hear, slow to speak, slow to wrath" (James 1:19). We would be much less likely to break this commandment, which forbids the giving of false testimony, if we would be slower in the matter of throwing our tongue into high gear when we ought to be turning off the motor. There are a number of important questions by which we can test the information that we pass on concerning others.

A. *Do we know for certain that it is true?*

B. *Is it kind and helpful?*

C. *Is it necessary for me to communicate this information?*

D. *Would I be willing to stand and verify that which I speak with my lips?*

E. *Would Christ be pleased with my conversation?*

## Conclusion

James said concerning the tongue, "But the tongue can no man tame; it is an unruly evil, full of deadly poison" (James 3:8). He declares that it is impossible for us to domesticate the tongue to the extent that it will become tame and harmless. While we cannot tame it, we can bridle it and control it. The best way to control the tongue is to let the Holy Spirit fill our hearts with love for others. If the heart is filled with genuine love, the tongue will be much less likely to be guilty of bearing false witness against one's neighbor.

## WEDNESDAY EVENING, FEBRUARY 25

*Title:* The Parable of God's Joy

*Scripture Reading:* Luke 15:1–24

### Introduction

Each of Jesus' parables has all of the marks of a good short story. Jesus was a master artist; he could take a few words and paint a beautiful picture. Most beautiful were his pictures of God. The three parables of Luke 15 set forth that which brings greatest joy to the heart of the heavenly Father.

### I. God rejoices like a good shepherd who finds his sheep (Luke 15:4–7).

In the Middle East shepherds love their sheep and call them by name. They spend long hours under the hot sun together. To a good shepherd the loss of a sheep is more than a financial loss; it is also a personal loss that brings grief and sorrow to the shepherd's heart. Worry, apprehension, and even fear would fill a shepherd's heart when he knew that one of his sheep was not in the fold. It was an occasion of great joy to rescue a helpless sheep who had fallen behind the flock, dropped in a hole, or drifted away. He would put the sheep on his shoulder and rejoice in the privilege of carrying him to the safety of the sheepfold.

Jesus concludes from this story that God experiences more joy over the homecoming of one wayward sheep than he does over ninety-nine self-righteous people who feel no need for God's grace and mercy. God rejoices greatly over just one who comes to him.

### II. God rejoices like a diligent woman who finds her lost coin (Luke 15:8–10).

The woman was so happy that she not only rejoiced in her heart but called in all of her friends and neighbors and shared her joy with them. Jesus said that God is like that. When a sinner decides to forsake the love of sin and returns to God for mercy and forgiveness, he is filled with joy (Luke 15:10).

### III. God rejoices like the waiting father who eagerly yearns for the return of a beloved son (Luke 15:20–24).

Have you missed the picture of the waiting father who day after day glanced out of the window and down the road looking eagerly for a familiar figure? Have you failed to hear his prayers at night for the welfare and the return of his prodigal son? Have you neglected to see the tears shed because of the absence of one who was so dear?

The day came when the waiting father saw a familiar figure appear in the distance. He lifted his hand to shade his eyes that he might be certain. Yes, it was the son for whom his heart hungered and for whom he had yearned and prayed day by day. Instead of concealing his joy and wiping away the tears, instead of retreating to some back room, he rushed out the door and down the road with terms of endearment and welcome.

The wayward but returning son had repented in his heart and had carefully memorized his expression of confession and his plea for pardon and for restoration, not as a son, but as a hired servant. The loving father cut him off by shouting instructions to the servants to bring forth the best robe and put it on him and to bring a ring and put it on his hand and shoes on his feet. These were symbols of honor, sonship, and happiness.

For months the father had had a calf in a stall being prepared for a feast, a feast that he was planning for the time of the hoped-for return of his son.

Jesus is trying to tell us that there is nothing that brings greater joy to the heart of God than for one to return from the far country.

**Conclusion**

One step away from God is the far country. Today God will rejoice like the shepherd and the woman and the father in Jesus' parables if you will return.

SUGGESTED PREACHING PROGRAM FOR

# MARCH

## ■ Sundays Mornings

The suggested theme for this month is "The Prophets Speak to the Present." While the prophets were predictors concerning the future, their primary function was to speak for God. They brought the message of God to bear upon the issues that faced the people of their day. As the spokesmen of God, they continue to have a message that is relevant for today.

## ■ Sunday Evenings

"Sermons from the Sermon" is the theme for Sunday evenings this month. Included are five messages based on texts found in the Sermon on the Mount.

## ■ Wednesday Evenings

The guiding theme for the Wednesday evening services this month is stewardship. Stewardship concerns every area of life. In the background of each suggested message is the basic philosophy of Jesus expressed in the beatitude "It is more blessed to give than to receive" (Acts 20:35).

---

## SUNDAY MORNING, MARCH 1

*Title:* Are We at Ease in Zion?

*Text:* "Woe to them that are at ease in Zion, and trust in the mountain of Samaria, which are named chief of the nations, to whom the house of Israel came!" (**Amos 6:1**).

*Scripture Reading:* Amos 6:1–8

*Hymns:* "Holy, Holy, Holy," Heber

"The Way of the Cross Leads Home," Pounds

"We Praise Thee, O God," Mackay

*Offertory Prayer:* Holy Father, we recognize this as the day that you have made. We will rejoice and be glad in it. We praise you with songs from our hearts. We praise you with testimonies from our lips. We praise you with our tithes and offerings as we acknowledge you as the Giver of every good and perfect gift. Bless the use of these offerings that others might come to know of your love and grace through Jesus Christ our Lord. Amen.

### Introduction

Amos preached in a postwar period, a day of unsuspected peril. It was a day of unrivaled national power and unparalleled material prosperity. Religious activities were popular.

With penetrating insight, the prophet from Tekoa diagnosed the sickness of his nation and pronounced its early death. In less than forty years his nation was to die and be buried in the Assyrian exile. The sickness that buried his nation can do the same thing to our country unless we find a cure.

**I. The charge of spiritual complacency: "Woe to them that are at ease in Zion, to them that trust in the mountain of Samaria" (Amos 6:1).**

A. *The condition of complacency is described.*
   1. Their customs, dress, and perfumes were the richest (6:4).
   2. They enjoyed the richest foods and rarest delicacies (6:4).
   3. The pursuit of pleasure was uppermost in their thoughts (6:5).
   4. They drank their wine out of bowls (6:6).

B. *The causes of complacency.*
   1. Israel was enjoying an unprecedented era of prosperity. Two possible reactions:
      a. People may react as Israel did. They became proud and boastful. They lived extravagantly and took all of the credit for themselves (6:9, 13).
      b. They should have reacted with an attitude of humility. A person's response to prosperity will both reveal and determine his or her character.
   2. They trusted in military resources for security (6:1).
   3. They dismissed all serious thought (6:3).
   4. The pursuit of prosperity was of primary importance (6:4).
   5. They were not grieved because of the sickness of their nation (6:6).

**II. The curse of complacency.**

A. *In Amos's day.*
   1. Complacency led to the death of his nation.
   2. Complacency caused the people to reject their divine mission.
   3. Complacency denied to them their destiny.

B. *In our day.*
   1. Complacency robs God of energetic and consecrated servants.
   2. Complacency robs us of joy unspeakable here and rewards unbelievable hereafter.
   3. Our complacency prevents some from going to heaven when this life is over.

**III. The cure for complacency.**

A. *Attempt to comprehend the love of God.*

B. *Contemplate the value of salvation to another individual.*

C. *Meditate on the issues and the values of eternity.*

D. *Listen to the command of the Master.*

### Conclusion

Unsaved friend, if you are at ease concerning your spiritual state, it would be wise for you to become alarmed. Preoccupation with material things can cause you to become complacent and unconcerned about your spiritual welfare until it is too late. Seek the Lord today while he may be found. Call upon him while he is near. It is dangerous and deadly to be unconcerned about your relationship with God.

---

## SUNDAY EVENING, MARCH 1

***Title:*** The Inner Spirit of a Genuine Christian

***Scripture Reading:*** Matthew 5:1–9.

### Introduction

The Beatitudes are not just pious platitudes or nice generalizations. In the Sermon on the Mount, Christ gave us a wonderful picture of what a real Christian is like. Have you been guilty of assuming a familiarity with the Beatitudes to the extent that you have given them no serious thought? By carefully considering the Beatitudes, we can measure our worthiness to wear the name of Christian.

The word *blessed* means more than the superficial idea of happiness or material well-being. It refers to proper attitudes and actions that issue in spiritual well-being. The emphasis is not on the blessing to be received; it is on the condition of the heart and mind that makes it possible for a person to experience the blessings of God.

The Beatitudes were not directed to an unbelieving world. They were given in a teaching-learning situation to Christ's disciples. These inner attitudes do not come to us automatically at our conversion. Consequently, each of us as disciples should sit at the feet of Jesus and listen attentively and responsively as he describes the inner attitude of an ideal citizen of his kingdom.

### I. A consciousness of spiritual poverty: "Blessed are the poor in spirit: for theirs is the kingdom of heaven" (Matt. 5:3).

A. *Are you overwhelmed with a consciousness of spiritual poverty?* Do you feel like a pauper in the things of God? Do you feel destitute as far as spiritual achievement goes?

B. *Are you filled with pride concerning your spiritual attainments?* In the parable of the Pharisee and the publican, Jesus described a proper attitude of spiritual poverty in the person of the publican. He used the role of the proud Pharisee to indict many of us for our self-righteousness and lack of humility.

### II. A great grief for sin and failure: "Blessed are they that mourn: for they shall be comforted" (Matt. 5:4).

The grief that Jesus here speaks about is not that which is normally expected at the death of a loved one. It is a personal grief that is the result of the awareness of the spiritual poverty referred to in the previous beatitude.

A. *Is there a sense of sorrow in your heart because of your own personal transgressions and failures?* Grief over personal sin is a basic requirement for continued spiritual growth. To neglect Christ's forgiveness is to be overwhelmed with ingratitude and self-righteousness.

B. *Do you grieve because of the sins and failures of others, or do you find it easy to be critical?* In this picture of the inner attitude of a genuine Christian, Jesus is referring to a condition of the heart that is described by the psalmist: "The sacrifices of God are a broken spirit: a broken and a contrite heart, O God, thou wilt not despise" (Ps. 51:17). In this psalm David is grieving because of his sin. His grief led to confession, and his confession made possible his cleansing.

### III. A meek and teachable spirit: "Blessed are the meek: for they shall inherit the earth" (Matt. 5:5).

A. *Meekness is not to be confused with weakness.* Jesus is not encouraging an attitude that says, "Excuse me for living."

B. *Meekness refers to an open mind and a teachable spirit, which are essential if one is to be possessed by the mind of Jesus Christ.* To be meek is to be the very opposite of the egotistical know-it-all who has the last word on every subject.

Those who enjoy horseback riding know that some horses have what is called a tender mouth, while others are tough mouthed. Those with a tender mouth are sensitive and responsive to the movement of the reins. This is the attitude toward God of one who is meek.

### IV. An intense hunger and thirst after righteousness: "Blessed are they which do hunger and thirst after righteousness: for they shall be filled" (Matt. 5:6).

To be able to appreciate this beatitude, one needs to have suffered the pangs of hunger and the torment of an unsatisfied thirst. Jesus uses these two deep appetites of life to illustrate the deep spiritual hunger of a genuine disciple to be right with God and his fellow human beings in all things.

We live in a world in which there is a tremendous hunger for wealth and an insatiable thirst for pleasure. There is a continuous struggle for success. Jesus declares in this beatitude that his disciples will be characterized by an intense hunger and thirst after righteousness.

A. *Right with God.* While we are justified by faith in Jesus Christ and are given a right standing before God on the basis of that faith, we need always to bring every facet of our life into harmony with the benevolent will of God. Do you really want to be right with God?

B. *Right with our fellow humans.* The genuine disciple will put forth continuous effort to maintain right relationships with his or her fellow humans. The Bible emphasizes that we cannot enjoy the favor of God if we mistreat our fellow humans.

**V. An intelligent sympathy: "Blessed are the merciful: for they shall obtain mercy" (Matt. 5:7).**

Jesus declares that his disciples will be compassionate toward others. As the recipients of mercy, they are to be merciful toward others. They are to demonstrate mercy and kindness toward the unfortunate. To be merciful is to be habitually looking at others through the eyes of Jesus Christ. He saw the internal as well as the external needs of people. The parable of the good Samaritan is a demonstration of mercy.

**VI. A devoted and undivided loyalty to God: "Blessed are the pure in heart: for they shall see God" (Matt. 5:8).**

To be pure in heart or motive is to have unhindered access to the throne room of the Eternal. In this beatitude the word "pure" refers to that which is unalloyed, unadulterated, unmixed—an undivided allegiance to the will of God.

The background of this beatitude is the throne room of a Mideastern monarch. A king was always safely guarded from attack by an enemy. Only those of unquestioned loyalty to the king were ever granted the privilege of entering the throne room. Similarly, today there are only a few individuals who do not have to have an appointment to see the president of the United States. They have this privilege because of their unquestioned allegiance and loyalty to him.

This beatitude is referring to a present experience with God rather than to a future prospect of seeing God after we reach heaven. Jesus is declaring that his disciples can experience the real presence of God in the here and now if they are utterly devoted to him.

**VII. Peacemakers are regarded as the children of God: "Blessed are the peacemakers: for they shall be called the children of God" (Matt. 5:9).**

This beatitude refers to something much closer to home than the work of a diplomat in his or her efforts to establish peace among the nations of the world. Jesus is declaring that those who possess the inner spiritual characteristics described in the previous verses will experience the apex of spiritual achievement by leading others to know God through faith in Jesus Christ. In modern terminology, he is declaring that the natural function of a genuine Christian will be to produce other Christians.

A. *Peace between God and humans.* As the servants of Jesus Christ, we are to announce the good tidings that God is not at war with humans—that God loves people and is communicating this love in the gift of his Son Jesus Christ. By his death on the cross, Jesus has removed the sin that alienates us from God. We are authorized to announce that peace and harmony and happiness are possible for all who will receive him (2 Cor. 5:18–20).

B. *Peace between humans.* The ideal citizen of the kingdom of God will seek to promote peace and harmony on all levels and in all relationships. This peace should be based on justice, kindness, mercy, and concern for the welfare of others.

### Conclusion

To come face-to-face with the claims and the requirements of these beatitudes is to recognize how far short we fall of being all that we are capable of being as followers of Jesus Christ. The Holy Spirit seeks to make possible the inner attitudes that are essential if we are to become truly Christlike in our conduct. We must be Christlike on the inside before we can be Christlike on the outside. May God help each of us as we give careful and considerate attention to cultivating these inner attitudes set forth by our Savior.

## WEDNESDAY EVENING, MARCH 4

***Title:*** Give Your Stewardship Testimony

***Text:*** "Take heed that ye do not your alms before men, to be seen of them: otherwise ye have no reward of your Father which is in heaven" **(Matt. 6:1)**.

### Introduction

Our Scripture text and the verses that follow it have been interpreted as meaning that we should always be secretive concerning our gifts. A serious study of this verse in its context, however, will reveal that Jesus was talking to his disciples primarily about the motive behind their deeds of righteousness as citizens of the kingdom of heaven. He uses three illustrations to emphasize the importance of proper motivation. These illustrations are the giving of alms (Matt. 6:1–4), the offering of prayers (vv. 5–15), and the practice of fasting (vv. 16–18). In each of these areas illustrative of service to others, service to God, and personal spiritual discipline, Jesus warned against the desire for human applause as the primary motive for actions (vv. 1–2, 5, 16).

A desire for the approval of God rather than the applause of people is to be our primary motive. Jesus was not insisting that every contribution be secret. Nor was he insisting that prayer be restricted to private communion with God. He was declaring strongly that we must have the right motive.

In the preceding chapter, Jesus made a statement that would seemingly contradict Matthew 6:1–4, for he said, "Let your light so shine before men, that they may see your good works, and glorify your Father which is in heaven" (Matt. 5:16). In this verse Jesus says that we must let people see our good works. He is talking about influence rather than motive. Consequently, in certain circumstances we would be guilty of disobeying our Savior and we would be mistreating our fellow Christians if we were secretive about our gifts. Therefore, if you can do so with the right motive, you should give a stewardship testimony.

### I. Give your stewardship testimony and register your love for your Savior.

The Lord has freely given his life on the cross for us because of love. If you have found love in your heart that motivates you to be a tither so that others might come to know Christ, then your testimony concerning this love can possibly increase the love of others for him.

**II. Give your stewardship testimony and strengthen the faith of other disciples.**

We should be no more hesitant to give a stewardship testimony concerning the faithfulness of God and the provisions of God on a material level than we would be to give a testimony as to how God has answered our prayers.

Some people have the faith to become good stewards merely because the Bible says that we should be. Others need the testimony of more mature Christians who have tested promises of God and have found them to be true. By giving our testimony, we can strengthen the faith of others in the promises of God.

**III. Give your stewardship testimony and encourage others to put their heart into the kingdom of God (Matt. 6:9–21).**

Jesus was declaring that our hearts follow our investments. Until we begin to invest in the kingdom of God, our hearts will remain outside the kingdom. If we can encourage others to become generous, consistent contributors, or investors, in God's work, we will have rendered them a real service by helping them get their hearts in the right place.

**IV. Give your stewardship testimony with your eye on the open windows of heaven (Mal. 3:10).**

If you can encourage another to trust God and to try God's promise to tithers, you will be the means that will make it possible for God to open up the treasure house of heaven and pour out into the heart of someone else his rich blessings. There are many who need the benefits of your experience. They need the encouragement of your faith. Faith comes by hearing, not only the Word of God, but also the word of God's children who have found that God is honest and that he can be depended on to be faithful to his every promise.

**Conclusion**

Your motive is the main thing. If you cannot talk concerning your personal experiences as a tither without a desire for human applause, then you had better seal your lips. But if your motive, deep within your heart, is to glorify God and be a blessing to others, then for you to remain silent in a time of opportunity to witness is criminal.

## SUNDAY MORNING, MARCH 8

***Title:*** Unheeded Chastisement

***Text:*** "I gave you empty stomachs in every city and lack of bread in every town, yet you have not returned to me" **(Amos 4:6 NIV)**.

***Scripture Reading:*** Amos 4:6–12

***Hymns:*** "Praise to the Lord the Almighty," Neander

"Jesus, Keep Me Near the Cross," Crosby

"There Is a Name I Love to Hear," Whitfield

**Offertory Prayer:** With gratitude for both spiritual and material blessings, we approach your throne, O Lord; and we acknowledge you as the Giver of every good and perfect gift. We thank you for life. We express our gratitude for the privilege of being able to work so as to provide for our families. We rejoice in the privilege of bringing material gifts for dedication upon your altar. Accept these symbols of our gratitude and dedication, and bless them in the work of your kingdom through Jesus Christ our Lord. Amen.

### Introduction

The prophet Amos lived in a time of great material prosperity. It was a postwar period, and the people thought that God had indicated his pleasure in them by giving them victory. They thought everything was exactly as it should be.

There were primarily only two classes of people in the land—the very rich and the very poor. The rich enjoyed great luxury and indulged in all the pleasures that money could provide. The poor were continually oppressed, and injustice was practiced in the courts.

True religion had been compromised to the extent that it was a mere form of religion. The religion of the people produced no moral effects in their lives.

The nation depended on financial and military might for existence among the nations of the earth. It seemed that all was right with the world. The prophet of God, however, was able to see signs of decay, evidences of poison in the bloodstream, and inevitable calamities ahead for these people who were unable to read the signs of the times.

### I. Divine chastisement was unrecognized and unheeded.

A. *God sent famine upon them.* "And I also have given you cleanness of teeth in all your cities, and want of bread in all your places: yet have ye not returned unto me, saith the Lord" (Amos 4:6).

B. *God withheld the rains.* "And also I have withholden the rain from you, when there were yet three months to the harvest; ... yet have ye not returned unto me, saith the Lord" (Amos 4:7–8).

The people simply thought that they had had a drought. When rain was needed, it did not come. Many people incorrectly assume that the laws of nature take care of such things as Amos is speaking about.

C. *God sent agricultural failure.* "I have smitten you with blasting and mildew: when your gardens and your vineyards and your fig trees and your olive trees increased, the palmerworm devoured them: yet have ye not returned unto me, saith the Lord" (Amos 4:9).

The people thought that the season had produced an unusually large number of insects. Many times God is like a dentist; he has to inflict pain that better things may result.

D. *God chastised his nation with war.* The people were so dull that they did not recognize that God was trying to tell them something. "I have sent among you the pestilence after the manner of Egypt: your young men have I slain with the sword, and have taken away your horses; and I have made the stink of your camps to come up unto your nostrils: yet have ye not returned unto me, saith the Lord. I have overthrown some of you, as God overthrew Sodom and Gomorrah, and ye were as a firebrand plucked out of the burning: yet have ye not returned unto me, saith the Lord" (Amos 4:10–11).

## II. God continues to chastise.

A. *God chastises nations.* One cannot study the Bible without recognizing that the biblical writers believed that God had the power to sway the destiny of nations. The God of grace and justice rewards the nations that fear him and serve him and punishes the nations that ignore him and oppress the helpless.

The study of history reveals that those who usurp the place of God and ignore the laws of justice and mercy are eventually destroyed. History has been described as "His story." The Bible declares and history verifies the truth that "the wicked shall be turned into hell, and all the nations that forget God" (Ps. 9:17). There are nations today strutting across the stage of human history that must either change or experience the radical justice of a holy God.

B. *God chastises individuals.* A church member was injured quite seriously while driving under the influence of alcohol. His chest was crushed and his limbs were broken, and his life hung by a narrow thread. Someone could have said that the accident was due only to the loss of his mental faculties while intoxicated. His explanation was different. After months of lying on his back looking up, looking backward, looking inward, and looking forward, with the language of faith, he declared that the loving heavenly Father had caused him to have the accident to bring him to his senses. He rededicated his life and renewed his vows and resumed the discipline of discipleship. As the years went by, he became a trusted and respected servant of Jesus Christ as well as a blessing to his family, his church, and his community.

An unbelieving husband and wife were blessed with the birth of a precious baby. The years went by and they refused to worship and bring the child to church. While still an innocent child, the girl became ill and died. Shortly thereafter both the father and mother were converted and became faithful in both worship and work for God. With the language of faith, we would declare that they had to experience loss to experience the highest possible gain.

## III. The purpose of chastisement needs to be understood.

A. *Chastisement is the proof of the fatherhood of God.* "If ye endure chastening, God dealeth with you as with sons; for what son is he whom the father chasteneth not?" (Heb. 12:7).

1. Where discipline is lacking, true fatherhood is wanting.
2. Because we are his sons, God chastises and educates us.

B. *In the distresses and trouble of life, God deals with us in terms of his love.* "For whom the Lord loveth he chasteneth, and scourgeth every son whom he receiveth" (Heb. 12:6).

C. *God disciplines and chastises his children according to the dictates of perfect wisdom, in order that we might be changed into the image of his holiness.* "Furthermore we have had fathers of our flesh which corrected us, and we gave them reverence: shall we not much rather be in subjection unto the Father of spirits, and live? For they verily for a few days chastened us after their own pleasure; but he for our profit" (Heb. 12:9–10).

D. *Chastisement properly understood and accepted produces peace and righteousness.* "Now no chastening for the present seemeth to be joyous, but grievous: nevertheless afterward it yieldeth the peaceable fruit of righteousness unto them which are exercised thereby" (Heb. 12:11).

## Conclusion

The psalmist said, "It is good for me that I have been afflicted: that I might learn thy statutes" (Ps. 119:71). God seeks men by means of his grace and goodness.

The apostle Paul asked, "Despiseth thou the riches of his goodness and forbearance and longsuffering; not knowing that the goodness of God leadeth thee to repentance?" (Rom. 2:4).

By the goodness of his love and by his mercy revealed in the gift of his Son, Jesus Christ, God seeks us. If we turn a deaf ear and heart toward God's goodness, he may seek us through affliction and trouble. He uses this method only as a last resort, to bring the greatest possible good to us after his entreaties of mercy have been spurned. Isaiah challenges each of us: "Seek ye the LORD while he may be found, call ye upon him while he is near" (Isa. 55:6).

## SUNDAY EVENING, MARCH 8

***Title:*** The Cure for Worry

***Text:*** "Seek ye first the kingdom of God, and his righteousness: and all these things shall be added unto you" **(Matt. 6:33)**.

***Scripture Reading:*** Matthew 6:25–34

### Introduction

Jesus sought to impart to his disciples a faith in the goodness of God that would cure most of the heartaches and headaches that plague us today. In attempting to bestow the gift of this great faith, he pointed out the perils of letting earthly possessions be our greatest treasure (Matt. 6:19–23). He also pointed out the impossibility of a man being both the servant of God and the servant of material things (Matt. 6:24).

### I. To be conquered by worry is sinful.

A. *Cares and worries are idolatrous (Matt. 6:24).*

B. *Cares and worries about the means of living are secondary (Matt. 6:25).*

C. *Cares and worries are useless (Matt. 6:27).*

D. *Cares and worries are pagan (Matt. 6:32).*

E. *Cares and worries are injurious (Matt. 6:34).*

### II. If we are to overcome care and worry ...

A. *We must evaluate ourselves (Matt. 6:26).* We need to listen to a sermon from the sparrows. The sparrows work, but they do not worry. It is not work that upsets us and robs us of sleep at night. Rather, it is worry that creates tension that destroys our health and happiness and effectiveness.

We need to listen to a lecture from the lilies (Matt. 6:28–29). There are many profitable lessons that we could learn from the beautiful lily that grows out of the mud and dirt to become a thing of beauty exceeding the glory of Solomon.

The God who takes care of the sparrows and provides for the lilies will most definitely take care of his children who trust him, love him, and who seek to obey him and do his good will.

B. *We must accept ourselves (Matt. 6:27).* "God grant me the serenity to accept the things I cannot change; courage to change the things I can; and the wisdom to know the difference."

There are some things in life that are absolutely unchangeable, and the only proper response to these is that of acceptance. We must not fret and worry ourselves into frustration about the things over which we have no control either in the present, the past, or the future.

C. *We must dedicate ourselves (Matt. 6:33).* If we would conquer our cares and overcome our worries, we must dedicate ourselves to something bigger than ourselves. We must put first things first. The priority of God's claim must be recognized. A complete surrender to God and a joyful cooperation with him in the bringing of his rule of love into the hearts and lives of others will do much to help us to forget all of our anxieties.

### Conclusion

The God who has given us life also will provide day after day the things necessary for the sustaining of life. Instead of concerning ourselves with the means of living, we would be wise to concern ourselves with the purpose for which we live. To concentrate upon living each day to the fullest for the glory of God will cure us from the harmful effects of worry and make possible for us the abundant life in the here and now.

---

## WEDNESDAY EVENING, MARCH 11

***Title:*** The Widow's Gifts

***Text:*** "There came a certain poor widow, and she threw in two mites, which make a farthing" (**Mark 12:42**).

### Introduction

The account of the widow bringing her offering is one of the most beautiful scenes in the life of Jesus. Two things stand out in this picture: the Lord and the treasury. Christ was watching the proceedings with genuine interest as the collection was being taken.

### I. As Lord of the treasury, Christ was interested: "He sat over against the treasury."

Why was Jesus interested in the people's gifts?

A. *Money placed therein was a recognition of God's ownership and of people's stewardship.*

B. *Humanly speaking, money is the means by which the kingdom of God is to go forward.*

C. *Money is pent-up power or force. It can be used to blight or to bless.*

D. *What we do with our money is an index to our character.*

1. Some are pleasure seekers.
2. Some are power seekers.
3. Some invest in God's work and reveal that their heart belongs to God. The offering plate becomes a throne before which our character is tested. We judge ourselves, and the Christ also judges us. He sees what we give, and we win his approval or his disapproval.

### II. Jesus saw several things as he sat by the treasury.

A. *He saw much that was commendable. The rich and the poor alike were present.*

B. *The rich men were present, and they were liberal in their gifts.*

C. *There was one poor giver present who did not cast in much.*
   1. She was a poor widow.
   2. She had suffered.
   3. She knew the pinch of poverty.
   4. She had no fear of her home being burglarized.
   5. From a human point of view, her future was very uncertain.

**III. The language of the treasury: "Money talks."**

A. *The two mites spoke of a greater love.*
   1. The widow did not give because she was seeking applause.
   2. The widow did not give because she could afford to be generous. Love was her compelling motive. "Though I bestow all my goods to feed the poor, and though I give my body to be burned, and have not love, it profiteth me nothing" (1 Cor. 13:3).

B. *The two mites spoke of greater sacrifice.* The others gave out of their abundance, while the widow gave out of her poverty. What would be your reaction if you had a rich uncle and he sent you a gift—a sixty-cent candy bar?

C. *The two mites speak of a great fidelity to God.*
   1. Faithful in material things.
   2. Faithful in spiritual things.

**IV. Lessons for the present that bring encouragement.**

A. *This incident puts the very poorest of us on an equal footing with the richest.*

B. *This incident reveals to us that Christ looks first at the spirit behind the gift.* The spirit is more important than the sum.

C. *This incident reveals that the very smallest gifts, if they are our best, win the approval of Christ.*

**Conclusion**

How great is your love for God? Your love for your church? Your love for a lost world? How great is your willingness to sacrifice that others might come to know of the love, mercy, and grace of God? The measure of our sacrifice is the measure of our love and fidelity.

---

## SUNDAY MORNING, MARCH 15

***Title:*** "Be Not Thou Rebellious"

***Text:*** "But thou, son of man, hear what I say unto thee; Be not thou rebellious like that rebellious house" **(Ezek. 2:8)**.

***Scripture Reading:*** Ezekiel 1:28–3:3

***Hymns:*** "I Gave My Life for Thee," Havergal

"I Surrender All," DeVenter

"Rescue the Perishing," Crosby

***Offertory Prayer:*** Holy Father, today we bring to you the fruits of our labors in tithes and offerings. We bring these monetary gifts as an indication of our desire to give our hearts and minds and bodies completely to you, for you have been merciful and gracious to us. Every good gift comes from you, and with a heart filled with gratitude, we now worship you with our gifts. Amen.

### Introduction

God warned the prophet Ezekiel against the peril of being rebellious to the divine command even as his nation had rebelled. Israel had rebelled against God's will. Israel had been stubborn, hard-hearted, and disobedient and thus failed to enter into their spiritual legacy.

Are you aware that it is possible to rebel against the good will of God for our lives even as it was possible for Ezekiel to rebel? Israel's rebellion had manifested itself in disobedience and in a continuous transgression of the law of God. Are you guilty of rebellion against God?

### I. Rebellion may occur because of the difficulty involved in doing God's will.

A. *People sometimes shrink away from a great undertaking.*

B. *Often our love of comfort and ease will cause us to slip away.*

C. *There is no easy situation in God's service.*

D. *Success is never automatic or accidental; it always involves self-discipline and diligent effort.*

### II. Rebellion may be the result of a lack of faith or confidence in God.

The besetting sin of the Israelites was the sin of little faith. They staggered back before the promises of God and neglected to put confidence in his promises.

A. *Satan seeks continually to undermine our faith in God.*

B. *Satan seeks to misrepresent the character of God (Gen. 3:4–5).*

C. *Many have a weak faith because they have never put enough confidence in God on a continuing basis to develop the faith that they are capable of having.* Each of us can have a great faith if we will put forth the effort to do that which God commands us to do, trusting him for the help that we need for its achievement.

### III. Rebellion may be due to ignorance of God's purposes for ourselves and others.

Humans prefer to walk by sight rather than by faith.

A. *We cannot see the end from the beginning.*

B. *God sees the big picture, and he has a great overall plan for our lives and the lives of others.*

C. *God's purposes for us are always motivated by his love for us.* May God grant that we have the faith to believe this.

### IV. Rebellion may be due to a false or shallow concept of happiness.

A. *We all are tempted to live only for the present.* We are tempted to believe that happiness is to be found in material things and in sensual pleasures. We find it easy to think only in terms of self, and this causes us to give God and others a low priority in our thoughts and actions.

B. *The highest happiness a person can experience is to be in fellowship with God and in cooperation with his good purpose for others.* God would have us to relate our lives to others in terms of unselfish and generous concern for their well-being. This higher happiness is something that one discovers only in experience.

### V. The way of rebellion is hard.

For a person to rebel against God is to reject one's divine destiny and the highest possible happiness that the human heart can know.

Saul, the first king of Israel, rebelled against the will of God for his life. He rationalized and offered sacrifices of fine cattle as a substitute for obedience to God's will. Samuel, the prophet, came into Saul's camp with a message from God to the rebellious king: "Hath the LORD as great delight in burnt offerings and sacrifices, as in obeying the voice of the LORD? Behold, to obey is better than sacrifice, and to hearken than the fat of rams. For rebellion is as the sin of witchcraft, and stubbornness is as iniquity and idolatry. Because thou hast rejected the word of the LORD, he hath also rejected thee from being king" (1 Sam. 15:22–23).

The way of rebellion is the way to death. The way of cooperative surrender to the will of God is the way to happiness and helpfulness.

### Conclusion

God has revealed the extent of his love for us in the gift of his Son. God freely gave his Son for us. If we will tarry at the cross and measure the love of God for us, we will be less hesitant to surrender our all to him.

---

## SUNDAY EVENING, MARCH 15

***Title:*** The Model Prayer

***Text:*** Matthew 6:9–13

### Introduction

The Sermon on the Mount contains much of our Lord's teaching concerning the nature and purpose of prayer. It also discloses many of the conditions that must prevail if we are to pray effectively. We must not pray like hypocrites (Matt. 6:5) or like heathens (6:7–8). The Sermon on the Mount also contains some very practical, positive teachings concerning prayer. Prayer is everyone's gift, privilege, and responsibility. The power of prayer is the power that is least exercised by the average believer.

A disciple prayed, "Lord, teach us to pray." Jesus replied by giving the model prayer. Instead of calling this "The Lord's Prayer," we would be more accurate if we called it the disciples' prayer or the children's prayer or the family's prayer or the kingdom prayer. It is a perfect pattern, an accurate blueprint, a wonderful recipe that we should follow in the offering of prayer.

### I. The spirit of the model prayer.

A. *It encourages a filial spirit— "Father."*
B. *It encourages an unselfish spirit— "Our Father."*
C. *It encourages a reverent and worshipful spirit— "Hallowed be Thy name."*
D. *It encourages an evangelistic and missionary spirit— "Thy kingdom come."*
E. *It encourages an obedient and submissive spirit— "Thy will be done in earth, as it is in heaven."*
F. *It encourages a humble and dependent spirit— "Give us this day our daily bread."*
G. *It encourages a confessing and forgiving spirit— "Forgive us our trespasses as we forgive those who trespass against us."*
H. *It encourages a cautious and trusting spirit— "Lead us not into temptation, but deliver us from evil."*
I. *It encourages a confident and adoring spirit— "For thine is the kingdom, and the power, and the glory, forever, Amen."*

### II. The objective of the model prayer.

A. *It addresses the fatherhood of God.*
B. *It honors the holiness of God.*
C. *It seeks the glory of God.*
D. *It trusts the daily love of God.*
E. *It confesses the forgiveness of God.*
F. *It craves the deliverance of God.*
G. *It acknowledges the brotherhood of man.*

### III. The elements of the model prayer.

There are at least three elements in the model prayer that should be included in your prayers.

A. *Communion must be established through recognition, surrender, and confession.*
B. *Petitions concerning personal needs are to have attention only after consideration has been given to God's holiness, sovereignty, and good purpose on the earth.*
C. *Intercession permeates the prayer.* He to whom the prayer is addressed is "our Father." The petitions for daily bread, forgiveness, and deliverance are plural.

### Conclusion

In this model prayer there are three looks: the up-look, the in-look, and then the out-look. We must look up to God first, and then we can see our real needs as well as the needs of others. Let us seek to follow the perfect pattern given by the Savior when we kneel before the throne of grace in prayer.

## WEDNESDAY EVENING, MARCH 18

***Title:*** The Gifts of God

***Text:*** "Thanks be unto God for his unspeakable gift" (**2 Cor. 9:15**).

### Introduction

If we will consider the nature of God's gifts to us, our faith will be encouraged, our love will be deepened, and our "thanksliving" will be enhanced.

### I. The gifts of God are perfect (James 1:17).

A. *They are never harmful.*

B. *They are always beneficial.*

### II. The gifts of God are precious (1 Peter 1:18–19).

A. *The gifts of God are beyond our ability to compute in value.*

B. *The richest and best gifts that come to us in life are from God.*

### III. The gifts of God are permanent.

A. *Some gifts are of temporary value—flowers, candy, or perfume.*

B. *God gives to us that which is of eternal significance (John 1:28).*

### IV. God's best gifts are personal.

A. *Many of God's gifts are presented to everyone (Matt. 5:45).*

B. *God's best gifts are those that are received personally by those who respond to him in faith (John 3:16).*

### V. God's most wonderful gift is Jesus.

A. *You cannot buy this gift.*

B. *You cannot merit this gift.*

C. *You cannot steal this gift.*

### Conclusion

God is eager to give to each of us the fullness of the presence and power of the Christ who died but who lives again and who will live in our hearts if we will receive him by faith.

## SUNDAY MORNING, MARCH 22

***Title:*** Return, Thou Backsliding Israel

***Scripture Reading:*** Jeremiah 3:12–14

***Hymns:*** "Throw Out the Lifeline," Ufford
"I Need Thee, Precious Jesus," Whitfield
"I Am Resolved," Hartsough

***Offertory Prayer:*** Holy Father, today we come to give our tithes and offerings to you for you have given so much for us and to us. We love you because you first loved us. Through our tithes and offerings, we not only worship you, but we preach to the ends of the earth the message of your grace and mercy. Today we pray your blessings upon the missionaries stationed around the world who are seeking to communicate the message of your love to others. Bless them with good success. We pray in Jesus' name. Amen.

## Introduction

The term *backsliding* is used in several different ways in the Old Testament. It is used with reference to disobedience, unfaithfulness, and failure to measure up to an ideal.

One of the cardinal teachings of God's Word is that concerning the safety of those who have fully trusted Jesus Christ as Lord and Savior. This can be observed in a number of Scripture passages (e.g., John 3:16, 36; 5:24; Rom. 8:16).

## I. What about the man who claims to be saved and yet lives a sinful life?

A. *There is a possibility that he has never been saved.*
   1. First John 2:19.
   2. First John 3:8–10.

B. *There is a possibility that he is in a backslidden condition.*
   1. The flesh is the same.
   2. The Devil must be dealt with.
   3. The world is antagonistic.

C. *Examples of backsliders in the Bible.*
   1. David.
   2. Peter.
   3. Jonah.
   4. The churches of Asia Minor (Rev. 2–3).

## II. When is a Christian in a backslidden condition?

A. *Often backsliders are unconscious of their true condition.* The Devil blinds the minds of the saved as well as of the lost (2 Cor. 4:4).

B. *We have some false ideas about backsliders.* Many say that only alcoholics, immoral persons, gamblers, and criminals are backsliders. These are sins of the flesh. There are also sins of the spirit (2 Cor. 7:11).

## III. How can people know if they are backsliders?

A. *If they willingly tolerate even "small" sins in their lives.*

B. *If their lives are not characterized by an intense hunger and thirst after righteousness.*
   1. Matthew 5:3–6.
   2. Psalm 42:1–2.

C. *If their hearts are not filled with love for others (John 13:35).*

D. *If they put the material before the spiritual (Matt. 6:24).*

E. *If they are not rendering service to the heavenly Father.*
   1. "Ye have not chosen me, but I have chosen you, and ordained you, that ye should go and bring forth fruit, and that your fruit should remain" (John 15:16).
   2. "For we are his workmanship, created in Christ Jesus unto good works, which God hath before ordained that we should walk in them" (Eph. 2:10).

F. *If they do not recognize their lives as being a stewardship from God (1 Cor. 6:20).*

### IV. The solution to the backsliding problem is repentance.

A. *Recognize your sin.*
B. *Acknowledge your guilt before God.*
C. *Confess and forsake your evil ways.*
D. *Return to the cross.*
E. *Return to the church.*
F. *Return to the Bible.*
G. *Return to your duty and opportunity.*

### Conclusion

The wise man said, "The backslider in heart shall be filled with his own ways: and a good man shall be satisfied from himself" (Prov. 14:14). Because backsliding is very dangerous, and because the joys of forgiveness are so wonderful, we pray that you will let God heal you of your backsliding (Hos. 14:4) in order that you might regain the full joy of salvation.

---

## SUNDAY EVENING, MARCH 22

***Title:*** "As We Forgive Our Debtors"

***Text:*** "And forgive us our debts, as we forgive our debtors" **(Matthew 6:12)**.

***Scripture Reading:*** Matthew 6:14–15; 18:21–22

### Introduction

Repeatedly our Lord spoke of the need for his disciples to have a forgiving spirit.

Forgiveness was an unknown virtue in the ancient world. The pagan ideal was to do as much injury to your enemies as possible.

Forgiveness is a friendly act on the part of God. It is that action in which God restores the offender to a state or condition in which there is no obstacle that prevents the offender from enjoying communion with God. Forgiveness makes peace of mind possible because of the consciousness of divine mercy. Forgiveness removes the fear of punishment and creates love within the heart.

Jesus taught his disciples that even as God had forgiven them of their offenses and transgressions, so they must be willing to forgive others who had offended them.

Peter considered himself to be very generous by his offer to forgive an offender as many as seven times. Jesus shocked him and the other disciples by encouraging an attitude of unlimited forgiveness (Matt. 18:22). Jesus' attention was focused on the harmful effects of an unforgiving spirit in the heart of the offended rather than on a tolerant attitude toward offenders.

**I. The results of an unforgiving spirit.**

A. *One cannot experience the joy of forgiven sins.*
B. *One cannot experience the joy of answered prayer.*
C. *An unforgiving spirit drives people farther and farther apart.*
D. *An unforgiving spirit makes progress in the Christian life impossible.*
E. *An unforgiving spirit will rob a person of self-respect.*
F. *An unforgiving spirit will cause one to consciously live short of the Christian ideal.*
G. *An unforgiving spirit makes it impossible for one to see his own sins and shortcomings.*
H. *An unforgiving spirit causes one to live by the principle of hate rather than love.*

**II. The refusal to forgive places the present and the future under the tyranny of the past.**

**III. The difficulty of forgiving sins.**

A. *Sin is a serious matter.*
B. *On many occasions forgiveness is undeserved.*
C. *To forgive is not a natural human reaction.* "To err is human, to forgive is divine."
D. *Some of the injuries that come to us are malicious and deliberate.* Our natural inclination is to retaliate.

**IV. Results of a spirit of forgiveness.**

A. *The one who forgives purges himself of the poison produced by hatred and resentment.*
B. *The forgiver gains a peace of mind and health of spirit not enjoyed by the unforgiving.*
C. *The one who forgives experiences a sense of cleanness and calm.*
D. *It makes possible a "beautiful spirit" that others can imitate to their profit.*
E. *A spirit of forgiveness is bound, as a general rule, to create a change of spirit in others.*
F. *To forgive is a healing, creative experience.*

**V. Encouragement to forgive others.**

A. *The command of the Savior (Luke 17:1–4).*
B. *The example of our Savior (Luke 23:34).*
C. *Our own experience of forgiveness (Col. 3:13).*

### Conclusion

It is never easy to forgive those who have offended you and have brought injury into your life, but by the grace of God and with the help of Jesus Christ, you can find both the wisdom and the strength that you need to forgive. First, as a matter of principle, renounce the right to retaliate. Let God deal in vengeance if such is necessary. Second, pray for the strength to forgive and put forth an effort to remove resentful feelings toward the offender. Finally, with God's help, restore friendly relations. Let the light of God's love fall on the offender through you.

## WEDNESDAY EVENING, MARCH 25

***Title:*** What Kind of Gifts Do You Give?

***Text:*** "Freely ye have received, freely give" **(Matt. 10:8)**.

### Introduction

Most of us celebrate the birthdays and anniversaries of our family and friends by giving gifts. Deciding on the proper gift can be a difficult task, for it is not always easy to know what gift would please a certain person. Perhaps we need to go beyond the giving of trinkets and gadgets and also present others with gifts that show our love and thoughtfulness.

### I. Plan to give love.

Christian love has been defined by someone as "a persistent, unbreakable spirit of goodwill," and everyone needs this. It will be highly prized by those who receive it and will bring joy and gratitude to their lives. By the grace of God and with the help of the Holy Spirit, each of us can plan to bestow this gift upon our friends.

### II. Plan to give kindness.

Kindness is love in action. It is sincere courtesy. Kindness can be expressed in many ways. Kindness on your part will make life more beautiful for others.

### III. Plan to give understanding.

Deliberately put forth an effort to wear the other person's coat and to stand in his or her shoes. Put forth an effort to understand the other person's problems and difficulties. With the love of the Good Samaritan, determine to be of help.

### IV. Plan to give praise.

Commendation when commendation is due will lighten the load of the other person. It will challenge him or her to more significant achievement. It does not cost you anything except the time involved in taking notice and in expressing appreciation. Your expression of praise will serve as a bugle call to the other person's drooping spirit.

**V. Plan to give encouragement.**

Everyone needs encouragement, and everyone can give encouragement.

### Conclusion

God has given us wonderful gifts, and he has bestowed these upon us freely. There are many things that each of us can give, and we should plan to give them on all occasions.

## SUNDAY MORNING, MARCH 29

***Title:*** The Plan of the Divine Potter

***Text:*** "The vessel that he made of clay was marred in the hand of the potter: so he made it again another vessel, as seemed good to the potter to make it" **(Jer. 18:4)**.

***Scripture Reading:*** Jeremiah 18:1–17

***Hymns:*** "Holy Ghost, with Light Divine," Reed

"Make Me a Channel of Blessing," Smythe

"Have Thine Own Way," Pollard

***Offertory Prayer:*** Holy Father, we thank you for your blessings upon the work of our hands during the past week. We thank you for the ability to work and for the power to make progress in providing for our families. We bring to your altar a portion of that with which you have blessed us, and we present it to you as a token of our gratitude and as an expression of our desire to share the glad tidings of your love with all men everywhere. Bless these tithes and offerings to your purpose. In Jesus' name. Amen.

### Introduction

The biblical background for the great hymn "Have Thine Own Way" is found in the message that came to Jeremiah the prophet while he was visiting a pottery. God spoke to Jeremiah through the elements of nature and the events that were taking place in his nation.

Jeremiah was a shy, retiring young man when the call of God came to him with a revelation of the divine purpose for his life. After several excuses and some hesitation, Jeremiah felt compelled to become a spokesman for God and to warn the people of the consequences of their sin.

Jeremiah preached the love of God, and the people turned a deaf ear to his message. Jeremiah preached and appealed to their reason, but they refused to think logically. Jeremiah preached judgment and condemnation, and still the people continued to live lives of sin.

Jeremiah's day was similar to our day in many respects. The people were guilty of idolatry while at the same time they were regular in their attendance at temple worship. They were materialists and lived as if this world were the totality of human existence. They were lovers of sensual pleasure and were in continuous pursuit of some new excitement. Most of the people gave no serious thought to the condition of the nation, the circumstances of their own lives, or what the future might hold for them.

Jeremiah went to the potter's house and saw him as he worked at his wheel. The potter had pliable clay on a revolving wheel that he manipulated with his foot. As Jeremiah gazed upon this scene, there dawned upon his mind several great truths that were of significance both for then and for now.

**I. Jeremiah saw a potter who had a purpose.**

A. *The potter was carefully working with his fingers and with chosen instruments to accomplish a purpose that he had in his mind.* He had a specific plan for the vessel on the wheel.

In western Kentucky there is a small pottery that is in many respects very similar to the one Jeremiah visited. The potter there places a piece of clay on the revolving wheel, which is propelled by electricity. He produces various vessels according to the orders of his clients. It is interesting to see how he chooses a certain lump of clay for a particular vessel. After placing it on the wheel, the shapeless mass begins to take form under his fingers. It may become a small flower pot or a tall vase. Under his hand it could even become a birdhouse or a serving dish. The plan of the potter, combined with the pliability of the clay, determines what the vessel is to become.

B. *Jeremiah saw God as the divine Potter.* As Jeremiah watched the potter, he was given spiritual insight. He saw Jehovah God as the Potter and Israel, his nation, as the clay. Jeremiah believed that his God was sovereign and supreme and that he was also wise and benevolent. He believed that all of the purposes of God toward Israel were good. To hold this belief about God while at the same time being overwhelmed with the fact that his nation faced judgment disturbed him. God used this experience in the potter's house to help Jeremiah understand.

1. The divine Potter has a purpose for nations. This was true with regard to ancient Israel, and it is true in our modern world. Both the blessings of God and the judgment of God come upon nations as well as upon individuals.
2. The divine Potter has a purpose for individuals. It is the will of God that each of us be converted and that we live a consecrated life to the glory of God and to the good of our fellow humans. God has a general will for all of us and a specific will for each one of us.
3. The divine Potter has a purpose for churches. As the Christ walked in the midst of the seven golden lampstands (Rev. 1–3), even so he walks in the midst of churches today. And he wants each of them to serve as his body in their particular sphere of influence.
4. The divine Potter has a plan for your family. He wants to lead and guide you so that you can walk together in a creative relationship that helps

each member of the family to experience their full potential. That the divine Potter has a plan for each of us can be both disturbing and challenging. This truth should disturb us from a state of lethargy and should stimulate us to be cooperative. We are on the wheel of God (Phil. 1:6; 2:13). God is seeking to make a graceful, beautiful, and useful vessel out of each of us.

**II. Jeremiah observed that there is a possibility of perverting the purpose of the potter.**

A. *As the potter worked, the vessel was marred in his hand.* The vessel could not become what the potter had planned for it to be.

B. *Jeremiah saw that Israel was the clay on the wheel and that his nation had resisted the touch of the divine Potter.* Israel had refused to recognize God's divine plan. They had accepted God's blessings without recognizing their position of responsibility to God and their destiny.

Little thought is given to the divine plans for our nation. Few would even recognize that God has a plan for the nation as well as for the individual.

As an individual have you resisted the molding touch of the divine Potter upon the vessel of your life? Have you starved your soul by neglecting a devotional study of the Word of God and the place of prayer? Have you refused to equip yourself for a greater service by declining opportunities for training? Have you turned a deaf ear to the voice of God's Spirit as he has called you either to a deeper devotion to God or to a ministry of mercy toward others?

If we believe that God is love and that all of his ways are wise, then we would be wise to cooperate completely with the leadership of the Holy Spirit.

*God has a plan for all my life;*
*He wants to lead through storm and strife.*
*He promises His grace divine;*
*His providence today is mine.*
*God has a plan, the Scriptures state;*
*I must with this cooperate.*
*Half-heartedness will not suffice*
*When I behold his sacrifice.*

*—Charles M. Elam*

**III. Jeremiah saw the infinite patience and persistence of the potter.**

"And the vessel that he made of clay was marred in the hand of the potter: so he made it again another vessel, as seemed good to the potter to make it" (Jer. 18:4).

A. *The divine Potter would not throw the lump of clay on the junk pile after it was marred in his hand.* Instead, he crushed it and placed it on the wheel again to make another vessel out of it.

Jeremiah was led to see that the fall of his nation and the captivity of its people was not an indication of the decline of God's power, nor was it a defeat of God's purpose. He saw this catastrophe as a part of the process by which God would continue his purpose for Israel and would still make his nation a vessel usable for redemptive purposes.

Today trouble often falls across our pathway. There are times when we are both distressed and depressed. On such occasions it would be profitable if we could see ourselves on the wheel of the divine Potter. The apostle Paul had this great truth in mind when he declared that God works in all things for good "to them that love God, to them who are the called according to his purpose" (Rom. 8:28).

B. *God gives both individuals and nations a second chance.* God gave Israel another chance to be his people among the nations of the world. To a degree they succeeded and to a degree they failed.

In spite of the failures in your past, the God of infinite mercy and patience still has a work for you. The message about God that Jeremiah learned when he visited the potter's house is both comforting and challenging. It would declare to us that there is still hope.

## Conclusion

Is there a limit to the divine patience? Is it possible for a nation or an individual to pass the point of no return as far as God is concerned? Some evidence indicates that there is a limit, and other evidence encourages us to have hope always. Through Jeremiah, God said to Israel, "I will scatter them as with an east wind before the enemy; I will shew them the back, and not the face, in the day of their calamity" (Jer. 18:17). This verse would cause us to realize that it is very dangerous for us to presume upon the mercy and patience of God.

The apostle Peter encourages his readers to believe that there is hope as long as there is life. "The Lord is not slack concerning his promise, as some men count slackness; but is longsuffering to usward, not willing that any should perish, but that all should come to repentance" (2 Peter 3:9). God does not delight in the death or defeat of any man or nation. God would have all come to repentance—to be as pliable clay on the wheel that we might be vessels of beauty, honor, and usefulness.

## SUNDAY EVENING, MARCH 29

***Title:*** The Golden Rule

***Text:*** "Therefore all things whatsoever ye would that men should do to you, do ye even so to them: for this is the law and the prophets" (**Matt. 7:12**).

### Introduction

Our text is one of the greatest verses in the Bible. It is not only a summary statement of all that Jesus said concerning our treatment of our fellow humans, it also declares that it covers all that the Law and the Prophets have taught on this matter.

The Golden Rule calls for positive action on the level of the second great commandment, "Thou shalt love thy neighbor as thyself."

Our text, commonly called the Golden Rule, reveals the superiority of Christ to all other great teachers. The Hebrew teacher Hillel said, "Do not do to thy neighbor what is hateful to thyself." The Greek philosopher Socrates said, "What stirs your anger when done to you by others, that do not to others." Confucius gave what some have called the Silver Rule: "What you do not want done to yourself, do not do to others."

Some have said that these great teachers said the same thing that Christ said in the Golden Rule, but a careful examination of the Golden Rule in contrast with these statements reveals one radical difference: While these statements are negative and passive, Christ's command to his disciples is positive and active. These great teachers say, "Stand still and do not do what you do not want someone else to do to you." Christ says, "Go and do what you would that others should do to you." Christians are not merely to refrain from harming their fellow humans; they are to go and relate to others in the manner in which they would have others relate to them.

### I. A very significant "therefore" (Matt. 7:11–12).

A. *In speaking to his disciples, Jesus was encouraging them, on the basis of God's good gifts to them (Matt. 7:11), to give themselves in acts of positive goodness toward others. Paul made this same appeal to the Roman Christians (Rom. 12:1).*

B. *We cannot expect to continue to receive the good gifts of God if we do not relate ourselves to others in terms of positive kindness and helpfulness.*

C. *We are to treat our fellow humans as we desire to be treated by our heavenly Father.*

D. *Because God has dealt so bountifully with us, we should follow his example and practice generosity and liberality toward our fellow humans.*

E. *We are not to let our conduct be determined by how men treat us but rather by how God has treated us.*

### II. A standard of complete unselfishness.

A. *Man by nature is a selfish creature.* Most of our troubles are due to our selfishness. Most of our squabbles with others, whether they be at home, at church, at play, or at work, are due to selfishness.

B. *Jesus challenges us to rise above our tendency to be self-centered in our human relationships.* We can easily determine what our duty toward our neighbor is if we will determine, honestly and sincerely, how we would like our neighbor to treat us.

C. *By this rule, Jesus provides us with a clue to the maintaining of a good conscience in all of our contacts with our fellow humans.* To follow this rule is to have a conscience that does not condemn us.

D. *This rule applies not only to giving but to forgiving.* "Forbearing one another, and forgiving one another, if any man have a quarrel against any: even as Christ forgave you, so also do ye" (Col. 3:13). It is utterly vain for us to speak like angels in prayer if we then act like demons in our transactions with our fellow humans.

## III. A commendation of the Golden Rule: "For this is the law and the prophets."

A. *In the Golden Rule, Jesus summed up the substance of the teaching of both the Law and the Prophets concerning a person's relationship with his or her fellow humans.* If you would keep the ethical requirements of the Ten Commandments, apply this principle in everyday life.

B. *The Golden Rule provides us with the very essence of our Christian duty toward our fellow humans.* Consider for a moment what the practice of this principle could mean in your home, between husband and wife, between parents and children. Contemplate what the practice of this principle could mean in your community and in your business.

Abraham practiced this principle in his relationship with Lot (Gen. 13:5–18).

Joseph practiced this principle toward his brothers in spite of their mistreatment of him (Gen. 45:1–15).

## Conclusion

We cannot have the religion of the Sermon on the Mount without the Christ of the Mount. Only those who have experienced the love of God in Christ Jesus can even begin to love others as themselves. Only by the grace of God can one rise up to the high level of living the Golden Rule in every relationship.

In spite of the fact that we have failed in the past and may fail in the future, let us ever pray and strive that we might be able to do unto others as we would have them do unto us—in all things and always.

SUGGESTED PREACHING PROGRAM FOR

# APRIL

## ■ Sunday Mornings

"But Now Is Christ Risen from the Dead" (1 Cor. 15:20) is the theme for this month's Sunday morning sermons. The second Sunday in the month is Easter Sunday, the day of all days, the festival of all festivals for the Christian. Easter Sunday comes just once a year, yet we celebrate the resurrection of Christ every seven days. We cannot overproclaim that Christ is alive. Is it possible that we have preached the cross more than we have the resurrection? A study of the preaching in the book of Acts will reveal that the resurrection was the climactic truth in the preaching of the apostles. We would be wise to follow their example.

## ■ Sunday Evenings

"Encouragements to Evangelistic Efforts" is the theme for the Sunday evening messages.

## ■ Wednesday Evenings

"Fountains of Living Water" that can quench the thirst of the soul can be found in the five psalms that are suggested as a basis for the Wednesday evening messages.

---

## WEDNESDAY EVENING, APRIL 1

***Title:*** God's Ideal Man

***Scripture Reading:*** Psalm 1

### Introduction

Psalm 1 probably provided the scriptural basis for Jesus' Sermon on the Mount. Both Psalm 1 and the Sermon on the Mount describe the attitude and actions of God's ideal person. Both set forth the ideal person's character, influence, conduct, and destiny.

The Sermon on the Mount closes with a description of the destiny of humans. Those who both hear and heed the Word of God, like the blessed man described in Psalm 1, are likened to a wise man who built his house on a rock foundation. His house was stable and secure in the time of testing. Those who hear but refuse to heed the Word of God, like the ungodly man described in Psalm 1:4–6, are likened to a foolish man who built his house on sand. In the time of testing, they will discover that they do not have that which gives them permanence and stability.

Psalm 1 presents the portraits of two men. The blessed man guards his direction, his leisure, and his company; and he loves and meditates on the Word of God day and night. The ungodly man is just the opposite. He walks in the counsel of the ungodly, stands in the way of sinners, and sits in the seat of the scornful. Instead of being secure, fruitful, and happy, he is blown about by the winds of life and is finally destroyed for the lack of a sure relationship with God.

In a few well-chosen words, the psalmist sketches two sharply contrasting pictures. The first picture is of a happy and successful man. The second picture is of a man whose life ends in dismal failure. Because all of us hunger for success and want to avoid failure, let us focus our attention on the first in order that we might avoid the destiny of the second.

### I. The pathway to spiritual success.

The portrait of God's ideal man describes him both negatively and positively.

A. *There were at least three great refusals in his life.*

1. He refused to walk in the counsel of the ungodly. In times of uncertainty, he did not seek the advice of the ungodly. Deliberately rejecting the ideas and philosophies of the ungodly, he refused to adopt the principles or to follow the practices of those who had eliminated God from their thinking.
2. He refused to stand in the way of sinners, seeking no intimacy with them as companions. He refused to associate with rebellious offenders against God. Evidently he was aware of the destructive effect of a continuing contact with evil.
3. He refused to sit in the seat of the scornful. He did not listen to those who were experts at sneering and scoffing at and joking about sacred things.

B. *At least two prominent, positive qualities affected his life.*

1. His greatest delight was in knowing and doing the will of God (Ps. 1:2). Evidently he rejoiced in the precious promises of God. He responded with gratitude to the purpose of God's grace that was behind the law of God in the first place.
2. He meditated on the law of the Lord day and night. This means that he gave the truth of God his serious consideration. He mulled it over in his mind throughout the day in order that its meaning might saturate his whole being.

### II. The pathway to spiritual failure.

While the psalmist does not describe specifically the pathway to spiritual failure, we are left to infer from the spirit of the psalm that the ungodly man was just the opposite of God's ideal man.

A. *He rejected the law of God as the guiding principle for his life.*

B. *He directed his life on the basis of the counsel of the ungodly.*

C. *He did not hesitate to tarry in the way of sinners.*
D. *It is possible that in addition to listening to the scorn of the scoffers that he likewise thought lightly and spoke flippantly of the things of God.*

**III. Contrasted destinies.**

A. *The godly man is pictured as an evergreen tree planted by the rivers of water.* It is a picture of vitality, prosperity, fruitfulness, and permanency.
B. *The ungodly man discovers that instead of standing secure like a tree planted by the rivers of water, he is blown about like the chaff when the storms of life sweep across the plains.* He discovers that when the world caves in, instead of being alive, he is dead, dry, wind-driven, insecure, and helpless. He has no fruit or vitality or stability, and his life ends in failure.

### Conclusion

Each of us would be wise to compare our choices with the choices of the men described in this psalm. We should earnestly seek to imitate the example of the blessed man in order that we might escape the destiny of the ungodly man.

---

## SUNDAY MORNING, APRIL 5

*Title:* The Meaning of the Resurrection for Today

*Text:* "And they said one to another, Did not our heart burn within us, while he talked with us by the way, and while he opened to us the scriptures?" **(Luke 24:32)**.

*Scripture Reading:* Luke 24:28–48

*Hymns:* "All Hail the Power of Jesus' Name," Perronet
"Christ the Lord Is Risen Today," Wesley
"He Lives," Ackley

*Offertory Prayer:* Our heavenly Father, today we rejoice in your grace and thank you for the hope, comfort, and happiness the resurrection has brought to our hearts. We thank you for the assurance that through Christ we have victory over death and the grave. In gratitude and worship, and because of our desire that others come to know of his death and resurrection and his abiding presence, we bring these tithes and offerings for the work of your kingdom. In the name of the living Lord. Amen.

### Introduction

The resurrection of Christ from the tomb of Joseph of Arimathea is something far more than an isolated event of the ancient past that has no significance or meaning for today. Far from being a mere historical event removed from us by more than two thousand years, the resurrection of Christ is a present reality in the light of which we must live and act today.

Only as we see the significance of the resurrection of Christ for the past, the present, and the future can we truly understand and appreciate the message of Easter.

The resurrection of Christ is something other than a trick of supernatural magic performed by God to excite the emotions of his disciples and to amaze and antagonize his enemies. Christ's resurrection speaks of something far more meaningful than "the promise of pie in the sky by and by," as some have charged. The empty tomb of Christ contained a message that was vitally necessary for that age, for this age, and for every age until Christ comes back to receive his own.

**I. The resurrection of Christ explained the meaning of his death on the cross.**

As Jesus approached the end of his ministry, he began to prepare his disciples for his sacrificial and substitutionary death on the cross. Such a concept was so foreign to the popular ideas concerning the Messiah that it was impossible for Jesus to convince them fully of the necessity of his death. They did everything they could to persuade him to stay away from Jerusalem and the possibility of coming into contact with those who wanted to kill him. In spite of their efforts, Jesus persisted in his plans to go to Jerusalem. This trip was to result in the false accusations and the unjust trials that were part of the process leading to his crucifixion.

A. *For his disciples, Jesus' death was a great personal sorrow.* They had become deeply devoted to him during their days of association together. Their hearts were crushed with grief because of his death and their personal loss.

B. *Jesus' death was for his disciples a great personal disappointment.* They were hoping to reestablish the kingdom of David and the sovereignty of the nation of Israel. As they saw Jesus feed the hungry, heal the sick, and raise the dead, they were convinced that there was no way by which he could be defeated if he would raise an army. They were normal human beings who hoped for a position of prominence once that political kingdom was established. His crucifixion obliterated these hopes and dreams.

C. *Jesus' death was for them a great public tragedy, for Jesus was a very popular leader.* He had been publicly condemned as a criminal. The final and ultimate indignity to which he was subjected was death by crucifixion. We can easily understand why they fled in fear and despair.

We read that following his resurrection, "he opened their minds so that they could understand the Scriptures" (Luke 24:45 NIV). From the law of Moses, and the Prophets, and the Psalms, it was revealed that Jesus' substitutionary death on the cross had been in the plan of God from the very beginning. His death was the supreme demonstration of the determination of God to redeem people from the tyranny and the waste of sin. The resurrection revealed the great price paid for our redemption.

1. Redemption by love (Rom. 5:8).
2. Redemption by substitution (1 Peter 3:18).
3. Redemption by suffering (1 Peter 2:23–24).

**II. The resurrection of Christ was to the early disciples a dramatic demonstration of his deity.**

It was this conviction that gave purpose to the church and glued the apostles together as a witnessing body to the great redemptive acts associated with the cross and the empty tomb. The disciples believed Jesus to be the unique Son of God. They had witnessed his marvelous miracles, the perfect purity of his life, and his compassionate concern for sinners. They were convinced that Jesus was no ordinary man. Nicodemus had declared Jesus to be a "teacher come from God" (John 3:2). Jesus had accepted this and other similar statements as the truth.

From a distance these disciples had witnessed the shameful treatment of the Christ by sinful humans. Their hearts were broken by his agonizing death on the cross. They were bewildered and depressed, fearful and fainting. They fled into hiding for fear of losing their lives as well. It was the resurrection that changed this situation.

In Paul's epistle to the Romans he reveals that it was the resurrection that authenticated as divine truth all that Jesus had claimed and promised. He says that Jesus was "declared to be the Son of God with power, according to the spirit of holiness, by the resurrection from the dead" (Rom. 1:4).

A. *The resurrection declared Jesus of Nazareth to be the Son of God.* His divinity was no longer a matter of faith alone to these disciples. They now knew it to be a fact. Jesus appeared among the disciples when Thomas was present, and Thomas was bold to say, "My Lord and my God" (John 20:28).
B. *The resurrection declared Christ to be a sinless Savior.* Because Jesus had died a substitutionary death for our sin instead of some personal sin, Luke, the author of the book of Acts, declares that it was not possible for death to hold him (Acts 2:24).
C. *The resurrection assured the apostles that Christ was a divine Savior who had died for their sins and arose that they might have life (1 Cor. 15:3–4).*

**III. The resurrection of Christ gave the disciples a companion for the road of life.**

Jesus did not arise from the dead merely to give us a new doctrine, although believing in his resurrection is at the very heart of our faith. He arose from the dead to assure his disciples that he had not forsaken them and that he would continue to be with them in a very real and wonderful sense through the ministry of the Holy Spirit (John 14:18).

A. *At the very center of the disciples' faith was the conviction of the abiding presence of the living Lord who had defeated sin, death, the grave, and all the powers of evil.* This living Lord was invested with all heavenly power and authority. The effects of this conviction explain the continuation of Christianity as a living faith today.
B. *Christ's living presence controlled the disciples in moments of moral weakness.*
C. *Christ's living presence challenged the disciples in the hour when tremendous effort and courage were needed.*

D. *Christ's living presence comforted the disciples in their times of trial and trouble.* They demonstrated that Christianity is something far more than a man doing the best that he can. Christianity is the vital contact and fellowship of men and women with the living Christ.

A trainer of seeing-eye dogs told his blind companion as they walked across the street with her new guide dog, "Walk closer to him. He cannot guide you if you hold him at arm's length." The same is true for Christians. We must consistently and deliberately stay close to the living Christ if we want to enjoy the companionship and the infallible leadership of him who never leads us wrong.

**IV. The resurrection disclosed to the disciples and to us the power that is available to us as we seek to lift the loads of life.**

Paul prayed for the Ephesians that they might know "his incomparably great power for us who believe. That power is like the working of his mighty strength, which he exerted in Christ when he raised him from the dead and seated him at his right hand in the heavenly realms" (Eph. 1:19–20 NIV).

We are in need of something more than intellectual, political, or financial power if we are to do God's work effectively in this world today. We must have access to and utilize spiritual power that Jesus declared would be available through faith in him and cooperation with the Holy Spirit. We can praise God for the availability of this divine energy for those who are obedient.

**V. The resurrection of Christ is a wonderful disclosure of the gift of immortality.**

Jesus had spoken to his disciples concerning the reality of eternal life, which he was able to bestow on those who trusted him. It is very unlikely that they understood what he meant by these words until after he had conquered death and the grave. He said to them:

> "I tell you the truth, whoever hears my word and believes him who sent me has eternal life and will not be condemned; he has crossed over from death to life. I tell you the truth, a time is coming and has now come when the dead will hear the voice of the Son of God and those who hear will live. For as the Father has life in himself, so he has granted the Son to have life in himself....
>
> "Do not be amazed at this, for a time is coming when all who are in their graves will hear his voice and come out—those who have done good will rise to live, and those who have done evil will rise to be condemned" (John 5:24–29 NIV).

When Jesus described himself as the Good Shepherd, he said that he would give his life for his sheep, and he also declared, "No man taketh it from me, but I lay it down of myself. I have power to lay it down, and I have power to take it again" (John 10:18). Only after the resurrection could the disciples possibly understand or fully believe that Jesus had this power.

In writing to Timothy, Paul interpreted the resurrection in terms of its being a demonstration of the life and immortality that Jesus gives to those who believe the gospel (2 Tim. 1:9–10).

When the transfigured and glorified Christ appeared to John on the Isle of Patmos, he claimed to have sovereignty over death because of his resurrection and exaltation by God (Rev. 1:18).

On the basis of both the promises and the performance of Jesus, his friends can face death with the confidence that death shall have no final victory. In anticipation of his victory over death, Jesus had said, "Because I live, ye shall live also." This truth has cheered the hearts of martyrs as they faced execution by their persecutors.

### Conclusion

Christ Jesus is risen from the dead. He is present here today. He is able to save you from sin's penalty, which is death. He is able to save you from sin's power and give you victory. He is able to bring the spirit of God's holiness and happiness into your heart and life. Today you would be wise to respond to him in faith and let him become your Savior. Decide now to sit at his feet continually and let him be your Teacher. He is the Leader who will never lead you wrong. He, and he alone, can give you victory over death and the grave and the privilege of fellowship with a loving God for eternity.

---

## SUNDAY EVENING, APRIL 5

***Title:*** The Methods of the Witnessing Church

***Text:*** "And daily in the temple, and in every house, they ceased not to teach and preach Jesus Christ" **(Acts 5:42)**.

### Introduction

People are on a perpetual quest for an easier way to get the job done. In nearly every area of human interest and activity, great attention is given to methods, techniques, and procedures. The church must continually reexamine and reevaluate and improve its methods and techniques of communicating the gospel to our generation.

The book of Acts presents a thrilling success story of the early church as it communicated the saving truths of the gospel to its generation. We read of great advances in Jerusalem, in Judea, and in Samaria. These early witnesses advanced into Asia Minor and crossed over into Europe; and in the lifetime of the apostles, they bore a winning witness to the then-known world.

We live in a "how-to-do-it" age. Someone has said, "Build a better mousetrap, and the world will beat a path to your door." Today let us examine the methods used by the early church as it sought to witness to the people of the first century of the Christian era. A study of the book of Acts will reveal that they used simple

rather than complex methods. Their techniques were solid rather than superficial. They were constructive and complementary instead of being competitive with each other. And they used at least seven different methods for witnessing.

**I. Talking (*lalein*).**

The Greek word means "to tell, to speak, to carry on a Christian conversation" (Acts 5:20, 40; 11:20). If we are to communicate the saving gospel of Jesus Christ to our generation, we cannot depend on the pulpit or the Sunday school classroom to get the job done. But think of what would happen if each disciple of our Lord were to develop the art and the inclination to carry on a Christian conversation concerning spiritual things with those about him. It should be as normal for us to talk about our Savior as it is for us to talk about our doctor or our dentist or our insurance man or our banker or our family members. If all followers of our Lord were to do this simultaneously, we could evangelize the whole world in less than one decade.

**II. Witnessing (*marturein*).**

The word means "to bear witness, make a solemn declaration, give evidence, bear testimony" (Acts 1:8; 2:32; 3:15; 4:33; 5:32).

The witnessing that the early followers did was that of a testator rather than a spectator. It could be claimed that the disciples were eyewitnesses to the redemptive acts of Jesus, but his commandment for them to witness refers to a verbal testimony. They were to communicate to others what they had seen and heard.

By its very nature, witnessing is always personal. We cannot bear witness to that which we have not seen or heard or experienced ourselves. Some will be shocked to know that it is our own personal experience with Jesus Christ that he would have us to share with others. It is our personal witness that the Holy Spirit can take and bless and use to bring conviction and conversion to the hearts of unbelievers.

**III. Preaching (*kerussein*).**

The Greek word means "to preach, to proclaim, to publish, to herald with authority" (Acts 3:20; 8:4–5).

In the days before newspapers and television, a king would have his proclamation read throughout the kingdom. The representatives of the king would enter a city, and one of the soldiers would sound a trumpet. After the people assembled, the proclamation would be read. The man who read the proclamation was called a *kerux*, or herald. He was the one who proclaimed the message of the king with authority.

As the early disciples of our Lord were scattered, they went forth announcing what God had done and what he offered to those who would repent and believe. As his official spokespersons, they were announcing the terms by which people could be saved.

Many times this preaching was done by one individual to another, and it was not simply pious platitudes or moral instructions. It was the announcement of what God had done and of what he would do if people would repent in faith.

**IV. Evangelizing (*euangelizesthai*).**

The Greek word means "to evangelize, to address with good tidings" (see Acts 5:42; 8:4, 25, 35, 40). In each of the verses listed above, the word that is translated "preach" is actually the word "euangelizesthai," and it means to announce the good tidings of God's love and mercy and grace as revealed in and through Jesus Christ for sinners. Dr. C. E. Autrey has translated this word "gossiping the gospel." The early disciples were everywhere talking continuously about the wonderful things that God had done.

Each member of the modern-day church needs to rediscover the meaning of the gospel and do the work of an evangelist. No one likes to be the bearer of bad news; everyone likes to communicate good news; and this is our task.

**V. Prophesying (*propheteuein*).**

The Greek word means "to speak for God under the inspiration of the Holy Spirit" (Acts 2:17–18; 4:8, 31; 13:1). Primarily the prophets were spokesmen for God rather than predictors of the future. They were men of God speaking the truth of God to the hearts of men and women. It is possible for all of us, according to Acts 2:17–19, to be spokespersons for God. God meant for us to follow in the tradition of the prophets and to be spokespersons to our generation.

**VI. Teaching (*didaskein*).**

The Greek word means "to teach, to disciple" (Acts 2:42; 5:21, 25). This word is used thirty times by Luke, fifteen times concerning the work of Jesus and fifteen times concerning the work of the apostles. The prominence of this method in both the life of the Savior and in the work of the apostles should cause every pastor to realize that he must major on teaching in his ministry. Preaching that does not contain a strong element of teaching is poor preaching. Good teaching is also good preaching.

These truths should challenge each believer seriously to consider opportunities for teaching both in the church classroom and on a person-to-person basis as we have opportunity.

**VII. Pleading (*parakalein*).**

The Greek word means "to beseech, to entreat, to exhort" (Acts 2:40; 20:18–21; 26:3). The early church bore a winning witness because the concern and compassion of the Savior for the lost world filled their hearts. Both in public and in private, in a face-to-face and heart-to-heart relationship, they pleaded with their families and friends to respond to Jesus Christ as Lord.

The early church had no beautiful sanctuaries, expensive educational facilities, mighty organs, or trained choirs. They had no buildings or budgets, and yet they changed the course of history using the seven methods that are available to each of us today.

### Conclusion

Have you ever wished that you could preach like a skilled evangelist or sing like a gospel recording artist? We all wish there were more people with these talents, but our Lord may not want us to be either. He does, however, want each of us to use the methods that are available to us. These he will bless, and these he will use to bring salvation to the hearts of those about us. May God help us as individuals and help our church to use these seven simple but satisfactory methods that the Holy Spirit has blessed through the ages, and may God bless you as you use these methods.

## WEDNESDAY EVENING, APRIL 8

***Title:*** The Faith That Conquers Fear

***Text:*** Psalm 27:1–2

### Introduction

One of the great problems of every person is that of fear. Fear can be defined with a long list of synonyms, such as alarm, care, despondency, dismay, dread, fright, gloom, horror, panic, or terror. As children many of us were awakened from sleep by the terror of a nightmare. And there are adults today who look upon life as a continuous nightmare because fear has captured their souls.

A study of the Bible will reveal that fear has been a companion of man from the beginning of time. There are seventeen different nouns and thirteen different verbs for the idea of "fear" in the original language in which the Bible is written.

The heavenly Father wants to deliver his children from fear. Nearly a hundred passages in the Bible exhort us to "fear not."

The book of Psalms especially encourages us to put our faith in God that we might overcome our fears. We find, for example, "Yea, though I walk through the valley of the shadow of death, I will fear no evil: for thou art with me; thy rod and thy staff they comfort me" (23:4) and "The LORD is on my side; I will not fear: what can man do unto me?" (118:6). The words of our text, "The LORD is my light and my salvation; whom shall I fear? The LORD is the strength of my life; of whom shall I be afraid?" (27:1), provide us with an explanation of the conquering faith of David. The entire psalm is a hymn of praise to the goodness and greatness of God. It contains a revelation of God that each of us needs greatly for the living of these days.

### I. Fear is a current problem for many of us.

A. *We fear disappointment by others.*

B. *We fear failure because of suspected inadequacies of a personal nature.*

C. *We fear the possibility of being eliminated by the giant system of life that treats people as numbers rather than persons.*

D. *We fear the possibility of a dreaded disease or an untimely accidental death.*
E. *We fear the possibility of an international catastrophe.*
F. *We fear financial insecurity.*
G. *Some of us fear the approach of death and the prospect of meeting our Creator.*

## II. Our God wants to deliver us from the bondage and agony of fear.

"God hath not given us the spirit of fear; but of power, and of love, and of a sound mind" (2 Tim. 1:7).

A. *Fear is a thief of happiness.* No one can enjoy the happiness that God wants him to have if he feels the agony of fear at the same time.
B. *Fear robs us of the possibility of worthy achievements in life.* Fear of failure causes us to hesitate to set achievement goals that are within the reach of our abilities.
C. *Fear produces failure.* He who takes counsel of his fears will always stagger back from that which appears to be impossible or difficult. He who never attempts that which is exceedingly difficult is defeated by lack of faith.

## III. The faith that throws off fear.

A. *The faith that throws off fear is the faith that trusts God in the here and now (Ps. 27:1).* Many of us have thought of God as being on the scene in the ancient past. Others think of him as appearing on the scene at some time in the future. Those who experience victory are those who trust him as being present in the present. He is the God of today as well as the God of yesterday and the God of tomorrow. He is more concerned about our today than he is about our yesterday. He is more concerned about our today than he is about our tomorrow, because our tomorrow is largely wrapped up in the decisions of today.
B. *The faith that throws off fear is the faith that trusts God because of yesterday (Ps. 27:2).* Because God had been so very faithful in the past, the psalmist was encouraged to believe that God would continue to be gracious. He was able to trust God in the present because of his personal experience with God in the past.

   It would be good for us to open our eyes and see the activity of God on our behalf in the past. This activity is recorded in the Bible and on the pages of Christian history. It can be discovered on the pages of our own personal experience if we have eyes to see.
C. *The faith that throws off fear is the faith that trusts God for tomorrow (Ps. 27:3).* The psalmist faced the uncertain future with a calm confidence in the abiding presence of the good God who had blessed him from childhood to full maturity in times of great danger and difficulty.

## Conclusion

The psalmist had a faith that conquered fear because of at least two things. First, he responded to God's movements toward him. As he became aware of

God's will, he sought to do God's will. Second, he deliberately sought the presence and the guidance of God throughout all the days of his life. He wrote, "One thing have I desired of the LORD, that will I seek after; that I may dwell in the house of the LORD all the days of my life, to behold the beauty of the LORD, and to inquire in his temple" (Ps. 27:4).

You and I can have the faith that conquers fear if we will respond to God's movements toward us and if we will deliberately seek his guidance for our lives.

## SUNDAY MORNING, APRIL 12

***Title:*** The Risen Christ and Mary Magdalene

***Text:*** "Now when Jesus was risen early the first day of the week, he appeared first to Mary Magdalene, out of whom he had cast seven devils" **(Mark 16:9)**.

***Scripture Reading:*** John 20:1–18

***Hymns:*** "Hallelujah! Christ Is Risen," Wordsworth

"Low in the Grave He Lay," Lowry

"Crown Him with Many Crowns," Bridges

***Offertory Prayer:*** Heavenly Father, as we come bringing tithes and offerings, we offer to you the thoughts of our minds, the love of our hearts, and the strength of our hands. We offer you the praise of our lips and the testimony of lives that have been uplifted by the living presence of your Son, Jesus Christ. We thank you for every good and perfect gift that comes to us in life. As we offer our gifts to you, we thank you in anticipation of your continued mercies through Jesus Christ our Lord. Amen.

### Introduction

The Scriptures testify that forty days transpired between the resurrection of the living Christ and his ascension back to the heavenly Father. Luke, the beloved physician, who made a detailed search concerning all that Jesus began both to do and to teach, records that Jesus "shewed himself alive after his passion by many infallible proofs, being seen of them forty days, and speaking of the things pertaining to the kingdom of God" (Acts 1:3).

The New Testament records at least ten different postresurrection appearances of our Lord to his disciples. On the first Easter Sunday, the risen Lord appeared to Mary Magdalene and to the other women. He walked from Jerusalem to Emmaus with two disciples. Also on that first Easter Sunday, he appeared to Simon (Luke 24:34). He appeared in the Upper Room to ten of the apostles as two believers from Emmaus described their fellowship with him.

There is nothing that the modern church or the individual Christian needs more than a fresh and vivid awareness that our Savior and Lord conquered death and the grave. There are at least three things that this awareness could and would do for us.

First, we need to discover that Christianity is a vital relationship with the living Lord. Great men come and go on the stage of history. They make an impact for a day. They achieve eminence, and the world acclaims them. Biographers seek to interpret their thoughts and actions. The great ones die, and monuments are erected to their memory. Jesus of Nazareth also marched into the central place on the stage of human activities. He also died, but he did not disappear, for he arose and reappeared. He remains on the stage eternally the same.

People's beliefs about Christ and their understanding of him may change from age to age, yet they do not change Jesus Christ. He is God's final and sure word to humankind. He is God's grace for our saving. He is God's mercy for our healing. He is God's truth for our leading. He is forever alive and available.

Second, we need to understand that worship is an experience with the living Lord. Worship is something more than just going to church and hearing the singing of the choir and the sermon of the preacher. Real worship is an experience with the one who has promised always to be present "where two or three are gathered together in my name" (Matt. 18:20). To rediscover the living presence of Christ would both strengthen our faith and deepen our devotion.

Third, to experience Christ's living presence would cause us to rediscover our mission to the world. Christ did not come into the world merely to give us a ticket to heaven and deliverance from hell. He came to redeem our lives from the power of evil and to utilize our lives in service to others. For most, this ministry to others is the opportunity and responsibility to be a personal witness—that is, a communicator of what God has done in the past and what he can do in the present and future for those who will trust him.

How can we rediscover the presence of the living Lord who arose triumphant over death and the grave? There is no simple answer to this question. We can learn something as we study the record of how Jesus appeared to his disciples.

### I. The risen Christ appeared first to Mary Magdalene.

It is significant that Jesus appeared first of all to a woman. The Scriptures say, "Now when Jesus was risen early the first day of the week, he appeared first to Mary Magdalene, out of whom he had cast seven devils" (Mark 16:9). We can assume that because Jesus appeared to Mary Magdalene that he also wants to make himself real to us. Mary Magdalene was no great person of prominence. She had no material wealth or academic credentials. She had no political power. She was a sinner saved by grace like the rest of us. By appearing to her first, perhaps the Savior was demonstrating his availability to all who have hungry hearts and are willing to believe and trust.

### II. The risen Christ comes to us in times of our deepest need.

Mary Magdalene and the other women came to the sepulcher at dawn on the first day of the week following the entombment of the Christ that they might complete their loving service of anointing and embalming his body (Luke 24:1).

At first they were shocked and horrified to see the stone rolled away and the body of their Lord missing. No doubt a thousand questions tormented their minds in a moment as they considered the possibility that indignity had been added to the insult of crucifixion. They were astonished beyond words when they were informed by angelic beings that he was risen, and they rushed to inform the apostles. It was some time during the early morning that the Christ appeared to Mary Magdalene, while she was desolate, heartbroken, and overwhelmed with the thought that "they have taken away my Lord, and I know not where they have laid him" (John 20:13).

Christ, the living Lord, took the initiative in making himself real to his disciples. And he will walk into our thoughts as we study the Scriptures. If we will study them regularly and reverently, he will reveal his presence. In the great hymns he will speak to our hearts if we listen for the message from God. He will come to strengthen us in the times of our weakness and to guide us in the time of uncertainty if, by faith, we trust and obey him.

**III. The risen Christ is often unrecognized.**

"And when she had thus said, she turned herself back, and saw Jesus standing, and knew not that it was Jesus" (John 20:14).

A. *At first Mary Magdalene did not recognize the risen Christ.* She was so consumed with her grief that her eyes were closed as far as recognizing him. This has been the case with many of us. He comes to us today as he came to Mary Magdalene.

B. *The two disciples from Emmaus did not recognize Jesus at first.* Luke's gospel says that the power to recognize him was withheld until after he had communicated a message that they needed (Luke 24:16–31).

C. *The seven apostles, who were fishing in the sea of Tiberius, did not recognize Jesus at first.* Perhaps it was the distance, but most likely they were unable to see him because of an undue concern for their own personal problems.

**IV. The risen Christ calls his own by name.**

"Jesus saith unto her, Mary. She turned herself, and saith unto him, Rabboni; which is to say, Master" (John 20:16). When Jesus had described himself as a good shepherd, he said, "I am the good shepherd, and know my sheep, and am known of mine" (John 10:14). The good shepherd was able to call his sheep by name.

The God who numbers the hairs on our heads very definitely knows our names. He even knows our middle names and our nicknames. This thought should encourage our faith and cause us to love our Lord more because of his individual and personal concern for each of us.

**V. The risen Christ conveys a message to be delivered: "Go to my brethren, and say unto them, I ascend unto my father, and your father; and to my God, and your God" (John 20:17).**

To have an experience with the living Christ is to make a discovery that must be shared. We are not to boast of our faith, but neither are we to conceal it. We

are to witness to others of what the living Lord means to us so that we may be the means whereby they might have faith and so that our own faith might be strengthened.

### Conclusion

Paul based his faith in Christ on the solid foundation of the testimony of others and on his own personal experience with the living Christ. He declares that Jesus was seen by Cephas and then by the Twelve. On one occasion he was seen by over five hundred brethren at once. He also was seen by James and by all of the apostles assembled together (1 Cor. 15:3–8).

This living Christ has walked down through the corridors of time to this hour and to this service. He stands at the heart door of each of us. Some of us need to let him in as Savior and Redeemer that we might have forgiveness of sin and the gift of new life.

Most of us have already welcomed Christ, but we need to let him occupy completely. Let us give him first place in every area of our lives. Let us do it right now.

---

## SUNDAY EVENING, APRIL 12

***Title:*** Matthew the Publican Becomes Matthew the Apostle

***Text:*** "As Jesus passed forth from thence, he saw a man, named Matthew, sitting at the receipt of custom: and he saith unto him, Follow me. And he arose, and followed him" **(Matt. 9:9)**.

***Scripture Reading:*** Matthew 9:9–15

### Introduction

There is a great difference between Matthew the publican and Matthew the apostle. He is a demonstration to us of the difference Christ can make if a person hears and responds to Christ's invitation of discipleship.

Matthew was a tax collector for the Roman government. The Romans placed a tax on all property, real and personal. Usually high Roman officials were given the responsibility of collecting this burdensome tax from the suppressed people, but in most cases they in turn would hire others to do it. Occasionally they would auction off to the highest bidder various cities or areas of the country for a set sum of money with the understanding that the purchaser would have the right to collect the taxes. His profit would be the amount that he was able to collect in excess of what he had paid.

In many instances those who purchased the right to collect these taxes were citizens of the country in which the taxes were to be collected. This was true in Israel, and Matthew was among this despised group.

These tax collectors, or publicans, were universally feared and hated throughout the empire. In no place were they hated more than in the land of Palestine. They were classified with sinners and harlots in the minds of the people. This explains part of the dismay and surprise of the Pharisees when they saw Jesus attending a banquet in the house of Matthew following his conversion.

**I. The character of Matthew before his call.**

A. *He was engaged in what was considered by all a disreputable business.*

B. *Evidently he did not care too much about his reputation, for to be a publican was to be the object of criticism in the community.*

C. *He evidently was afflicted with an insatiable desire for money.* However, it could be that he was a very practical man who logically arrived at the conclusion that he could make more money as a tax collector than he could in any other manner. If this were the case, then we may see some striking resemblances between ourselves at times and this man.

D. *He was not considered a true patriot of his country.* By being a tax collector, Matthew identified himself with the Roman army of occupation. By the very nature of the case, it would have been necessary for him to have sought to maintain the favor of his superiors rather than looking out for the best interests of his fellow citizens.

E. *By every accepted standard, he was considered an irreligious man.*

**II. The call to a higher life (Matt. 9:9).**

A. *Matthew provides us with a dramatic demonstration of the truth that Jesus did not come to save just the innocent or the pure and refined.* Over and over again, Jesus declared that he had come into the world to save sinners: "They that be whole need not a physician, but they that are sick ... for I am not come to call the righteous, but sinners to repentance" (Matt. 9:12–13).

B. *Without doubt, Matthew had heard much about Jesus before they met that day in the place where toll was collected.* It is quite possible that Matthew had heard both the preaching and the teaching of Jesus and that he had seen the results of Jesus' miraculous power to heal. Perhaps he recognized the unique character of Jesus to the extent that he wanted to respond to the divine claims upon his life.

C. *Matthew's wealth had not satisfied the hunger of his soul.* No amount of wealth can satisfy the deepest hunger of the heart.

D. *Jesus the Savior could see in Matthew the publican great possibilities for good.* As the naturalist can see the oak in an acorn, so could Jesus see the apostle in Matthew.

E. *The choice of Matthew, a man hated and despised by his contemporaries, illustrates the power of the living Christ to transform and to elevate to higher possibilities the life of an individual who will respond to him.*

**III. The cost to Matthew of following Jesus.**

A. *Luke's gospel records that Matthew "left all, rose up, and followed him" (Luke 5:28).*

1. He forsook his business.
2. He forsook his hopes of wealth.

3. He forsook his companions, such as they were.
4. He forsook his luxuries.

B. *He forsook a life of disloyalty to his country, turning away from great temptations to dishonesty and bad companionship.*

A sincere Christian was earnestly seeking to persuade a friend to become a follower of Jesus Christ. When the inquirer was confronted with the question, "What will it cost me to become a Christian? What will I have to give up in order to become a follower of Jesus Christ?" the Christian replied by saying, "To become a Christian the only things you must give up are those things that are going to ruin you if you don't."

**IV. The compensation of following Jesus.**

A. *Matthew forsook the assurance of worldly success, but in doing so he gained both inward satisfaction in this life and eternal success as a worker in God's kingdom.*

B. *From every standpoint Matthew became a better man and was no doubt surprised to discover later on that he was to be the author of the first gospel.* When he left the toll gate, he brought with him his pen. Instead of using this pen to write names and figures in a tax book, under God's guidance he wrote a gospel.

C. *By deciding to follow Jesus, Matthew discovered a fuller and richer life as well as a glorious companionship with the Christ.*

D. *Matthew discovered a better work than he had ever dreamed of before.* Being a follower of Jesus Christ was not to be compared with his previous position as a tax collector.

### Conclusion

In compassion the living Christ confronts you as he did Matthew. He challenges you to forsake the lower and to choose the higher way of life. He wants to utilize your talents for a nobler service than what you have planned. With your life he can also write a message of love and mercy and helpfulness on the lives of others. May you have eyes to see Jesus as he passes by, and may you have ears to hear him when he invites you to follow.

## WEDNESDAY EVENING, APRIL 15

*Title:* The Happy Duty of Daily Praise

*Text:* "Every day will I bless thee; and I will praise thy name for ever and ever" **(Ps. 145:2)**.

*Scripture Reading:* Psalm 107

### Introduction

The psalmist calls upon us to be faithful in offering praise to God for all of his many blessings to us. In Psalm 107 we notice the recurring refrain: "Oh that men would praise the LORD for his goodness, and for his wonderful works to the children of men!" (Ps. 107:8, 15, 21, 31). Most of us are guilty of neglecting this area of Christian service—the expression of gratitude and praise.

The world needs to see a demonstration of a religion that produces joy. We will never truly rejoice in the Lord if we neglect to think of God's many blessings and to praise him for his goodness. The world goes on in spiritual darkness because we have neglected to praise our God for his goodness and for his wonderful works.

### I. The daily praise of God is a natural act for a true child of God.

A. *One does not have to be a professional Christian worker to sing the praises of our great and wonderful God.*
B. *We praise our mothers for we are grateful.*
C. *We praise our doctors because of their ability to meet our needs in the time of illness.*
D. *We praise our friends.*
E. *Why not praise our Savior?* By our silence we leave the impression that Christianity is not truly worthwhile and that Christ does not really make a difference.

### II. The daily praise of God will prove to be very beneficial to each individual.

A. *It will help us to have joy in our hearts even when the world situation is distressing.*
B. *It will help us to overcome the competitive and materialistic spirit of our age.*
C. *It will remind us of the faithfulness and goodness of God.*
D. *It will create within us an attitude of gratitude.*
E. *It will contribute to a spirit of optimism regarding the future.*

### III. The daily praise of God will bring blessings to others.

A. *It will encourage unbelievers to have faith in Christ.*
   1. Give the testimony of your heart concerning what Christ means to you as you have opportunity.
   2. Give the testimony of your heart concerning what the church means to you and your family as you have opportunity.

B. *Your praise will encourage believers to have a greater faith.*

### Conclusion

David firmly resolved to praise God with all of his heart. "I will extol thee, my God, O king; and I will bless thy name for ever and ever. Every day will I bless thee; and I will praise thy name for ever and ever" (Ps. 145:1–2). David's resolution to praise God was very personal, but at the same time it was public, for there was no way he could praise God and be secretive about it. He praised God for the blessings of the past. He praised God for blessings in the present. He praised God in anticipation of blessings that were to come in the future.

For the good that it can bring into your own life and for the good that it can bring into the lives of others, let us give voice to the gratitude of our hearts in joyful praise.

## SUNDAY MORNING, APRIL 19

*Title:* "It Is the Lord"

*Text:* "Therefore that disciple whom Jesus loved saith unto Peter, It is the Lord" (**John 21:7**).

*Scripture Reading:* John 21:1–14

*Hymns:* "Jesus Shall Reign Where'er the Sun," Watts
"Wherever He Leads I'll Go," McKinney
"O for a Closer Walk," Cowper

*Offertory Prayer:* Holy Father, we bring to you a portion of that which you have given to us, for you are the giver of every good and perfect gift. We bring these gifts, not because you are in need, but because deep in our hearts we need to give both to you and to those about us. Help us to give joyfully even as you have given your rich gifts to us joyfully. You have bestowed your gifts upon us in a generous, lavish manner. Help us in turn to be cheerful givers of our best in every relationship of life. Through Jesus Christ our Lord. Amen.

### Introduction

In every age the scientific minds of humans have searched for logical explanations for the mysteries of life. This was true two thousand years ago when Christ our Lord conquered death and the tomb. Luke, the writer of the book of Acts, reveals that the Lord responded to the desire of his disciples for proof. "To whom also he showed himself alive after his passion by many infallible proofs, being seen of them forty days, and speaking of the things pertaining to the kingdom of God" (Acts 1:3).

Today we can be grateful that Jesus Christ completely convinced his disciples of his victory over death and the grave. We can be assured that it took absolute concrete evidence to convince them that Christ was risen, for he was confined to the tomb by at least five different powers. The cold hand of death gripped him firmly. Linen grave clothes were wound tightly about his body. There was a great stone rolled before the entrance to the tomb to prevent entrance or exit, and the official seal of the Roman government had been affixed to the tomb. Roman guards were posted near the tomb to make certain that no one came to retrieve Christ's body.

The first piece of evidence that was presented as proof that Christ had conquered death and the grave was the empty tomb. Many testified that the tomb was empty. The women found it empty. The disciples found it empty. The angel declared that it was empty. The Jewish Sanhedrin admitted that it was empty.

The evidence of the empty tomb is not all that proves Christ had conquered death and the grave. The New Testament mentions at least ten different appearances of our Lord to his disciples. In these appearances he gave to them absolute assurance of his living presence. He gave them an apprehension of the purpose for his death on the cross, and he gave them a divine authority to go to the ends of the earth proclaiming the significance of his death and resurrection.

Today we examine one of the appearances of the risen Savior to see what it has to say to our lives.

**I. The risen Lord manifested himself deliberately (John 21:1).**

A. *Jesus showed himself "again."* This was not his first appearance, and neither was it to be the last. He deliberately chose this occasion to convey a message to his followers.

B. *"On this wise showed he himself."* John, the writer of this gospel, was impressed by the special manner in which Jesus showed himself. He receives the impression that something is to be remembered from the manner in which the Christ revealed himself.

**II. The risen Christ came to the disciples on the level of their experience. This is very significant, and we should take note of it.**

A. *There was nothing unique or significant about the place where Jesus appeared.* There were thousands of places similar to this. It was not necessary for the disciples to travel to some shrine or some historical place to have an audience with the Christ.

B. *Christ appeared while the disciples were doing what they had previously done to earn a living.* Are we to assume from this that the risen Christ may approach us while we are busy with the common tasks of life? Does this mean that Jesus might visit your home or place of business? I believe it does.

C. *The risen Christ does reveal himself at unique times and places.* "For where two or three are gathered together in my name, there am I in the midst of them" (Matt. 18:20). We can expect the Lord to be present in the classroom. We can expect the living Lord to be present in the place of prayer and worship when God's people come together to praise him, adore him, and worship him. As we become more experienced and mature in the Christian life, there are certain places where we have had experience with God. To return to one of these places is to encourage the faith and response that makes it possible to have a fresh experience with the living Christ.

D. *Christ comes to all of us on the level of our own experience.* It would be discouraging to think that the risen Christ could come to us only on the level of the highest possible spiritual experience. The truth is that it is his coming to us on the common road of life that lifts us to these high experiences of spiritual awareness.

**III. The risen Christ was concerned about the disciples' well-being.**

From this we can assume that he continues to be interested in the welfare of his disciples.

A. *Have you caught any fish?* Jesus stood on the shore at a distance from where the disciples were casting their nets after a night of futile effort. They were exhausted and depressed because they had caught nothing. Through the fog they observed someone standing on the shore who shouted, "Have you caught any fish?" Their negative reply probably expressed the weariness of their bodies.

B. *Jesus prepared a hot breakfast for his disciples.* "As soon as they were come to land, they saw a fire of coals there, and fish laid thereon, and bread" (John 21:9). While they were dragging in the fish they had caught as a result of following Jesus' suggestion, he rekindled the fire and began to prepare breakfast with some of the fish that had been caught previously and were in the process of being cured for sale. He also suggested that they bring some of the fish they had caught (John 21:10).

C. *From the thoughtfulness of the risen Savior, we can assume that he comes to us with purposes of love.* He is always concerned about that which is best for us. Life would be much more beautiful and satisfying if we would recognize and respond graciously to his every suggestion instead of foolishly resenting his presence on the basis of a false assumption that he is an intruder.

### IV. The risen Christ made a suggestion to his disciples.

A. *They had labored through the night and were weary and exhausted.* In spite of their efforts, their nets were still empty.

Life can be an empty net. Have you failed to achieve your potential? Have you neglected or refused to do God's will?

B. *A command was given.* "Cast the net on the right side of the ship and ye shall find" (John 21:6). On a previous occasion Jesus had advised his disciples to "launch out into the deep, and let down your nets" (Luke 5:4).

C. *Have you been casting your net on the wrong side of the ship of life?* Is it possible that this explains why you have an empty net?

1. Do you need to cast your net on the other side of the ship of life as far as your home is concerned?
2. Do you need to cast your net on the other side of the ship as far as your business is concerned?
3. Do you need to cast your net on the other side as far as your church is concerned?

### V. Obedience to the risen Christ transformed failure into success.

A. *There is no substitute for obedience, whether that obedience be to God or to the laws of the state.* Obedience needs to be taught and learned in the home.

B. *Obedience to the living Lord produces harmony in life.* To be disobedient is to create tensions that can know no peace.

C. *Obedience to the living Lord brings fruitfulness and good success.* The disciples discovered that their net was full when they responded immediately to the command of the Savior.

### Conclusion

The living Lord appeared to these disciples and met their immediate need both for fish and their need of food for their stomachs. He had a hot breakfast waiting for them when they arrived on the shore. The richest gift that he gave to them was his own companionship and the continued commission to communicate the gospel of God's love for a lost world.

What is your need? Is it salvation from the penalty of sin or salvation from the power of sin? Do you need guidance and wisdom or self-confidence? The risen Christ comes to you repeatedly on the level of your own experience. May God grant to you the eyes to see him and the faith to respond to his gracious invitation and loving commandments.

## SUNDAY EVENING, APRIL 19

***Title:*** Barnabas: The Good Man

***Text:*** "He was a good man, full of the Holy Spirit and faith, and a great number of people were brought to the Lord" **(Acts 11:24 NIV)**.

***Scripture Reading:*** Acts 11:19–26

### Introduction

Our text is a short biography of a man named Barnabas. The word "good" is used sparingly in the Bible. It is a term that we have cheapened. It was not used carelessly by Luke. He says nothing about Barnabas being crafty, level, smooth, smart, wise, witty, aggressive, influential, powerful, or successful. To say that a man is good is to say something more than that he is righteous or just.

### I. Barnabas was full of the Holy Spirit.

A. *He was God-conscious.*

B. *He did not ignore the work of God's Spirit.*

C. *He was under the direct control of God's Holy Spirit.* People can be God-possessed today.

### II. Barnabas was full of faith.

A. *Jesus was real to him.* To Barnabas, Jesus was not an empty abstraction or a far-off visionary theory.

B. *He looked to Christ for salvation.*

C. *He looked to Christ for leadership.*

D. *People of heroic faith move the world (Phil. 4:13).* Abraham was a man of such faith. Paul had a great faith.

### III. Evidences, proofs, and fruit indicate that Barnabas was a good man.

A. *Barnabas was a man of the noblest generosity (Acts 4:36–37).*

1. The bondage of money is the most selfish bondage that ever grips a human soul.
2. There are dangers involved in becoming prosperous. Dr. George W. Truett said, "A man wrong on the question of his money is likely to be seriously wrong on every other question in religion."

B. *Barnabas was a missionary to the core.* He became vitally interested in the Gentiles (Acts 11:20).

C. *Barnabas always saw the best in others.*

1. Saul (Acts 9:27–28).
2. John Mark (Acts 15:36–39).

D. *Barnabas was free from the mean spirit of jealousy or envy (Acts 11:25–26).* It is remarkable what can be achieved if our primary concern is not who is going to get the credit for it.

### Conclusion

To be good is of primary importance for each of us as witnesses of the kingdom of God. We cannot all be clever, smart, intellectual, or famous, but with God's help each of us can be good, kind, gracious, and helpful. By faith, faithfulness, and cooperation with the Holy Spirit, we can become good men and women.

---

## WEDNESDAY EVENING, APRIL 22

***Title:*** What Kind of Revival Do We Need?

***Text:*** "Wilt thou not revive us again: that thy people may rejoice in thee?" **(Ps. 85:6)**.

### Introduction

*Revival* is an Old Testament word. Revival and evangelism are two different things. Revival, rededication, renewal, or repentance, or a combination of these, must take place before the church can bear an effective witness that will cause great hosts of people to seek Jesus Christ as Savior.

Revival is a work of the Spirit of God among God's own people whereby they get right with God and with each other. We are in need of something more than a revival of church attendance or tithing.

### I. We need a revival that will cause us to recognize the abiding presence of God.

A. *God is our Creator.* He is sovereign, holy, and just. He will one day be our Judge.

B. *God is gracious toward us.* He demonstrates his love through forgiveness, patience, and helpfulness.

### II. We need a revival that will cause us to rediscover the lordship of Christ.

A. *Jesus Christ is Lord because of who he is.*

B. *Jesus Christ is Lord because of what he has done.*

C. *Jesus Christ is Lord because of what he can do (Phil. 4:13).*

Christ the Lord has been endowed with the right to command. He has the right to issue orders to each of us. We should remember that he is the Lord of love who demonstrated his compassion for us by dying in our place on the cross.

**III. We need a revival that will cause us to rediscover the blessing and power of prayer.**

A. *Jesus our Savior found prayer both necessary and profitable.*

B. *Prayer had a vital place in the life of the early church (Acts 6:4).* Prayer has been described as the mightiest force in the world. When we come to God in prayer, we not only come into connection with the power behind the universe, but we make it possible for God to release his power in and through us.

**IV. We need a revival to revitalize our faith so as to reshape our lives.**

A. *Real faith is something much more than a mental assent to the existence of God (James 2:19).*

B. *A genuine faith will always express itself in faithfulness.* Someone has said, "The faith that falters before the finish had a flaw from the beginning."

**V. We need a revival to renew our devotion to our Lord so as to cause us to redefine the goals of our lives.**

Jesus said, "If ye love me, keep my commandments" (John 14:15).

A. *Jesus would have us to serve him because of love rather than because of fear.*

B. *We need to recognize our debt of gratitude to our Lord for all that he has done for us.* We enjoy the gift of everlasting life because Jesus was willing to die on the cross for us.

C. *Because Jesus died for us we should live for him.* Our goals in life should be defined in terms of obedience to the one who loved us so lavishly.

**VI. We need a revival that will recover a lost passion and restore a sense of loving loyalty to the church.**

A. *Jesus Christ came into this world to seek and to save the lost.* He gave himself to this task to the extent that he died on the cross to achieve it. We need to let his concern for the lost become our concern for the lost.

B. *As individual members of the church, we need to recognize the importance of our being loyal and faithful in rendering the ministry that the Holy Spirit would lead us to give.*

### Conclusion

With your heart and faith, join with the psalmist in praying, "Wilt thou not revive us again: that thy people may rejoice in thee?" (Ps. 85:6). God will rejoice to give us these blessings. Others will experience great joy as we experience this kind of a spiritual revival.

## SUNDAY MORNING, APRIL 26

***Title:*** The Risen Christ and Doubting Thomas

***Text:*** "Then saith he to Thomas, Reach hither thy finger, and behold my hands; and reach hither thy hand, and thrust it into my side: and be not faithless, but believing. And Thomas answered and said unto him, My Lord and my God" (**John 20:27–28**).

***Scripture Reading:*** John 20:24–31

***Hymns:*** "I Know That My Redeemer Liveth," Pounds

"One Day," Chapman

"Glorious Is Thy Name," McKinney

***Offertory Prayer:*** Holy Father, we come together in the name of the living Lord, who died for our sins on the cross. We rejoice in him who conquered death and the grave and who revealed by his resurrection the reality of life immortal. Today we not only bow in worship before him, but we bring to him our gifts to express our affection and to indicate our desire to assist in a ministry of proclaiming the good news of the Easter faith to the ends of the earth. Accept these tithes and offerings and bless their use in helping a lost world to come to know Jesus Christ as the Lord of love and the Giver of all life. Amen.

### Introduction

The apostle John is known as the apostle of love, but he is also known as John the evangelist. He revealed his evangelistic purpose for writing the gospel that bears his name in the words, "These are written, that ye might believe that Jesus is the Christ, the Son of God; and that believing ye might have life through his name" (John 20:31). The last example that John used to accomplish his purpose of convincing people that Jesus of Nazareth is the Christ, the Son of God, was the account of the appearance of the risen Lord to the disciples a week following the resurrection (John 20:26–29).

For some reason, Thomas had been absent on the first Easter Sunday evening when Jesus first appeared to the apostles as a group. While it is impossible to know for sure why he was absent, we probably would not be far from the truth if we assume that he was absent because he had fallen into a state of spiritual despondency. Such an attitude of despondency can be easily understood if we will attempt to grasp the depth of the disappointment into which the death of Christ had plunged all of his disciples. His death was for them a humiliating public disgrace, for he had died as a condemned criminal in the cruelest manner that could be inflicted upon a breaker of the law. His death plunged their political hopes into complete eclipse, for they had dreamed of glory with him in a restored kingdom of Israel.

If we would properly understand and benefit from Thomas's experience with the living Lord, it would be good for us to recall his devotion and at the same time his frustration as he contemplated Jesus' departure from Galilee for Jerusalem.

Jesus had said that he would be betrayed and crucified. Thomas knew that this was a real possibility. When Jesus had declared his intention to return to Bethany, the disciples sought to dissuade him from his plans (John 11:8). When Thomas discovered that Jesus was determined to go, he said to his fellow disciples, "Let us go also, that we may die with him" (John 11:16). Because of Thomas's devotion and his disappointment, we can easily understand why he could have fallen into deep despair and thereby missed the first appearance of our Savior. Before we scorn Thomas for his doubts, let us compare our love with the love that Thomas showed when he followed Christ from Galilee to Judea convinced that he might die for his Lord.

**I. The appearance of the risen Christ to the disciples and to Thomas (John 20:26–27).**

Because of the testimony of glad hearts, Thomas was present a week following the first Easter Sunday evening when Christ appeared in the Upper Room.

A. *Thomas experienced the unchanging love of his Master.*
   1. Jesus expressed gentle and patient concern for one individual's faith (John 20:27). We can be assured that each of us is precious in his sight.
   2. Jesus never rejects sincere inquiry. The living Lord's love met Thomas's doubts, and he used every possible way to dispel them.

B. *Thomas became aware of the penetrating knowledge of his living Lord.* The risen Christ was aware of Thomas's demand. "Except I shall see in his hands the print of the nails, and put my finger into the print of the nails, and thrust my hand into his side, I will not believe" (John 20:25). In order that Thomas might be absolutely certain of Christ's victory over death and the grave, the Lord said to Thomas, "Reach hither thy finger, and behold my hands; and reach hither thy hand, and thrust it into my side: and be not faithless, but believing" (John 20:27).
   1. We can be grateful that Thomas demanded a personal certification or validation to dispel his doubts.
   2. Thomas wanted unimpeachable evidence that Christ had really conquered death and the grave. Those who believe in the scientific method can be grateful that at least one of the apostles was determined to be absolutely certain that Christ had really conquered death and the grave.

C. *Thomas was given a sympathetic and complete confirmation for his faith.*
   1. Not one single demand was unmet.
   2. Each specification was met with tenderness and understanding by the triumphant Savior.

**II. The recognition and response of Thomas to the risen Christ.**

"My Lord and my God" (John 20:28). For Thomas the resurrection meant that his Lord, the Son of God, had come back to life. This experience was a life-transforming encounter with the living Christ.

A. *Previously Peter had received a remarkable revelation and had given voice to a great confession of faith in response to the question of Jesus, "But whom say ye that I am?" and Simon Peter answered and said, "Thou art the Christ, the son of the living God" (Matt. 16:15–16).*

B. *Thomas responded to this revelation of the risen Christ with a great confession of his lordship and his divinity: "My Lord and my God" (John 20:18).*
   1. In confessing Christ's lordship, Thomas was recognizing his authority to command and to expect obedience.
   2. The continued existence of the church in the world for over nineteen centuries after Christ's death and resurrection is proof that the living Lord has walked down through the corridors of time.
   3. The miracle of salvation in people's lives through trusting in the living Lord should encourage us to believe that he can perform miracles in our lives if we trust him.

### Conclusion

The joy in the hearts of believers and the deep hunger in the hearts of those who have not yet believed is an indication that the living Christ has come into our midst this morning. He has come to bless the redeemed and to give faith to those who are willing to trust him. With Thomas, make him your Lord and your God today.

---

## SUNDAY EVENING, APRIL 26

***Title:*** The Wisdom of Andrew

***Text:*** "The fruit of the righteous is a tree of life; and he that winneth souls is wise" **(Prov. 11:30)**.

***Scripture Reading:*** John 1:35–42

### Introduction

Do you ever study the New Testament with a desire to find someone in whose path you would like to follow? We should seek to follow Jesus in all areas of our lives. We can also be inspired by following the example of some of his noblest servants. Andrew, one of his early disciples, is a case in point.

Consider Andrew. He must have been a happy individual. He had an experience with Jesus Christ that he was eager to share with others. Each biographical reference to Andrew in the New Testament pictures him as bringing someone to Jesus Christ. He is worthy of our admiration, and we would do well to follow his example. He made the best possible investment of his energies and opportunities, and he lived to see some of the fruit of his efforts.

Andrew is famous primarily because of his habit of bringing others to Christ. This would qualify him to be listed among the wise if we use the measuring stick of the book of Proverbs: "The fruit of the righteous is a tree of life; and he that winneth souls is wise."

**I. Andrew was wise—he brought himself to Christ.**

A. *Andrew heard the preaching of John the Baptist (John 1:35).* John came preaching a message of repentance, urging people to prepare their hearts for the coming of the Messiah. Andrew believed the preaching of John and became identified as one of John's disciples.

B. *Andrew believed the preaching of John concerning Jesus (John 1:36).*

C. *Andrew responded to the ministry and message of Jesus Christ at the very beginning of Jesus' earthly ministry (John 1:37–40).* As a result of the day that was spent in conversation with him who John had described as the Lamb of God, Andrew became convinced that he was indeed the promised Messiah, and with his mind and with his heart he received him as such.

1. Through Christ he found a new life.
2. Through Christ he found a new joy.
3. Through Christ he found a new power.
4. Through Christ he found a new purpose for living.

The wisest thing that any person can do is welcome and receive Jesus Christ as Messiah and Lord. May God help you to make this decision if you have not already done so.

**II. Andrew was wise—he brought his brother to Jesus.**

"He first findeth his own brother Simon, and saith unto him, We have found the Messiah, which is, being interpreted, the Christ. And he brought him to Jesus" (John 1:41–42).

A. *Andrew had made a discovery in Jesus that he felt compelled to share.* This was a natural thing for him to do. All Christians should be eager to share the joy they have experienced through faith in Christ.

B. *Andrew first sought his brother.* This is a pattern that modern-day believers should follow. We should share our faith in God with those who are nearest and dearest. In some instances this would be a relative, but in other instances it would be those with whom we labor or those with whom we enjoy leisure.

C. *There was no cause for embarrassment in Andrew's life that would lead his brother to disbelieve his testimony.*

1. Is there something in your life that would cause your companions to respond with disbelief if you were to tell them that you are a Christian?
2. Does your child see evidences of the work of God operating in your life?
3. Does your life authenticate and verify the testimony that your lips could bear concerning your discovery of Jesus as the Messiah?

The modern church will never reach the world for Christ by conducting worship services on Sunday mornings and Sunday evenings. Individual believers must, like Andrew, share their discovery with others.

### III. Andrew was wise—he found a boy and brought him to Jesus (John 6:5–12).

It was Andrew who knew about the boy who had brought a lunch of five barley loaves and two fish. It was Andrew who raised the question concerning the insignificance of such a lunch as they faced the hungry multitude of five thousand men plus women and children.

Have you ever gone to the trouble of taking a boy to the lake to fish or to the field to hunt or to the gymnasium to play ball in order that you eventually might lead him to know Jesus Christ as his personal Savior?

A. *Every boy is important.*
   1. A boy is important to his home.
   2. A boy is important to his school.
   3. A boy is important to his community.

      On April 21, 1866, a Sunday school teacher named Edward Kimball passed and repassed a shoe store in Chicago. Finally, he mustered up enough courage to go inside and speak to a young clerk and ask, "Dwight, don't you think it is about time you gave your heart to the Lord?" This led to the conversion of the young man who was to become the famous evangelist Dwight L. Moody.

B. *To bring a boy to Christ is to accomplish more than we realize.*
   1. This means that he can become a Christian citizen.
   2. This means that some woman will have a Christian husband.
   3. This means that some family can have the blessing of a Christian father and home.

### IV. Andrew was wise—he brought strangers to Jesus (John 12:20–22).

When the Greeks came to see Jesus, they came to Philip, and Philip shared this information with Andrew. It was Andrew who then took the initiative in leading these Gentiles to Jesus Christ. We must not limit our witness to those with whom we are closely associated. The Holy Spirit of God will lead total strangers with hungry hearts to us if we are sensitive and responsive both to his leadership and to the heart needs of those with whom we come into casual contact day after day.

### Conclusion

Have you brought yourself to Jesus Christ? If not, then be wise like Andrew and bring yourself to him in faith and commitment.

Do you have a dear one or a near one whom you should bring to Jesus? Do you have a relative, a close friend, or a business associate whom you should bring to Jesus? If so, then dedicate yourself now to cooperate with the Holy Spirit and determine to put forth an effort to be like Andrew and bring that person to Jesus.

Do you know a boy or girl whom you could or should bring to Jesus? May God make you wise to see your opportunities, and may he give you ears to hear his Spirit and the often unrecognized inquiries of those who are still seeking him.

## WEDNESDAY EVENING, APRIL 29

*Title:* An Appropriate Question

*Text:* "What shall I render unto the LORD for all his benefits toward me?" **(Ps. 116:12)**.

### Introduction

Psalm 116 is the beautiful testimony of a grateful heart. It is the testimony of a good steward. This psalm contains the testimony of every sincere believer who lives long enough to experience the rich blessings of God's grace.

After drawing up a list of the many reasons why his heart was filled with love for God, the psalmist asked a question that you and I should ask ourselves: "What shall I render unto the Lord for all his benefits toward me?"

This question was a personal question. For us it should be a present question. It is a proper question for each of us. For some of us it is a pressing question, for we do not have as much time in which to demonstrate our love for the Lord as we might think.

### I. We can give to our Lord the faith he deserves.

"But without faith it is impossible to please him; for he that cometh to God must believe that he is, and that he is a rewarder of them that diligently seek him" (Heb. 11:6). For us either to neglect or to refuse to trust the promises of God is both to insult our God and to deprive ourselves of the blessings of God and of the activity of God in our own lives. If we would praise him and demonstrate our love for him, we must trust him implicitly as did Abraham who was known as the father of the faithful (Rom. 4:20).

### II. We can give to our Lord the love he deserves.

The first and greatest commandment requires that we love God supremely and without reservation (Matt. 22:37). If we were to enumerate the many ways in which God has demonstrated his love for us as the psalmist did, we would find him to be altogether lovely. We would find it impossible not to ask the question contained in our text. Because God is so lovable, we should find it easy to love him with all of our hearts.

### III. We can give to our Lord the obedience that is essential.

Jesus said to his disciples and to us, "If ye love me, keep my commandments" (John 14:15). The heavenly Father much prefers that love be the motive behind our service rather than fear. The Lord would have us to labor in his vineyard because of love rather than out of fear of the consequences of disobedience.

There is no substitute for obedience. World evangelism both in the home community and to the furthest point on the globe waits upon the obedience of those who consider themselves to be disciples.

### IV. We can give our Lord a dedicated body (Rom. 12:1).

The body of the believer is the temple of the Holy Spirit. The body is the tool that the inner man is to use in doing the work of God. Paul encourages the believers in Rome to dedicate their physical bodies as an act of worship, as a gift on the altar in service of Jesus Christ. When he wrote to the Corinthians, he declared that the spirit as well as the body belonged to God and that each believer should magnify and glorify God and make God known in and through his body.

### Conclusion

Faithfully, joyfully, and unreservedly we should give ourselves both in praising our God and in seeking to persuade others to trust him and love him. As we do so, we bring the greatest possible glory to God and render the greatest possible service to our fellow humans.

SUGGESTED PREACHING PROGRAM FOR

# MAY

## ■ Sunday Mornings

This month we will begin a series using the theme "Practical, Probing Questions for Serious Consideration."

## ■ Sunday Evenings

The guiding theme for the Sunday evening services this month is stewardship. Stewardship concerns every area of life. In the background of each suggested message is the basic philosophy of Jesus expressed in the beatitude "It is more blessed to give than to receive" (Acts 20:35).

## ■ Wednesday Evenings

The Wednesday evening messages will deal with the theme "Modern Messages from the Book of Jonah."

## SUNDAY MORNING, MAY 3

*Title:* What Does It Mean to Be a Christian?

*Text:* "The disciples were called Christians first in Antioch" (**Acts 11:26**).

*Hymns:* "More Like the Master," Gabriel

"Take the Name of Jesus with You," Baxter

"Living for Jesus," Chisholm

*Offertory Prayer:* Our Father, we sit at the feet of Jesus and hear him say that it is more blessed to give than to receive. Help us to believe this truth to the extent that we determine to become a giver in every area of our lives. Today we give to you our tithes and offerings. Bless us with a spirit of generosity as we do so. Grant to us the excitement of seeing good things happen through the wise and consecrated use of these funds for the advancement of your kingdom. In the name of our Savior. Amen.

### Introduction

The title *Christian* is a fallen term. It has been cheapened by common usage. It is now an expression that covers a multitude of religious ideas, error as well as truth, paganism as well as the revelation of God's divine truth. This term *Christian* has been stretched to the extent that it covers rationalistic modernism on one hand and a frothy sentimentalism on the other. It is ascribed to that which in some instances is gross worldliness and in other instances to that which is anything short of pharisaic self-righteousness. The term *Christian* is used to describe that which is coldly ritualistic and also that which is nothing more than heated emotionalism. Is it possible that Christianity is failing to make a distinctive impact due to our failure to understand what it means to be a Christian?

Some apply the term *Christian* to all who have high moral standards and believe in the existence of God. Others claim this title simply because they are members of a church. Still others claim the privilege of wearing this title because they have had a conversion experience. Ideally, they have a right to do so. However, the great test comes in what others think of our witness. When they see our lives, are they able to call us Christian? Do they see the evidences of the presence of Christ in our lives? If so, only then should we apply or claim this title for ourselves.

The disciples were first called Christians at Antioch. This was probably a term of derision because they were followers of the crucified Galilean. Evidently they thought and talked and acted in a manner that reminded their contemporaries of the Christ. What would your neighbors say about you? Is it possible for them to see features and characteristics in your life that resemble Jesus Christ? A government official in India once said to some Christian leaders, "If Christians would act like Jesus Christ, India would be at his feet." It is time for us to cease being satisfied with a low level of Christian living. We must demonstrate that genuine Christianity is something more than cushioned pews, enjoyable music, a comforting sermon on Sunday, and business as usual during the week.

### I. To become a Christian, one must be saved.

It is absolutely impossible for one to be a Christian who does not have a personal redemptive relationship with Jesus Christ.

Jesus said to Nicodemus, "Ye must be born again" (John 3:7). A person must repent—change his or her mind about the nature of God, sin, self, and others. Inseparable from genuine repentance, sincere faith must be placed in Jesus Christ as the Lord of life (Acts 20:20–21). As a person responds to the gospel with repentance and faith, the Spirit of God brings about the miracle of the new birth within the soul. The believer becomes a child of God (Gal. 3:26). He or she is now a new creation (2 Cor. 5:17).

The new birth alone does not produce Christlikeness. The new birth makes possible a growth and development into Christlikeness. It is impossible for one to be genuinely Christian who has not had an experience of commitment and conversion.

### II. To be genuinely Christian, one must be surrendered.

Jesus was surrendered completely to the will of God. "Jesus saith unto them, My meat is to do the will of him that sent me, and to finish his work" (John 4:34). His surrender led to Gethsemane and Calvary. He prayed, "Father, if thou be willing, remove this cup from me: nevertheless not my will, but thine, be done" (Luke 22:42).

Jesus said to the Galilean fishermen, "Follow me, and I will make you fishers of men. And they straightway left their nets, and followed him" (Matt. 4:19–20). As they forsook their nets, they began the journey that would lead them to the place where others would be able to bestow upon them the title of Christian.

To be considered Christian, a convert must be identified with Christ through baptism. This is a visible symbol of an institutional relationship to Christ in which the individual accepts the demands and discipline of his lordship. To be genuinely Christian, the convert must be sincerely committed to the task of living the teachings of Jesus Christ. There will be a deep concern about keeping God's holy law. The Sermon on the Mount will be something more than just a beautiful passage of Scripture.

Commitment to the will of God will express itself in the home, throughout the community, within the business, and in every other area of life.

### III. If a person is genuinely Christian, he or she will serve.

Jesus said, "My father worketh hitherto, and I work" (John 5:17). "I must work the works of him that sent me, while it is day: the night cometh, when no man can work" (9:4). Someone has said that the best biography of Jesus is that which describes him as one "who went about doing good" (Acts 10:38). There are many inactive church members, but an inactive Christian is a contradiction of terms, for when we cease to serve, we cease to be truly Christian.

Genuine Christians deliberately give themselves to doing good and do so with humility and gratitude and without display. "As we have therefore opportunity, let us do good unto all men, especially unto them who are of the household of faith" (Gal. 6:10).

### Conclusion

Who is sufficient for this ideal? It is impossible for the convert to be fully surrendered and graciously serving without the leadership and the assistance of the Holy Spirit of God. A part of the wonder and the miracle of the new birth is the coming of the Holy Spirit to dwell within the heart of the believer (Gal. 4:4–6). The Holy Spirit dwells in the heart to produce the fruit of a Christlike spirit and a Christlike life (5:22–24). An old spiritual expresses the sincere desire of every believer:

*Lord, I want to be a Christian*
*in my heart, in my heart,*
*Lord, I want to be a Christian*
*in my heart.*

We must become Christlike within our hearts and minds before we can be called Christians.

## A Definition of a Christian

A Christian is born of God, engrafted into Christ, and an inhabitation for the Holy Spirit. His nature is renewed, his mind illumined, his spirit changed.

He is not what he was, for grace hath made a difference; he is not what he desires to be, for grace is not yet perfected; he is not what he shall be, for grace shall be consummated in glory.

The knowledge of Christ is his treasure; the mind of Christ his evidence; the love of Christ his song; conformity to Christ his life; to be with Christ his preeminent desire.

By faith he rests on Christ, receives Christ, and looks to Christ. He heareth Christ's words, treadeth in Christ's steps, and seeketh Christ's approbation.

He speaks the language of the Savior's kingdom, reveres the Savior's statutes and laws, obeys his ordinances, wears his costume, and lives to his glory.

The life of Christ within him is the principle of his being, and because Christ ever lives, he shall live also. In the Christian, Christ lives and speaks and acts.

He is Christ's representative on earth, his witness before men, and his follower before God. The Christian hearkens to Christ's teachings, rests on Christ's sacrifice, avails himself of Christ's meditation, and cheerfully obeys Christ's royal laws. He inquires what would Christ have me know, what do, and what enjoy.

To know Christ, is Christianity intellectual; to obey Christ, Christianity practical; to enjoy Christ, Christianity perfected. As bread to the hungry, as water to the thirsty, as the rock in the sultry day, is Christ to the Christian.

The Christian is in the world but not of it, among the world yet separate from it, passing through the world but without attachment to it.

The Christian is a man and may err, an imperfect man and may sin, but a renewed man and shall have his fruits unto holiness and in the end everlasting life.

The Christian is a warrior and must fight; but he is a conqueror and must prevail.

The Christian sojourns on earth but dwells in heaven; a pilgrim in the desert but an enrolled denizen of the skies.

The Christian is the impress of Christ, the reflection of the Father, and the temple of the Holy Ghost.

Contrast him with the infidel in his faith, with the profligate in his life, with the merely moral in his heart, and with the Pharisee in his spirit. His pedigree, from Jehovah; his nature, from heaven; and his name, from Antioch. O Christian, great is thy dignity, refulgent thy glory, interminable thy blessed hope. All things art thine; thou art Christ's and Christ is God's.

—*Author Unknown*

## SUNDAY EVENING, MAY 3

***Title:*** Extravagant Devotion Needed

***Text:*** "And Jesus said, Let her alone; why trouble ye her? she hath wrought a good work on me" **(Mark 14:6)**.

***Scripture Reading:*** Mark 14:1–19

### Introduction

Jesus was a welcome guest in the home of Mary, Martha, and Lazarus of Bethany (Luke 10:38–42). John 11 tells us of the raising of Lazarus from the dead. Immediately following the raising of Lazarus a feast was prepared where Jesus was the guest of honor (John 12:1–8). It was during this supper that Mary demonstrated her lavish, extravagant devotion toward the Christ.

### I. Extravagant devotion seeks an appropriate means of expression.

A. *Love will find a way.*

B. *Gratitude will manifest itself.*

C. *Christ recognized Mary's gift as a lovely work done in view of his coming death and burial (John 12:7).*

1. Love.
2. Gratitude.
3. Worship.

D. *Christ had confidence in his kingdom's progress and permanence (Mark 14:9).*

### II. Extravagant devotion leads to extravagant loyalty.

A. *The sinful woman (Luke 7:44–47).*

B. *John 15:15.*

### III. Extravagant devotion blesses the lives of others.

A. *Mary's act of devotion blessed the heart of Jesus as he faced death.*

B. *Mary's precious spikenard continues as an endless living stream to inspire the hearts of others.*

C. *The fragrance of Mary's spikenard still fills the room of those who read and listen.*

How long has it been since others have been blessed by some fragrance from your life?

### IV. Do you have the Judas mind or the mind of Mary?

It could be said concerning many of us that we measure our devotion to the Lord and his cause with a medicine dropper. A medicine dropper is normally used to administer limited dosages to those who are sick.

Instead of permitting the devotion of our hearts to flow with the vigor of an artesian well, we continually restrict it and almost completely choke it off. Such was not the case with Mary, the sister of Martha and Lazarus. Her kind of love is the need of the kingdom at this time.

Judas was a shrewd businessman who knew the price of things. He was completely practical about everything. He disapproved of Mary's act as a foolish waste.

### Conclusion

Jesus disagreed with Judas and commended Mary. Jesus loved people extravagantly to the extent that he gave his life for them. God loves us extravagantly. He gave his Son to die on the cross for us.

The measure of our sacrifice is the measure of our worship. The measure of our sacrifice is the measure of our concern for others.

## WEDNESDAY EVENING, MAY 6

***Title:*** "Arise, Go to Nineveh"

***Text:*** "Arise, go to Nineveh, that great city, and cry against it; for their wickedness is come up before me" **(Jonah 1:2)**.

### Introduction

The prophets of the Old Testament were the spokesmen of God to his people. They were men who received a unique call to a high and holy task. While certain similarities characterize these prophets, each of them was unique in the particular emphasis of the message he delivered to the people.

The book of Jonah is different from the other prophetic books in that it is all in the third person. The entire book takes the form of a short story and describes God's dealings with one of his spokesmen. Many have missed the main message of the book because of their curiosity and speculations concerning the size and type of the fish that swallowed Jonah. Instead of being concerned about whether God is able to make a fish big enough to swallow a man, we ought to concern ourselves with the message of the book both to the prophet as an individual, to the nation as a people, and to our present generation.

Before we consider our text, we should note several great truths concerning the book. This book reveals the necessity of God's people putting forth an effort to bring about the salvation of the whole world. It also contains the greatest revelation of God's love to be found in the Old Testament. In its emphasis on concern for others, the book of Jonah is more like the New Testament than any other Old Testament book.

Several great truths in the text have significance for each of us.

### I. The fact of divine communication is revealed.

The book of Jonah declares that the great God of Israel communicates with his creatures. In one way or another, the Word of God can come to us. God spoke to people in the past, and he continues to speak to people in the present.

**II. The possibility of the human reception of divine communication is revealed.**

Jonah had no question at all concerning the divine communications. With all of his mind, he perceived what the will of God was for him. He would declare to us that each of us has the capacity for two-way communication with God.

**III. The divine authority to command is assumed.**

God took the initiative and issued the command to the prophet. God is Creator, Redeemer, and Sustainer. On the basis of these three claims, he has the right to command our person, our energies, and our time. He issued the command to Jonah, and he issues commands to us.

**IV. A spirit of urgency characterizes this command: "Arise, go, ... cry against it."**

A. *Jonah was given a revelation of the compassionate heart of God.* Jonah's main emphasis was to be primarily of the coming judgment, and yet even this message contained an element of hope.

B. *Jonah discovered that God's love reaches out to all people.* It was revealed to him before the coming of Christ that God's love is all-inclusive. With God there is no favored group or party. The circle of his love included the cruel citizens of Nineveh.

C. *Jonah discovered that all people have the capacity to receive and to respond to God's grace.* This is a truth that we need to face up to today. We need to let this truth grip our hearts and command our energies.

**V. Jonah's response was unworthy.**

A. *His was an opportunity to turn the entire city to God.*

B. *His was the opportunity of becoming the city's greatest benefactor.*

C. *His was the opportunity of being a vital part of the greatest enterprise on earth—God's redemptive program.*

D. *His was the opportunity of earning a great spiritual inheritance.*

**Conclusion**

What has your response been to the call of God on your life? Have you made a worthy response? Have you obeyed gladly? May God help you to arise immediately and do that which the Lord would have you to do.

## SUNDAY MORNING, MAY 10

***Title:*** Are You a Real Christian Mother?

***Text:*** "When I call to remembrance the unfeigned faith that is in thee, which dwelt first in thy grandmother Lois, and thy mother Eunice; and I am persuaded that in thee also" **(2 Tim. 1:5)**.

***Scripture Reading:*** 2 Timothy 1:1–12

***Hymns:*** "Great Redeemer," Harris

"I Love Thy Kingdom, Lord," Dwight

"Faith of Our Mothers," Patten

***Offertory Prayer:*** Holy Father, on this lovely Lord's Day we are reminded of the lavishness of your generosity to us. We praise you, and we respond to you with the glad commitment of our lives to your purpose for us. May your blessings be on the use of our tithes and offerings in preaching the gospel to those who are spiritually poor, in binding up the brokenhearted, in proclaiming deliverance to those who are the captives of sin, and in bringing sight to the eyes of those who are blind. Bless these offerings to the end that the world might better know that it can be saved by your grace. Through Jesus Christ our Lord. Amen.

### Introduction

Sociologists, psychologists, psychiatrists, law enforcement officers, educators, and social workers are reminding us repeatedly of the importance of the home. The influence of the home for good or bad has been the subject of many books, countless articles, and innumerable speeches.

While the family unit is made up of a man, a woman, and children, the woman is at the center, and the lives of others are good to the degree to which the woman takes her calling seriously, making their welfare her major concern. In the twenty-first century, mothers face myriad complex problems and challenges. Although the mothers of yesterday faced some problems that are practically nonexistent today, the modern mother faces problems undreamed of a short time ago.

### I. If you would provide for your children a Christian mother, consider motherhood as a Christian calling.

A. *There is a call to the ministry of preaching.* There is a call to the ministry of religious education. There is a call to the ministry of sacred music. And there is a call to the ministry of missions at home and abroad.

B. *Let us recognize the high call to Christian motherhood—the fulfilling of God's plan and purpose for you.* With Paul, press toward the mark for the prize of the high calling of God in Christ Jesus (Phil. 3:14).

C. *Eunice and Lois are still recognized today because they did an outstanding job in training a son and grandson.*

1. The Christian mother should be a leader in worship.

2. The Christian mother can be a professor of biblical knowledge. "And that from a child thou hast known the holy scriptures, which are able to make thee wise unto salvation through faith which is in Christ Jesus" (2 Tim. 3:15).
3. The Christian mother should be a teacher of Christian ideals.
4. The Christian mother should be an example of Christian graces. "But continue thou in the things which thou hast learned and hast been assured of, knowing of whom thou hast learned them" (2 Tim. 3:14).

**II. If you would provide your children a Christian mother, recognize your need for help.**

A. *You need the help of God.*
   1. Make much of the Bible in your personal life.
   2. Be familiar with the closet of prayer. "But thou, when thou prayest, enter into thy closet, and when thou hast shut thy door, pray to thy Father which is in secret; and thy Father which seeth in secret shall reward thee openly" (Matt. 6:6).
   3. Walk by faith, claiming the promises of God.
   4. Follow the leadership of the Holy Spirit.

B. *You need the help of your husband.*
   1. He should be a Christian.
   2. He should be a good steward.
   3. He should be a servant of Jesus Christ.

C. *You need the help of the church.*
   1. There is no substitute for public worship.
   2. Yours should be a wholesome and enthusiastic participation in the church's program of education, training, missionary activities, and worship.

**III. If you would provide for your children a Christian mother, dedicate yourself to God.**

A. *Eunice and Lois sent Timothy forth as a servant of Jesus Christ.*
   1. He was a man of immeasurable unselfishness.
   2. He had the capacity for gentle devotion.
   3. He was warmhearted and loyal (1 Cor. 4:17).
   4. He possessed charm and gentleness with tenderness and patience.
   5. He was willing to sacrifice himself without reservation to the cause of Christ (1 Cor. 16:10).

B. *These qualities are such that only a consecrated mother and grandmother could bestow them upon a son.*

C. *"Seek ye first the kingdom of God . . ." (Matt. 6:33).*

### Conclusion

Perhaps the greatest contribution that you as a parent will make to the kingdom of God will be in the child or children you raise for his glory. May God bless you with the faith and grace that you need for serving him day by day through the years at this post of duty.

There can be no question concerning a mother's need for Christ as Savior. If you have not trusted him, then today would be a good day to decide to let him come into your life. And there is no question that for a mother to be the best possible mother, her husband needs to be a devout Christian. As the husband of your wife, you are the only man who can bestow this blessing upon her and upon your children. If you are not already doing so, then let today be the beginning.

Probably some here today have forsaken the devout teachings of a godly mother. The best way you could honor either your living mother or your departed mother is by renewing your vows to her Lord and begin serving him. Today would be a good time to begin.

---

## SUNDAY EVENING, MAY 10

***Title:*** Two Things God Needs

***Text:*** Matthew 28:18–20

### Introduction

The Great Commission is a New Testament statement of God's great eternal plan of redemption. It has always been his purpose and always will be.

Jesus issued the proclamation: "All authority is given unto me in heaven and in earth." This authority is the authority to command and to issue orders to his disciples. He has the authority to request, even demand, our total resources.

In our text the Lord reveals his worldwide, agelong program. He tells his disciples that in their going about from place to place, they should make disciples, and he promises to be with them if they obey his command.

The title of this message is a paradox. In one sense God is not dependent on us for anything. He is all-sufficient and could ignore us completely if he wished. On the other hand, and I say this with humility, God is completely dependent on us. He has chosen to limit himself to utilize our talents and our resources. The title of this message could be "The Helplessness of God."

For the accomplishment of God's great redemptive purpose, he needs two things: manpower and material resources.

### I. God needs manpower for the accomplishment of his purpose.

A. *God needs converted people.*

B. *God needs consecrated people with dedicated minds, hearts, and hands.*

C. *God needs consistent people.*

D. *God needs compassionate people with warm hearts and tender hands.*

E. *God needs courageous people.* Jesus said, "The harvest truly is plenteous, but the labourers are few" (Matt. 9:37). Paul challenged the Corinthians with the opportunity of "laboring together with God" (1 Cor. 3:9). The church has been and continues to be plagued by the curse of insufficient manpower.

## II. God needs material resources for the advancement of his kingdom.

In a very real sense, God does not need anything we have. He is no pauper. He is no beggar. Poet Harriet E. Buell has written:

*My Father is rich in houses and lands,*
*He holdeth the wealth of the world in his hands!*
*Of rubies and diamonds, of silver and gold.*
*His coffers are full, He has riches untold.*

If this is the case, then someone is certain to say, "Why does God need my financial resources?" We need to understand that our lives and our material resources are wrapped up in the same package. It is impossible to think of a person in total isolation from his or her material resources. People who separate God from the economic realm of life automatically place their hearts in material things rather than in the kingdom of God (Matt. 6:19–21).

From the beginning of time, God has commanded people to be givers—not because God was a pauper, but to save people from the tyranny of the material. By the commandment for people to be tithers, God was seeking to enter into the economic activities of people and to show them the sacredness of this area of life. By commanding his tithe, God was seeking to guarantee that we would invest our lives in spiritual rather than material things.

A. *The teaching of the tithe is as old as the Bible (Gen. 28:20–22).*
   1. The giving of the tithe is based on divine ownership.
   2. The giving of the tithe is based on human stewardship.

B. *The giving of the tithe works today.*
   1. Tithing helps spiritualize that which is considered secular.
   2. Tithing brings a new reality and vitality into worship as the tither brings a specific portion of his or her time, talents, and efforts in the form of a tithe.
   3. Tithing greatly helps in evangelizing a lost world through the support of missionaries both at home and abroad.
   4. For the members of a given church to begin tithing will revolutionize both the worship and witness of that church. Real spiritual renewal is experienced when people begin to bring themselves with their resources into the work of God.

## III. God needs people and money because people need God.

God loves and labors to bring his mercy and grace into the hearts and lives of lost men and women. He has given his Son to be their Savior. He has sent the Holy Spirit into the world to work within the hearts of both the saved and the unsaved. God needs every believer to be a messenger of his love and power to save.

### Conclusion

Give yourself and your substance to the service of God. God needs you, and he will use you if you will permit him to. Commit yourself to him now.

## WEDNESDAY EVENING, MAY 13

*Title:* A Mighty Tempest

*Text:* Jonah 1:1–15

### Introduction

The Devil will always have a ship ready when people want to sail away from God, but it will be the most expensive trip they ever take, for the trip will always cost far more than they thought when they began the journey.

In Jonah 1:2 we find the prophet's commission: "Arise, go to Nineveh, that great city, and cry against it; for their wickedness is come up before me." In Jonah 1:3 we find the prophet's resignation. Because of his great concern for the welfare of the people of Nineveh, God refused to accept Jonah's resignation.

The storm that swept across the sea and caused Jonah and his traveling companions so much trouble was no accident; it was a providential event designed to teach a rebellious prophet the futility of attempting to flee from a divine assignment.

### I. Are you in a disgraceful flight from duty?

A. *Has God called you to some place of duty and responsibility?*

B. *Has God revealed to you some great need that he would like to supply with your help?*

C. *Have you declined some position of responsibility in your church without an honest, legitimate excuse?*

D. *Have you neglected to render a ministry of mercy that is greatly needed by someone?*

E. *God has a work for each of his children of one sort or another.* He does not expect from any of us exactly the same as he does from others.

### II. The chastisement of God upon Jonah.

We should recognize the divine strategy that thwarted the plans of the disobedient prophet. By his disobedience the prophet also thwarted the plans of God. For Jonah's good, as well as for the good of the people of Nineveh, the chastisement of God came upon the wayward prophet.

The chastisement of God will come upon modern-day Jonahs if they flee from the task to which God calls them. This truth may explain some of the turmoil that may exist in your life. The writer of Hebrews discusses God's chastisement of his children.

A. *We are not to despise the chastisement of the Lord (Heb. 12:5).*

B. *Divine chastisement is motivated by love (Heb. 12:6).*

C. *Chastisement is a proof of sonship (Heb. 12:7).*

D. *Chastisement is to be taken very seriously (Heb. 12:9).*
E. *Chastisement is for our profit (Heb. 12:10).*
F. *We are not to permit chastisement to overwhelm us, though it may be painful as it was in Jonah's case (Heb. 12:11–12).*

### III. God's storms follow every sinning saint.

A. *God may send the storm of sorrow into your life.*
B. *God may send the storm of suffering into your life.*
C. *God may send the storm of financial stress into your life.*
D. *God may send the storm of spiritual insecurity into your life.* Have you lost the joy of your salvation? Has your religion become a burden instead of a lift? Is it a cold duty rather than a joyful privilege? If so, it may be that God has sent a storm into your life because of a disgraceful flight from duty.

### Conclusion

God never delights in sending storms into our lives. He much prefers that we sail the ship of life on a calm and peaceful sea. Because of his love for us, we can be assured that the storms will come if they are necessary. Instead of disobeying like Jonah, let us volunteer like Isaiah (Isa. 6:8).

---

## SUNDAY MORNING, MAY 17

***Title:*** What Grade Will You Make?

***Text:*** "Take my yoke upon you, and learn of me; for I am meek and lowly in heart: and ye shall find rest unto your souls" **(Matt. 11:29)**.

***Scripture Reading:*** Matthew 11:27–30

***Hymns:*** "We Would See Jesus," Warner
"Come, Thou Fount of Every Blessing," Robinson
"More about Jesus," Hewitt

***Offertory Prayer:*** Dear Father, you have given us the rich gifts of your grace. We thank you for the peace that passes understanding. We thank you for the assurance that we are your children. We thank you for the hope that cheers our hearts. We thank you for the blessings that come to us through family and friends. We thank you for the privilege of work. Today, out of the gratitude of our hearts, we offer to you our tithes and offerings. Bestow your blessings on these gifts that your will might be done on earth as it is in heaven. Amen.

### Introduction

Exam week is often a painful experience for both parents and pupils. I would suppose that the grading of papers is at least sometimes painful for teachers. A time of testing reveals something not only about the learning achievement of the pupil, but also about the effectiveness of the teaching methods used by the teacher. Let me challenge the students of the congregation to face up to the question of grades. What kind of grades are you making in school? Your grades will be determined by how you respond to the teacher and by how you apply yourselves to your learning opportunities.

Today I challenge each of you to think of Jesus Christ as the great Teacher for your life. We think of him as the divine Son of God, the Redeemer who came to die on the cross for the sins of the world, the conqueror of death and the grave, the coming one who will raise the dead and judge the wicked and reward the righteous. But today let us consider Jesus as heaven's infallible, inherent Teacher, who came to teach the truth about God, life, and eternity. As we think of a teacher, we must also think of students. We must recognize learning opportunities and responsibility. Let us disturb ourselves with the question, "What grade will I make in the school of Christ?"

As we study the life of Christ, we may be surprised to discover that Jesus was generally recognized as a teacher. His disciples and his contemporaries considered him to be a teacher. He was called Teacher, Master, or Rabbi. All of these titles contain the idea expressed by Nicodemus when he said, "Rabbi, we know that thou art a teacher come from God" (John 3:2). Jesus is never addressed as a preacher, but at least 45 times in the four Gospels he is called "Teacher." The title "Master" occurs 66 times in the King James Version, and in 54 of these instances the Greek word means teacher or schoolmaster.

Jesus said, "You call me 'Teacher' and 'Lord,' and rightly so, for that is what I am" (John 13:13 NIV). Jesus' choice of the term "disciple" to designate his followers indicates that he considered himself a teacher. They were not called "subjects," "servants," "retainers," or "comrades." "Disciple," meaning "pupil" or "learner," is used 243 times.

How have you responded to the Teacher? Have you been listening attentively? Have you given attention to reading the text from which he would instruct you? What grade are you making?

**I. The invitation to enroll.**

In the gracious words of the text, Jesus would invite the entire world, one by one, to experience conversion. While he may have been referring to the yoke worn by oxen, it is more likely that he was thinking in terms of himself as a teacher with a group of students. To accept the yoke or to bear the yoke was to describe the teacher-pupil relationship. The gracious words of the invitation and the text must not be limited to a simple call to conversion, for these words of invitation include the opportunity to learn and to grow and to experience the fullness of God's great salvation. This will be the experience of each person who interprets the Christian life as an opportunity for continuous growing and serving.

A. *Learning must not be limited to listening.* While it is important that we listen attentively, it is a proven fact that one can hear and grasp all that a speaker says by using only 20 percent of his mental capacity. If the rest of the intellect and the emotions are not concentrated on the subject that is being considered, the potential learning experience is almost completely nullified.

B. *Learning must not be limited to looking.* Priceless, indeed, is the capacity to see. One good picture is said to be worth more than a thousand words, but one can look and observe without reaching the highest level of learning. We need to observe the Christ in every phase of his life, but if we do nothing more than look, we will not be fully responding to his gracious invitation to enroll in the school of Christian discipleship.

C. *Learning must not be limited to a pleasant emotional experience.* Many of us go to church or to a Bible class and thoroughly enjoy the songs or the sermon or the lesson. We experience a spiritual uplift. This type of experience is of great value, yet we may not learn anything of real significance from it.

**II. The invitation to continue in learning.**

Luke, the writer of Acts, comments that the enemies of the early church "took knowledge of them, that they had been with Jesus" (Acts 4:13). Jesus' personality and teaching had placed a distinguishing mark upon them. Later on in the book of Acts, the enemies of Christ again observed conspicuous results in those who enrolled and then continued in the school of Christ, for the record says, "The disciples were called Christians first in Antioch" (Acts 11:25).

A. *We learn through identification.* Parents have a profound effect on every facet of a child's life because of their identification with each other. The family is the first school that the child knows anything about. Here there is an identification between the teacher-parent and the child-pupil.

In high school a boy learns how to play football, not by reading a textbook, but by identifying with a coach in a learning-working relationship.

The crowd with which we identify, whether we are young or old, creates a learning experience.

If we would respond to Jesus Christ, heaven's Teacher of the heavenly way of life, we must be solidly identified with him. This requires more than a confession of faith and church membership. A regular exposure of our mind and heart to him in worship is essential as is careful, attentive listening to his words of truth and wisdom.

We need to observe and contemplate both the character and conduct of Jesus Christ in his relationship with others if we would truly consider ourselves his disciples, his followers, students in his school. What grade are you making?

B. *We learn through participation.* Not only in the public school system but in the church school as well, hands-on, activity-based teaching is recognized as an effective method for communicating truths to the minds of children.

When Jesus said, "Come unto me," he was inviting us to participate in a learning experience. He instructed the man out of whom he had cast a legion of devils to "go home to thy friends, and tell them how great things the Lord hath done for thee" (Mark 5:19). This was an invitation to a laboratory experience in which the man would relate what God had done. In so doing he would discover also what God could do with him in the lives of others.

If we are to learn, we need both to identify and participate. What grade are you making?

### III. The invitation is still open.

College catalogs contain a paragraph that gives the time limit for enrolling in courses of study. They specifically state that beyond a certain date the opportunity to enroll is closed. Today we can thank God that the opportunity to enroll in the school of Christ continues to be open to those who are among the living. You do not have to wait until next semester; you can come to Christ today and begin to learn.

### Conclusion

A tragic mistake made by many is that of assuming that conversion automatically produces spiritual maturity, but Jesus tells us that we need to learn. You must not delay coming to Jesus Christ because of immaturity or fear of failure. You must come as one admitting your spiritual poverty and ignorance and your desire to learn and become rich in spirit.

Neglecting to enroll in the school of Christ is costly. Enroll today. Let him be not only your Savior and Redeemer but your Coach and Teacher too. To do so is to make a wise decision that you will never regret.

---

## SUNDAY EVENING, MAY 17

***Title:*** Is It Possible to Be a Hilarious Giver?

***Text:*** 2 Corinthians 9:7

### Introduction

The word that is translated "cheerful" in our text is the Greek word *hilaron*. It is the word from which we get our English word *hilarious*. Paul declared that "God loves the hilarious giver." Webster defines this word as "noisily merry, boisterous." Some people seriously question whether it is possible for any except the rich to be hilarious givers. Hilarious giving is not, however, to be restricted to the affluent.

### I. Under certain conditions hilarious giving would be impossible.

A. *Hilarious giving is impossible if life is considered only in terms of an abundance of things (Luke 12:15).* Jesus warned us against considering the acquiring of an abundance of material things as the primary objective for living. He declared and people have affirmed that an abundance of material things does not guarantee happiness.

B. *Hilarious giving is impossible if life is lived in only one dimension (Luke 12:21).* The rich fool lived as if he were a creature of time alone. He completely ignored eternity. Paul commended the Philippians because of their investments in his missionary work. He affirmed that by these contributions they would reap spiritual dividends of eternal significance (Phil. 4:17). He who has no faith in eternity will find it impossible to invest his resources or energies in that which is not tangible and visible.

C. *Hilarious giving is impossible if God is considered as an untrustworthy cheat.* Malachi, God's prophet, indicted the people of his day for stealing from God. They had refused to bring their tithes and offerings into the storehouse of God. In the final analysis their refusal to tithe was an indication of their lack of faith in the goodness of God. If faith in the generosity of God had filled their hearts, they would have joyfully brought their tithes into God's storehouse.

Today the primary reason for the failure of some to tithe is found in their lack of faith in the good God who has promised to open the windows of heaven and pour out an abundant blessing upon those who tithe. God does not lie. You can trust him to keep his promise.

D. *Hilarious giving is impossible if you do not have faith in the generous provisions of God (Matt. 6:26–30).* One of the excuses that is most often given for stinginess is that of personal need and a fear of failure to be able to provide the necessities of life in the future. Jesus encouraged his disciples to avoid worry by exercising faith and putting forth an honest effort.

1. Jesus would encourage the worrier to listen to a sermon from the sparrows (Matt. 6:26).
2. Jesus would encourage the worrier to listen to the lecture from the lilies (Matt. 6:28–30).

**II. Why does God love the hilarious giver?**

Is it because he is poor and his treasury is empty? Does God love the hilarious giver because he is hungry and in need of our generosity? These are foolish questions.

A. *Hilarious giving indicates a growth in godliness.* God is a hilarious giver. Lavishly he has given his blessings to us. Extravagantly he has been merciful to us. As the heavenly Father, he would be delighted by a similar attitude on the part of his children.

B. *Hilarious giving is an indication of gratitude.* The beloved apostle said, "We love him, because he first loved us" (1 John 4:19).

C. *Hilarious giving indicates a deep concern for a lost world.* God so loved the world that he gave his Son. Christ so loved the world that he gave his life. We should so love this world that we give of our time, talents, testimony, and treasure in a cheerful manner.

**III. Hilarious giving insures an abundant harvest (2 Cor. 9:6).**

It is a law of nature and it is a law of the spirit that we reap in proportion to the quantity of the seed that we sow.

A. *He who sows sparingly shall reap sparingly.* No wise farmer will be stingy with his seed. According to his best wisdom, he will use a sufficient amount of seed to reap the greatest possible potential from his field.
B. *He who sows bountifully shall reap also bountifully.* The farmer who plants a full measure of seed into the soil can normally expect an abundant harvest. This is a law that works not only in farming but in every area of life. We reap according to what we sow.

### Conclusion

God sees the hilarious giver as one who will enjoy the privilege of reaping a full harvest in life. God sees the hilarious giver as one who is investing in time with the interest of eternity in mind. May God give each of us the grace, the faith, and the wisdom to be hilarious givers.

## WEDNESDAY EVENING, MAY 20

***Title:*** The High Cost of Disobedience

***Text:*** Jonah 1:1–17

### Introduction

It is unfortunate that the remarkable teachings of the book of Jonah have been lost in the constant wrangling over the story of the great fish, which is but an event mentioned and soon dismissed. The book of Jonah is one of the least understood books of the Bible, yet it is so simple that a child can understand its profound truths. Although Jonah lived many hundreds of years ago, his book has a message for our day that is as fresh as the ink on this morning's newspaper.

The book of Jonah reveals the great redemptive purposes of God for all peoples of all nations. It rebukes the narrow spirit of nationalism, of racial hatreds, and of contempt for alien peoples whenever and wherever found. It discloses that the hearts of the most depraved and degenerate can be touched and cleansed by the power of God's Spirit. Moreover, the book of Jonah is a striking indictment of our sin of disobedience to the Great Commission (Matt. 28:18–20). Christ launched a world conquest of righteousness and meant for each of us to have our lives invested and deeply involved in winning a wicked, wayward world back to God.

### I. As God commanded Jonah, Christ has the right to command us.

A. *He is the Creator (John 1:3).*
B. *He is the Sustainer of this universe (Col. 1:17).*
C. *He is our Redeemer.*
D. *He is Lord of Lords (Phil. 2:11).*
E. *"Now the word of the LORD came unto Jonah the son of Amittai, saying, Arise, go to Nineveh."*

1. Nineveh was a great, sinful city (Jonah 1:2).
2. Nineveh was the object of God's loving concern (Jonah 4:11).

   Jesus' great commission contains his will for each of us. As we go about from place to place in our personal world, we are to invest our time, talents, ability, and resources in a manner so as to persuade all to become believers in and followers of him. He would have each of us live a devout life, and he would challenge each of us to be a student of the Bible and to live for others. Also, he would encourage us to be completely Christian in our home life and in benevolent ministries in our community. Finally, he would challenge us to be a part of world missions by means of our tithes and offerings.

**II. The cost of disobedience continues to be high.**

Jonah paid a high cost for being disobedient to the great commandment of his God.

A. *The cost of disobedience to Jonah.*
   1. It cost him the joy of cooperating with God.
   2. It cost him the joy of participating in the highest possible service that can be rendered to a city.
   3. It cost him the joy of receiving God's approval.

B. *The cost of your disobedience to you.*
   1. The way of disobedience is always down.
   2. One always "pays the fare thereof."
   3. God will cast a storm upon your sea.
   4. It will cost you fellowship with God and his blessed protection.
   5. It will cost you the joy of a clean conscience before God.

C. *The cost of your disobedience to God.*
   1. You limit his love.
   2. You limit his power.
   3. You limit the spread of his kingdom on earth.

D. *The cost of your disobedience to others.*
   1. You withhold from them the Savior.
   2. You withhold from them a challenging example.
   3. You withhold from them a blessed memory.

**Conclusion**

The way of obedience to the loving commandments of God is the high road of happiness. God's commandments are not grievous and galling. They may appear to be such, for at times they involve difficulties and hardship, and we cannot see ahead to the joy that will come to us as a result of obedience. May God give to each of us the wisdom and grace to be obedient.

## SUNDAY MORNING, MAY 24

***Title:*** "Lord, What Wilt Thou Have Me to Do?"

***Text:*** "And he trembling and astonished said, Lord, what wilt thou have me to do? And the Lord said unto him, Arise, and go into the city, and it shall be told thee what thou must do" **(Acts 9:6)**.

***Scripture Reading:*** Acts 9:1–16; 2 Timothy 4:6–8

***Hymns:*** "Majestic Sweetness Sits Enthroned," Stennett
"Fairest Lord Jesus," Anonymous
"Wonderful, Wonderful, Jesus," Russell

***Offertory Prayer:*** Holy Father, today we thank you for the beauty of springtime and for the glory of growing things. We thank you for the hope of a harvest that shall come as a result of planting seeds in the soil. We thank you for the privilege of being able to work and for the joy of receiving an increase. In this time when seeds are being planted and there is an evidence of new life on all sides, help us by means of both our efforts and our gifts to sow the seed of divine truth in the hearts and lives of people. Bless these offerings to the end that there might be an abundant increase in your kingdom. Through Jesus Christ we pray. Amen.

### Introduction

The passages of Scripture that we are considering today contain Paul's first recorded statement as a child of God and one of his last utterances as a veteran soldier of the cross.

Paul's ability to make the triumphant statement in his letter to Timothy is a direct result of his making the earlier statement, at the beginning of his discipleship, in utter sincerity. The question, "Lord, what wilt thou have me to do?" not only expressed the sentiments of Paul at the moment, but it is a description of his continuing attitude throughout the balance of his life.

Paul's question is appropriate for each of us under all circumstances and all times.

### I. The question, "Lord, what wilt thou have me to do?" acknowledges the absolute lordship of Jesus Christ.

The term *lord* does not have the meaning today that it had during the days of Paul. For a man to be lord meant many things. *Lord* was the normal address of respect in everyday Greek during those days. It was also a title of authority that distinguished between a master and a slave.

*Lord* was also used to describe absolute possession or ownership. It could refer to ownership of a house, a piece of property, an animal, or a slave. It was also used in legal terminology to designate one who served as a guardian for those who had no legal rights, such as women and children. This term was also the standard title of Roman emperors. The highest use of this term is found in the Greek translation of the Hebrew Bible where the Greek word *Kurios*, translated Lord, was regularly used as the name of Israel's God. It was in this context that Paul addressed the risen Christ who confronted him as he pursued his mad career of persecuting the church.

A. *During his earthly ministry nature had recognized and responded to the lordship of Jesus Christ.* The winds and the waves obeyed his command.

B. *The animal world recognized and responded to his lordship.* In Mark's gospel there is a statement in the account of Jesus' temptation experience that is often overlooked. Mark says, "He was there in the wilderness forty days, tempted of Satan; and was with the wild beasts; and the angels ministered unto him" (Mark 1:13).

Why did Mark call attention to the fact that Jesus was "with the wild beasts"? The passage implies that Jesus was in their favor and that their normal fear of man was absent. It is also significant that when Jesus made his triumphal entry into Jerusalem that he rode on a colt that had never been ridden before (Luke 19:30–37). Those who have had any experience with riding colts know that this would have been unusual. Is it possible that even the colt recognized the lordship of Jesus?

C. *The demons recognized the lordship of Jesus.* Repeatedly throughout the New Testament, we observe Jesus commanding evil spirits to surrender their sovereignty over the lives of those who had been enslaved by evil. They recognized him and resented him, but they also obeyed him (Mark 5:7–13).

D. *Jesus accepted recognition as Lord by his disciples.* He said, "Ye call me Master and Lord: and ye say well; for so I am" (John 13:13). On another occasion he rebuked them because they did not assume the responsibilities of his lordship. "And why call ye me, Lord, Lord, and do not the things which I say?" (Luke 6:46).

E. *In writing his epistle to the Philippians, Paul declared that everyone should recognize and respond to the lordship of Jesus.* "Wherefore God also hath highly exalted him, and given him a name which is above every name: That at the name of Jesus every knee should bow, of things in heaven, and things in earth, and things under the earth; And that every tongue should confess that Jesus Christ is Lord, to the glory of God the Father" (Phil. 2:9–11).

## II. The question, "Lord, what wilt thou have me to do?" was the expression of a surrendered heart.

A. *By this question Paul was giving voice to his inward repentance toward God and the beginning of his faith toward Jesus Christ as Savior.* While there are many factors that contributed to this change of attitude toward God and new openness to Jesus, there came the decisive moment when Paul responded with the surrender of his heart to Jesus.

B. *Henceforth the will of Christ was to be sovereign and supreme in every area of Paul's life.*

C. *Unreserved and unfaltering allegiance to the will of God as he understood it was to be the dominant passion of Paul's life.*

## III. The question, "Lord, what wilt thou have me to do?" was the beginning of a great career.

A. *Paul actively identified himself with the greatest person and with the greatest cause on earth.* The person was Jesus Christ, and the cause was the kingdom of God, which was to find spiritual visibility in the establishment of churches in many different cities and countries between this moment and the moment of Paul's martyrdom in Rome.

B. *Have you found some great person with whom you can identify?* We cannot live our lives in isolation from others. Life is made up of relationships, and relationships are created by choice. Each of us would be wise to choose to identify with persons who can challenge us to become what God would have us to be.

C. *Have you chosen a cause in which to invest your time, energy, and financial resources?* Life is made up, not only of relationships to persons, but to institutions. What place have you given to the church? Dr. M. E. Dodd once said, "A dollar invested in a New Testament church will rise higher, sink deeper, spread wider, go farther, and last longer than a dollar invested in any other institution on earth."

If this is true concerning dollars, it is also true concerning energy, effort, and time. Many are making the sad mistake of giving first-rate loyalty to third-rate causes and giving third-rate loyalty to the church, which is a first-rate cause. Because Paul was responding to the will of his Savior, the church was foremost among all institutions in his concern and in his effort.

## IV. The question "Lord, what wilt thou have me to do?" opens the door so that the will of God may be known.

The will of God is not something to be feared. It is something to be discovered and grasped. The will of God is not that which a cruel, compassionless fate would impose upon us; rather, it is the high and holy plan of the loving God.

A. *Our life is at its highest and best when it is lived in the circle of the divine will.*

B. *Paul described the will of God as good and perfect (Rom. 12:2).*

C. *If we are willing to do God's will, it is possible for us to know God's will.*

1. God's will can be discovered by reverently reading the Word of God.
2. God's will can be discovered in the closet of prayer.
3. God's will can be discovered through worship.
4. God's will can be discovered by counseling with devout and mature Christians.
5. God's will can be discovered through serious, prayerful thought.

### Conclusion

"Lord, what wilt Thou have me to do?" is everyone's question, and it should be your question. It is urgent because you need to know what the Lord would have you do today.

If you do not know Jesus Christ as Savior, it is the will of God that you be saved. If you are here as a negligent follower of Christ, it is the will of God that you rededicate your life and become a devout follower and servant. Let his will become your will today. Let his way be your way today and always.

---

## SUNDAY EVENING, MAY 24

***Title:*** Try Giving Yourself Away

***Text:*** "It is more blessed to give than to receive" **(Acts 20:35)**.

### Introduction

The title of the message tonight is the title of a book by David Dunn—*Try Giving Yourself Away* (Englewood Cliffs, N.J.: Prentice-Hall, 1956).

In this book David Dunn tells us how he found the secret of happy living. He had been brought up, as most of us have, believing that success and happiness were to be found in getting. In the first chapter he tells how he discovered the secret of happiness by accident. One night while lying awake in his berth on the Twentieth-Century Limited between Chicago and New York, he began to wonder about where the eastbound and the westbound Centuries passed each other during the night. It occurred to him that this thought might have advertising potential, so he wrote a letter expressing the idea "with no strings attached." He received an expression of thanks, and a second letter followed that revealed that his idea was to be used as the subject for the New York Central calendar for the coming year.

That was in 1924. During that year he had the privilege of seeing again and again the night picture of the oncoming engine of one Century and the lighted observation platform of the other, passing on a curve. Each time he saw this picture, it brought joy to his heart. It was his picture, and he had given the idea away "with no strings attached." This was but the beginning of a life of giving that brought supreme happiness to the giver.

Have you discovered the joy of giving? Jesus did. He believed in giving to the extent that he gave his all.

### I. Try giving yourself away: become a genuine follower of Jesus Christ.

A. *Jesus came into the world that he might be a giver.* He gave health to the sick, sight to the blind, hearing to the deaf, hope to the despairing, forgiveness to the guilty, strength to the weak, courage to the fearful, and life to the dead.

B. *Jesus lived to give.*

C. *Jesus died to give.*

**II. Try giving yourself away and be obedient to the teachings of Christ.**

A. *"Freely ye have received, freely give" (Matt. 10:8).*

B. *"And whosoever shall give to drink unto one of these little ones a cup of cold water only in the name of a disciple, verily I say unto you, he shall in no wise lose his reward" (Matt. 10:42).*

C. *"Give, and it shall be given unto you; good measure, pressed down, and shaken together, and running over, shall men give into your bosom.* For with the same measure that ye mete withal it shall be measured to you again" (Luke 6:38).

D. *"It is more blessed to give than to receive" (Acts 20:35).*

**III. Try giving yourself away if you want to discover the way of abundant living.**

Jesus said, "I am come that they might have life, and that they might have it more abundantly" (John 10:10). This abundant life is not found merely by receiving him as Lord and Savior. We must move beyond and think as he thought and act as he acted. Jesus found happiness in giving himself completely to the purpose of God and to the well-being of humankind.

A. *First, we need to give ourselves completely to God.*

B. *We need to recognize and to accept giving as a way of life.*

C. *We will discover that if we give lavishly we will live life abundantly (Luke 6:38).*

**Conclusion**

Do you look upon your life as a goblet to be filled? If so, most likely your goblet will never overflow. Do you look upon your life as a channel or a conduit through which the blessings of God may flow to bless the lives of others? If so you may never be rich in the eyes of people, but you will possess an inward joy that brings true satisfaction to the heart. Live each day determined to be a giver.

## WEDNESDAY EVENING, MAY 27

***Title:*** Sitting under a Gourd Vine

***Text:*** Jonah 4:1–11

**Introduction**

The book of Jonah has many lessons for today's Christians. The principle truth of the book is that God's compassion for souls is universal in its range and all-inclusive in its concerns (Jonah 4:11). Because of God's deep concern for all, there are other truths that we need to recognize: (1) God has a redemptive purpose for each of us; (2) God has the right to command each of us; (3) it is foolish to disobey or to ignore the will of God for our lives; (4) and God will give the disobedient a second chance if they are willing to cooperate.

The book of Jonah is a most uncomplimentary biography of one of God's prophets. We are safe in assuming that someone other than Jonah is the author of the book, for it would be almost impossible for a man to describe himself as Jonah is described in this book. The book closes with Jonah in disgrace. The picture of the prophet we see in the final chapter is indeed pitiful.

**I. Jonah sat under a gourd vine.**

A. *Jonah was very angry with God because Nineveh had been spared, for he had hoped that it might be destroyed.* Nineveh was the archenemy of his country. His people had suffered greatly because of the cruelty of its people.

B. *Jonah had placed limits on the love of God.* He found it impossible to believe that God could love the hated Ninevites.

C. *Jonah had absolutely no concern about the spiritual welfare of the people of Nineveh.* In fact, he would have been delighted if God had rained fire and brimstone down on the capital city of Assyria.

D. *The Lord said to Jonah during this fit of anger, "Doest thou well to be angry?"* To try to communicate the divine concern for the people of Nineveh, God provided a gourd vine that shaded the prophet from the sun and wind. Jonah was grateful for the vine and enjoyed it because of the comfort that it brought to him. When the vine was destroyed by a worm, Jonah was again upset, and God rebuked him for being more concerned about a vine then he was about the people of Nineveh.

**II. Are you sitting under a gourd vine?**

A. *If we consider ourselves as the sole object of God's love, we may be sitting under a gourd vine with Jonah.*

B. *When we fail to respond to God's divine purpose for us as individuals, we may have taken our seat with Jonah.*

C. *If we have no sense of personal responsibility for the spiritual welfare of others, we may discover that we are enjoying the shade of Jonah's vine.*

D. *If we are not diligently seeking to be genuinely Christian in all of our conduct, it may indicate that we love the shade of the gourd vine.*

E. *Are you enthusiastically evangelistic?* Are you seeking to share your faith with others? Are you concerned about the need of the world for Christ?

**III. Do you, like Jonah, love the gourd vine?**

A. *Have the sinful pleasures of the world caused you to compromise your Christian convictions to the extent that you have no testimony?*

B. *Does your love for comfort and ease prevent you from rendering service for the Lord and his church?*

C. *Have you let the love of money capture your heart to the extent that you have no time for the work of God?*

**IV. The results of sitting under the gourd vine.**

God was greatly displeased with Jonah, as he was displeased with the nation of Israel. The book does not describe the final consequences of Jonah's life. Today we can only grieve about Jonah's failure.

We should be even more concerned about the consequences of our sitting under a gourd vine.

A. *We can miss the true purpose for our being if we refuse to follow the wishes of our loving Lord.*
B. *We will deprive God of the glory due him if we neglect to communicate to others his universal and specific concern for them.*
C. *Unsaved people will perish if we neglect to proclaim the gospel.*

### Conclusion

May God save each of us from the sad destiny of Jonah who loved the comfort of the gourd vine more than he did the Ninevites.

---

## SUNDAY MORNING, MAY 31

***Title:*** Do You Have an Excuse?

***Text:*** "Moses said unto God, Who am I, that I should go unto Pharaoh, and that I should bring forth the children of Israel out of Egypt?" **(Exod. 3:11)**.

***Scripture Reading:*** Exodus 3:1–13

***Hymns:*** "We're Marching to Zion," Watts
"Jesus Calls Us," Alexander
"Living for Jesus," Chisholm

**Offertory Prayer:** Holy Father, help us to recognize that our money is stored-up energy and that by means of our monetary gifts we can render services of kindness to those who suffer both physically and spiritually. Help us to recognize the necessity of our participating in the work of your kingdom by means of our financial contributions. Help us not only to bring dedicated hearts and helping hands but to bring of our financial increase and present it as an act of worship upon your altar. In Jesus' name we pray. Amen.

### Introduction

People are born excuse makers. They have been such since the beginning of time. Adam blamed both Eve and God for his fall into sin (Gen. 3:12). His descendants have followed his example by blaming someone else when things go wrong.

While some excuses are perfectly legitimate, it should be recognized that the development of the habit of making excuses is very dangerous. Most excuses contain an element of dishonesty. If we develop the habit of always making excuses, we can rob ourselves of the habit of correcting our mistakes, which always leads to further failure. Making excuses is a form of escapism in which we refuse to accept responsibility for either our actions or our decisions.

When you are brought face-to-face with an opportunity to render some service to God or to be helpful to others, do you instinctively seek an excuse to avoid, postpone, or escape?

If you find that you have developed the habit of making excuses, you can be both comforted and disturbed. You can be comforted by the fact that you are not alone, but you should be disturbed, for this habit can prove to be extremely dangerous to yourself and detrimental to others.

Our Scripture reading for today concerns a man who at first traveled the road of excuse making. Moses repeatedly offered excuses as to why he was not the proper person to do what God was calling him to do. Are we imitating his example? It would be wise for us to reexamine our excuses. Are they acceptable to God? Are they acceptable to us personally when we give them serious thought? Would they be acceptable in the eyes of friends?

### I. God needed the help of Moses to set his people free.

A. *God appeared to Moses at the back side of the desert in a bush that burned with fire but was not consumed.* When Moses approached, God spoke to him:

> *I am the God of thy father, the God of Abraham, the God of Isaac, and the God of Jacob. And Moses hid his face; for he was afraid to look upon God. And the Lord said, I have surely seen the affliction of my people which are in Egypt, and have heard their cry by reason of their taskmasters; for I know their sorrows; and I am come down to deliver them out of the hand of the Egyptians, and to bring them up out of that land unto a good land and a large, unto a land flowing with milk and honey. (Exod. 3:6–8)*

Not only did God declare his intention of delivering the oppressed Israelites who were being treated cruelly as slaves, but he revealed the role that Moses was to play in this deliverance. "Come now therefore, and I will send thee unto Pharaoh, that thou mayest bring forth my people the children of Israel out of Egypt" (Exod. 3:10).

B. *The words of God to Moses reveal the intention that the Lord Jesus had for his disciples as he commissioned them to serve as his witnesses in a sin-enslaved world.*

1. Jesus needs the cooperation of his disciples to deliver people from the slavery and waste of sin.
2. Jesus continues to look to his followers in leading the unsaved out of the slavery of sin and into the freedom of sonship and faith.

### II. Moses began to make excuses.

A. *Moses replied to God as many modern people respond to their spiritual opportunities and responsibilities.* In today's language he said, "You can just count me out. I have sheep to care for. I have my own family to consider. What you are proposing would be exceedingly difficult and inconvenient. I am not at all disposed to do this thing at this time."

B. *Moses knew his own limitations.* He carefully evaluated his own abilities and provided a list of his disqualifications.

1. He first pled his lack of fitness for the task: "Who am I, that I should go unto Pharaoh, and that I should bring forth the children of Israel out of Egypt?" (Exod. 3:11). Moses was saying, "Anybody but me. I am just not cut out for that job. It's just not my cup of tea."

2. Moses next pled his lack of an exhaustive knowledge of God: "Behold, when I come unto the children of Israel, and shall say unto them, The God of your fathers hath sent me unto you; and they shall say to me, What is his name? what shall I say unto them?" (Exod. 3:13). Moses was declaring that he had not been to Bible college or seminary. He had no experience as a Sunday school teacher or deacon. He was pleading inexperience and immaturity.
3. Moses next pled his lack of authority and prestige: "Behold, they will not believe me, nor hearken unto my voice: for they will say, The LORD hath not appeared unto thee" (Exod. 4:1). Moses was forgetting God as he offered these excuses. He was assuming that his success was going to be determined by his own human ability rather than by the power of God. Many people today make this same fatal mistake and offer the same silly excuse that Moses offered.
4. Moses also pled a lack of speaking ability. "O my Lord, I am not eloquent.... I am slow of speech, and of a slow tongue" (Exod. 4:10). Many people today offer the excuse that they are not public speakers. They declare that because they do not have the ability to sweep an audience off its feet with their oratory, they are automatically eliminated from responsibility as the servants of the Lord.

### III. Moses' excuses provoked the anger of God (Exod. 4:14).

A. *Moses' excuses were an insult to the truthfulness of God, for in each instance God promised to make him adequate for the task to which he was being called.* Moses' excuses were actually declarations of his lack of faith in the promises of God.

B. *God was angry for Moses' sake.* God was just as interested in Moses achieving his greatest possible potential as he was in delivering the Israelites from Egyptian bondage. God was unhappy with this man who was staggering back in unbelief and depriving himself of the opportunity to achieve his divine destiny. God is angry with us when we make excuses, for we also stagger around in mediocrity and nothingness when we could achieve something really worthwhile in the service of God.

C. *God was angry with Moses for the sake of the suffering Israelites.* Moses was uniquely equipped by virtue of his personal knowledge of the court of Pharaoh and by virtue of his forty years in the wilderness to be the deliverer of these downtrodden people who were so dear to the heart of God. A loving God could not stand by in impassive unconcern toward a man who was refusing to assist in a noble venture. Neither will God be happy with us if we refuse to become involved in meeting the needs of our present world.

### IV. Moses finally, rather grudgingly, faced up to the responsibility and opportunity.

"And he said, O my Lord, send, I pray thee, by the hand of him whom thou wilt send" (Exod. 4:13). In modern terminology Moses was saying, "If there is no one else to do it and if I can't get around it, then I'll go."

There are at least two truths from this early example of Moses that can be inspiring and challenging to children of God in today's world as they face up to the fact that God needs them and that God wants to use him in delivering others from the slavery of sin and leading them to the promised land of abundant living.

A. *The first truth is that one does not have to be perfect to serve God effectively.* Moses was far from perfect, yet God used him in a mighty way. God can use each of us and will, particularly if we voluntarily commit ourselves to cooperative activity with him.

B. *The second thrilling truth is that God uses those who are available.* While one's ability is of tremendous importance, one's availability is the matter of supreme importance to God. God has chosen the simple things to accomplish mighty and wonderful things (1 Cor. 1:26–29).

### Conclusion

One of the most powerful parables that fell from the lips of our Savior concerned those who made excuses. He tells the story of a man who prepared a great supper and invited guests (Luke 14:16–24). One offered the excuse that he could not come because he had to attend to a piece of property. Another offered the excuse that his occupation stood in the way of his coming to the banquet. A third declared that he could not come because he had an obligation to his family. If a man develops the habit of making excuses, he can always find an excuse for saying no to God.

It would be wise for us to quit making excuses. We should be honest with our Lord, with ourselves, and with others. Let us cooperate with God. Let us face our responsibilities and quit blaming others for our failures. Let us quit living under a list of excuses.

## SUNDAY EVENING, MAY 31

***Title:*** Generous Sowing Means a Generous Harvest

***Text:*** "The point is this: he who sows sparingly will also reap sparingly, and he who sows bountifully will also reap bountifully" **(2 Cor. 9:6 RSV)**.

***Scripture Reading:*** 2 Corinthians 9:6–12

### Introduction

In 2 Corinthians 8–9 the apostle Paul is writing to the disciples of our Lord in the city of Corinth regarding a generous offering they have made plans to provide for the poor saints in Jerusalem. He has commended them for their generosity and their eagerness to be a part of providing relief for those who were in genuine need.

The apostle was particularly interested in this being a generous and worthy offering because it would not only relieve the conditions of distress in Jerusalem, but it would also serve as a bridge to unite Jewish believers with those who were converts from paganism and idolatry to the Christian faith. Paul knew that if a generous offering came from Gentile converts, this would be very helpful in breaking down the cultural and religious barriers that separated Gentile believers from Jewish believers (cf. Acts 6:1; Gal. 2:9–10).

In these two chapters Paul deals with the subject of the proper motivations for generous giving, and he also discusses the principles of proper giving to God and for the needs of others.

This section of the epistle contains pleas for generosity and for enthusiasm in the giving of the offering. Furthermore, it contains a plea for a great faith in God, and it also has a word of encouragement concerning their entering into a real partnership with God and others in relieving the needs of those in poverty.

Paul encourages his readers to be generous by reminding them of one of the basic laws in agriculture. The gardener or the farmer will reap in direct proportion to his using a proper amount of seed for the planting of a garden plot or field. He emphasizes that it is foolish to be stingy with the seed in sowing time. He who is stingy is robbing himself of the potential harvest in the future. The apostle applies this to the practice of giving for the glory of God and for the good of others. This principle works in every area of life.

### I. We reap in the measure that we have given ourselves to Bible study (Josh. 1:8).

Many people are not even acquainted with biblical characters, much less the great events of biblical history. They have no knowledge of the provisions of God's great salvation, which is offered through the ministry of Jesus Christ and through the abiding presence of the Holy Spirit. Their lives are greatly impoverished because they have never given themselves to the study of God's Holy Word. If we neglect to feed ourselves on the truth of God's Word, we cannot possibly grow up in the salvation God has provided (1 Peter 2:1–3). The psalmist describes the happy and successful person as one who delights in and meditates on the great truths of God's Word (Ps. 1:1–3).

### II. We reap in the measure that we have given ourselves in prayer (Matt. 6:6).

Jesus dogmatically declared that spiritual rewards come to those who develop the habit of going apart into the private place for communion with the Father God. These rewards and blessings are too numerous to list, but many people miss them because they never give themselves to prayer. James writes in his epistle, "You do not have, because you do not ask" (4:2 RSV). This does not mean that we can get anything we ask for. It does mean that God has many things for those of us who ask. On the other hand, those who neglect prayer miss the blessings that come from prayer. We reap according to the measure in which we have sown.

### III. We reap in the measure that we give voice to our Christian testimony (Ps. 126:6).

One of the greatest sins that we are guilty of is being silent about the goodness and grace of God revealed in and through Jesus Christ. It appears that some of us are either ashamed of our relationship with Jesus Christ or afraid to speak about his presence in our lives. The Holy Spirit can use our personal testimony to impart the gift of faith to nonbelievers about us. When we neglect to "plant the seed" of our personal testimonies concerning what God has done in our own lives, we are depriving others of the blessing they could receive. At the same time, we are robbing ourselves of the joy of the harvest God wants us to experience.

**IV. We reap in the measure that we give of our material resources in the service of God and for the good of others (2 Cor. 9:8).**

The apostle Paul did not believe that God was a beggar or that God's treasury was in danger of going bankrupt. He did not believe that God became richer because of the gifts of his people. Instead, he encouraged these people in Corinth to become generous givers because God is a generous giver. The apostle declares, "God loves a cheerful giver" (9:7 RSV). God does not love the generous giver because the gifts enrich the heavenly treasury; God loves the cheerful giver because that giver is becoming like God. When we give out of a heart of love and meet the needs of others, God sees in us those character traits that remind him of his own nature. To be generous is to be godly. To be stingy is to be ungodly.

Paul declares in verse 8 of this chapter that God responds to the generosity of his children by blessing them in the manner in which they have given of themselves into his service and for the good of others. God blesses not just by addition, but by multiplication. Paul declares that God will bless the generous person with divine generosity and that his or her needs will be met.

As noted previously, the Greek work translated *"cheerful"* is the source of the word *"hilarious."* One cannot be a hilarious giver if he or she has a great feeling of insecurity. Those who find their security in the possession of material things can never be hilarious givers, because they can never accumulate enough to be totally secure. Paul is encouraging the people to find their security in God, and then, out of the resources with which he blesses them, to be hilarious helpers of others.

**Conclusion**

It is never wise to be stingy with seed at planting time. A farmer is very generous with his seed because he recognizes that if the seed is not planted, there can be no harvest. This law works in the realm of the spirit exactly as it does in the realm of nature. We can become hilarious givers of ourselves and of our substance if we will trust God to give us an abundant harvest.

Suggested Preaching Program for

# JUNE

## ■ Sunday Mornings

Continue with the theme "Practical, Probing Questions for Serious Consideration."

## ■ Sunday Evenings

The Sunday evening messages for this month are based on Psalm 23. These messages should reveal the grace and goodness of God so as to encourage a greater faith, a deeper love, and a more devout life.

## ■ Wednesday Evenings

"The Growing Christian" is an appropriate theme for this series on the need for every disciple's continuing growth to spiritual maturity.

---

## WEDNESDAY EVENING, JUNE 3

*Title:* Provision for Spiritual Growth

*Text:* "Wherefore laying aside all malice, and all guile, and hypocrisies, and envies, and all evil speakings, as newborn babes, desire the sincere milk of the word that ye may grow thereby" (**1 Peter 2:1–2**).

### Introduction

A false idea held by many is that the child of God is born full grown. They believe that once a person becomes a convert, instantaneously and automatically he becomes a mature Christian. Consequently, mature Christian conduct is expected from those who are in reality mere babes in the family of God. But spiritual birth does not automatically produce spiritual maturity. In the words of our text, Peter speaks to new converts concerning their continuing need to put off and lay aside attitudes and actions that are contradictory to the spirit and teachings of Christ. He affirms that they will be able to put off these harmful attitudes as they grow spiritually.

Many new converts have been greatly distressed by their failure to measure up to what they believe they should be as followers of Jesus Christ. They have mistakenly labored under the impression that once you become a child of God, Christian character and maturity will naturally follow. Some have been terribly distressed to discover that in spite of the fact that they have a new nature within their heart, evil continues to plague them.

As children of God, each of us needs to recognize that spiritual growth is both a responsibility and a continuing opportunity. We also need to face up to our responsibility toward younger Christians, those who are but babes in Christ, and do all that we can to help them in their progress toward spiritual maturity.

All people are creatures of God, but only those who are born again are children of God. If the children of God would become the servants of God, they must grow. Our text speaks of the provisions for our growth. It speaks of our Father, our food, and our future as the children of God.

### I. Our Father.

A. *We are God's little ones—babes in Christ.* We may be old in sin, but we are young in Christ at the time of our spiritual birth.

B. *This text should teach us humility.* Ours is the privilege of being the children of the eternal God. John rejoiced in the assurance of sonship: "Behold, what manner of love the Father hath bestowed upon us, that we should be called the sons of God: therefore the world knoweth us not, because it knew him not. Beloved, now are we the sons of God, and it doth not yet appear what we shall be: but we know that, when he shall appear, we shall be like him; for we shall see him as he is" (1 John 3:1–2).

C. *This text should impart hope to each of us.* We are not what we ought to be. Neither are we now what we can be. The heavenly Father has made provisions for our growth. As time passes by, it will be possible for us to resemble both the heavenly Father and our older Brother.

D. *This text reveals to us the attitude that we should have toward the heavenly Father.*
   1. As his children we should love him.
   2. As his children we should trust him implicitly.
   3. As his children we should obey him.

### II. Our food.

A. *The Father has made provisions for his children.*
   1. In the church he has provided for us a family in which to grow toward spiritual maturity and effectiveness.
   2. In the Bible he has provided us the milk, the meat, and the bread we need for spiritual energy.

B. *The sincere milk of the Word.*
   1. "Being born again ... by the word of God" (1 Peter 1:23).
   2. Purify your soul by obeying the truth of the Word of God (1 Peter 1:22).
   3. The Word of God has the life of God in it (1 Tim. 3:16–17; 1 Peter 1:23).
   4. The Word of God endures forever (1 Peter 1:25).

C. *Desire the sincere milk of the Word.* It is a law of nature and also a law in the spiritual realm that shortly after birth the newborn has an appetite for food. The child of God will desire the milk of God's Word.
   1. We must know the truth of God revealed in his Word.
   2. We must obey the truth of God learned from a study of his Word. When we study and obey the Word of God, our faith grows, our love deepens, and we gain spiritual strength and vitality.

### III. Our future.

Peter reveals the noble destiny that God has planned for his children. It is God's will that the followers of Christ assume both the privileges and the responsibilities that had been bestowed upon Israel as a nation.

A. *You are a chosen generation.*
B. *You are a royal priesthood.*
C. *You are a holy nation.*
D. *You are a people for God's own possession.*
E. *You are to show forth the praises of the One who has called you out of darkness into light.*

### Conclusion

The noble destiny that God has purposed for us reveals the necessity for our growth toward spiritual maturity.

---

## SUNDAY MORNING, JUNE 7

***Title:*** Can I Be Sure That I Am Saved?

***Text:*** "These things have I written unto you that believe on the name of the Son of God; that ye may know that ye have eternal life, and that ye may believe on the name of the Son of God" (**1 John 5:13**).

***Scripture Reading:*** 2 Timothy 1:1–12

***Hymns:*** "Praise to God, Immortal Praise," Barbauld

"I Am Thine, O Lord," Crosby

"Blessed Assurance, Jesus Is Mine," Crosby

***Offertory Prayer:*** Heavenly Father, today we thank you for the inward disposition that causes us to want to worship you. We rejoice in the glad consciousness of forgiven sin. We are grateful for the assurance that we are children of your love. Today we bring our tithes and offerings to express our love and gratitude and to proclaim your grace to others. Through Jesus Christ our Lord. Amen.

### Introduction

The hearts of all people hunger for an assurance that both their souls and lives are acceptable to God. As we think of one day meeting our Creator, it is only natural that we desire to have assurance that we will be acceptable to him on that occasion.

Many people sincerely believe that it is impossible to have the assurance in this life that we are acceptable in the sight of God. Such people labor under the impression that the only way to be acceptable to God is to live a life without flaw and full of good works. Scripture, however, tells us that all have sinned and come short of the glory of God. It is only by the blood of Jesus Christ that we can be made acceptable in God's sight.

John stated the reason for writing his first epistle: "These things have I written unto you that believe on the name of the Son of God; that ye may know that ye have eternal life, and that ye may believe on the name of the Son of God" (5:13). He addressed his words to disciples of the Lord Jesus, those who were already in possession of the gift of eternal life. Some, however, were not certain that it was faith in the Christ that had brought to them the precious gift of eternal life.

We can conclude from 1 John that it is not presumptuous for the believer to say with humility and gratitude, "I know that I am saved." God wants his children to know without doubt that they belong to him.

**I. Assurance of salvation is essential.**

A. *The lack of assurance of salvation makes Christian love, joy, and peace impossible (John 14:15; 15:11).* The heavenly Father does not want us to serve him out of a fear of the consequences of not serving him. Our Lord encouraged his disciples to respond to his commandments on the basis of love, gratitude, and joy. He who lives in constant fear that he will be shut out of the presence of God in eternity will find it very difficult to love God warmly. The peace that God wants us to have is unknown to him who has no assurance of salvation.

B. *The lack of assurance of salvation makes effective work unlikely.* To be an effective salesperson, a person needs to be convinced of the worth of his or her product on the basis of personal experience. Secondhand knowledge of the product will undermine the salesperson's effectiveness as he or she tries to present the product to potential customers. The same thing is true in the realm of the Spirit. People who do not know Jesus Christ as their personal Savior and who do not have the assurance of a living relationship cannot possibly be convincing witnesses for the Lord Jesus.

C. *The lack of assurance of salvation dishonors the power of God (John 10:27–30; 2 Tim. 1:12).* To commit oneself to Jesus Christ as Lord and Savior and then to doubt either God's willingness or ability to effect that salvation is to cast reflection on the saving power of the Lord Jesus. The sincere believer in Jesus Christ should never say, "I hope I am saved."

D. *The lack of assurance of salvation clouds the pathway ahead.* To live daily in the fear that something might happen to prevent us from meeting God as one of his dear children is too frightful to contemplate. Earthly parents who love their children are eager for their children to have a sense of security in the family relationship. The heavenly Father is even more eager for us to be able to face the struggles and troubles of life with the inward strength that a sure relationship with him can bring.

**II. Factors that contribute to a lack of assurance.**

Many factors can contribute to a lack of assurance of salvation in the hearts of sincere believers. Some of these need to be recognized and evaluated.

A. *A misunderstanding of the way of salvation causes many sincere believers to be unsure of their salvation.* Instead of recognizing that eternal life is the gift of God through faith in Jesus Christ (Rom. 6:23; Eph. 2:8–9), many believe that salvation comes as a result of the grace of God plus human works. Those who believe in this manner can never have a happy assurance of salvation.

B. *Some people lack the assurance of salvation because of the absence of a tremendous conversion experience.* Many who received Jesus Christ as Lord and Savior at an early age cannot bear testimony to a revolutionary conversion experience such as that of one who was converted as an adult. Some have falsely assumed that because of their inability to describe in detail a soul-shaking conversion experience, they have never been converted. These should recognize that it would be illogical to expect a child to have a conversion experience that was as unique as that of the apostle Paul as described in Acts 9:1–18. The primary concern should be whether we have a sincere trust in Jesus Christ at the present.

C. *The neglect of Christian duty and personal spiritual growth will always make it impossible for a child of God to have the joy of salvation.* In the conversion experience itself, the Holy Spirit comes into the heart of the believer to work the work of God and to reproduce the character of Jesus Christ (Phil. 1:6; 2:13). When the believer neglects to cooperate with this inward work of God, the chastisement of the heavenly Father falls upon that person (Heb. 12:6–11). In almost all instances, this chastisement begins with a removal of the joy and assurance of salvation. This is the heavenly Father's way of encouraging his children to confess and forsake sin and to encourage them to live in harmony with the new nature that came to them in the spiritual birth.

If you once had the assurance of salvation and no longer enjoy that blessing, then you should examine your own heart and life. You need to reaffirm your faith and rededicate yourself to the spiritual discipline that will help you to achieve God's plan for your life.

**III. The basis for a believer's assurance of salvation.**

A. *There can be no assurance of salvation apart from an absolute confidence in the Word of God (1 John 5:13–14).* The mistake that many believers make is in basing their assurance of salvation on their feelings or emotions. Because our feelings ebb and flow and never remain stable, we should recognize that this would be a shaky basis upon which to place our confidence.

Feelings are deceptive. Many feel that they are saved when in reality the Scriptures would teach that they are unsaved. At the same time there are many who feel that they are unsaved when in reality they have in their life many evidences that would indicate that they possess eternal life through their faith in Jesus Christ.

B. *God has promised to save the believer (John 3:16, 18, 36).* With all of our hearts, we need to believe that God is able, eager, and willing to do that which he has promised for those who trust Jesus Christ as Savior. If you are among those who are trusting him, then have faith to rejoice in the assurance that condemnation for sin has been removed (John 3:18) and that eternal life is already a present possession (John 3:36).

C. *There are other indications on which we can base our assurance of salvation.* John sets forth in his first epistle a list of identifiable marks or distinctive characteristics of those who are the children of God. These characteristics are inward and spiritual but express themselves in an outward manner. I list five for prayerful consideration.
   1. An inward desire to be obedient that expresses itself in obedience (1 John 2:3, 5). We can know that our faith is a saving faith if it gives us an inward desire to be obedient to the known will of God. If we don't have this desire, we can know that we are still in need of a spiritual birth that will make us members of the family of God.
   2. An inward love for the brethren (1 John 3:14). Those who do not love their brothers and sisters have not known and do not know the God of love. Having within our hearts a love for others, particularly for the people of God, is a sign that we are God's children.
   3. A life that is lived by the principle of love (1 John 3:18–19). Because we have experienced the love of God within our own hearts and lives, we will relate to others out of self-giving love. This type of love is possible because of the work of the Holy Spirit within the hearts of believers (Rom. 5:5). To love in word only is not a distinctive mark by which we could be encouraged to believe that we are the children of God.
   4. The testimony of the Holy Spirit (1 John 4:13; Rom. 8:14–17). As the parents of a new baby speak words of endearment that provide the infant with a feeling of security, even so the Spirit of God who comes into the heart of new converts bears a spiritual testimony to their souls that convinces them of their divine adoption.
   5. The testimony of divine Scripture (1 John 5:11–12). To have assurance of salvation, we must believe in the truthfulness of the Scriptures. The divine record is that God gives us eternal life and that this life comes to us through faith in his Son.

## Conclusion

You must have a conversion experience before you can have the assurance of salvation. Many have wanted the assurance prior to the experience. Faith in Christ as Savior and Lord produces the experience, and information concerning what God has done and is doing for the believer makes blessed assurance of salvation possible. This assurance then makes peace of heart, overflowing joy, genuine love, and effective service possible.

## SUNDAY EVENING, JUNE 7

*Title:* "The LORD Is My Shepherd"

*Text:* "The LORD is my shepherd; I shall not want" **(Ps. 23:1)**.

### Introduction

Psalm 23 is one of the simplest yet loveliest poems ever written. Its lines are as simple as childhood rhymes, yet its meaning is as deep as an archangel's anthem. We could well afford to deprive ourselves of some of earth's most magnificent libraries rather than deprive ourselves of this precious little poem. Psalm 23 is the reflective thinking of an aged man who had been forgiven and who had discovered some wonderful truths about God. It is a confession of faith, a profession of faith, and a proclamation of faith. It is an anthem of grace. It is a shout of joy—an exclamation from the heart of a man who is overflowing with love and gratitude for his God.

Dr. J. P. MacBeth points out three distinct themes in Psalm 23. In verses 1–4 our God is the Shepherd. The scene is a pasture, and we are his sheep. In verse 5 the scene is a banquet, and God is the Host and his people are the guests. In verse 6 the scene is our eternal home, and God is the Father and we are his children. The Shepherd becomes the Host, and the Host becomes the Father. The pasture becomes the table, or the banquet room, and the banquet room becomes the eternal home of the heavenly Father. The sheep become the guests, and the guests become the children. It is wonderful for our Savior to be pictured as a Shepherd. It is better to think of our God as a Host. It is even more wonderful to think of him as being our eternal, loving, heavenly Father. The pasture scene is beautiful, the banquet room is even more beautiful, but the eternal home of the redeemed is beyond compare. It is very fruitful and productive to think of ourselves in terms of the sheep, and it is a greater privilege to be a guest, but it is even more wonderful to be a child in the home of the heavenly Father.

In the New Testament we read about the Good Shepherd, the Great Shepherd, and the Chief Shepherd. As the Good Shepherd in Psalm 22, Jesus gives his life for the sheep. As the Great Shepherd in Psalm 23, he lives to guide, nourish, protect, and help the sheep. In Psalm 24, as the Chief Shepherd, he comes to receive unto himself those who have trusted him, those who love him and have followed him.

Psalm 23 is in some respects a theological treatise, for it talks about God. It gives us a man's experience of God. This psalm is not about man. It is not man-centered; it is God-centered. You can discover much about the greatness, the goodness, the character, the nature, and the purpose of God in the psalm.

In this beautiful psalm we find that there is progression or advance from one scene to the other. The psalmist is trying to get across to us the same thought that our Savior labored to plant in the hearts of his disciples when he taught them to think of God in terms of a loving, devoted, merciful heavenly Father. Only in one recorded instance did Jesus ever address God in a different manner. That was when he was on the cross with the sin of a needy world bearing down on his soul. When he was dying under the penalty of our guilt, he cried, "My God, My God, why hast thou forsaken me?"

In every other instance, Jesus addressed the Creator, the Eternal One, as Father. He is a Father who is infinitely wise, bountifully good, and perfectly kind. He sees the end from the beginning, and his purposes toward us are always purposes of love. The psalmist was trying to get across in prophetic symbolism that which Jesus was to teach explicitly during his earthly ministry.

Evidently Jesus was using Psalm 23 as a text for his comments recorded in John 10.

### I. The Good Shepherd and his sheep.

A. *The Good Shepherd leads his sheep.* He is not a driver. He is a leader. He is always out in front.

B. *The Good Shepherd feeds his sheep.*

C. *The Good Shepherd protects his sheep.* One day when David was a shepherd boy, a bear came out of the wilderness to attack the sheep. With his club, David stood between the sheep and the bear and finally was able to slay the bear. On another occasion, a lion came out of the thicket to attack the sheep. Instantly, David, with his club, was between the sheep and the lion and was able to slay the lion.

Jesus Christ, the Good Shepherd, took his club, the cross, and stood between his sheep and sin, Satan, death, and the grave. He literally died for the salvation of his sheep. The Good Shepherd gave his life completely for his sheep. Oh, how he loves us! How he wants to protect us! How grateful we should be that though he had the power to lay down his life for us, he also had the power to take it up again.

The Good Shepherd understands his sheep. He died for his sheep and rose again to lead his sheep.

### II. The sheep of the Good Shepherd.

In the Good Shepherd chapter, John 10, Jesus makes seven remarks about sheep.

A. *The sheep know their Shepherd.*

B. *They know his voice.*

C. *They hear his voice.*

D. *The good sheep follow the Shepherd.*

E. *They love the Shepherd.*

F. *They trust the Shepherd.*

G. *They obey the Shepherd.*

Each of us who names the name of Christ should pray that we might be good sheep, even as he is a Good Shepherd.

### III. Do you know the Good Shepherd?

There is a tremendous difference in the way people read Psalm 23. Some read it and say, "The Lord is a shepherd." Others read it and say, "The Lord is the Shepherd." Some can read it and say, "The Lord is my Shepherd." There is a great deal of difference in saying, "There is a car," "There is the car," and "This is my car." And it makes all the difference in time and all the difference in eternity if you can read this psalm and from the heart say, "The Lord is my Shepherd."

A. *I shall not want for forgiveness.*

B. *I shall not want for spiritual vitality.* I shall not want for spiritual restoration. I shall not want for guidance.

C. *I shall not want for courage.*

D. *I shall not want for sustenance.*

E. *I shall not want for a home at the end of the way, for the Lord is my Shepherd.*

### Conclusion

Jesus Christ has a shepherd's heart, and he loves you. He has a shepherd's eye; he sees your needs. He has a shepherd's strength; he is able to deliver you. He has a shepherd's faithfulness; he will never leave you nor forsake you. He has a shepherd's tenderness; he will give you personal attention if you will trust him in your heart. If you have not yet trusted him, give your heart to Christ today. Jesus said, "Him that cometh unto me, I will in no wise cast out." So come to him today.

## WEDNESDAY EVENING, JUNE 10

***Title:*** The Necessity of Spiritual Growth

***Text:*** "But grow in grace, and in the knowledge of our Lord and Savior Jesus Christ. To him be glory both now and for ever" **(2 Peter 3:18)**.

### Introduction

It is a tragedy both on the physical level and the spiritual level for one to fail to grow or neglect to grow.

When we were children, most of us had the fear that we would never grow up to adulthood. We could hardly wait until maturity was a reality. We were sympathetic toward those who for one reason or another did not fully develop physically or mentally.

It is absolutely necessary that we follow a program that will make spiritual maturity possible. This is true for many reasons.

### I. A baby Christian cannot do the work of a mature Christian.

Even as a growing boy would be terribly frustrated if he thought that he would never be able to do the work of a man, the baby Christian would be upset if he did not have hope of someday being able to do the work of a full-grown Christian. Growth is absolutely essential if we would do the work God would have us to do and which in our heart we want to do.

### II. A baby Christian cannot understand the deep things of God.

Often parents will say to a child, "You are not old enough to understand." In many instances this is true. The same is true on the spiritual level. The writer of the book of Hebrews grieved over the spiritual immaturity of those to whom he was writing. He declared that their lack of growth made it impossible for them to understand the things he was trying to communicate to them. He rebuked them because, at a time when they should have had the capacity to be teachers, they needed to be taught themselves. Instead of being able to eat the strong meat of the Word of God, they were infants on a milk diet. He wrote, "We have much to say about this, but it is hard to explain because you are slow to learn. In fact, though by this time you ought to be teachers, you need someone to teach you the elementary truths of God's word all over again. You need milk, not solid food! Anyone who lives on milk, being still an infant, is not acquainted with the teaching about righteousness. But solid food is for the mature, who by constant use have trained themselves to distinguish good from evil" (5:11–14 NIV).

### III. A baby Christian who does not grow cannot escape discontentment and unhappiness.

Did you ever know a boy who was rejoicing that he was not growing toward manhood? How many girls have you known who wept when it was time to quit playing with dolls and to start looking at boys? Many of the conflicts that plague the fellowship of the church are the direct results of the wretched unhappiness of those who are still in the spiritual nursery when they ought to be mature enough to vote in the spiritual realm. Paul declared that one of the problems that disrupted the fellowship of the church at Corinth was the immaturity of many of the members: "And I, brethren, could not speak unto you as unto spiritual, but as unto carnal, even as unto babes in Christ. I have fed you with milk, and not with meat: for hitherto ye were not able to bear it, neither yet now are ye able. For ye are yet carnal: for whereas there is among you envying, and strife, and divisions, are ye not carnal, and walk as men?" (1 Cor. 3:1–3).

### IV. A baby Christian will receive only a baby's reward.

There are laws that forbid the employment of children until they reach an age where work will not be detrimental to their growth and education. When young people reach the age where they can become employees, they usually start out at the bottom of the wage ladder, for they have little or no experience and therefore probably do not merit a high wage.

Did it ever occur to you that if you never grow and develop so as to become an effective servant of the Lord, you will not receive greater responsibility and greater rewards? As training and preparation prepare one for a better income, so growth, training, and experience make possible a greater responsibility here and a greater reward in heaven for the children of God.

### Conclusion

Are you a babe in Christ? You do not have to remain a babe. Are you an adolescent who is in a process of growing toward spiritual maturity? Are you rejoicing in the privilege of being spiritually mature and effective in the service of the Lord? If so, do not rest upon your laurels, for you can continue to grow in the grace and knowledge of our Lord and Savior Jesus Christ.

## SUNDAY MORNING, JUNE 14

***Title:*** What Do We Owe Our Children?

***Text:*** "And these words, which I command thee this day, shall be in thine heart: And thou shalt teach them diligently unto thy children, and shalt talk of them when thou sittest in thine house, and when thou walkest by the way, and when thou liest down, and when thou risest up" **(Deut. 6:6–7)**.

***Scripture Reading:*** Colossians 3:16–21

***Hymns:*** "This Is My Father's World," Babcock

"Fairest Lord Jesus," Author Unknown

"Happy the Home When God Is There," Ware

***Offertory Prayer:*** Holy Father, in the beauty of summer we thank you for the sunlight of your love, which shines into our hearts through Jesus Christ. We offer to you the love of our hearts and the praise of our lips. We bring to you the strength of our hands. Accept these tithes and offerings as a portion of our very life, and bless them to the spreading of the gospel, to the healing of the sick, to the relief of the poor, and to the glory of your holy name. Amen.

### Introduction

The title "What Do We Owe Our Children?" may provoke a negative reaction from parents and at the same time arouse the curiosity of the young. It is normal for children to feel that their parents and, for that matter, the whole world, owe them something. The immature are always self-centered. They think in terms of what others can and should do for them. Wise parents will guide their children away from selfishness yet will realize that they really do owe a number of things to their children. There are certain obligations, responsibilities, or debts that are involved in the parent-child relationship.

### I. Children deserve to be desired.

It is a tragedy for a child to be born into a home where she is not wanted and where she is not fully accepted. A child will be much better able to withstand the shocks and deprivations of life if she has the inward assurance that she was desired and that she is fully accepted by her parents. It is tragic for a child to feel unwanted because she has overheard parents say that they wanted a child of the opposite sex.

**II. Children need the devotion of their parents.**

"As sunshine is to the plant, so love is to children." Affection and devotion are as necessary for the emotional well-being of children as food is essential for physical growth.

**III. Parents should disciple their children.**

In the Great Commission, Jesus commanded his disciples to so conduct themselves that in their traveling about they would make disciples. In no place do we have a greater obligation to be obedient than within the home. By both profession and practice, parents should conduct themselves and instruct their children so that at the earliest possible time their children can make a personal response to Jesus Christ as their Lord and Savior. This is a responsibility that must not be repudiated or shifted to someone else.

**IV. Children must have moral discipline.**

The word *discipline* is related to the word *disciple,* which means a learner. Discipline refers to control, educating. With reference to the family, it means the control and directing of the members of that group, especially children.

A. *The big problem is parental discipline.*
B. *The disciplining of children must be a partnership.*
C. *Discipline should be consistent.*
D. *Discipline in the home must be firm, but it need not be harsh.*

**V. Parents should dedicate their children.**

A. *Hannah dedicated Samuel unto the Lord (1 Sam. 1:28).*
B. *Parents brought their little children to Jesus for his blessings (Matt. 19:13–15).*
C. *While parents cannot make spiritual decisions for their children, they can release their parental claims upon those children by recognizing that God's claims come first.*

**VI. Parents should develop their children.**

"Train up a child in the way he should go: and when he is old, he will not depart from it" (Prov. 22:6).

A. *Mentally.*
B. *Socially.*
C. *Economically.*
D. *Spiritually.*

**VII. Parents should defend their children.**

A. *The world, the flesh, and the Devil will devour and destroy our children unless there are some built-in defenses that will make this impossible.* Parents can build in these defenses against destruction.

B. *First, we need to be somebody for God.* By virtue of our parenthood, we are appointed as the stewards and custodians of the spiritual welfare and destiny of our children. If we respond to God's love and grace and power, we can be proper parents and meet our obligations to our children.

C. *We must do something for God.* Life is made up of being and doing. We must be somebody if we want to do something significant.

The best defense that we can provide for our children is inward rather than external.

### Conclusion

We can meet our obligations and opportunities as parents through faith and faithfulness. We should put our faith in our Lord, and then we should follow him faithfully.

---

## SUNDAY EVENING, JUNE 14

***Title:*** The Pause That Refreshes

***Text:*** "He maketh me to lie down in green pastures: he leadeth me beside the still waters" **(Ps. 23:2)**.

### Introduction

In Psalm 23:2, our text for this evening, the sweet singer of Israel spiritualizes the relationship of sheep to their shepherd in such a manner as to sing an anthem of praise to the Lord.

It is almost impossible to get a hungry sheep to lie down in the midst of green grass. A hungry sheep will continue to eat. Even if it is forced to lie down, it will continue to nibble the grass that is nearby. In verse 2 we have the picture of a sheep that has been completely satisfied and perfectly filled. The psalmist is describing the spiritual nourishment that is provided for the child of God who is willing to wait upon God through the study of his Word and through prayer and communion and fellowship with God. We cannot find strength sufficient to walk through the valley of the shadow of death unless we are willing to take time to lie down in the green pastures of the divine Word and by the still waters of prayer.

### I. The Good Shepherd causes his sheep to lie down.

A. *The Good Shepherd teaches his sheep to lie down.* We find it difficult to take the pause that refreshes. All of us find it exceedingly difficult to lie down in the midst of the green pastures and beside the still waters that we might have our spiritual batteries recharged and the vital energies of life restored.

The complaint most frequently heard when visiting the sick concerns having to lie in bed: "I am so tired of doing nothing. I just cannot wait until I am up and around again." Quietness is a rare commodity in modern life.

We awaken to the beeping of an alarm clock. We drive to work to the tune of honking horns. We spend the day listening to the whirr of machinery or the electronic sounds of computers and cell phones. We return home to relax in the presence of a blaring television. This goes on day after endless day. The Lord says that people need to be quiet: "Be still, and know that I am God" (Ps. 46:10). One of the reasons why so many of us know so little about God is that we cannot hear God speak above the noise. God does not shout; he speaks in a still small voice.

The mother of a young child reveals her affection and devotion not by shouting at the infant but by speaking loving words while clasping the child to her bosom. When the psalmist says, "He maketh me to lie down in green pastures, he leadeth me beside the still waters," he is speaking about an experience of communion and fellowship in which the Good Shepherd reveals his love to the waiting sheep.

It is difficult to get sheep to lie down and be still. It is much easier to get them to do something. Members of the average church will work, fight, sing, teach, preach—do almost anything but lie down in green pastures beside the still waters and seek seasons of quiet and periods of retirement for secret communion with God.

B. *Most of our hymns emphasize activity.* They are militant, working, active hymns: "Work, for the Night Is Coming," "The Fight Is On," "Onward Christian Soldiers," "Stand Up, Stand Up for Jesus," "Fight the Good Fight," "Keep the Faith." Many times we march into battle for the Lord without the inward strength we need to win the conflict.

Perhaps all of us could wisely pray:

*Slow me down, Lord. Ease the pounding of my heart by the quieting of my mind. Steady my hurried pace with a vision of the eternal reach of time. Give me, amid the confusion of the day, the calmness of the everlasting hills. Break the tensions of my nerves and muscles with the soothing music of the singing streams that live in my memory. Help me to know that magical, restoring power of sleep. Teach me the art of taking minute vacations—of slowing down to look at a flower, to chat with a friend, to pat a dog, to read a few lines from a good book.*

*Remind me each day of the fable of the hare and the tortoise that I may know that the race is not always for the swift and that there is more to life than increasing speed. Let me look upward into the branches of the towering oak and know that it grew because it grew slowly and well. Slow me down, Lord, and inspire me to send my roots deep into the soil of life's enduring values, that I may grow toward the form of my greater destiny. Amen.*

—*Wilferd A. Peterson*

I have known husbands and wives who came to the place where they were ready to throw in the towel and quit. Tracing back to the root of their problems, we discovered that they had neglected this privilege that the psalmist has talked about in our text. I have known individuals who worked under pressure to the extent that they came to the breaking point.

They failed to recognize that it is a part of God's plan for us to lie down in the green pastures and rest beside the still waters.

## II. The Good Shepherd maketh me to lie down.

The casual reader of this psalm would get the impression that the good shepherd casually leads his sheep to the pastures and from the pastures to the place of rest. The actual picture presented in the original language is difficult to convey in English.

The word "maketh" is what Hebrew grammarians call the "hiphil frequentative imperfect." It refers to a repeated action. And it is a tense that involves forcible, compelling action. It declares that the shepherd makes the sheep to lie down. The shepherd knows that sheep cannot endure the heat of the day and the strain of the march across parts of the desert unless they have had a proper time to rest.

Our Good Shepherd knows that in the midst of the strain, the activity, and the restlessness of our lives, it is absolutely necessary for us to take periods of quiet and rest. Without such, it will be impossible for us to walk in the paths of righteousness continuously. The overworked watch spring snaps, and the overworked motor burns out.

A. *From the very beginning, it has been in the plan of God that people should rest as well as work.*

> *"Remember the sabbath day, to keep it holy. Six days shalt thou labour, and do all thy work: But the seventh day is the sabbath of the LORD thy God: in it thou shalt not do any work, thou, nor thy son, nor thy daughter, thy manservant, nor thy maidservant, nor thy cattle, nor thy stranger that is within thy gates: For in six days the LORD made heaven and earth, the sea, and all that in them is, and rested the seventh day: wherefore the LORD blessed the sabbath day, and hallowed it."* (Exod. 20:8–11)

B. *The New Testament does not lay down any rigid legal descriptions about the observance of the Lord's Day.* The Sabbath was one of God's mercies to people that they might be relieved from the pressures of life. The person who works seven days a week continuously is committing suicide. We must have a day of rest and worship.

C. *Sometimes we are forced to rest.* A visitor to the Middle East tells of visiting a Syrian shepherd. He noticed that in the morning the shepherd would take food out to a sick sheep in the sheepfold. Finally, he went out and noticed that this sheep had a broken leg. He inquired as to how it happened. The shepherd said, "I broke it." The visitor said, "What, you broke the leg of your sheep?" The shepherd replied, "Yes, I had to do it. This was a stubborn, disobedient, wayward sheep. Where we walk and graze, it is dangerous. I had to do this to the sheep to preserve his life, for sooner or later he would have plunged over a precipice, or he would have been devoured by a beast. He also had a tendency to lead other sheep astray, and so I had to break his leg to teach him that I love him and that I am going to take care of him and that he ought to listen to my voice."

### Conclusion

How often do you lie down in the green pastures and by the still waters? How often do you read God's Holy Word meditatively and prayerfully? How often do you go into the closet of prayer, both to present your requests and to listen for God's message for your heart? Have you cultivated and maintained regular public worship habits? These are the ways by which we can choose to lie down and receive the rest and relaxation that will enable us to do God's good will.

---

## WEDNESDAY EVENING, JUNE 17

***Title:*** The Foes of Spiritual Growth

***Text:*** "Wherefore laying aside all malice, and all guile, and hypocrisies, and envies, and all evil speakings. As newborn babes, desire the sincere milk of the word, that ye may grow thereby" **(1 Peter 2:1–2)**.

### Introduction

The words of our text imply that the laying aside of harmful attitudes and evil actions should be simultaneous with the process of spiritual growth. Spiritual growth, like growth in the plant and animal kingdoms, is always a struggle. Plants and animals do not find growth easy, for they must overcome enemies, adverse conditions, and diseases. If we are to grow toward spiritual maturity as the children of God, we must recognize the foes to that growth.

### I. We have an evil nature within that makes spiritual growth a real struggle.

Paul discusses the struggle between our new nature and our old nature (Rom. 7:18–25). He declares that it is only through Jesus Christ that the new nature can experience victory over the old fleshly nature (Rom. 7:24–25).

In writing to the Galatian Christians, Paul speaks of the antagonism that exists between the Holy Spirit and the lower nature of humans (Gal. 5:17). He declares that the only way we can grow spiritually and achieve victory in the Christian life is by walking in a conscious awareness of the presence of the Holy Spirit who has come to dwell within our hearts (v. 16). He describes the fruit of the indwelling Spirit as "love, joy, peace, longsuffering, gentleness, goodness, faith, meekness, [and] temperance" (vv. 22–23).

### II. The evil world about us is a foe to spiritual growth.

The world system, society as it exists contrary to the will of God, makes spiritual growth exceedingly difficult. There is nothing in the natural world or in organized society that is conducive to spiritual growth. We must not expect the world about us to encourage our efforts or to applaud our struggle toward spiritual maturity.

**III. The Devil is a foe of spiritual growth.**

Speaking from personal experience, Peter warns us against the attack of the Devil. We can rest assured that the Satan will do everything he possibly can to hinder us from spending time with the Word of God that we might nourish our souls. He will keep us busy in order to keep us away from the worship and fellowship of the church. He will promise us both profit and pleasure if we will do his bidding. He is determined to try to keep us in spiritual infancy.

**IV. Our natural tendency to neglect, postpone, and avoid struggle can be a foe to our spiritual growth.**

If children are to be healthy and to enjoy proper growth, they must have a proper diet and regular exercise. If students are to make steady progress toward academic excellence, they must do their homework day by day. If we are to make continual progress, we must not neglect that which is absolutely essential for health and success in the family of God.

**V. The poor example of others can be a foe to our growth.**

If a person has never had the opportunity to measure himself by a mature Christian, he may become content with the spiritual stature of a midget. Let us beware lest we make the fatal mistake of measuring ourselves by those who do not measure the full thirty-six inches to the yard. We need to allow Jesus Christ to be our ideal and to let the Sermon on the Mount be our scale for measuring spiritual maturity.

**Conclusion**

While there are many foes to growth, we can be assured that we can overcome these and make progress toward spiritual maturity if we will sincerely desire the milk of the Word and determine to walk in the light provided by him who is the Light of the World.

## SUNDAY MORNING, JUNE 21

***Title:*** Are You a Godly Father?

***Text:*** "Listen, my sons, to a father's instruction; pay attention and gain understanding" **(Prov. 4:1 NIV)**.

***Scripture Reading:*** Proverbs 4:1–14

***Hymns:*** "God, Our Father, We Adore Thee," Frazer

"A Child of the King," Buell

"Make Me a Channel of Blessing," Smyth

***Offertory Prayer:*** Our gracious and loving Father, help us to recognize all of the evidences of your continuing concern for us. Help us to see how graciously and bountifully you have blessed us with all spiritual blessings. Today we thank you for our daily bread and for all of the material blessings of life. We dedicate our tithes and offerings to your glory and to the advancement of your kingdom. Through Christ our Lord. Amen.

**Introduction**

Billy Graham said, "A good father is one of the most unsung, unpraised, and unnoticed, yet one of the most valuable assets in our society." God intended for fathers to do more than "bring home the bacon." From a biblical standpoint, the father is to be a provider, a protector, a priest, a guide, a teacher, and a disciplinarian.

Potentially, the father is the best possible teacher about God that a child can have, for the father is the human counterpart of God. When Jesus taught his disciples to pray, he said, "After this manner therefore pray ye: Our Father, which art in heaven" (Matt. 6:9). He taught his disciples that they were to think of the eternal God in terms of a wise, devoted, generous, forgiving father. The child who never has the privilege of knowing a loving father has a serious handicap when it comes to understanding the nature and character of God.

Dr. R. G. Lee tells the story of a father whose young son was stricken with diphtheria and placed in isolation in the hospital. It was necessary for the parents to wear a mask while visiting their son. The little boy inquired, "Why are you dressed that way?" The father replied, "I want to protect others, for you are very sick." After some hesitation, the little fellow replied, "Daddy, am I going to die?" The dad, who had taught his boy never to tell a lie, said, "That is what the doctor says." After a great deal of inward agony, the father put a question to his boy: "Son, you are not afraid, are you?" From the sick bed the little boy replied, "Daddy, if God is like you are, I won't be afraid."

The home is the most basic institution in our society. The responsibility for the spiritual stability and success of families is too much for mothers to bear alone. If we are to provide our children with godly fathers, we must consider certain essentials.

**I. Make certain that you give your heart and soul to Jesus Christ.**

A. *This is essential if you are to be the best possible husband.*

B. *This is essential if you are to be the best possible father.* There is no way by which you can practice the teachings of the Sermon on the Mount unless you have the Christ in your heart as Savior, Lord, and Teacher.

C. *Much time is required for the task of being a good husband and a good father.* It is not commendable for a man to hold down an extra job merely to provide more luxuries for his family. They need *him,* not the material assets he can provide.

**II. Be an example in all things.**

A Chinese proverb says, "One picture is worth a thousand words." Today it is recognized by all that visual education is one of the most effective methods of teaching. One good example may make a greater impact than a hundred lectures.

A father should seek to provide an atmosphere that is conducive to good character development in the lives of his children.

A. *Be an example in reverence and worship.*
B. *Be an example of truthfulness in speech.*
C. *Be an example of honesty in all legal and financial obligations.*
D. *Be an example in both attitudes and ambitions.*

### III. Provide proper discipline.

A. *Ephesians 6:4.*
B. *Proverbs 13:24.*
C. *Proverbs 23:13.*
D. *Proverbs 29:17.*

### Conclusion

In our quest to provide material benefits for our children, let us not be neglectful to provide that which is the greatest benefit of all—a godly father who loves Jesus Christ sincerely and steadfastly and who seeks to demonstrate this faith in every area of life.

Today make the decisions that are necessary for your children to have the invaluable benefit of a godly father.

---

## SUNDAY EVENING, JUNE 21

***Title:*** "He Leadeth Me"

***Text:*** "He leadeth me beside the still waters.... He leadeth me in the paths of righteousness for his name's sake" **(Ps. 23:2–3)**.

### Introduction

There are three thrilling truths in our text concerning the Good Shepherd's infallible leadership. First, the Good Shepherd is identified as heaven's infallible leader. Second, the Good Shepherd is declared to be a capable leader. Third, the Good Shepherd is of necessity a dependable leader.

### I. The Good Shepherd is our leader.

"I am the light of the world: he that followeth me shall not walk in darkness, but shall have the light of life" (John 8:12).

A. *Meditate for a moment on these words: "He leadeth me."*
   1. He is the Creator of the heavens and the earth.
   2. He is the one who upholds all things by his power.
   3. He is the unerring, unchangeable, all-seeing, all-knowing, all-powerful one, and "He leadeth me."

B. *The Good Shepherd leads rather than drives.* "He goeth before them, and the sheep follow him: for they know his voice" (John 10:4). The Good Shepherd will not ask his sheep to go anywhere that he himself does not go.

C. *How does the Good Shepherd lead?*
   1. He leads by example.
   2. He leads by the direction in the Gospels.
   3. He leads by the counsel of a Christian friend.
   4. He leads by the message of a lesson or sermon.
   5. He leads by the inward impulses of the Holy Spirit.

**II. The Good Shepherd is a capable leader.**

Our text tells us that the Good Shepherd is a trustworthy, capable, competent leader. David said, "He leadeth me in the paths of righteousness." The Good Shepherd helps us to get on the path of straightness that leads to the right destination.

A little book loved by children tells the story of a playful locomotive. The locomotive got along wonderfully as long as it stayed on the tracks, but one day it noticed the butterflies out in the fields smelling the flowers and decided that it too wanted to go out into the pasture to smell the flowers. When the little locomotive got out into the pasture, it mired down and was unable to roll like it did when it was on those two steel tracks.

The psalmist says that the Good Shepherd helps us to stay on the track so that we can get to the desired destination in life. The Good Shepherd will never lead us astray.

**III. The Good Shepherd is of necessity a trustworthy and dependable leader.**

For many years I thought that the Good Shepherd led his people in the paths of righteousness "for his name's sake"—that is, for the advancement of his kingdom. While this is true, this is not what the psalmist had in mind here. The thought that the Good Shepherd leads us for his own glory does not even begin to exhaust the meaning of the text.

A. *The good name of God is involved in the leadership that the Good Shepherd offers to his sheep.* The integrity of God is at stake. The very character of God is involved in where he leads those who trust him and obey him.

B. *The angels could not give worship and praise and respond with deep adoration to a God who would mislead his people.* By the quality of the leadership and by the destiny to which he has led, the Good Shepherd has maintained the respect and the appreciation of his followers throughout the ages.

C. *The Good Shepherd will never do anything that is inconsistent with divine integrity.* He will never lead his people down a dead-end street; he will never lead them to waste their energies or to make bad investments. Someone has casually said, "God maintains an excellent credit rating." He values the integrity of his name, for his name stands for his person and character.

D. *The Good Shepherd will lead you right in the here and now and lead you to the heavenly home in the hereafter if you are willing to trust him and follow him.*

### Conclusion

Who is your leader? Do you follow the crowd? Do you follow the whim of the moment? You would be wise to follow him who said, "He that followeth me shall not walk in darkness, but shall have the light of life" (John 8:12).

## WEDNESDAY EVENING, JUNE 24

***Title:*** The Joys of Spiritual Growth

***Text:*** "But grow in grace, and in the knowledge of our Lord and Savior Jesus Christ. To him be glory both now and for ever" **(2 Peter 3:18)**.

### Introduction

There are many joys for the Christian. We can praise God for the joy of having our sins forgiven. We can rejoice in the blessed assurance of divine sonship. We can face the future with optimism because of our assurance that death has been conquered and that the grave will have no final victory over us. Our hearts can overflow with joy as we contemplate the fact that the Christ is preparing for us a home at the end of our earthly journey. Along with these joys we can be grateful for the joy that we experience as we recognize the signs of our daily growth toward spiritual maturity.

### I. Our spiritual growth brings joy to the heavenly Father.

Earthly parents know an indescribable joy when they bring their firstborn home from the hospital. With feelings of delight, they look into the face of the baby whom they recognize as belonging to them. As the weeks go by, they observe the increase in the baby's weight and the improvement in coordination. It is indeed a happy day when the child recognizes a parent and responds with a smile. Indescribable would be the agony in the hearts of those parents if something were to happen to prevent the continuance of this growth. It is natural for parents to take delight in every stage of the progress of their children from childhood to adulthood.

The heavenly Father also is delighted to see his children grow. As children rejoice in the approval of their parents, even so the child of God can rejoice in the joy of the heavenly Father.

### II. Our spiritual growth makes possible the joy of effective service.

No one likes to be a loser. No one rejoices in being a failure. One of the greatest joys the human heart can know is that of significant achievement in any chosen field of endeavor. This is also true in the realm of the spirit. Paul challenged Timothy: "Study to shew thyself approved unto God, a workman that needeth not to be ashamed, rightly dividing the word of truth" (2 Tim. 2:15). Not only did Paul want Timothy to be an effective servant of the Lord, but he wanted him to experience the joy of being an effective interpreter of the Word of God to the hearts and lives of others.

### III. Our spiritual growth makes personal happiness possible.

Can you remember how, when you were a child, you measured yourself by your parent and were pleased to discover how you had grown? Can you remember a time as a student making a good grade on an exam and feeling pleased with your progress?

Spiritual growth could produce harmful pride as well as an attitude of self-righteousness if it were not for the fact that spiritual growth is made possible only by the presence of the Holy Spirit. The Holy Spirit knows not only how to challenge us in the upward struggle but also how to keep us humble in the midst of God's goodness toward us. It is altogether proper that as we experience the joy of progress in other areas of life we also know the joy of experiencing progress in our spiritual growth.

### IV. Christian growth makes the joy of an abundant harvest possible.

Paul encouraged the Galatian Christians toward spiritual growth and significant achievement with the promise of a sure reward if they did not faint and fall away before the harvest season: "And let us not be weary in well-doing: for in due season we shall reap, if we faint not" (Gal. 6:9).

Success along the way from day to day is in many respects its own reward. As students rejoice over success in their studies, children of God can rejoice day by day in the assurance that they are making spiritual progress. For students, graduation day will come, and they will receive the commendation of their professors and the trustees of the institution where they have studied. For children of God, the day of rewarding will come when it is possible for them to hear words of commendation from the heavenly Father. We should so grow and serve and live and labor that on that last great day each of us can hear the Father say, "Well done, thou good and faithful servant" (Matt. 25:21).

### Conclusion

We must not be content with mere membership in the family of God. We must not be satisfied with remaining in the nursery. By God's grace each of us can grow toward spiritual manhood and womanhood for the glory of God, for the good of others, and for the personal satisfaction the heavenly Father would like us to have.

## SUNDAY MORNING, JUNE 28

***Title:*** Are You a Good Citizen?

***Text:*** "Let every soul be subject unto the higher powers. For there is no power but of God: the powers that be are ordained of God" **(Rom. 13:1)**.

***Scripture Reading:*** Romans 13:1–7

***Hymns:*** "God of Our Fathers, Whose Almighty Hand," Roberts

"America the Beautiful," Bates

"My Country! 'Tis of Thee," Smith

***Offertory Prayer:*** Holy Father, we thank you for your bountiful blessings toward our native land. Help us to see the bounty of your provisions for our earthly welfare in its natural resources. We thank you for those who have lived and labored and even suffered that we might enjoy the liberties and the freedoms that are ours. Today as we bring our tithes and offerings, we use this tangible way to express to you our gratitude. It is our desire that all people everywhere hear the good news concerning Jesus who alone can deliver us from the tyranny of sin and grant us the freedom and liberty of becoming your sons. Amen.

### Introduction

As Christians we have dual citizenship. We are citizens of our native land, but we are also citizens of the kingdom of heaven. Paul challenged the disciples in Philippi to respond to the obligations of their heavenly citizenship while living as citizens of the Roman Empire. To be a poor citizen of one's native land is also to be a poor citizen of the kingdom of God. While the two are not to be equated, it should be recognized that as Christians we have a greater responsibility for being good citizens than we would have as non-Christians.

### I. The Christian and the state (Rom. 13:1–7).

A. *This passage does not deal with the whole problem of a Christian's relationship to the state.*

B. *Nothing is said concerning the form of government.* What is insisted is that state government is of God and that all who are under it should respect it.

C. *Nothing is said about political parties or the matter of voting for governmental leaders.* We are left to infer that Christians should use their influence to secure good rulers and to exclude bad ones.

D. *Our first allegiance is to God, and only if the state requires of us something that would violate our loyalty to God are we to resist (Acts 4:19–20; 5:29).*

### II. The duties of Christian citizenship.

A. *We should be subject to the state because it is a divine institution (Rom. 13:1).*

B. *Resistance to constituted authority is resistance to God, and it will be punished (Rom. 13:2).*

C. *Rulers, viewed ideally, are God's ministers appointed to encourage that which is good and to punish that which is evil (Rom. 13:3–4).*
D. *Only evildoers have anything to fear from properly constituted authority (Rom. 13:4).*
E. *We should be subject to the state, not only from fear of the consequences of disobedience, but because it is right to obey (Rom. 13:5).*
F. *Taxation is an illustration of the state's power to impose duties upon us and of our duty to submit (Rom. 13:6).*
G. *We should fulfill our many obligations to the state (Rom. 13:7).*

### III. Citizens of the kingdom of heaven (Phil. 3:20).

A. *Heavenly citizenship cannot be purchased or merited.* It is ours by spiritual birth into the family of God through faith in Jesus Christ.
B. *We should set our affections upon things above (Col. 3:1).*
C. *We should seek God's kingdom and his righteousness first (Matt. 6:33).*
D. *We should walk on earth worthy of our heavenly citizenship.*

### Conclusion

Because of our gratitude for God's blessings that have come to us in the past and because of our obligations to the future, let us rededicate ourselves to the task of being good citizens of our native land.

## SUNDAY EVENING, JUNE 28

***Title:*** "He Restoreth My Soul"

***Text:*** "He restoreth my soul; he leadeth me in the paths of righteousness for his name's sake" **(Ps. 23:3)**.

### Introduction

The words "He restoreth my soul" are among the most precious in Psalm 23. They speak to us of one of the most gracious works of all the works of the Good Shepherd. In this statement the psalmist is saying that the Shepherd brings the soul back again to a state of balance. Spiritual vim, vigor, and vitality are restored, and one is able to walk in the way of righteousness.

The psalmist speaks from experience when he says, "He restoreth my soul." David could remember the time when he had drifted far away from the guidance and leadership of the Good Shepherd. He could remember the days of grief and the days of sorrow and shame. Because of sin, he had been deprived of God's fellowship and of the joy of prayer. There had been no answers to David's prayers, and he felt utterly forsaken by God. This loneliness, this feeling of shame, led to confession and repentance and to restoration. David could say with the joy bells of heaven ringing in his heart, "He restoreth my soul."

**I. The tendency of human nature is to err and stray like sheep.**

The Good Shepherd's ministry of restoration is absolutely necessary. All of us have an innate tendency to go astray. We find it much easier to do those things that are wrong than things that are right. Were it not for the ministry of restoration in which the Lord comes again and again to restore us to the paths of straightness, all of us would utterly go astray.

A. *The Good Shepherd's ministry of restoration is continuous.* Over and over he comes to guide us, direct us, and help us.

B. *The Good Shepherd's ministry of restoration is gracious.* He does it because of his love and grace and not because of something within us that merits his mercy of restoration.

C. *The Good Shepherd's ministry of restoration is purposeful.* He does it that we might walk in the paths of righteousness for his name's sake.

1. When the soul grows sorrowful, the Good Shepherd revives and restores that soul by coming and bringing comfort, consolation, and help.
2. When the soul is sinful, the Good Shepherd comes and awakens within that soul an awareness of shame that there might be confession and cleansing so that the soul might be restored to the services of God.
3. When the soul is discouraged, the Good Shepherd comes to impart cheer and confidence and courage and help by giving to that individual an awareness of God's abiding presence.
4. When the soul is weak, the Good Shepherd comes to impart strength and power. Paul had moments of despondency and discouragement. There were times when he felt defeated, and yet in those moments there came to him an awareness of the presence of his Savior, and he was able to say, "I can do all things through Christ which strengtheneth me" (Phil. 4:13). Paul was convinced of his own spiritual and emotional weakness, but, at the same time, he was convinced of his adequacy and sufficiency with the help of the Lord.
5. When the soul wanders away, the Good Shepherd comes seeking to restore the wayward sheep to the paths of righteousness.

Every person present today is present because of the ministry of restoration of our Savior. We certainly would have gone astray and we would not be here today if the Good Shepherd had not come to us again and again, restoring us to the place of service, the place of safety, satisfaction, and happiness. With David, we should all praise him, glorify him, and give him the credit for every spiritual achievement and every degree of success we have attained.

Jonah the prophet was disobedient and had an unchristian spirit toward the unregenerate world. But after he had been restored to the place of service, he said, "Salvation is of the Lord" (Jonah 2:9). There is absolutely no place for boastfulness in the lives of Christians concerning their own achievements and their own attainments in the Christian life.

After Peter had denied the Lord three times, the Bible says, "Jesus turned and looked at Peter" (Luke 22:61). There was no scorn or attitude of "I told you so." There was something in that look that literally broke the heart of Peter, and he went out and wept bitterly. There was love, affection, and devotion in the look of the Savior that day at a wayward, disobedient, Christ-denying disciple. Later on, the resurrected Christ sent a special message through the angel and the women to Peter (Mark 16:7).

On the first Easter, Jesus appeared to Peter privately and secretly in order that Peter might confess his sins (Luke 24:34). Later, in the presence of the apostles, Jesus gave Peter a threefold opportunity to say, "I love you" (John 21:15–17). In this manner he was given an opportunity to forever erase his threefold denial of the Master.

If you have drifted, the Good Shepherd is seeking you today. If you have lost the joy of your salvation, he is seeking you today. If there is a shadow cast across your fellowship with God or if you have been living a life of disobedience, a life of inactivity, a life of unhappiness, or a life of failure, the Good Shepherd is seeking you today.

**II. The sources of spiritual decline.**

The sources of spiritual decline are not mentioned in the text. I have heard people say, "I just do not know why I drifted." It is our nature to drift. We have a sinful nature that will lead us astray. We need to recognize this truth about ourselves. Only through the grace of the Good Shepherd, who continually restores us, are we here today.

A. *Sheep have no sense of direction.* If a dog, a cat, or a horse gets lost, it can usually find its way back home, for those animals seemingly have a built-in compass. Such is not the case with sheep. It is our nature to drift into sin and to go deeper and deeper into sin unless the Good Shepherd comes and by one means or another draws us back to the place of safety and service.

B. *Sheep have very poor eyes.* Sheep cannot see farther than about fifteen yards. They do not select a direction by sight. Instead, they follow the sound of a familiar voice. Jesus said, "My sheep hear my voice, and I know them, and they follow me" (John 10:27). Concerning the sheep and their shepherd, Jesus said, "He goeth before them, and the sheep follow him: for they know his voice. And a stranger will they not follow, but will flee from him: for they know not the voice of strangers" (John 10:4–5). Sheep have to stay close to the shepherd to hear his voice. They follow the sound of his voice rather than the vision of their eyes.

Spend some time meditating on the fact that it is much safer, wiser, and practical to follow the voice of the Good Shepherd as he speaks to our hearts than it is to try to plan and to foresee the path that we should follow in the distant future. When the child of God falls into deep sin, it is because he has neglected or refused to heed the loving voice of the Good Shepherd.

C. *A number of things can cause us to drift away from the Shepherd.*
   1. The neglect of spiritual nourishment through a daily devotional study of the Word of God inevitably leads to a famished soul. Many suffer from spiritual malnutrition due to an inadequate spiritual diet. Neglect of the Word of God has caused a loss of spiritual vim, vigor, and vitality. Many of us are spiritually anemic due to the absence of the iron of God's truth in our daily diet.
   2. Unconfessed and unforsaken sin will cause the sheep to drift farther and farther away from God. Our first natural impulse is to hide, conceal, deny, or explain away our sins. It is always easy to find an excuse, to blame someone else. The Bible says, "The ways of a man are clean in his own eyes" (Prov. 16:2). You can always find a reason why you did what you did if you want to. The wise thing to do is to be honest with yourself and say, "I have sinned. May God forgive me and give me grace to forsake it." If we neglect to confess and forsake sin, it will cast a shadow across our fellowship with God.
   3. Companionship with the pleasure-loving crowd of the world will lead ultimately to the compromise of moral principles and moral ideals. This will lead people to do things they know they ought not to do.
   4. The neglect of known duties will cause people to decline spiritually, to drift away and be in need of spiritual restoration. The tragedy is that many people have drifted away and are in desperate need of spiritual restoration, yet they do not recognize this need.

### III. The symptoms of spiritual decline.

For every illness there are always certain symptoms in evidence. When people are spiritually ill and have drifted away from the Lord, there are a number of symptoms by which we can detect their spiritual condition.

A. *A critical, complaining attitude is an indication that there is something wrong in a person's heart and life.* When you are unhappy with yourself, you are usually unhappy with everyone else. When you get to the place where you can see only that which is wrong in others, this indicates that there is something seriously wrong with you. You stand in need of being restored through repentance and confession and rededication to the will of God. A person who is close to God is going to see the best in others rather than the worst.

B. *An indifferent spirit that leads to inactivity is a symptom of spiritual illness.*

C. *A lack of awareness of the lostness of lost people indicates that a person is seriously ill spiritually.* How long has it been since you have shown interest in an unsaved friend? How long has it been since you have tried to persuade someone to forsake the life of no faith and to trust Christ as his or her own Savior?

**IV. The methods of restoration.**

The Good Shepherd uses many different factors in his ministry of restoration. Moffatt translates our text in this manner. "He revives life in me." Have you ever neglected a flower or plant at home? It became limp and wilted, but probably in a matter of hours after you supplied water, it was growing beautifully again. That is what God does to the soul.

A. *The Good Shepherd sent a prophet named Nathan to David not to criticize but to restore.*

B. *The Good Shepherd sent an angel with a special word to Peter not to criticize but to restore.*

C. *Sometimes the Good Shepherd uses chastisement.* He may send a storm into your life as he did with Jonah.

D. *The Good Shepherd may use the word of a friend, the chorus of a long-forgotten hymn, a sentence or paragraph from a book, the memory of devout parents, the visit of a Sunday school teacher, or a word of encouragement from one of the deacons in the church.*

E. *The Good Shepherd can use the hunger for a lost joy or the call of the divine Spirit.* He can use anything or everything to draw you back to the place of safety, service, and spiritual satisfaction.

**Conclusion**

Jesus told the parable of the lost son, which can also be seen as the parable of the loving father. The father remained at home and loved his wayward son more than he loved his own life. He waited eagerly and prayerfully for the return of his wayward son. When his son did return, he rejoiced greatly and hosted a lavish banquet for him.

If you have drifted far away from the Father in heaven, I challenge you to let the Lord restore you. I challenge you to rededicate your heart and life and begin again where you left off. Do what the Lord wants you to do. He will bless you and help you. He will use you to be a blessing to others.

## Suggested Preaching Program for

# JULY

## ■ Sunday Mornings

Continue the series called "Practical, Probing Questions for Serious Consideration."

## ■ Sunday Evenings

Continue the series on Psalm 23.

## ■ Wednesday Evenings

"Discovering and Removing the Obstacles to Effective Prayer" is the theme for Wednesday evenings.

---

## WEDNESDAY EVENING, JULY 1

***Title:*** The Hindrance of Idolatry

***Text:*** "Son of man, these men have set up their idols in their heart, and put the stumbling block of their iniquity before their face: should I be inquired of at all by them?" **(Ezek. 14:3)**.

### Introduction

In the text God presents the question to the prophet Ezekiel concerning some of the elders of Israel who had been approaching the throne of grace in prayer. God inquires concerning the right of these men to have entrance to and an audience in the throne room of prayer. A negative reply is the only proper answer.

It could be that idolatry is that which has prevented you from receiving an answer to the request you have presented before the throne of God's grace in prayer.

Do I hear you raise the questions, "What is idolatry? Who is an idolater?"

You may assume that because you do not bow down before some heathen shrine or offer sacrifices on the altar of a hideous image that there is no possibility of your being an idolater. But an idol is anything that usurps the place that belongs to God in a person's heart. To yield the throne of one's heart to something or someone other than God is to be guilty of breaking both the first and the second of the commandments given to Moses. It was primarily idolatry that caused the people of Ezekiel's day to experience the judgment of God that led to their captivity in Babylon. They still were blind to their own sin of idolatry, and consequently they were deprived of the privilege of productive communication with God in prayer.

### I. Have you made an idol out of your marriage companion?

It must be admitted that there are men who put forth more effort to please their wives than they do to please God. There are women who are more eager to have the approval of their husbands than they are to have God's approval. If God has the place that belongs to him, the marriage will be much happier than it can possibly be when either party has usurped the place that belongs only to God.

### II. Have you made an idol out of success?

The inward desire to achieve success is commendable. Something is radically wrong with the person who has no desire for significant achievement. But the subtle temptation to achieve success at any cost can lead into idolatry without our recognizing it.

### III. Have you made an idol out of love of comfort?

All of us enjoy a soft chair. We must admit that we prefer a cushion to a cross. The love of comfort and ease can prevent us from studying and training for effectiveness in service and may even prevent us from serving God at all.

Does the love of comfort and leisure keep you away from the house of worship on the Lord's Day?

### IV. Have you made an idol out of yourself?

Is self on the throne, or does Christ occupy the throne? If Christ is not on the throne, then self has usurped the place that belongs to God.

### Conclusion

Only when we treat God as God can we pray effectively. God is no errand boy. To pray effectively, we must pray, "Thy kingdom come. Thy will be done in earth, as it is in heaven" (Matt. 6:10), rather than, "My kingdom come, my will be done."

---

## SUNDAY MORNING, JULY 5

***Title:*** Are You at Your Post of Duty?

***Text:*** "Son of man, I have made thee a watchman unto the house of Israel: therefore hear the word at my mouth, and give them warning from me" **(Ezek. 3:17)**.

***Scripture Reading:*** Ezekiel 3:10–19

***Hymns:*** "Come, Thou Almighty King," Anonymous

"Be Ye Doers of the Word," Linthicum

"Onward Christian Soldiers," Baring-Gould

***Offertory Prayer:*** Holy Father, we thank you today for the gift of faith that makes it possible for us to respond to you in spirit and in truth. We thank you for the fellowship that we enjoy with you from day to day. We are grateful that our hearts hunger for you and that in worship we find that which meets the deepest need of life. As we have received from you, even so today we bring to you our tithes and offerings in a spirit of worship that indicates our hope and our desire to give ourselves completely to you and to your will for us. Bless these gifts to the work of your kingdom. Through Jesus Christ our Lord. Amen.

## Introduction

People in America and in Western Europe can sleep soundly at night in the assurance that others stand at the post of duty constantly watching the skies lest an attack be made on their homeland. Our security in the Western hemisphere depends largely on their being faithful at their post of duty.

God placed Ezekiel in charge of a spiritual radar station among the Jewish exiles who had been carried into Babylon as the captives of Nebuchadnezzar. As a watchman over the house of Israel, he was to fill a spiritual role that had its counterpart in the defense of the city or the nation.

In the ancient world, people built high, thick walls around their cities to protect themselves from enemy attack. Usually the city, or at least the portion of it that was the refuge in time of trouble, was located on the highest part of a hill or mountain. Watchtowers were built on strategic points on the wall, and watchmen were stationed in these towers to keep the entire countryside under surveillance. A watchman was charged to watch and listen and blow a blast on the trumpet to warn the people when there was any evidence of danger. To be derelict in this duty was to experience severe condemnation from superiors.

There are some striking similarities between God's commission to Ezekiel and our Lord's commission to his disciples. Christian witnessing to the unsaved is not optional; it is obligatory upon every follower of Jesus Christ.

Jesus spoke words to his disciples that are as binding upon us today as they were on the day when they fell from his lips. "Then said Jesus to them again, Peace be unto you: as my Father hath sent me, even so send I you. And when he had said this, he breathed on them, and saith unto them, Receive ye the Holy Ghost; Whose soever sins ye remit, they are remitted unto them; and whose soever sins ye retain, they are retained" (John 20:21–23). As each Christian bears a witness to the unsaved, he or she becomes the means whereby that one can experience the forgiveness of sin. For us to be careless or indifferent or silent is like a watchman in Ezekiel's day ignoring the presence of danger to his country.

These words of the Christ to Christian watchmen are universal in application. They continue to be binding upon us.

## I. The watchman must watch.

We must be observant.

A. *We must see ourselves as saved persons.*

B. *We must see ourselves as servants of God.*

C. *We must see the sad condition of unbelievers.*

1. They are unsaved sinners.
2. They are spiritually dead.
3. They are completely helpless to save themselves.
4. They are the objects of God's loving concern. "Say unto them, As I live, saith the LORD God, I have no pleasure in the death of the wicked; but that the wicked turn from his way and live: turn ye, turn ye from your evil ways; for why will ye die, O house of Israel?" (Ezek. 33:11).

### II. The Christian watchman must listen (Ezek. 3:10–11).

A. *We must listen to the Word of God.*
B. *We must listen to the Holy Spirit who dwells within.*
C. *We must listen to the requests for spiritual testimony and information that come from hungry hearts.*

### III. The Christian watchman must speak.

A. *We can speak by the life that we live, but our actions alone are not enough.*
B. *We can speak by deeds of mercy, but these alone are not enough.*
C. *We can speak by our loyalty to the church, but this alone is not enough.*
D. *We must actually communicate the message of God's love for sinners, for God has no other means of saving the unsaved.*

### IV. Where is your post of duty?

A. *Your post of duty is where you are.*
   1. At home.
   2. In business.
   3. In recreation.
   4. In school.

B. *Your post of duty is where you ought to be.*
   1. Where God's love leads.
   2. Where human need is present.

### Conclusion

Have we faced up to the seriousness of our responsibility for the spiritual welfare of others? Are we aware that others can be ushered into eternity unprepared to meet God and that our neglect to witness could be one of the contributing factors to that unpreparedness? It is too fearful to contemplate that we might have the blood of a soul upon our hands (Ezek. 3:18).

Instead of being motivated out of a sense of duty, the joy of leading someone to know Jesus Christ should be a continuing challenge that will cause us to do our best to persuade others to trust Christ.

## SUNDAY EVENING, JULY 5

***Title:*** "I Will Fear No Evil"

***Text:*** "Yea, though I walk through the valley of the shadow of death, I will fear no evil: for thou art with me; thy rod and thy staff they comfort me" **(Ps. 23:4)**.

### Introduction

Let us go once again to the green pastures of Psalm 23. I encourage you to lie down by the still waters, feast your soul on the Bread of Life, drink from the fountain of living waters, have your soul restored, be instructed in the paths of righteousness, and have your fears dissolved, that you might face life courageously and boldly, confident that the Good Shepherd will abide with you as he did with David in ages gone by.

The psalmist pays tribute to the fact that the shepherd ministers to the sheep throughout their entire lives. He assists with the birth of lambs and ministers to the young. He provides for them and protects and guides them throughout their entire lifetimes. The prophet Isaiah had this in mind when he spoke concerning the ministry of the Good Shepherd: "He shall feed his flock like a shepherd: he shall gather the lambs with his arms, and carry them in his bosom, and shall gently lead those that are with young" (Isa. 40:11).

The totality of life is referred to in this psalm. If you study Psalm 23, you will find that the shepherd leads his sheep out in the early morning into the pastures. During the heat of the day, he carries them to a place of rest, relaxation, and refreshment and causes them to lie down. He then leads them into the paths of righteousness. Finally, he leads them through the dark, gloomy canyons that lead to the safety of the sheepfold at the other end of the road.

### I. The dark valley of danger in life.

The next verse tells us that occasionally the straight and narrow path of righteousness leads through a dark, gloomy, discouraging, and fearful valley. The psalmist says, "Yea, though I walk through the valley of the shadow of death, I will fear no evil."

There are some who labor under the mistaken impression that if you live a good Christian life; go to church on Sunday; treat your spouse, family, and neighbors right; and fear God and try to keep his commandments, all of life will be beautiful, a happy flower garden with one delight after another—no discouragement, no disease, no sorrow, no grief, no sadness, no failures.

This is a rather romantic, unrealistic, and immature attitude toward life. It does not square with the facts. Nowhere in all of God's Book are we promised that if we will live a good life everything will be rosy and happy, joyful and successful. Over and over again we find promises in God's Word to the effect that if we seriously try to walk in the paths of righteousness, our Lord will be with us throughout all of our days to provide us the inward strength that we need to face the difficulties, responsibilities, and burdens of life.

Psalm 23, particularly verse 4, has been so associated with death in the minds of many people that they have lost the joyful, triumphant, victorious note that was in the heart of the psalmist when he recorded, by inspiration, these precious words. We have done the same thing to a number of great hymns. "Near to the Heart of God" is a joyful, beautiful message in song. We have used it at funerals to the extent that we have made a dirge out of it. This is tragic. "Rock of Ages" is a thrilling, triumphant hymn of security and joy because of the strength of our Savior. Some people place a shroud on their spirit when they sing it.

**II. A bold confession of faith.**

The psalmist, in this passage of Scripture, is not gloomy and sad and morbid; he is filled with optimism, faith, and courage. He shouts, "Yea, though I walk through the valley of the shadow of death, I will fear no evil." It is as if he were saying, "I have lain with him in green pastures. I have walked with him in the paths of righteousness. I have experienced restoration of the vital energies of life. As I face the future, I am confident and courageous that, come what may, I will be able to meet it."

The psalmist gives us a bold, triumphant confession of faith based on experience. When he was just a boy caring for his sheep, a lion attacked one of his sheep. David was a good shepherd, and he did not flee as a hireling would. Nor was he overcome with fright. His love for the lamb caused him to come to the rescue, and with the help of God, he was able to kill the lion. Later David killed a bear that attacked his flock. And as he grew older and his faith developed even more, he was courageous enough to face the giant Goliath in the name of his God. David had tested God and proved him. He was speaking from experience, and he was confident that he would be able to face the future with adequate resources at his disposal. We have no need to be overcome with fright if we will stay close to the Shepherd.

The Good Shepherd has been with every person here who has exercised faith in the promises of God. Those who have stayed close to the Good Shepherd can bear joyful testimony that he was with them in their time of great need. The psalmist is not here saying that he is going to assume a nonchalant, careless attitude toward whatever the future might hold. He is not saying that there will be no uncertainty, but he is saying that he is confident that with the help of God, he will be adequate for any emergency.

**III. A great tribute of praise.**

Not only does the psalmist give us this confession of faith based on experience, but he speaks with a shout of praise. He is giving God the credit, the glory, the praise for all that he has been able to achieve in life. He is praising God not only for what he has done but for what he is persuaded God will do in the future.

Someone has said, "Today is the tomorrow that we worried about yesterday." Most of the things that we worry about never happen. We should face the future with the confidence that he who holds the future will be there to meet our deepest need when that time comes.

I do not like to bring bad news to anyone, but all of us should be realistic enough to know that at some point we will come to a dark, gloomy, dangerous valley through which we will have to walk. Unless we have had experience with the Good Shepherd on the sunny days of life, we may be overcome with fright and uncertainty when we come to the dark valleys.

### IV. A personal challenge to others.

The psalmist speaks with the voice of commendation.

A. *He is encouraging each of us to let the Good Shepherd become our Shepherd.*

B. *He is encouraging each of us to follow the Shepherd closely.*

C. *He would insist that we develop such an intimate relationship and fellowship with the Good Shepherd that we will be able to face the dark and dangerous periods of life with courage and confidence.*

A mother was to have serious surgery. She had three daughters at home, the eldest about sixteen. The welfare of those daughters weighed heavily on her heart. She had hoped that her surgery might be delayed until her daughters were older. Finally, it was necessary that she have the surgery. After entering the hospital, she said to her family, "It is going to be all right." She reached over to pick up a magazine from a table. In the center of the page, blocked in with heavy lines, were the words: "Yea, though I walk through the valley of the shadow of death, I will fear no evil." The mother read that verse aloud and then placed the magazine back on the table and closed her eyes calmly and courageously.

The psalmist is not talking about death; he is talking about the shadow of death, the valley, some gloomy period in life. Death for a Christian is not a dark valley; it is a door that opens to the sunny hills of God.

A woman called her pastor one day and told him about a neighbor who was dying. She said, "She is frightened. She knows that she is going to die, and she is afraid to die. Could you come?" He went to the woman's home and found that when she moved to the city she had left her church membership back in her home town. She had drifted along, and her faith was not as strong as it could have been. He sought to restore her faith and her courage. He began to quote verses of Scripture. Finally, as he quoted, "The Lord is my shepherd, I shall not want," he noticed her lips beginning to move. She was repeating it silently and slowly with him. He quoted the entire psalm, and her faith and courage came back. She was happy and contented and relieved, and throughout the afternoon again and again she expressed her confidence and her joy over the fact that she was now ready to meet her Savior. Three days later the pastor conducted her funeral service.

### Conclusion

Do you know the Good Shepherd as your Savior? Are you following him closely? If you are, when you come to the dangerous, gloomy period of life, you will find him there as close as your breath. I challenge you today to decide to follow him closely and to trust him implicitly.

## WEDNESDAY EVENING, JULY 8

***Title:*** The Hindrance of Unconfessed and Unforsaken Sin

***Text:*** "Behold, the LORD's hand is not shortened, that it cannot save; neither his ear heavy, that it cannot hear: But your iniquities have separated between you and your God, and your sins have hid his face from you, that he will not hear" (Isa. 59:1–2).

### Introduction

During the days of Isaiah, the people offered many prayers to God. They were greatly disappointed when they did not receive the desired answers. As they analyzed the reason for their failure to receive from God, someone finally arrived at the conclusion that possibly God's arms were short so that he could no longer save, and his ears were deaf so that he could no longer hear their prayers.

Through the prophet Isaiah, God sought to correct this mistaken conclusion. He declared that he was not deaf nor blind nor weak as far as answering their prayers was concerned. He informed them that it was the presence of unconfessed and unforsaken sins in their lives that hindered them from receiving that for which they had prayed.

### I. The presence of sin in the heart and life always hinders us from receiving God's best gifts.

The psalmist declared, "If I regard iniquity in my heart, the LORD will not hear me" (Ps. 66:18). For God to continue to bestow his best gifts upon those who persist in sin would be both to condone and encourage their continuance in such. Sometimes our prayers receive a negative response, which is God's means of encouraging us to forsake that which is destructive to us and harmful to others. Is there sin in your life that needs to be recognized, confessed, and forsaken?

### II. Are you guilty of sins of commission—repeatedly (Isa. 1:16–18)?

### III. What are your sins of omission that are impoverishing your life as well as the lives of others (James 4:17)?

### IV. Are there sins of disposition that cause you to be in disfavor with God as well as with others (2 Cor. 7:1)?

### Conclusion

One of the greatest truths of the Bible concerns forgiveness and cleansing from sin (1 John 1:9). Claim the promises of this verse for your own heart. Let God forgive you. After God has forgiven you, be sure and forgive yourself and face the future with a clean heart.

## SUNDAY MORNING, JULY 12

***Title:*** If Life Caves In, What Then?

***Text:*** "I can do all things through Christ which strengtheneth me" **(Phil. 4:13)**.

***Scripture Reading:*** Matthew 7:24–27

***Hymns:*** "How Firm a Foundation," Keith
"God Will Take Care of You," Martin
"Wonderful, Wonderful Jesus," Russell

***Offertory Prayer:*** Holy Father, this is a day that you have made. We will rejoice and be glad in it. We recognize your goodness toward us, and gratitude rises up within our hearts and expresses itself not only through the praise of our lips but also through the actions and services that our hands can render. Accept our tithes and offerings as expressions of our love and as a symbol of our desire to be completely yours. As the Christ gave himself for us, so help us to give ourselves to your service. In Christ's name. Amen.

### Introduction

By using the title "If Life Caves In, What Then?" I am not encouraging you to believe that life is going to cave in on you. Many people live in terror of what may happen, and that is heathenish. They waste a great deal of energy worrying about that which is not going to happen. Someone has said, "Today is the tomorrow that we worried about yesterday."

Some of us have made such an idol out of happiness that we do not know how to deal with unhappiness. Occasionally it does seem that life is caving in on us.

I have seen life cave in on many people. When a young man's fiancée was killed in an automobile accident, it seemed to him that life had caved in. A couple's youngest son greatly disappointed them with his irresponsible attitudes and actions, which led to the accidental death of one of his classmates. For them, life had caved in. A young wife was injured in a diving accident and was almost totally paralyzed. In addition to this tragedy, her husband forsook her and their child. For her, life caved in. A fifty-year-old man lost his job and because of his age was unable to get another job to support his family. For him, life had caved in. A young soldier, while rescuing a wounded buddy, was horribly and irreparably disfigured. In spite of the best efforts of the plastic surgeons, they could not restore a nose and ears and fingers that had been burned away in an explosion. For him, life had caved in.

What will you do when death comes to take away your dear and beloved companion? How would you react if you were to find yourself suffering the heartbreak of knowing that your companion had been unfaithful to the marriage vows? If your children bring heartaches, disappointments, and possibly disgrace, how will you pick up the pieces?

We have often heard it said that it is too late to buy insurance after the house has burned down. As the farmer said to his boy, it is too late to close the gate after the cattle are out and gone. And so we need to make some preparation in case life should cave in upon us.

Each of us should face up to the fact that we can individually be responsible for causing life to cave in on ourselves. Many of the tragedies and troubles that plague us are but the consequences of errors in our judgment or faulty choices that we made without considering the destiny to which the choice would lead. Today we will concentrate on preparing for troubles that may come over which we have no control.

**I. Face life with real faith.**

Paul, the author of our text, declared, "I can do all things through Christ which strengtheneth me." He believed and demonstrated that a man can be victorious over the circumstances that befall him provided he faces life with a courageous and steadfast faith. We need to have a faith that will sustain us and strengthen us in the time of crisis. We should not be satisfied with a faith that needs to be defended and propped up. A complete faith is a faith that recognizes that genuine piety does not provide us with an immunity against pain and sorrow. We must recognize that life may cave in on us even if we are some of the very best of God's children.

A. *We must have faith to believe that God is a good God and that all of his purposes toward us are purposes of love.* "He that spared not his own Son, but delivered him up for us all, how shall he not with him also freely give us all things?" (Rom. 8:32). The Devil will win his victory over us when life caves in if he can cause us to believe that God is not a good God. He has sought to deceive people in this manner since the beginning of human history (Gen. 3:4–5). We must believe that God is a good God in spite of the fact that at times he appears otherwise. God is not our enemy. He wants to shower upon us the abundance of heavenly love.

B. *We must have faith to believe that God is at work for our good in all things that happen (Rom. 8:28).* Many have misquoted and misunderstood this verse. Some have interpreted it to say, "Everything happens for the best." That just is not so. Many things happen for the worst, for they shatter and wreck and ruin and bring awful agony into human lives. There are others who interpret this verse to say, "Whatever happens is the will of God," and this is not so. This would mean that God is responsible for evil, and God is not responsible for evil. We should not blame him for the fact that life caves in on us at times.

This verse expresses the faith of the apostle to the effect that God will be at work in everything that happens to those who love him in order to rescue and to restore and to bring every possible good out of that which appears to be a complete disaster. We can count on God to help us with our burdens, our problems, our questions, and our sufferings. Someone has jokingly said, "If life hands you a lemon, make lemonade." The apostle is declaring that if life hands you a lemon, then God will be there to help you make the best lemonade that can possibly be made!

C. *We must have faith to believe that God will not permit impossible burdens to come upon us (1 Cor. 10:13).* The Bible provides a continuing testimony that God will be with us to provide us with strength and wisdom and grace that are sufficient to bear the burdens of life. Nowhere in the Bible are we promised complete immunity from trouble if we have faith. Instead, we are promised the strength of God's presence through which we can be adequate. Paul believed that God would provide for all of our needs through Jesus Christ (Phil. 4:19).

D. *We must have faith to believe that there may be a redemptive purpose in some of our sufferings.* Paul spoke of a thorn in the flesh that was a continuing source of agony to him. With all his heart he prayed at least three times for the removal of this thorn (2 Cor. 12:7–8). As he struggled he discovered that there was a benevolent purpose behind this hardship (2 Cor. 12:9).

It is altogether proper that we seek to learn everything possible through the experiences that come to us. Hosea is a case in point. His contribution to the divine revelation came through the wound that was inflicted upon his heart by the moral and spiritual breakdown of his wife.

Only by means of a genuine faith in the greatness of God can we hope to overcome the world and be triumphant even amid tragedy.

## II. Avoid faulty ways of facing tragedy.

Some unknown writer has penned the following poem:

*Don't talk about your troubles*
*And tell them o'er and o'er,*
*The world will think you like 'em,*
*And proceed to give you more.*

Sometimes tragedy can be compounded by the fact that we use faulty methods of dealing with the tragedies that befall us. There are certain ways of facing tragedy that need to be avoided.

A. *Feelings of guilt and self-condemnation overwhelm some people when tragedy comes.* In many instances we have to face the fact that we are at least partially responsible for life caving in on us. To accept proper responsibility is a wholesome thing, but we must not permit feelings of guilt and self-condemnation to destroy us.

It is impossible to change or even to alter the events of yesterday. We can only deal with the consequences of yesterday. Instead of cultivating our sense of guilt with continuous self-condemnation, we need to enter into the forgiveness of God. Also, we need to forgive ourselves. It is neither Christian nor logical to continue to condemn oneself for past mistakes.

B. *We must not react to tragedy with bitter resentment and hatred.* It is easy to hate and to hold resentment toward someone who has been responsible for tragedy or disappointment in our lives. We need to recognize that hate is a corrosive force; it is a malignant thing that distresses the heart if we permit it to remain in our lives.

C. *It is normal to experience some self-pity and moods of depression when tragedy strikes.* All of us have felt sorry for ourselves at times. All of us will feel sorry for ourselves at some future time, but we need to recognize that this is not the best way to deal with tragedy. We must gain the victory over self-pity and depression.

D. *Some resort to an artificial escape from tragedy through alcohol or drugs.* We need to be on guard lest our emotions deceive us. Instead of giving way to some faulty way of facing tragedies, we need to look to God. The psalmist said, "I will lift up mine eyes unto the hills, from whence cometh my help. My help cometh from the Lord, which made heaven and earth" (Ps. 121:1–2).

## III. Grow a faith that can sustain you.

A. *We must become doers of the Word as well as bearers of the Word (Matt. 7:24–27).* Living the life of faith provides one with inward resources that are adequate for the time of testing.

B. *We should face the daily trials of life with joy (James 1:2).* This kind of joy is possible only to one who has faith to believe that God is present in any circumstance to provide an opportunity for growth and service.

C. *Face your problems on your knees (James 1:5).* Most of us are short on wisdom, so James encourages us to ask God for divine insight and understanding. Wisdom is available to those who trust God and ask for his guidance.

D. *Enjoy God's blessings day by day in the present.* Cultivate an attitude of gratitude. Deliberately look for that which can bring joy and thanksgiving into the heart.

E. *Live life one day at a time.* Do not worry about tomorrow. The sparrows could preach us a powerful sermon at this point. They work and do not worry. Life may never cave in on you, so do not worry about what may not happen.

## Conclusion

The secret key to the door of happiness is in the capacity, disposition, and determination to be a giver of joy and happiness to others in all circumstances. You can face life courageously and victoriously if you will determine with God's help to always be a giver. Some of God's richest blessings to the world have come through those for whom life caved in.

## SUNDAY EVENING, JULY 12

***Title:*** "Thy Rod and Thy Staff, They Comfort Me"

***Text:*** "Yea, though I walk through the valley of the shadow of death, I will fear no evil: for thou art with me; thy rod and thy staff they comfort me" **(Ps. 23:4)**.

### Introduction

The "comfort" in our text is the comfort against fear. Fear enters the hearts of people when they become aware of the presence of danger. Since we all live in the presence of danger, we all stand in need of the comfort the psalmist discovered in the rod and the staff of the shepherd. Many of us fear disease. Some of us get cold chills when we hear the word *cancer.* Others of us are afraid of failure. Some are afraid of being in an automobile accident, and many are afraid they will be a victim of violence. Only people who have access to the inward resources of God can walk through the world today with confident courage and perfect poise.

### I. The meaning of the terms.

A. *"The valley of the shadow of death."* To receive the comfort of this text, one must know the meaning of "the valley of the shadow of death." God spoke to his people during the days of Jeremiah and described the exodus journey from Egypt to the Promised Land in terms of a journey through the valley of the shadow of death. This land is said to be "a wilderness, through a land of deserts and of pits, through a land of drought, and of the shadow of death, through a land that no man passed through, and where no man dwelt" (Jer. 2:6). Our text teaches us that there will be times in life when we will have to walk through a dark, gloomy, dangerous valley—not necessarily death itself, but some dark tunnel through which we cannot see the way.

B. *"I will fear no evil."* The psalmist was declaring his faith when he said, "I will fear no evil." The reason for this confidence was the very presence of God. "I will fear no evil: for thou art with me." Have you studied this psalm closely enough to recognize the change when you come to verse 4? Until this verse the psalmist had been talking *about* God. Starting at verse 4, he talks *to* God. God is close and dear to him.

C. *"Thy rod and thy staff."* The psalmist uses terms that are not very familiar to people in the twenty-first century. He speaks of the shepherd's rod and staff and how they comfort him.

D. *"They comfort me."* The word "comfort" is an interesting word in the Bible. It means "with strength." To comfort means to give strength, to comfort by increasing the power. The psalmist was persuaded that God would strengthen him and stimulate him so as to enable him to do what needed to be done.

### II. The significance of the symbols.

Much of the unrest of our souls and minds, much of our spiritual immaturity, and much of our ineffectiveness in service are due to a hazy and indistinct grasp of the teachings of God's Word. Every phrase and every passage of God's Word has a unique and particular significance. It is important that we understand the spiritual significance of these symbols of the Shepherd.

It was customary during the days of David for a shepherd to carry a rod and a staff. May God help you to apply them to our Savior and to your own heart and life today.

A. *The shepherd's rod.* Many times the Bible speaks of the fact that God will cause his sheep to pass under the rod. In David's time the sheep passed one at a time under the shepherd's rod on entering or leaving the fold so that they might be counted. In the evening the shepherd would bring his sheep in from the pastures to the sheepfold where the sheep could rest. The shepherd would lead his flock to the door of the sheepfold, and then, one by one, name by name, he would tap each one of them with his rod and count them off as they entered the sheepfold. If there was one sheep missing, the shepherd was made aware of it so that immediately he might go out in search of the wayward sheep.

In the morning the shepherd would come down to the sheepfold, the keeper of the sheepfold would open the door, and the shepherd would call his sheep out by name, tapping them with his rod as they came out, to make certain that all of them left the fold. By this accurate individual count every evening and morning, the shepherd could determine when a sheep was missing.

Thus this verse says to me that the Good Shepherd in heaven will soon be seeking me if I go astray. It says to me that the Good Shepherd takes an individual interest in each of his sheep and that he knows them by name and calls them by name.

The shepherd also used the rod to defend his sheep in times of danger. He stood between his flock and the wild beasts. Our Savior stands between us and the Enemy. He is able to give us comfort if we will let him.

B. *The shepherd's staff.* The staff was the symbol of the shepherd's constant care. After the flock was led out of the sheepfold, the shepherd's staff was used as a means of guidance. The shepherd would lift his staff and point, and by means of the pointing staff, the sheep knew the path of safety to get to the greenest pasture and the best water. A sheep keeps its head close to the ground, and because it has poor eyesight, it cannot see very far ahead. If it can see the shepherd's staff, lifted and silhouetted against the sky, it knows the direction in which to go. If we will follow the guidance of our living Lord, we will never fall over a precipice to death and destruction. We will never fall into the pits of evil, for he leads us only in the paths of righteousness that lead to the right destination.

The staff was also often used as a means of rescuing a fallen sheep. Sheep would fall into a pit or slide down a bank and be utterly helpless to escape. All of us will face such times. We can rejoice to know that in that time our Lord will come and use the staff of his Word, the staff of a Christian friend, or some other staff to rescue us.

### Conclusion

Do you know the Shepherd? Are you willing to give your heart to him? Are you willing to trust him? He will never lead you wrong; he will always lead you right.

---

## WEDNESDAY EVENING, JULY 15

***Title:*** The Hindrance of Mistreating Your Mate

***Text:*** "Likewise, ye husbands, dwell with them according to knowledge, giving honour unto the wife, as unto the weaker vessel, and as being heirs together of the grace of life; that your prayers be not hindered" **(1 Peter 3:7)**.

### Introduction

There are many misconceptions concerning the privilege of prayer. Prayer was never intended as a means by which selfish persons could seek that which they desired for their own self-centered purposes. Instead, prayer is the divinely ordained channel by which the children of God are to receive the things needed for the advancement of God's kingdom and for meeting the responsibilities, obligations, and difficulties of life.

Every prayer promise is conditional. In no instance are we given a signed blank check upon which we can requisition our selfish desires.

A study of the Bible reveals that a number of different attitudes or actions can deprive us of being effective when we pray. Tonight we will see that a husband or wife may fail to receive an answer to prayer because he or she has mistreated a companion.

### I. That your prayer be not hindered.

The apostle Peter specifically informs husbands that if they mistreat their wives, they close the door to the throne room of God and deprive themselves of God's presence and provisions. The same instruction is applicable to the wife.

### II. The mistreatment of another always affects our fellowship with God.

In the Sermon on the Mount, Jesus said that one cannot purchase the favor of God with an offering or enjoy fellowship with God if he is guilty of mistreating a fellow human being (Matt. 5:23–25). The Creator of all men and the Father of those who have faith will not permit one of his children to mistreat another without suffering his chastisement. God loves each of us equally and is concerned about our well-being. If it seems that the heavens are made of brass and that God has refused to hear your prayers, it could be very profitable to examine your personal relationships, not only with others, but in particular with your marriage companion and other members of your household.

### III. Examine your attitudes and actions.

A. *Are you impatient with others?*
B. *Have you been unkind toward others?*
C. *Have you been envious of others?*
D. *Have you been generous with others?*
E. *Have you been discourteous to others?*
F. *Have you been distrustful of others?*
G. *Have you been helpful rather than a hindrance?*
H. *Have you been complimentary rather than critical?*
I. *Have you practiced forgiveness, or do you carry grudges?*

### Conclusion

Love that can be defined as a persistent spirit of goodwill is the Christian attitude that each of us should maintain toward others. To catch and maintain this attitude will assist you greatly both in the matter of entering the presence of God in prayer and in receiving the things that he has for you.

---

## SUNDAY MORNING, JULY 19

***Title:*** Why Do Good People Suffer?

***Scripture Reading:*** Romans 8:35–39

***Hymns:*** "I Must Tell Jesus," Hoffman
"Count Your Blessings," Oatman
"Jesus Is All the World to Me," Thompson

***Offertory Prayer:*** From your bountiful and gracious hand, O God, we have received a multitude of blessings. We acknowledge that every good and perfect gift comes from you. We thank you for the glad consciousness of forgiven sin. We thank you for the assurance of divine adoption. Today we offer to you the fruits of our labors as an expression of the love of our hearts. Bless these tithes and offerings in a manner that will cause others to experience your mercy, your forgiveness, and the joy of fellowship with you. In Christ's name. Amen.

### Introduction

There is no complete and final answer to the mystery of why people suffer. What we do know, however, is that suffering has permanent effects that can be either negative or positive. For some, suffering is a shattering experience that produces bitterness and cynicism. For others, suffering has a mellowing effect and results in a gracious and compassionate heart. Some allow suffering to drive them away from God. Others would say that if it had not been for suffering, they never would have found God.

### I. There is more suffering in our world than we realize.

Most of us have missed the application of the parable of the good Samaritan (Luke 10:30–37). We have hastily identified with the Good Samaritan or with the victim and have refused to see ourselves wearing the cloak of the priest or the robe of the Levite who passed by on the other side of the road. We find it convenient to be blind to the suffering about us on all sides.

A. *There is great physical suffering in our world.*

B. *There is a greater amount of mental illness and suffering than we realize.*

C. *Some of the most intense agony that can be experienced is emotional.* A homiletics professor said to his students, "Remember, every time you preach there is someone with a broken heart in your congregation." The professor would have been closer to the truth if he had said, "Remember, every time you preach every row contains someone with a broken heart."

D. *Perhaps the greatest suffering is spiritual.* People find life frustrating and painful because they have never found the inward peace and strength that are the results of knowing Jesus Christ in a vital living relationship.

### II. Some false solutions to the problem that must be rejected.

All of us have attempted to solve problems in a wrong way. We have also accepted a partial answer as being the complete answer. At times all of us have oversimplified. Particularly is this the case as people have dealt with the problem of pain and suffering.

A. *Some believe that all suffering comes from God.* This idea must be rejected. The Devil, from the beginning of time, has sought to misrepresent the character of God. He slandered God in the garden of Eden by implying that God wanted to restrict and hinder humans from experiencing their highest possible destiny. At every opportunity Satan would suggest that God is responsible for the tragedies and pain that people experience.

B. *Some believe that all suffering is due to sin that has been committed by the sufferer.* This was the belief of the friends of Job who declared that the reason he was suffering was because he was a great sinner (Job 4:7–9). The book of Job refutes the idea that all suffering is the result of some specific sin or sins in the lives of those who suffer.

While most of us would agree that sin will result in suffering, we need to recognize that all suffering is not a result of some sin that has been committed by the person who is in pain. Many of us have wondered when trouble came, "What have I done to deserve this?" While this is an appropriate question on many occasions, and the answer can be found, it should be recognized that at times the one in pain could not possibly be held responsible for the suffering that he or she is enduring.

C. *Some believe that all suffering is mere illusion.* They deny the reality of pain, saying that suffering is in the mind. Doctors confirm that much of our illness is in the mind. The field of psychosomatic medicine is a field by itself. The mind does play tricks on us. In many instances the only way to cure our illness is to change our thinking, but to deny the reality of suffering is illogical.

## III. Partial explanations for the problem of suffering.

Many of us like to find simple, pat answers to complex questions. This is difficult to do, particularly as one faces the problem of suffering. Instead of one simple answer, usually there are many different factors that enter into our suffering.

A. *The Devil deserves the blame for much of what God is charged with.* While the book of Job reveals that nothing is permitted to come into the life of the child of God without the permissive will of God, it also says that Satan is behind much of our suffering (Job 2:7). Peter, who had some personal experience with the Evil One, warns against the peril of being devoured by the Devil (1 Peter 5:8). It is wise to recognize that the Devil tries to tempt us and ill advise us to bring great suffering into our lives. Parents should recognize these satanic designs upon their children and do all they possibly can to lead their children to a deep and vital faith in Jesus Christ. The responsibility for much of our suffering can be laid at the feet of him who sought to tempt and destroy our Savior.

B. *We are personally responsible for much of our suffering.* To blame all of our suffering on the Devil would be not only false, but it would be a way of denying our own responsibility.

1. Much of our suffering is the result of our ignorance.
2. Much of our suffering is due to negligence. If we neglect to do right, we cannot escape the consequences.
3. Much of our suffering is due to our carelessness. We must not blame God or the Devil for an automobile accident if we were not paying attention to our driving.
4. Much of our suffering is due to greed (1 Tim. 6:9).
5. Much of our suffering is in the form of worry. Anxiety is due primarily to our lack of faith in the goodness of God (Matt. 6:25–30). We need to work and not worry. We need to trust God to help us in whatever life may bring.

C. *Others are responsible for much of our suffering.* By no stretch of the imagination can we believe that God would punish us for the sins of others, but it is true that we suffer because of the sins of others. This is true in marriage, in the family, in the community, and throughout the whole world.

D. *The natural law of the universe is responsible for some suffering.* Natural law is benevolent as long as it is recognized and obeyed. To violate this law is not to break it but rather is to be broken upon it. Fire can warm, but fire can also destroy. Water can quench the thirst, but it can also fill the lungs and make breathing impossible. The laws of cause and effect are inseparably tied together.

E. *Some suffering does come from God (2 Cor. 12:7).* When God is responsible for suffering in our lives, his motive is benevolent and redemptive. It is our responsibility, with the help of the Holy Spirit, to discover the purpose or meaning behind this training or chastisement (Heb. 12:5–12).

## IV. How shall we react to suffering?

A. *Shall we react with self-pity?* Most of us do, and to some degree we will continue to do so. There have been times when all of us have felt sorry for ourselves. We should not be shocked if we pity ourselves in the future, but such a reaction will not solve the problem of suffering.

B. *Shall we react with blind, fatalistic resignation?* Some have and some will. Often when tragedy strikes, someone will hastily say, "It is the will of God, and we must accept his will." If this explanation is always given, what will this do to one's concept of God and to one's faith? God must not be blamed for something he is not responsible for. Many times he has been slandered when in reality he was not responsible at all for the suffering that someone was enduring.

C. *Shall we react with bitter resentment?* Some have and some will. To become hard-hearted and cynical builds a barrier in the mind that shuts God out and makes it impossible for the sufferer to utilize spiritual resources in his or her time of greatest need.

## Conclusion

Instead of seeking a simple explanation of why people suffer, we should seek for victory in our sufferings and over our sufferings. In one way or another, a solution can be found in the cross where God suffered in the person of Jesus Christ. God is no stranger to suffering, for there was a cross in the heart of God long before there was ever a cross on Calvary's hill. Christ suffered courageously and victoriously.

In the words of our text, the apostle Paul declares that no suffering of the past, present, or future can separate us from the love of God (Rom. 8:35–39). In writing to the Corinthians, he declared that no trial or trouble would come upon them that would be unbearable if they would utilize the spiritual resources that were available (1 Cor. 10:13).

With Christ on board the ship of our life, we can experience victory in and over suffering. Rebecca R. Williams put it this way:

*One ship drives east, and another drives west,*
*While the self-same breezes blow;*
*It's the set of the sails and not the gales*
*That bids them where to go.*
*Like the sails of the seas are the ways of our wills*
*As we voyage along through life;*

*It's the set of the soul that decides the goal*
*And not the storms or the strife.*

## SUNDAY EVENING, JULY 19

***Title:*** A Banquet Prepared by God's Grace

***Text:*** "Thou preparest a table before me in the presence of mine enemies: thou anointest my head with oil; my cup runneth over" **(Ps. 23:5)**.

### Introduction

In our earlier Sunday evening sermons on Psalm 23, we noted that there is a progression in the psalm. In verses 1–4 we find the relationship of God and his people treated under the figure of the shepherd and his sheep. When we come to verse 5, we find that the spirit, the atmosphere, and the relationship of the shepherd and the sheep is enriched in the progression. The shepherd becomes a host, and the sheep become the guests at a gracious and festive banquet.

It is wonderful to think of ourselves in terms of being the sheep of the Good Shepherd's pasture and to consider the safety, security, and satisfaction we enjoy under his guidance, leadership, and protection. It is even more wonderful to think of ourselves as guests at his table enjoying the bounty of his plenty and the fellowship that is ours as the children of God.

### I. The life of faith is a feast.

A. *A feast.* The psalmist says, "Thou preparest a table before me." The life of faith and surrender to God is treated under the figure of a feast in which fellowship is enjoyed. It is interesting to note as we study the life of our Savior how many of the wonderful experiences of his ministry took place around a banquet table. After Matthew's conversion one of the first things he did was to prepare a banquet for Jesus and invite a great host of people to come and meet his Savior. The scribes and Pharisees criticized Jesus, saying, "This man receiveth sinners and eateth with them." Evidently Jesus spent much time at the dinner table enjoying friendship and fellowship.

Jesus said, "Behold, I stand at the door and knock: if any man hear my voice, and open the door, I will come in to him, and will sup with him, and he with me" (Rev. 3:20). Once he who stands at the door of your heart knocking is permitted to come in, he becomes the Host and prepares the banquet, giving you the privilege of feasting on the bread of heaven and drinking from the fountain of living water.

B. *A prepared feast.* It is interesting to note that this is a prepared banquet: "Thou preparest a table before me in the presence of mine enemies." When we are having guests at our house, a number of things are taken into consideration. One of the primary concerns is what our guests would enjoy. Food is prepared with them in mind. We want the meal to delight and refresh them. The psalmist looked upon the life of faith and fellowship with God as being a feast in which God had prepared that which would delight the hearts of those who participated.

We should always remember that everything God brings into our lives is something prepared especially for us. Sometimes we may not be able to understand it, but after time has gone by, we can look back and see how certain things came into our life to prepare us for that which was yet out in front.

C. *Fellowship and feasting.* Usually only the best of friends get together around a banquet table, for here there is an intimacy and affection of fellowship that is precious and sweet. God wishes to cultivate and develop that kind of a relationship with his people. God is not a tyrant or a bully or a killjoy or a policeman. He is a loving host who has prepared a bountiful feast.

### II. A feast in the presence of our enemies.

The psalmist continues, "Thou preparest a table before me in the presence of mine enemies." Many of us could say, "So far as I know, I do not have one single enemy." But the psalmist could not say that, for there had been times when men had tried to destroy him. He speaks from real experience when he says, "Thou preparest a table before me in the presence of mine enemies."

In the ancient East a traveler enjoyed the complete protection of his host until he departed from his tent. There were no motels and hotels, and they did not even have locks on their doors to shut their enemies out. However, they had customs and traditions that were just as inviolable as the locks on our buildings today. Once a man came under the tent of even a stranger, he enjoyed the protection and the security of that tent and its owner until his departure. To injure a guest was the mark of deepest depravity in the ancient East. So here we have a picture of great significance. The psalmist is saying that throughout life, when I reach the safety of the heavenly Father's tent, I can lie down in perfect peace and safety even though my enemies be but a few feet away.

There are some things that we cannot escape. There are even some enemies who dog our heels day and night. Some enemies are common to all of us. Many years ago Dr. J. H. Jowett preached a remarkable sermon on this text called "The Guest of God." He listed three enemies who confront each of us and from whom we can have safety and security in the tent of our heavenly Father. They are:

A. *The sin of yesterday.* There is not one among us who is not a sinner. No two of us have sinned alike. In the life of every person, there is sin of which he or she is ashamed. Some sins have been forgotten, yet like a hound at our heels, they sometimes return to plague us. The Scriptures teach us that sin by its very nature pursues the sinner. We are taught to believe that sin and its punishment are wrapped up in the same package. The Bible says, "Be sure your sin will find you out" (Num. 32:23). It does not say that your sin will be found out, but it says, "Be sure your sin will find you out." The Bible teaches us that "their works do follow after them."

There are many of us who have sometime in the past done some vile act that degraded and defiled us and that sometimes returns to torment us. At times even memory is an accusing finger that would destroy our peace, our happiness, our joy, and our fellowship with God. Dr. Jowett declared that in the presence of this enemy, the sin of yesterday, it is possible for us to have full, free, and complete forgiveness through the blood of Jesus Christ that cleanses us from all sin. The God of heaven forgives us for the sin of yesterday. He holds it against us no longer, for it was taken care of in the death of Jesus Christ.

B. *The temptation of today.* The second enemy that faces everyone of us is the temptation of today. Sin is a peril, a menace, an enemy that would invade the pulpit as well as the pew. Sin would enter the heart and life of the most aged saint, as well as the life of the inexperienced, unwise juvenile.

Temptation stands by the wayside of every person's life. With deceptive deliberateness evil would enter my life or your life, the lives of our children or the lives of our parents, and literally ruin us if we do not stay close to the Master and follow his guidance and avail ourselves of his power. Sometimes temptation is sly like a fox; at other times it roars like a lion with mighty power to engulf and to overthrow and to completely submerge those in its wake. Temptation is ever present, and it crouches very near even when we pray.

Through the lust of the flesh, the lust of the eyes, and the pride of life, temptation lurks in the pathway of each of us. Paul had this in mind when he said, "I keep under my body, and bring it into subjection: lest that by any means, when I have preached to others, I myself should be a castaway" (1 Cor. 9:27).

Every man, woman, boy, and girl stands always on the brink of disaster. We need to recognize this fact that we might be cautious and might trust the Good Shepherd, being instantly responsive to his leadership and guidance. We do not wait until our children are on the edge of a cliff to warn them of the danger of falling over. Neither does the Good Shepherd. He gives us warning after warning. The Christian who falls into great sin does so because he or she has deliberately refused to heed the warning voice of the one who leads us in the paths of righteousness. Everyone of us has an enemy in the temptation of today. The enemy that sows all of these evil thoughts and possibilities is the Devil.

C. *The death that awaits us tomorrow.* The last of the enemies each of us has is the death that awaits us tomorrow. The Bible says, "It is appointed unto man once to die" (Heb. 9:27). The Bible also says that death is our last enemy. Jesus Christ came and tasted death for every person that he might deliver us from the fear of death (Heb. 2:14–15). "The sting of death is sin" (1 Cor. 15:56). If sin were not a part of our human experience, then death would cease to be a horrible thing that many of us fear. It is sin that causes us to fear the experience and consequences of death. If it were not for sin, our attitude and our viewpoint and our evaluation of the death experience would be entirely different. Jesus Christ came and died for us that he might take the sting out of death.

In the presence of these three great enemies—the sin of yesterday, the temptation of today, and the death that awaits us tomorrow—God prepares for us a feast in which it is possible for us to sit down in the safety of fellowship with God. We can face the future with peace, poise, and courage.

### III. "My cup runneth over."

"Thou preparest a table before me in the presence of mine enemies: thou anointest my head with oil; my cup runneth over." We do not have anything in our contemporary lives that compares to the act of anointing a guest with oil. In the days of the psalmist, a host who was prosperous would anoint a guest with fragrant oil. The rich fragrance was a constant reminder of the happiness of the host on the occasion of the guest's visit. God is delighted and happy to have us at his banquet table. We should be continually reminded of his goodness, joy, happiness, and delight in those who are the supreme objects of his concern.

As the psalmist considered his blessings, he declared, "My cup runneth over." A retired minister addressed seminary students in a chapel service, and he began his message by saying that someone greeted him with, "How are you, John?" He replied, "I am drinking out of the saucer. My cup runneth over." Here we have a picture of what God wants our lives to be—lives of drinking out of the saucer!

There are some whose cups never overflow because they go to the wrong source. Some never let their cups overflow because they have a pessimistic spirit that always causes them to see what is wrong rather than what is right. Some never let their cups overflow because of envy. One can always look around and see that which belongs to others and become envious. We should continually drink out of the saucer, because by God's grace ours is the privilege of having the glad consciousness of forgiven sin. Ours is the privilege of enjoying the precious relationship of being children of God. God has given us the gift of eternal life. We have access to inexhaustible spiritual resources. God has given us the privilege of service. All of us could say with the psalmist, "My cup runneth over."

### Conclusion

I challenge you today to open the door of your heart and let the Christ come in. Let him become the Host. When you become the guest, he prepares the banquet. Make that decision today.

## WEDNESDAY EVENING, JULY 22

***Title:*** The Hindrance of an Unforgiving Spirit

***Text:*** "And when ye stand praying, forgive, if you have ought against any: that your Father also which is in heaven may forgive you your trespasses. But if ye do not forgive, neither will your Father which is in heaven forgive your trespasses" (**Mark 11:25–26**).

### Introduction

A sincere and devout woman spoke to a small group in a prayer circle, requesting their prayers on her behalf. She described her need as follows: "I find in my heart an unforgiving spirit toward one who has brought great harm to a member of my family. I bear a grudge against this person, and I have found this grudge to be a barrier in my way when I try to approach God in prayer. Please pray for me."

It is possible that a grudge you bear toward someone will hinder you from entering the closet of prayer where you can have a transforming experience with God. Jesus declared that it is necessary not only to enter the private place of prayer but that we must also get the door shut (Matt. 6:6). In this specification Jesus is declaring that the barriers, hindrances, obstacles, and obstructions to fellowship must be removed. One of these barriers that all of us have to deal with from time to time is the matter of an unforgiving spirit.

### I. Injury by others is inevitable.

A. *People are natural mistake makers.*

B. *Seldom are we mistreated deliberately.*

C. *Occasionally we are injured by others unconsciously.*

D. *Quite often we are injured by others indirectly.*

### II. How do you react to injury?

A. *Do you give expression to your hostility on the spot with remarks that seem to be appropriate?*

B. *Do you follow the policy of doing unto others as they have done unto you?*

C. *Do you list your grudges in a little black book so that when an occasion arises you can pay back the injury with interest?* If these are your reactions, then you are acting in a manner that would be considered normal by the unregenerate person.

### III. Unlimited forgiveness (Matt. 18:21–22).

Peter's offer to forgive as many as seven times was thought to be the height of generosity. The disciples were shocked when Jesus instructed them to forgive until seventy times seven. His primary motive behind this requirement of unlimited forgiveness was for the spiritual well-being of the offended rather than for exempting the offender from punishment. Jesus was fully aware that the carrying of a grudge, the harboring of desire for revenge, and the refusal to forgive would eat like an acid and fester like an infection in the soul. He was also aware that God could not forgive those who were unwilling to forgive.

### Conclusion

Do you find it difficult to forgive? The basis for our forgiving others is found in God's forgiveness of us (Col. 3:12–23). The God who forgives is able to give you the grace to forgive others. Ask God to help you to be willing and able to forgive those who have trespassed against you.

## SUNDAY MORNING, JULY 26

***Title:*** What Is the Gospel?

***Text:*** "For I am not ashamed of the gospel of Christ: for it is the power of God unto salvation to every one that believeth; to the Jew first, and also to the Greek" (**Rom. 1:16**).

***Scripture Reading:*** Romans 1:14–16; 1 Corinthians 15:1–4

***Hymns:*** "Great Redeemer, We Adore Thee," Harris

"I Love to Tell the Story," Hankey

"We've a Story to Tell," Sterne

***Offertory Prayer:*** Heavenly Father, from your heart of love you have given us your Son to be our Savior. Through him you have given us forgiveness and new life. Through him life has become meaningful and joyful. Because of our love for you, we come bringing our tithes and offerings. Accept them as symbols of our desire to give ourselves completely to you. In Jesus' name. Amen.

### Introduction

Radio stations, TV stations, and newspapers are in a constant contest to outdo each other in conveying the news to their audiences. Within the past several years, tremendous advances have been made in the means of mass communication. Incidents on the other side of the world are reported instantaneously via satellite. Our eyes and ears are constantly assaulted with the gory details of crimes or tragedies that take place. With all of the news coming from the north, south, east, and west, many of us become hardened to the things that are going on about us from day to day. We hear too much bad news. Today we consider some good news: the gospel of Jesus Christ.

The English word *gospel* comes from the Anglo-Saxon *godspel*, which meant good tidings or God's story. In the New Testament it is the Christ-message, not the books that were written to spread that message. The gospel is not only good news; it is the greatest news and the latest news about God (John 3:16–17), a message that we need to proclaim continuously to the world.

Jesus began his earthly ministry preaching the gospel. "Now after that John was put in prison, Jesus came into Galilee, preaching the gospel of the kingdom of

God, and saying, The time is fulfilled, and the kingdom of God is at hand: repent ye, and believe the gospel" (Mark 1:14–15). Jesus brought his earthly ministry to a conclusion by commanding the infant church to "Go ye into all the world, and preach the gospel to every creature" (Mark 16:15).

Just what is the gospel that Jesus preached and the early church proclaimed? What was Paul talking about when he spoke repeatedly of the fact that he had been called to preach the gospel? Have we misunderstood this word? Have we failed to appreciate it? Have we neglected to respond to it? Have we neglected to be the instruments for its proclamation to the world?

### I. The gospel is good news about God.

The greatest contribution of Christ to the world is his revelation of the nature and character of God. Jesus said, "He that hath seen me, hath seen the Father." He also said, "I and my Father are one."

A. *Jesus revealed that God is love (John 3:16).*

1. Redeeming love.
2. Forgiving love.
3. Merciful love.
4. Saving love.

B. *Jesus revealed God as a heavenly Father.* In the four Gospels, Jesus speaks of God as "Father" 153 times. Only once did he address the heavenly Father as "God," and that was while he was on the cross.

At night a child will grip his daddy's hand as he walks through the darkness. He does this because he has security in the presence of his father. Jesus would encourage us to trust the Creator God as a loving Father.

A little girl at an airport terminal became frightened when her father assisted her grandmother on board the plane. The mother was unable to console her until the father returned and took her into his arms. The world today needs to know that our God has not taken a trip and left us to our own resources. Jesus said that not even a sparrow falls to the ground outside of the Father's knowledge.

### II. The gospel is headline news about Jesus Christ.

When Paul said, "I am not ashamed of the gospel of Christ," he was using a negative statement to declare a positive truth. He was affirming that Jesus Christ had never disappointed him and that he was proud of Jesus Christ. He actually gloried in the cross of Christ (Gal. 6:14). Paul was proud of who Jesus Christ was, what he had done, and what he could do.

A. *Christ lived a marvelous life.* Jesus set an all-time world record in character achievement. His life was sinless and perfect in God's sight.

B. *Jesus died a matchless death.* "Christ died for our sins." This is good news that should be proclaimed constantly.

1. Love took Jesus to the cross.

2. Love kept Jesus on the cross.
3. Love is what we see in the cross.

C. *Jesus ever lives to save unto the uttermost (Heb. 7:25).*

### III. The gospel is good news for everyone who believes (Rom. 1:16).

In many parts of the world, human life is cheap. In the eyes of the world, many people are poor and insignificant; nevertheless, Christ died for all. An unknown poet prayed as follows:

> *Lord, help me see in all I meet*
> *On country lane or city street*
> *Not just men and women passing by*
> *But those for whom my Christ did die.*

### IV. The gospel is headline news of salvation and redemption.

A. *The gospel is God's chosen instrument for delivering men from the penalty, power, pollution, and presence of sin.* While education is wonderful and powerful, it does not solve the problem of evil.

B. *The gospel is God's only instrument for saving people from the tragic tyranny and waste of sin.* The gospel appeals to the heart. It changes the heart. It transforms, reorganizes, and regenerates human souls.

C. *The gospel is God's power unto salvation to everyone who believes.* Only the gospel has the dynamic power to really save.

1. Power to save morally.
2. Power to save physically.
3. Power to save intellectually.
4. Power to save personally.
5. Power to save economically.
6. Power to save socially.
7. Power to save eternally.

The gospel is divine in its origin and contains within it the dynamic creative power of God. The gospel is the unique power of God by which he saves people from the tyranny and waste of sin. Only through a response to the story of his love and mercy can God bring about the miracle of salvation to the heart.

### Conclusion

Has the gospel of Jesus Christ awakened your heart to your need for salvation? The gospel of Jesus Christ invites you to something better and nobler. The gospel invites you to forsake the love of sin and to embrace Jesus Christ as your own personal Savior. May God help you to do it today.

## SUNDAY EVENING, JULY 26

***Title:*** The Home at the End of the Way

***Text:*** "Surely goodness and mercy shall follow me all the days of my life: and I will dwell in the house of the LORD for ever" **(Ps. 23:6)**.

### Introduction

Today we come to the last verse of Psalm 23: "Surely goodness and mercy shall follow me all the days of my life: and I will dwell in the house of the LORD forever." There are several thoughts in this verse, each of which could serve as a text for a sermon.

### I. Facing the future with faith.

A. *"Surely," the psalmist says— "without doubt, beyond question."* "Surely goodness and mercy shall follow me all the days of my life." He speaks with confidence, faith, courage, optimism, and hope as he faces the future. He has no question about the goodness, faithfulness, and love of God. Because of his great faith in a wonderful Shepherd, the psalmist is able to say, "Surely goodness and mercy shall follow me all the days of my life." Some modern versions translate "surely" as "only": "Only goodness and mercy shall follow me all the days of my life."

B. *"Goodness and mercy."* God always deals with his children on the basis of goodness and mercy. It is very possible that some shepherds of David's time had sheep dogs that followed along behind the flock to keep the sheep from straying and to protect them from wild beasts. Someone has casually suggested that if this were the case, then perhaps the Good Shepherd had one dog whose name was Goodness and one whose name was Mercy.

As the psalmist looked back over his lifetime of varied success and failure, he bore testimony that God always deals with his own in terms of goodness and mercy. If God were to deal with us in terms of justice, we would be destroyed.

Is your heart and mind filled with fear, anxiety, and uncertainty as you face the future? Many situations in our world today would frighten us to death if we forgot that God has everything under control. The psalmist faced the future with courage and optimism, for he was convinced that the God who had been so gracious to him in the past would continue to be gracious to him in the future.

### II. Faith's commitment for the present.

Concentrate now on the psalmist's wonderful confession of faith: "I will dwell in the house of the LORD forever." This statement approaches better than any other in the Old Testament the revelation of life beyond death. It is similar to what Jesus said in John 14: "Let not your heart be troubled: ye believe in God, believe also in me. In my Father's house are many mansions: if it were not so, I would have told you."

Many people think that here the psalmist is referring only to heaven, but actually he considered it possible to begin dwelling in the house of the Lord here on earth. In Psalm 27:4 we read, "One thing have I desired of the LORD, that will I seek after; that I may dwell in the house of the LORD all the days of my life, to behold the beauty of the LORD, and to inquire in his temple." Although David had committed some grievous sins, the Lord had mercifully forgiven him, and now he could say, "I am going to dwell in the house of the LORD forever."

The eternal home of the soul is a continuation of the home of the soul that we have here and now. By his grace, God wants us to taste the very joys of heaven in this life. He wants us to enjoy fellowship with the saints and develop friendships with our brothers and sisters in Christ. In twenty-first-century terminology, David was saying, "I am going to stay close to the church all of the days of my life. Then I am going to dwell in the house of the Lord forever."

From time to time, every pastor's heart is grieved by hearing a fallen church member give one of the following reasons for leaving the church: "Things didn't suit me in Sunday school class"; "I became unhappy with one of the deacons"; "I became dissatisfied with the pastor"; or "I did not like the way that certain things were done." Such people have left the church to the detriment of their own spiritual lives and to the poverty of their own souls and the souls of their family members.

One of the wisest decisions that any of us can make is to say, "Come what may, I am going to stay close to the church. I am going to be a vital part of the church. I am going to be loyal to the church all the days of my life, for the church is the nearest thing on earth to the home of the soul in heaven."

**III. Faith in the future home.**

Many people cannot read the Twenty-third Psalm without thinking morbid thoughts, for they associate this psalm with death. We need to have a Christian understanding of death. Death for the Christian is not earth's greatest tragedy. We do not grieve because people go to heaven; we grieve only because we have been left behind. To paraphrase, the psalmist was saying, "When my body is worn out and when I am no longer able to function in this life, I will go to dwell in the house of the Lord forever."

A. *The home at the end of the way is a prepared place for a prepared people.* In no other area of life does preparation pay off so much as being prepared for the home at the end of the way.

B. *Heaven is a prepared place where praises will be perpetual and where we will praise God without the limitations that we have known in this life.*

C. *Heaven is a prepared place of purity.* Through the years saints have been disturbed by the fact that even in their most sacred moments of prayer they have been interrupted by impure thoughts. In heaven that sinful nature will no longer be with us.

D. *Heaven is a prepared place where payment is made.* Jesus said, "For whosoever shall give you a cup of water to drink in my name, because ye belong to Christ, verily I say unto you, he shall not lose his reward" (Mark 9:41). Jesus said, "Behold, I come quickly; and my reward is with me, to give every man according as his work shall be" (Rev. 22:12). I believe that somehow we develop the capacity in this life for enjoying and appreciating the life beyond. When we get to heaven, everybody's cup will run over, but as Dwight L. Moody said, some of us will have small cups. The size of our cup is determined by the works we do and by the worship of our hearts in this life.

### Conclusion

This life is the vestibule, the preparation room for the life beyond. I challenge you this day to make the Good Shepherd your Shepherd. Let him become your Leader, Guide, Teacher, Friend, and Savior. Make that decision today.

---

## WEDNESDAY EVENING, JULY 29

***Title:*** The Hindrance of Unbelief

***Text:*** "Let him ask in faith, nothing wavering" **(James 1:6)**.

### Introduction

If you have been disappointed with the results of your efforts in prayer, it might be wise for you to examine the faith that you have exercised in the matter of prayer.

It is the testimony of all Scripture that God is a prayer-hearing and prayer-answering God. Jesus declares that the heavenly Father knows our needs even before we present our requests (Matt. 6:8). He says that the heavenly Father is even more eager than a generous earthly father to bestow good gifts upon his children if they come to him in prayer (Matt. 7:9–11). Since this is so, then why is it that we do not receive the things for which we make request in prayer? While there may be a number of different explanations, tonight let us consider the possibility that the hindering cause is the lack of faith on our part.

### I. Jesus clearly taught the necessity of faith in prayer (Mark 11:24).

A. *We must believe that God is able to answer prayer.*

B. *We must believe that God is eager to answer prayer.*

C. *We must believe that our request is in harmony with both the character and the will of our heavenly Father (1 John 3:22).*

### II. Illustrations of praying in faith.

A. *Elijah prayed in faith for the fire of God to fall (1 Kings 18:36–39).*

B. *Elijah prayed in faith for rain (1 Kings 18:41–46).*

C. *The centurion prayed for the healing of his servant (Matt. 8:5–10).*
D. *The publican prayed for mercy (Luke 18:13).*
E. *The early church prayed in faith for the coming of the Holy Spirit (Acts 1:14).*

### III. The prayer of faith.

A. *Study the prayers recorded in the Bible that God answered for patterns for your praying.*
B. *Heed the instructions concerning the proper manner of praying as given by our Lord (Matt. 6:9–13).*
C. *Pray for more faith (Luke 17:5).*
D. *Act on the faith that you already have (Matt. 17:19–20).*

### Conclusion

The writer of the book of Hebrews declares that without faith it is impossible to please God. He who comes to God in prayer must believe that God is and that he is the rewarder of those who diligently seek him (Heb. 11:6). The spiritual giants of the past have been those who out-believed and out-prayed their contemporaries. May God grant to us more faith as we give ourselves to prayer and witnessing.

SUGGESTED PREACHING PROGRAM FOR

# AUGUST

## ■ Sunday Mornings

The theme for the Sunday morning services this month is stewardship. Stewardship concerns every area of life. In the background of each suggested message is the basic philosophy of Jesus expressed in the beatitude "It is more blessed to give than to receive" (Acts 20:35).

## ■ Sunday Evenings

"Great Hymn Titles" is the theme for Sunday evenings this month.

## ■ Wednesday Evenings

The theme for the Wednesday evening services is "Responding to the Holy Spirit."

---

## SUNDAY MORNING, AUGUST 2

***Title:*** The Value of Making Vows

***Text:*** "I will pay my vows unto the LORD now in the presence of all his people" **(Ps. 116:14)**.

***Scripture Reading:*** Psalm 116

***Hymns:*** "Love Divine, All Loves Excelling," Wesley

"May God Depend on You?" Martin

"O Jesus, I Have Promised," Bode

***Offertory Prayer:*** Holy Father, today we thank you for all of your precious promises to us. We enjoy your gracious provisions for us. We thank you for abundantly providing the physical necessities of life. Today as we bring our gifts and offerings, we ask that you will bless them for the preaching of the gospel of grace to this community and to the world. In Jesus' name. Amen.

### Introduction

Our life is what it is because of our vows or lack of vows. Most of us avoid making vows for a variety of reasons: (1) we have a natural inclination to avoid obligations, (2) we have a natural love of the easy life, (3) we have a fear of the future that causes us to be hesitant about committing ourselves to any endeavor, and (4) we have a tendency to be selfish. We are inclined to put self at the center and then hope that everything will revolve around us.

We should recognize that our decisions determine our destiny. Visions must be matched with vows if our castles in the air are to become realities.

**I. The high cost of refusing to make vows.**

A. *Refusing to make vows exposes one to the danger of living an aimless life.* Vows should be made with a definite objective in mind (Prov. 4:26).

B. *Refusing to make vows exposes one to the danger of living a shallow life.* Vows help us to channel our efforts and energies toward that which is worthwhile. The peril of drifting is a very real threat to each of us. It is a tragedy to live a life that has no higher authority than the whim, mood, or impulse of the moment.

C. *Refusing to make vows exposes one to the danger of living a nonproductive life.*

**II. The necessity of making vows.**

A. *Vows are necessary for a sound economic system.*

B. *Vows are necessary for the stability of home life.*

C. *Vows are necessary for the preservation of a just and orderly government on the community, state, and national level.*
   1. Local officials.
   2. State officials.
   3. National officials.
   4. Members of the armed services.

D. *Voluntary vows are absolutely essential for progress in your personal life.*
   1. School life.
   2. Marriage.
   3. Economic affairs.

E. *Voluntary vows are absolutely essential for spiritual growth and success.*
   1. We must make vows concerning regular worship.
   2. We must make vows concerning a devotional study of the Bible.
   3. We must make vows concerning our prayer opportunities.
   4. We must make vows concerning our financial stewardship.

**III. The vows of the psalmist: "I will pay my vows unto the LORD now in the presence of all his people" (Ps. 116:14).**

A. *"I will walk before the LORD in the land of the living" (Ps. 116:9).* This is a vow that lifts us to a new level of spiritual experience.
   1. Stewardship.
   2. Influence.
   3. Example.
   4. Desire for divine approval.

B. *"I will take the cup of salvation, ..." (Ps. 116:13).* This is a vow that deepens our personal experience with God.
   1. The bitter and the sweet.
   2. The pleasant and the difficult.

3. God's full program for life.

C. *"I will . . . call upon the name of the* L*ORD" (Ps. 116:13).* This is a vow that transforms all of life. "I will stay in contact with divine headquarters so that I can be instantly at his service."

D. *"I will offer to thee the sacrifice of thanksgiving" (Ps. 116:17).* This is a vow that releases joy. Your life can be an anthem of praise.

### Conclusion

Your life is the result of choices, responses, and vows as you have faced your burdens and your opportunities. Your vows and inward decisions will determine your future.

May God help each of us voluntarily make personal vows that are purposeful and productive. Let us make vows that will be worthy of the praise of our Lord. To stagger back from the opportunity to make vows is to stumble into oblivion.

---

## SUNDAY EVENING, AUGUST 2

***Title:*** "Trust and Obey"

***Text:*** "So Abram went, as the Lord had told him" **(Gen. 12:4 RSV).**

***Scripture Reading:*** Genesis 12:1–8

### Introduction

The hymn "Trust and Obey" could well be the theme song of the life of the patriarch Abraham, for he is well known for his trust in God and obedience to him. Today we will look at his life to learn how we too can honor God with our trust and obedience.

The flood is over. Humankind has started again with Noah's family. Sin, however, does not cease its ugly work! Once more the world is in trouble. The Tower of Babel causes the populated world to be scattered in various directions. Idolatry has become the order of the day. What will God do? He has promised that he will not destroy the world by water again. The first worldwide judgment did not change things: man is still a sinner and must be redeemed to live righteously.

God begins a new approach: he will take a man and start a new race. Through this person's descendants, God will do two things. First, he will reveal his character as holy. This would be in contrast to that of the false gods who have no life and, therefore, no moral qualities to challenge humankind to proper conduct. Second, in the fullness of time, he will send a Redeemer to bring salvation and forgiveness to all people regardless of who or where they are.

Where can God find such a person? All the world is contaminated by sin. Here is a man named Abram in Ur of the Chaldees. Abram's father, Terah, is a moon god worshiper (Josh. 24:2), but Abram has not adopted this terrible habit. An old Jewish tradition tells us that Terah ran a store where idols were sold. His son Abram did not like the idols and protested often to his father. One day when the boy was left in charge of the store, he took a metal stick and broke the idols into pieces. When his father came home and saw the ruins, he asked his son what had happened. The boy replied, "They all got in a fight and destroyed each other." The father insisted, "But they can't fight. They have no life." The boy replied, "Then why do you worship them?" This is the kind of man God needed to begin his redemptive program, and he called Abram to a new job and gave him a new name—Abraham.

### I. Get into a new environment.

Though one's surroundings do not always determine his service, there are times when we need to get into a new location to start a new work.

A. *God had reserved the land of Canaan for the place he would put his new people.* He, therefore, relocated this man who would begin the new program. From secular history we know that there was a general migration westward of a number of Semitic people about this time. The Hyksos, a group from the same ethnic background as Abram, went as far as Egypt, where they were successful in taking over the throne and holding it for several centuries. The call to Abram, however, was personal. Although he went with his father and other kinspeople, he knew it was only a matter of time before he must go out on his own.

B. *God reveals himself to all people, but he selects certain ones at certain times for certain tasks.* He had chosen Abram but knew Abram must make a break with the old land. Too many memories remained there, and the temptation to yield to the customs of that environment might be too strong. Abram needed to move to a new area to serve God best. We, too, must leave the old behind.

### II. Learn that life is for being a blessing.

A. *To do what Abram did required an awareness that God was with him.* How long he pondered the decision, we do not know, nor can we be certain of how his father Terah and the others fit into the scheme of things. Despite these questions, one thing is certain. Faith and obedience played a major role in the starting event and all that subsequently took place.

The writer of Hebrews chose Abraham's faith as an illustration of his definition of this glorious trait that he calls "the substance of things hoped for, the evidence of things not seen" (11:1). Future things do not have an existence for someone unless he believes in them. Faith makes eternity as real as today. Why? Because it gives a reality to the new and limitless future where we will have time to forget the sorrows and live past the losses of our present world.

B. *As great as faith is, we need, however, to ask an important question about it.* Faith in what? The answer is simple: God's provision. What, though, did God offer Abram? This promise at first reading sounds fabulous, for God offered him so much; but look closer and see that the material things offered were not the most important.

God offered Abram an opportunity to bless the world. The superficial reader emphasizes that God promised to make of Abram a great nation, to bless him, and to make his name great. The perceptive reader, however, sees something more. God said, "Thou shalt be a blessing" (Gen. 12:2). In fact, the literal Hebrew is imperative: "Be thou a blessing." Read a little further. The immature reader only notices, "I will bless them that bless thee, and curse him that curseth thee" (v. 3). The dedicated Christian emphasizes, "In thee shall all the families of the earth be blessed" (v. 3).

C. *Which is more important, to be blessed or to bless?* Unfortunately, too many of us become Christians for the wrong motivation or at least for a lesser one. Initially, we want to escape hell and go on to heaven. Though this is a legitimate motive, it is not the highest one. We should come to Jesus because of who he is and because of the life of service he offers. Usually, however, we must grow much before we make this the supreme motive of our lives. Abram did receive blessings, but most of all, God chose him as an instrument. Through him the world would be blessed. This is the meaning of life, for it is the one thing Jesus emphasized above everything else.

### III. Serve where you are.

Although we emphasized at first the necessity of leaving home to gain a new identity, the time comes when we must settle down where we are and serve God in that place. We cannot be constantly moving every time things get tough.

A. *Abram served God where God put him.* At first, God willed that Abram stay in Haran for a period of time. Perhaps it was to care for his father who may not have shared Abram's vision to go on to Canaan. For whatever reason, Abram waited patiently for a further word from the Lord. In the book of Acts we learn that after Terah's death Abram heard a new command from God. He then left Haran and went to Canaan. Notice that Abram "went forth to go into the land of Canaan; and into the land of Canaan they came" (Gen. 12:5). Nothing stopped Abram from doing God's will as he understood it.

B. *One thing that characterized Abram was that wherever he went, he built an altar and called on the name of the Lord* (Gen. 12:8). We need to worship where we are. The other side often looks better, but we must adjust to where God puts us.

### Conclusion

Why has Abraham gone down in history as such a great person? He had faith! He trusted God and obeyed him! Abraham's faith was proved by his faithfulness. God counted this faith as righteousness, and through his seed salvation has come to the world. We, too, can be a blessing if we trust and obey.

## WEDNESDAY EVENING, AUGUST 5

***Title:*** The Unredeemed May Resist the Holy Spirit

***Text:*** "Ye stiffnecked and uncircumcised in heart and ears, ye do always resist the Holy Ghost: as your fathers did, so do ye" **(Acts 7:51)**.

### Introduction

On the day of Pentecost, Peter interpreted the events taking place as the beginning of a new era in the program of God. He declared that they were witnessing the fulfillment of a prophecy spoken by Joel to the effect that the day would come when God would pour out his Spirit upon all flesh. Joel had looked forward to the time when every believer would be equipped by the Holy Spirit to be a spokesperson of God's message to the world. The Holy Spirit came on the day of Pentecost so that every believer might be a witness of the wonderful works of God (Acts 2:11).

In seeking to bear a Christian witness to the unsaved, we must trust in the Holy Spirit to do the work of convicting and even converting the unbeliever. It is not our assignment to condemn sins; this can be accomplished only by the Holy Spirit. You should not be unduly discouraged if your message is not received with gratitude, because a study of both the Scriptures and the experience of the church through the ages reveals that the unredeemed will often resist and rebel against the efforts of the Holy Spirit to bring them to faith in Jesus Christ. Instead of interpreting their response as a rejection of you personally, you would do well to recognize that it is Christ they are actually rejecting.

### I. The unredeemed resist the Holy Spirit because they do not understand or appreciate the person of God.

God has been misrepresented to them. They have a false concept of the nature of God.

### II. The unredeemed resist the Holy Spirit because they resent the purpose of God.

The natural mind is at enmity with God because of the rebellion that is within the heart. Unbelievers see God as an intruder or thief who would rob them of that upon which they have set their hearts.

### III. The unredeemed resist the Holy Spirit because they do not really believe the gospel.

The gospel is more than good advice. It is the good news of God's love for sinners as revealed in and through Jesus Christ.

### IV. The unredeemed resist the Holy Spirit in a number of ways.

A. *They will refuse to attend worship services where it is possible for them to hear the Word of God.*

B. *They will avoid the Christian who is concerned to the extent that he or she will express hope that they might come to Christ.*
C. *They will offer all kinds of excuses for not trusting Jesus.*
D. *In some instances they will manifest anger.* He who is seeking to witness to this type of an individual needs to be very cautious, compassionate, and in tune with the Holy Spirit.

### Conclusion

Those who would be effective witnesses need to be aware of the manner in which people may resist the Holy Spirit. Instead of being depressed by the refusal of the unbeliever to respond to Jesus, we should give ourselves to more earnest prayer for guidance and help to lead the one who is resisting the Spirit to yield his or her heart to Jesus Christ.

---

## SUNDAY MORNING, AUGUST 9

***Title:*** A Command with a Great Promise

***Text:*** "Give, and it shall be given unto you; good measure, pressed down, and shaken together, and running over, shall men give into your bosom. For with the same measure that ye mete withal it shall be measured to you again" **(Luke 6:38)**.

***Scripture Reading:*** Acts 20:25–38

***Hymns:*** "Glorious Is Thy Name," McKinney

"Give of Your Best to the Master," Grose

"Take My Life and Let It Be," Havergal

***Offertory Prayer:*** Holy Father, we thank you for your generosity toward us. You have bestowed your mercy upon us in a lavish manner. You have bestowed spiritual blessings upon us extravagantly. You have given your Son to die for our sins. You have given your Spirit to dwell within our hearts. Help us this day to give you a faithful, trusting, loving heart. Help us to give you the thoughts of our minds and the strength of our hands. Accept our tithes and offerings as an indication of our desire to give our all to you. Through Jesus Christ. Amen.

### Introduction

Every command of our Lord involves a promise. To see only the command is to interpret life in terms of duty and responsibility. To see the promise without the command is to neglect to meet the essential condition for receiving the promise.

All of us have developed certain attitudes and concepts of life that make it difficult for us even to see some of God's promises. It would appear that we are blind to many things that God is trying to communicate to us. Is it not true that all of us have read certain passages of Scripture for years before the real message penetrated our consciousness? Our text is a case in point.

What do you hear the Savior saying when you read the following text? "Give, and it shall be given unto you; good measure, pressed down, and shaken together, and running over, shall men give into your bosom. For with the same measure that ye mete withal it shall be measured to you again" (Luke 6:38).

One person might reply, "This text teaches me that I should give full measure. It should be pressed down, shaken together, and overflowing." Another person might say, "I see in this a gimmick for the receiving of an offering." Both of these interpretations miss the point of the text by a country mile. The text contains one word of command and the balance of the text is a promise.

### I. The Lord commands his disciples to concentrate on giving.

"Give. . . ." From earliest childhood we are taught to be conservative with our money. We are taught that others would try to secure our money by one method or another. Because of this early teaching, combined with actual experience, most of us have developed what someone has called "a pocketbook-protection instinct." This instinct immediately begins to function when we hear the word *give.* Most of us experience a mental block at this point, and consequently most of us have failed to recognize the promise that is attached to this commandment.

A. *The reason for this command.*
   1. Giving is the way to real maturity. We are born with a selfish, acquiring instinct. We can claim to be mature only after we have learned to share.
   2. Giving is the way to happiness. While there is a happiness that comes as a result of receiving, the highest happiness that the human heart can know comes to those who are givers.
   3. Giving is the way to usefulness. Only as we give some service to others can we feel useful or can we be useful.

B. *The focus of the Christian's attention and effort is to be on giving.* This refers to every area of life and is not to be confined to the offering plate.
   1. Be a giver at home.
   2. Be a giver at school.
   3. Be a giver at work.
   4. Be a giver in business.
   5. Be a giver at church.

C. *The Christian's continual course of action is to be in terms of giving.* Many labor under the mistaken impression that the highest form of giving is in terms of gadgets or trinkets that can be purchased and wrapped up in a package. Often these are but poor substitutes for something else that is needed more.
   1. You can give love.
   2. You can give mercy.
   3. You can give forgiveness.
   4. You can give praise.
   5. You can give encouragement.
   6. You can give inspiration.

7. You can give gratitude.
8. You can give time.

## II. The Lord promises a rich reward from people.

"Give, and it shall be given unto you; good measure, pressed down, shaken together, and running over, shall men give into your bosom" (Luke 6:38). This is not only a promise. It is a principle that works in every area of life.

A. *The husband who lives to give happiness to his wife and family will find such returning to him in abundance.*

B. *The wife and mother who lives to be a giver will experience far more happiness than she who thinks only in terms of her own interests.*

C. *The businessman whose primary concern is to meet a need and render an excellent service to and for others will find his place of business crowded with customers.* His success will be beyond his expectations. He will find that people have repaid him "good measure, pressed down, shaken together, and running over."

## III. We must give lavishly if we would live abundantly.

A. *God gave lavishly and extravagantly when he gave his Son to be our Savior.*

B. *Jesus Christ gave himself freely and fully for us when he went to the cross to die for our sins.* As difficult as it may be for us to believe, there was more joy for him in connection with the cross than there would have been by avoiding the cross. "Who for the joy that was set before him endured the cross, despising the shame, and is set down at the right hand of the throne of God" (Heb. 12:2).

C. *If you would experience abundant life, you must come to accept the basic philosophy of Jesus: "It is more blessed to give than to receive" (Acts 20:35).*

Helen Steiner Rice has put this thought in poetic form:

*The more you give, the more you get,*
*The more you laugh, the less you fret—*
*The more you do unselfishly,*
*The more you live abundantly. . . .*
*The more of everything you share,*
*The more you'll always have to spare—*
*The more you love, the more you'll find*
*That life is good and friends are kind. . . .*
*For only what we give away,*
*Enriches us from day to day.*

## Conclusion

When Jesus Christ said, "Give," he was referring to everything that we are and have. If we want to experience abundant life, we must give every day. It is only as we give that we receive. The hand that greedily grips that which it possesses is automatically closed so that it is unable to receive.

## SUNDAY EVENING, AUGUST 9

***Title:*** "It Is Well with My Soul"

***Text:*** "Run now, I pray thee, to meet her, and say unto her, Is it well with thee? Is it well with thy husband? Is it well with the child? And she answered, It is well" (**2 Kings 4:26**).

### Introduction

The hymn "It Is Well with My Soul" expresses the joy of a Christian poet over the glad consciousness of a saving relationship with Jesus Christ. Assurance of salvation is possible for every believer (1 John 5:13).

Assurance makes peace of mind and heart possible and also makes effective service possible. There are many who lack assurance, for some lack salvation, some misunderstand salvation, some lack faith, and some have sin in their lives.

### I. It is well with my soul because salvation is by grace.

"By grace are ye saved through faith; and that not of yourselves: it is the gift of God: Not of works, lest any man should boast" (Eph. 2:8–9).

### II. It is well with my soul because of the presence of God's Spirit within my heart.

A. *"For as many as are led by the Spirit of God, they are the sons of God. The Spirit itself beareth witness with our spirit, that we are the children of God" (Rom. 8:14, 16).*

B. *"And hereby we know that he abideth in us, by the Spirit which he hath given us" (1 John 3:24).*

### III. It is well with my soul because of the keeping power of God.

A. *"For I know whom I have believed, and am persuaded that he is able to keep that which I have committed unto him against that day" (2 Tim. 1:12).*

B. *John 10:27–30.*

C. *Romans 8:35–39.*

### IV. It is well with my soul because of the testimony of God's holy Word.

Instead of basing our assurance of salvation on feelings, we should recognize that our feelings are determined by our understanding of certain facts. One must believe and accept the statements of Scripture in order to have assurance of salvation.

A. *John 3:18, 36.*

B. *John 5:24.*

### Conclusion

If the believer will give serious thought and study to the great salvation that comes through faith in Jesus Christ, he can join with Horatio G. Spafford in singing:

*When peace, like a river, attendeth my way,*
*When sorrows like sea-billows roll;*
*Whatever my lot, Thou hast taught me to say,*
*It is well, it is well with my soul.*

## WEDNESDAY EVENING, AUGUST 12

***Title:*** The Holy Spirit May Be Grieved

***Text:*** "And grieve not the holy Spirit of God, whereby ye are sealed unto the day of redemption" **(Eph. 4:30)**.

### Introduction

Paul encouraged the followers of Christ at Ephesus to conduct themselves in a manner so as not to grieve the Holy Spirit of God. The word *grieve* means "to make sorrowful." This reveals both the personality and the tenderheartedness of the Holy Spirit who dwells within each believer.

A study of the context of this challenge not to grieve the Spirit indicates the manner by which the Spirit can be grieved.

### I. If we do not walk worthy of our Christian calling, we will grieve the Holy Spirit.

"I, therefore, the prisoner of the Lord, beseech you that ye walk worthy of the vocation wherewith ye are called" (Eph. 4:1).

### II. If we do not walk differently from the unregenerate world, we will grieve the Holy Spirit.

"This I say therefore, and testify in the Lord, that ye henceforth walk not as other Gentiles walk, in the vanity of their mind" (Eph. 4:17).

### III. If we do not walk in love, we will grieve the Holy Spirit.

"Be ye therefore followers of God; ... And walk in love, as Christ also hath loved us, and hath given himself for us an offering and a sacrifice to God for a sweet-smelling savour" (Eph. 5:1–2).

### IV. If we do not walk in the light, we will grieve the Holy Spirit.

"For ye were sometimes darkness, but now are ye light in the Lord: walk as children of light" (Eph. 5:8).

### V. If we do not walk carefully, we will grieve the Holy Spirit.

"See then that ye walk circumspectly, not as fools, but as wise" (Eph. 5:15).

### Conclusion

As sensitive parents grieve when their children fail to respond to their opportunities, even so the Holy Spirit grieves when we neglect to respond in a manner that would enable us to experience and manifest the beauty of Jesus Christ in our lives. The Holy Spirit is saddened when we are not instantly obedient to his commands of love. He wants to guide us and use us to bless others. Instead of grieving him, let each of us respond so as to bring joy to the Holy Spirit.

## SUNDAY MORNING, AUGUST 16

***Title:*** Do You Love the Lord?

***Text:*** "I love the LORD, because he hath heard my voice and my supplications" **(Ps. 116:1)**.

***Scripture Reading:*** Psalm 116:1–19

***Hymns:*** "Love Divine," Wesley

"My Jesus, I Love Thee," Anonymous

"O Love That Wilt Not Let Me Go," Matheson

***Offertory Prayer:*** Holy Father, today we pray that you would open our eyes and help us to see how richly blessed we are by your grace. Deliver us from blindness to your generosity. Help us to recognize that we can prove our love for you by sharing the rich blessings that you have bestowed on us with others. We desire to share the story of your love with the multitudes who continue to dwell in spiritual darkness. Take these tithes and offerings and bless them in the hands and lives of missionaries who seek to communicate the message of your love to a lost world. Help each of us to give as an act of worship. Through Jesus Christ. Amen.

### Introduction

Do you find it difficult to love God with all of your heart, with all of your soul, and with all of your mind (Matt. 22:37)? Some find it exceedingly difficult to love God in this manner because of false concepts of God. Some think of him as being an absentee God who is far away. They fail to recognize that he is always present. Others think of God as being a bully. Jesus came that people might know him in a father-child relationship. Some consider God to be stern and harsh, but Jesus revealed him to be a tender, kind, and loving heavenly Father. Some think that God is too busy to be concerned about them. Jesus had time to take children into his arms and bless them. He declared that the God who is aware of the falling of a sparrow is also concerned about each of us.

There are some who look upon God as being spiteful and vengeful. Jesus revealed him to be full of mercy and grace. It is easy to love the God whom Jesus came to reveal once we discover his beauty and love. On one occasion Jesus said to Philip, "He that hath seen me hath seen the Father" (John 14:9).

Even though the psalmist lived hundreds of years before Jesus came to reveal the grace of God, he had discovered in his own experience the gracious love and continuing mercy of God. In fact, he sang a hymn of love in which he enumerated a long list of reasons why he loved God. The message of the morning, like the message of the psalmist, takes the form of a personal testimony.

### I. I love the Lord because "he hath heard my voice and my supplications."

David was declaring his love for the Lord because the Lord had answered his prayers. You and I should be able to bear the same testimony.

A. *David had prayed for help in times of trouble, and God had heard and delivered him.*

B. *David had experienced times of great uncertainty when he needed guidance. When he prayed, God directed his path.*

C. *David had prayed in times of weakness, and God had given him strength.* Particularly was this so when he fought Goliath the giant. David expressed his confidence in the strength that God would give in a conversation with King Saul. He said, "The LORD that delivered me out of the paw of the lion, and out of the paw of the bear, he will deliver me out of the hand of this Philistine" (1 Sam. 17:37).

From the beginning to the end of the Bible there is continuous testimony that our God is a prayer-hearing and prayer-answering God. Barren and empty is your life if you have never experienced a definite answer to your prayers. Your blessings at this point will be in proportion to your faithfulness in coming before God's throne of grace for help in time of need. "Ye have not, because ye ask not" (James 4:2).

### II. I love the Lord because "[he hath] delivered my soul from death."

"For what shall it profit a man, if he shall gain the whole world, and lose his own soul?" (Mark 8:36). Our most valuable possession is our soul, our very being.

A. *We are grateful to our physician, who saves us from the effects of disease.*

B. *We are grateful to our teachers, who challenged our minds and delivered us from the blight of ignorance.*

C. *We are grateful to those who have given us counsel that has saved us from professional or economic failure.*

D. *While we should be grateful and manifest love for those who have rendered great personal services, we should also recognize that Jesus Christ has rendered the greatest service to us by dying for our sins on the cross to deliver us from spiritual death.* Through faith in him we have the delightful privilege of passing out of the realm of death into the realm of eternal life. "Verily, verily, I say unto you, he that heareth my word, and believeth on him that sent me, hath everlasting life, and shall not come into condemnation; but is passed from death unto life" (John 5:24).

### III. I love the Lord because "[he hath] delivered ... mine eyes from tears."

When John saw the new heaven and the new earth, he declared, "God shall wipe away all tears from their eyes; and there shall be no more death, neither sorrow, nor crying, neither shall there be any more pain: for the former things are passed away" (Rev. 21:4).

Has it ever occurred to you that God has already wiped away many of the tears that would have flooded your eyes if you had not known him as a personal Lord and Savior? If it had not been for his guiding presence in your mind and heart, you would have walked in the way of the transgressor where there is no peace and happiness and contentment. You would have known the frustrations and agony of facing life without the resources that God has made available to you. There would have been no comfort in the time of sorrow. There would have been no guidance in the time of uncertainty. There would have been no hope in the time of defeat. Our Lord has already wiped many of the tears from our eyes by removing the cause for those tears. Because of this great ministry, we should find it easy to love him and to praise him.

### IV. I love the Lord because "[he hath] delivered ... my feet from falling."

The salvation that our Lord seeks to accomplish in our life extends beyond the forgiveness of sin. He is eager to deliver us from the power and practice of sin in our daily life. Not one of us has followed him faithfully all of the way at all times. In spite of our deafness to his gentle warnings and our momentary rebellions against his gentle guidance, we can all bear testimony to his abiding presence in every time of need.

A baccalaureate sermon was preached to a group of young graduates. The title of the speaker's address was "The Infallible Leadership of Jesus Christ." The speaker declared to the students that they could put their faith always in the guidance of Jesus Christ because he was an infallible leader who would always lead them right. Jesus declared, "He that followeth me shall not walk in darkness, but shall have the light of life" (John 8:12). If we walk in the light, we can be assured that Jesus will deliver our feet from the danger of falling into some abyss of evil.

### Conclusion

Do you love the Lord? There are many reasons why we should love him. We should love him because he is our Savior, our Leader, and our Friend. We should love him for the privilege of serving that he has granted to us. We should love him because he has promised to deliver us from death and the grave and to prepare for us a home at the end of the way.

There are those who do not love Jesus because they have not yet responded by faith to the love that he demonstrated on the cross when he died for their sins. They know that they should love him, and they intend to love him someday. These ones would be wise to trust him as their Lord today.

## SUNDAY EVENING, AUGUST 16

***Title:*** "Jesus Is the Friend You Need"

***Text:*** "Henceforth I call you not servants; for the servant knoweth now what his lord doeth: but I have called you friends" **(John 15:15)**.

***Scripture Reading:*** John 15:13–15

### Introduction

Perhaps no fact in the Bible is more convincingly established than that Jesus is the Friend of sinners. The Pharisees and scribes found fault with Jesus and criticized him severely because of his association with those who were considered irreligious. The parables of the lost sheep, the lost coin, the lost son, and the waiting father were his reply to the charge of being a friend of publicans and sinners.

The earth's greatest man is the sinner's best friend.

### I. Jesus proves that he is the sinner's friend.

A. *His words will convince you (Luke 15).*

B. *His life reveals this fact.*

C. *His compassion convinces us.*

D. *His death proves it.*

### II. The blessed privilege of Jesus' friendship.

In the words of the hymn writer, "Jesus Is the Friend You Need."

A. *Do you need a friend with infinite power?*

B. *Do you need a friend with infinite wisdom?*

C. *Do you need a friend with unlimited love?*

D. *Do you need an ever-present friend who can go with you all of the way? (Prov. 17:17; 18:24; Matt. 28:20; Gal. 2:20).*

Proverbs 18:24 says that "there is a friend that sticketh closer than a brother." Thomas Fuller said, "They are rich who have true friends." Henry Adams said that one friend in a lifetime is much, two are many, and three are hardly possible. Jesus is the greatest Friend we can have.

### III. The transforming friendship.

A. *Jesus offers his friendship as a gift.* We must respond in faith to receive it.

B. *Our obedience to Jesus shows that we are his friends (John 15:14).*

### Conclusion

Friendship with Jesus can begin right now. It is personal, it is real, and it is transforming. I. E. Reynolds would encourage you to begin this friendship with Christ tonight:

*When the sun shines bright and your heart is light,*
*Jesus is the Friend you need;*

*When the clouds hang low in this world of woe,*
*Jesus is the Friend you need.*

*If you're lost in sin, all is dark within,*
*Jesus is the Friend you need;*
*God alone can save thro' the Son He gave.*
*Jesus is the Friend you need.*

*When in the sad hour, when in death's grim pow'r,*
*Jesus is the Friend you need,*
*If you would prepare 'gainst the tempter's snare,*
*Jesus is the Friend you need.*

*When the cares of life all around are rife,*
*Jesus is the Friend you need;*
*Glory to His name, always He's the same.*
*Jesus is the Friend you need.*

## WEDNESDAY EVENING, AUGUST 19

***Title:*** Do You Quench the Spirit?

***Text:*** "Quench not the Spirit" **(1 Thess. 5:19)**.

### Introduction

The presence and power of the Holy Spirit carry with them new responsibilities. Where there is responsibility, certain perils are created. Each of us finds the peril of making a negligent response to the ministry of the Holy Spirit in our lives.

The purpose and power of the Holy Spirit is not something that we are merely to enjoy. Ours is to be a response of recognition, surrender, and cooperation.

The picture in our text is that of pouring water on a fire. The inspired writer is saying to us, "Do not pour water on the fire that the Holy Spirit kindles within your heart. Do not choke the life out of the impulses that come from the Holy Spirit."

### I. Do you ever feel a deep need to go apart for prayer and communion with God?

How many of us would have to plead guilty to disobeying the Holy Spirit's invitation to the closet of prayer? There are times when God has a rich blessing for us, and by means of the Holy Spirit he calls us to the place of prayer and communion that he might bestow this blessing upon us. When we quench the Holy Spirit's leadership at this point, we impoverish ourselves and rob others of the greater blessing that we could be to them had we responded to the invitation to pray.

### II. Do you ever feel a great heart hunger to study the Word of God?

Do you permit something else to occupy your time so as to make it impossible to open up God's Word that you might feast on the Bread of Life and quench your thirst with the Water of Life? Did it ever occur to you that the Holy Spirit was trying to lead you to some message that you desperately need and that could be revealed to you through the written Word of God? The Holy Spirit is able to open up the Scriptures and to make the truth of God relevant and real to the life situation in which we find ourselves. To neglect the daily devotional study of God's Word is to quench the Spirit.

### III. Have you experienced a deep inward impulse to speak to someone concerning spiritual things?

Do you suppose that such an impression could possibly come from the Devil? Satan would never motivate you to encourage another in a conversation concerning the grace and goodness of God.

The Holy Spirit dwells in your heart and would utilize your experiences, your conversation, and all of your contacts for the glory of God and for the spiritual well-being of others.

Generally you can assume that when a deep inward inclination causes you to become concerned about another, the Holy Spirit has been working in that person's heart also. He is seeking to use you as the medium through which a portion of the message of God can be communicated to the other person.

If you will respond by faith in an attitude of humility, you will experience the joy of being used by the Holy Spirit to bring the blessings of God into the lives of others.

### Conclusion

The Holy Spirit will utilize you in giving praise to God and bringing the blessings of God into the lives of others if you will but recognize his presence and cooperate with his leadership. Not to do so is to pour water on the fire. Not to do so is to choke the life out of something that God is seeking to bring to fruition.

---

## SUNDAY MORNING, AUGUST 23

***Title:*** The Habit of Giving Thanks

***Text:*** "In every thing give thanks: for this is the will of God in Christ Jesus concerning you" **(1 Thess. 5:18)**.

### Introduction

All of us are creatures of habit, and each of us has some good habits and some bad habits. We are what we are largely because of the habits we have developed. Some of these habits have been developed carefully and deliberately. Others we have just drifted into and adopted without deliberation. When I was a boy, my father would always say to me, "Now, Son, what are you supposed to say?" This was his reminder to me to say "thank you" when one of my uncles would give me a nickel. My attitude of gratitude occasionally produced another nickel. My father was trying to instill within me the habit of expressing thanks. The words of our text say, "In every thing give thanks." Let us develop the habit of giving thanks.

**I. The giving of thanks is a habit to be learned.**

A. *We do not become grateful instinctively.*

B. *We acquire the attitude of gratitude that expresses itself in words and actions.* We wonder why only one of the lepers returned to give thanks (Luke 17:11–19). Perhaps that one had developed the habit of recognizing good things and then expressing gratitude for them.

C. *We need to give attention to our habits.* We talk much about bad habits. We first make our habits, and then our habits make us. You are what you are because of the habits that you have developed. If you are ungrateful, it could be that you have never opened your eyes and developed the habit of expressing thanks for things that come to you.

***The Thankful Heart***

*For all that God in mercy sends—*
*For health and children, home and friends;*
*For comfort in the time of need,*
*For every kindly word or deed,*
*For happy thoughts and holy talk,*
*For guidance in our daily walk—*
*In everything give thanks!*

*For beauty in this world of ours,*
*For verdant grass and lovely flowers,*
*For songs of birds, for hum of bees,*
*For the refreshing summer breeze,*
*For hill and plain, for stream and wood,*
*For the great ocean's mighty flood—*
*In everything give thanks!*

*For the sweet sleep which comes with night,*
*For the returning morning light,*
*For the bright sun that shines on high,*
*For the stars glittering in the sky—*
*For these and every thing we see,*
*O Lord, our heart we lift to Thee;*
*In every thing give thanks!*

—*Ellen Isabelle Tupper,* Quest and Conquests

William Law said, "If anyone would tell you the shortest and surest way to happiness, he must tell you to make it a rule to yourself to thank and praise God for everything that happens to you. For it is certain that when whatever seems calamity happens to you, if you thank and praise God for it, you turn it into a blessing." We should look for things for which we can thank God.

**II. The giving of thanks is a habit that should be learned.**

A. *The giving of thanks will produce joy.* It should be maintained and developed not just to show courtesy but because it will produce joy for all concerned.

1. The expression of thanks and gratitude brings joy to the heart of the heavenly Father. I do not know of anything that brings more delight to my heart than to hear one of my children say, "Dad, I love you" or "Dad, I am grateful." I believe that something in the heart of God rejoices when we come to him saying, "Thank you." Most of us go to him with our hands out.
2. The offering of thanks brings great joy to others. How long has it been since you have thanked your husband or wife and showed your appreciation for him or her? How long has it been since you wrote a letter to your mother and expressed gratitude for all she meant and did for you?
3. Joy will come into your own heart when you stop to say thank you. A boy was counting up the good things and the bad things that had happened in his life. He counted the good things first and became so happy about them that he forgot the bad things.

B. *The giving of thanks will always strengthen faith in the goodness of God.* John R. Bisagno, author of *The Power of Positive Prayer,* says that the first step in effective prayer is praise. Go into the presence of God thanking him for all that he has done for you. It will do something for your heart, your faith, and your gratitude. Paul had this in mind when he wrote, "Be careful for nothing; but in everything by prayer and supplication with thanksgiving let your requests be made known unto God" (Phil. 4:6). If you do not thank God for his blessings upon you, you will weaken your own faith.

C. *To be habitually thankful is to deepen your love for God and for others.* This love can be cultivated, and it grows. One of the finest ways to cultivate love for each other is to develop the habit of giving thanks. An expression of gratitude does much for you and also for others.

D. *To be habitually thankful will encourage an optimistic and hopeful outlook on life.* We all have more pessimism than we should. We can always see the hole instead of the doughnut. This is because we are selfish.

The Latin word *optimus* means "best," while the Latin word *pessimus* means "worst."

E. *To be habitually thankful is to discover the beauty of living.* Life can be beautiful if we look for the flowers. If we develop the habit of being sensitive and aware of the good things that come along in life, life will be more beautiful.

**III. The habit of giving thanks can be developed. How do you develop this habit?**

A. *We must begin by being grateful today.* Gratitude is the memory of the heart. We should determine that we are going to be grateful, again and again, until it becomes the automatic expression of our soul. Surely every one of us, even the most unfortunate among us, have many things for which we can be grateful.

B. *We must search for things to be grateful for.*
C. *We need to express gratitude even for small things.* We can bring joy into the life of a waitress or clerk by being thankful for the service she has rendered. Teachers will be greatly delighted if we tell them that we sincerely appreciate what they are doing for us. How long has it been since you have sent a letter to someone expressing sincere thanks for what they have meant to you and have done for you?
D. *We must search for ways to express thanks.* "In every thing give thanks, for this is the will of God for you." God wants us to develop the habit of expressing thanks, for he is glorified not by our groanings but by our expressions of thanks.

### Conclusion

"The art of thanksgiving is 'thanksliving'—gratitude in action. It is applying Albert Schweitzer's philosophy: 'In gratitude for your own good fortune you must render in return some sacrifice of your life for other life.' It is thanking God for the gift of life by living it triumphantly. It is thanking God for all that men and women have done for you by doing things for others. It is thanking God for opportunities by accepting them as a challenge to achievement. It is thanking God for happiness by striving to make others happy. It is thanking God for beauty by helping to make the world more beautiful. It is thanking God for inspiration by trying to be an inspiration to others. It is thanking God for health and strength by the care and reverence you show your body. It is thanking God for each new day by living it to the fullest."

—*Wilferd A. Peterson,* The Treasure Chest

---

## SUNDAY EVENING, AUGUST 23

***Title:*** "Take Time to Be Holy"

***Text:*** "But as he which hath called you is holy, so be ye holy in all manner of conversation; because it is written, Be ye holy; for I am holy" **(1 Peter 1:15–16)**.

### Introduction

The hymn "Take Time to Be Holy" contains a challenge for the heart of every believer. It brings to our attention a needed challenge that is misunderstood by many people.

### I. Our God is a holy God.

The biblical concept of holiness is strange to the ears of modern people. By the word *holiness,* the biblical writers were referring to the very essence of deity.

God's holiness is that part of his nature that reacts against sin. They used this word to describe the unique difference that existed between God and man.

A. *Exodus 3:5–6.*
B. *Isaiah 6:1–6.*

### II. The holiness of God calls for holiness on the part of his people.

The concept of the holiness of God came to refer to his flawless character, his moral nature, and the moral requirements that he placed on his people. What was dedicated to God was considered holy unto God: it belonged to God, was available to him, and was for his use only.

### III. A holy nation.

The purpose of God for us is that we be a holy nation. This we cannot be accidentally or incidentally. The hymn writer challenges us.

A. *"Take time to be holy."*
B. *"Speak oft with the Lord."*
C. *"Abide in him always."*
D. *"Feed on his Word."*
E. *"Make friends of God's children."*
F. *"Help those who are weak."*
G. *"Forgetting in nothing his blessings to seek."*

### Conclusion

To be holy is to be dedicated to God and available for his use. To be holy is to know the joy and peace and usefulness for which every human heart hungers. (Quote the other stanzas of the hymn if you like.)

---

## WEDNESDAY EVENING, AUGUST 26

***Title:*** Full of the Spirit

***Text:*** "Be not drunk with wine, wherein is excess; but be filled with the Spirit" **(Eph. 5:18)**.

### Introduction

On the day of Pentecost, those who were assembled together in prayer waiting for the promise of the Father were filled with the Holy Spirit (Acts 2:4). Being filled with the Spirit was not a once-for-all experience reserved only for those who were present on the day of Pentecost. We read that Peter was filled with the Holy Spirit as he spoke to the rulers and elders (Acts 4:8). When the church prayed, they were all filled with the Holy Spirit (Acts 4:31). The first deacons were said to be full of the Holy Spirit (Acts 6:3). Stephen spoke with great power because he was full of the Holy Spirit (Acts 7:55). Barnabas was a man full of the Holy Spirit (Acts 11:24). We read also that Saul, who became Paul, was filled with the Holy

Spirit (Acts 13:9). We should not be surprised when we read in Paul's epistle to the Ephesians that he exhorted them, "Be not drunk with wine, wherein is excess; but be filled with the Spirit" (Eph. 5:18).

**I. To be filled with the Spirit is to be God-intoxicated.**

Evidently there are some similarities between being filled with the Spirit and being intoxicated with alcohol, for Paul would not have said, "Be not drunk with wine, wherein is excess; but be filled with the Spirit." Someone has listed these similarities as follows:

A. *Those filled with the Spirit are brave.*
B. *Those filled with the Spirit are happy.*
C. *Those filled with the Spirit are talkative.*
D. *Those filled with the Spirit are generous.*
E. *Those filled with the Spirit are unworried about tomorrow.*

**II. To be filled with the Spirit is to be emptied of self.**

When self is on the throne, the Christ is forced to the circumference of life.

A. *The Spirit leads us to put spiritual life ahead of material life.*
B. *The Spirit leads us to set our affections on things above rather than on the perishable things of the present.*

**III. The pathway to the fullness of the Spirit.**

A. *We must have faith to believe that the Holy Spirit has come to dwell within our hearts (1 Cor. 3:16).*
B. *The Holy Spirit is permitted to enter fully as we give ourselves to prayer (Acts 4:31).*
C. *The Holy Spirit can take charge completely only when we yield ourselves to a life of grateful obedience to the will of God (Acts 5:32).*

---

## SUNDAY MORNING, AUGUST 30

***Title:*** A Certain Rich Man

***Text:*** "There was a certain rich man, which was clothed in purple and fine linen, and fared sumptuously every day" **(Luke 16:19)**.

***Scripture Reading:*** Luke 16:19–31

***Hymns:*** "My Soul, Be on Thy Guard," Heath
"Ye Must Be Born Again," Sleeper
"Why Do You Wait?" Root

***Offertory Prayer:*** Our heavenly Father, our prayers ascend to you this day in the name of our Savior. We ask you to bless these tithes and offerings given to you out of grateful hearts. Bless them to your use and the building up of your kingdom. Amen.

## Introduction

Jesus, the master storyteller, related a disturbing and thought-provoking parable about a rich man, but many of us miss his point. The parable has been used to verify the fact of hell as the destiny of the unbelieving, and it has been used as a basis for discussing both the temperature and the geography of the home of the doomed. It should bring tears to the eyes of everyone who contemplates what it will mean for a person to enter eternity outside of the favor and the salvation of God.

It is very possible that Jesus told this parable, not to describe hell, but to insist on people making a proper response to the message of Moses and the prophets (cf. Luke 16:29–31). The primary message of the parable is to be found in the rich man, his condition, his response, and the catastrophe he experienced. Many of us miss the point of the parable because we identify with Lazarus. We read about how Lazarus was poor, sick, and ignored in this life and how he eventually died and went to heaven. Many of us say, "That is talking about me. I am poor and ignored and mistreated, and when I die I have hope of going to heaven." We never identify with the rich man, and consequently we fail to hear the warning that comes to each of us personally in this powerful parable.

## I. Consider the rich man's riches.

A. *Evidently he was rich in money.* We usually measure riches in monetary terms.

B. *He was rich in food and clothing, for the parable says that "he was clothed in purple and fine linen and fared sumptuously every day."*

C. *Perhaps he was rich in friends. Usually those who are wealthy have many wealthy friends.*

D. *He was rich in leisure in that it was not necessary for him to struggle to earn his daily bread to keep from starving.*

E. *He was rich in his family, for the parable says that he had at least five brothers in his father's house (Luke 16:19).*

F. *He was rich in good health, at least for a time. The parable indicates that he had a good appetite, which is usually an indication of good health (Luke 16:19).*

G. *He was rich in talents, for unless he inherited his estate, he had been successful in acquiring material goods.*

H. *If we would be honest, we would discover that the rich man, rather than Lazarus, is the ideal of most of us.* He is the one whom we are inclined to envy. For us to fail to recognize this and to identify with him in this parable is to miss the cutting edge of what Jesus Christ was trying to communicate.

## II. Consider the rich man's blindness.

Did I hear you say that you did not know that the rich man was blind? The parable does not say so, but he was.

A. *The rich man was blind to his opportunities.* He had the opportunity to meet the desperate needs of a man who was lying at his gate at the point of death, and he also had the opportunity to make preparation for eternity.

B. *The rich man was blind to the needs of others (Luke 16:20).* Perhaps the rich man turned his head to avoid looking at Lazarus, as the priest and the Levite had done concerning the man who was robbed between Jerusalem and Jericho in Jesus' parable of the good Samaritan (Luke 10:30–32). Perhaps he was so preoccupied with his business that he never even saw Lazarus.

C. *The rich man was blind to the issues of eternity.* He failed to recognize the eternal significance of both his attitudes and his actions in the present. How terrible it is to be blind. Are you rich and also blind to your opportunities, to the needs of others, and to the issues of eternity?

### III. Consider the rich man's deafness.

Did I hear you say that you did not know that the rich man was deaf? The parable does not say so, but he was.

A. *The rich man was deaf to the voice of God.* In speaking about his brothers and his desire that they repent, he revealed that he had opportunities to respond to the voice of God but for one reason or another had declined. For all practical purposes, he who hears and refuses to respond is acting as if he were deaf.

B. *The rich man was deaf to the cries of distress about him.* Lazarus the beggar lay at the rich man's gate full of sores and at the point of death. We can assume that as the rich man entered the gate, Lazarus would lift his hand and make some audible plea for alms.

How tragic is the deafness of those who consider themselves to be God's people today. We fail to hear the desolate cries of distress of those about us who are in spiritual darkness and loneliness and who in one way or another continuously give voice to the emptiness of life as they experience it away from God. We have the message of him who can bring light and life and love to them. We have acted as deaf people to our Lord's commission to evangelize the world, beginning at our own home and continuing to the uttermost part of the earth (Acts 1:8).

### IV. Consider the rich man's misery in time as well as in eternity.

The parable does not say anything about the rich man being miserable while on earth; it does emphasize that fact after he entered eternity (Luke 16:23–28). A study of the parable reveals the rich man's selfishness.

A. *The rich man was self-centered, and self-centeredness never produces the highest possible human happiness.* We are not stretching the evidence at all to assume that even though he was rich and fared sumptuously, he was also miserable. His self-centeredness in life is revealed by his blindness to the needs of Lazarus and his deafness to his cries for help while enjoying the bounty of his own riches. Someone has said that when an individual is wrapped up in himself, he makes a mighty small package.

B. *The rich man was self-centered in death.* Notice the plea that came from his heart: "Father Abraham, have mercy on me, and send Lazarus, that he may dip the tip of his finger in water, and cool my tongue; for I am tormented in this flame" (Luke 16:24). His sole interest was his own comfort, and he immediately requisitioned the assistance of Lazarus as a servant to contribute to his comfort. It had been his habit in life to issue orders and to use men for his own personal well-being. He continued to be self-centered in hell.

The rich man again requisitioned the services of a man who had laid at his gate for days, ignored and unhelped, to render a service for his five brothers. While the concern of the rich man for his brothers has been used to illustrate the compassion that we should have for others, it should be recognized that in his particular case it was but a further expression of selfish concern for his own.

### V. Consider the rich man's brothers (Luke 16:28–31).

A. *Mention has been made of our tendency to identify with Lazarus rather than the rich man.* Perhaps we would be getting very close to the heart of this parable if we considered the possibility of identifying with these five brothers who are still among the living. Are you one of the brothers of the rich man who was not only rich but blind and deaf as well as foolish to live a self-centered life?

B. *Do you make the decisions of life primarily on a materialistic basis?* Do you live by the philosophy that a person must have bread in order to live? Are you constantly concerned with the questions, "What will it cost me? What's in it for me?" Do you look upon success in terms of being clothed in purple and fine linen and faring sumptuously every day? Lord, forgive us and bring us to our senses.

C. *Do you place spiritual values in second place rather than first place?* Do the demands of your stomach have precedent over the needs of your soul? As a creature of eternity living in time, do you act as the grasshopper who lives for the present unaware of the fact that the frost is going to fall and the grass is going to die?

D. *Have you accepted a false scale of values that puts the material before the spiritual, the temporal before the eternal?*

E. *Have you for some reason neglected to repent? (Luke 16:30).* To repent is something infinitely more than just being filled with remorse for past failures. Positively, repentance is both the act and the continuing attitude of making Jesus Christ the Lord of our lives. To really repent toward God is to change your attitude from an attitude of ignoring him to recognizing and acknowledging him. Instead of resenting him and rebelling against him, it is to respond to his love with a glad surrender of both the will and the emotions.

### Conclusion

The rich man of the parable was rich in many things, but because of his blindness to the things that really mattered and because of his deafness to the call of God and the inner hunger of his own soul, as well as to the cries of distress of those about him, he was inwardly miserable in life and forever miserable in eternity.

May God help you to open your eyes to your spiritual poverty and to your need for the spiritual riches that can come to you through repentance toward God and faith in the Lord Jesus. May God help you to hear today the warning of the rich man that you might avoid his destiny. May God help you to hear the message of Moses and the prophets concerning the Savior who came and died for our sins. He is risen from the dead and will be your Savior today if you let him become the Lord of your life.

---

## SUNDAY EVENING, AUGUST 30

***Title:*** "I Will Sing of My Redeemer"

***Text:*** "And at midnight Paul and Silas prayed, and sang praises unto God: and the prisoners heard them" **(Acts 16:25)**.

***Scripture Reading:*** Acts 16:16–25

### Introduction

Did you ever hear prisoners who had been cruelly beaten and unjustly imprisoned sing of the grace and love of God? It was indeed a strange turn of events for the prisoners in the jail of Philippi when Paul and Silas were placed in the inner prison. Instead of complaints and curses, they heard these men give utterance to prayers and hymns of praise to God. Why were they able to react in this strange manner?

### I. Paul and Silas had discovered that God is love.

This is the supreme truth of Christianity revealed in the life, death, resurrection, and living presence of the Savior. As the well-known hymnwriter Philip P. Bliss wrote,

> *I will sing of my Redeemer*
> *And His heav'nly love to me;*
> *He from death to life hath bro't me,*
> *Son of God with Him to be.*

### II. Paul and Silas had experienced the forgiveness of sins.

They could rejoice that though they were condemned by the officials in Philippi, they were not condemned before the bar of God's holiness (Rom. 5:1; 8:1; John 3:17–18).

### III. Paul and Silas were assured that death had been defeated.

They were completely convinced that through faith in Jesus, who had conquered death and the grave, they likewise would have full and complete victory over death and the tomb. Jesus had demonstrated the reality of immortality, and they did not cower in fear before the prospect of death. Because of this confidence, they were able to sing.

### IV. Paul and Silas were experiencing the living presence of Jesus Christ.

The Savior had attached a thrilling promise to his command that his disciples busy themselves in the task of witnessing. His promise was, "Lo, I am with you alway" (Matt. 28:20). Although the prisoners could not see Jesus, he was very real to Paul and Silas. He is always real to those who through faith obey.

### Conclusion

When Charles Wesley contemplated the wonder of our great salvation, he wished, "O for a thousand tongues to sing my great Redeemer's praise. . . ."

## Suggested Preaching Program for
# SEPTEMBER

### ■ Sunday Mornings

Hebrews 11, Faith's Hall of Fame, provides examples of those who lived the life of faith in their generation. God would have us to listen to the testimony of each of these witnesses (Heb. 12:1) for a message that can deepen our faith and encourage greater faithfulness.

### ■ Sunday Evenings

"The Witnessing Church in the Books of Acts" is the theme suggested for Sunday evenings. The messages present the early church as it responded to the commission of the risen Lord to be witnesses to all people, from the hometown to the uttermost parts of the earth. It is hoped that by these messages individuals will be encouraged to witness.

### ■ Wednesday Evenings

"The Work of the Holy Spirit" is the theme for Wednesday evenings this month. Believers are encouraged to recognize and respond to the Holy Spirit who has come to abide within their hearts.

---

## WEDNESDAY EVENING, SEPTEMBER 2

***Title:*** What Should I Believe about the Holy Spirit?

***Scripture Reading:*** Acts 2:1–21

### Introduction

Some believe that the Holy Spirit is an influence. Others believe that the Holy Spirit is the Word of God. But we know that the Holy Spirit is the third person of the Trinity.

### I. The Holy Spirit is the divine Spirit of God.

A. *Mystery surrounds the Trinity—God the Father, God the Son, God the Holy Spirit.* W. Herschel Ford says, "The Holy Spirit is God in the human heart."

B. *Personality is ascribed to the Holy Spirit.*

1. The Holy Spirit helps us in our infirmities and helps us to pray as we should (Rom. 8:26–27). Only a person could do this.
2. The Holy Spirit is capable of being grieved (Eph. 4:30). Only a person can be grieved.
3. Peter said Ananias had lied to the Holy Spirit (Acts 5:3).

4. The Holy Spirit is said to exercise his will in the matter of his bestowal of spiritual gifts (1 Cor. 12:11).

C. *The personal masculine pronoun is used in referring to the Holy Spirit (John 14:16–17, 26; 15:26).*

**II. The Holy Spirit brings about the miracle of the new birth.**

A. *The Holy Spirit convicts of sin (John 16:7–11).*

B. *The conversion experience is described as a renewing of the Holy Spirit (Titus 3:5).*

C. *The Holy Spirit leads us to the Savior (1 Cor. 12:3; Rev. 22:17).*

D. *The Holy Spirit gives assurance of salvation to the believer (Rom. 8:16).*

**III. The Holy Spirit fills the place in the life of the believer that the living Christ filled in the life of the apostles (John 14:16–18).**

A. *The Greek word translated "another" means "another of the same kind."* The word translated "Comforter" refers to one "called to walk by the side of." Jesus is promising that God will give to them the Holy Spirit who will be to them what he had been.

B. *"Whom the world cannot receive."* The word translated "receive" can also mean "seize or arrest." Jesus is promising that the unregenerate world will not be able to arrest and crucify the Holy Spirit, for the Holy Spirit will dwell within believers' hearts.

C. *"I will not leave you comfortless: I will come to you" (John 14:18).* In these words Jesus is promising that by his ascension he will step through the curtain of invisibility that he might come back in Spirit to be with them always.

**Conclusion**

The Holy Spirit does not ordinarily work where his person and presence are ignored. Trust in him for guidance and cooperate with him as he seeks to do his work in you.

---

## SUNDAY MORNING, SEPTEMBER 6

***Title:*** The Life of Faith

***Text:*** "Without faith it is impossible to please him: for he that cometh to God must believe that he is, and that he is a rewarder of them that diligently seek him" **(Heb. 11:6)**.

***Scripture Reading:*** Hebrews 11:1–6

***Hymns:*** "Have Faith in God," McKinney

"My Faith Looks Up to Thee," Palmer

"Faith Is the Victory," Yates

"'Tis So Sweet to Trust in Jesus," Stead

***Offertory Prayer:*** Holy Father, you have given us a multitude of undeserved blessings. You have given us the opportunity to be alive. You have given us an experience of your grace and love, your power and mercy, which we are eager to share with all people everywhere. Help us to give unto them a living demonstration of what it means to be a Christian. Help us to give unto them the glad testimony of our lips. And now as we bring our tithes and offerings to you, we do so as an indication of our desire to be completely yours and in an effort to help others around the world come to know your love. Amen.

## Introduction

Do you face the future with your heart filled with fear, or do you face the future with your heart filled with faith in the goodness of God and in your own ability, with the help of God, to meet life in a victorious manner?

There are many things in today's world that could contribute to anxiety in the mind of each of us if we were to concentrate our attention on our difficulties and problems rather than on our responsibilities and opportunities.

In the midst of a great worldwide depression, President Roosevelt said in his inaugural address, "The only thing we have to fear is fear itself." When people forget God, they either tremble in fear as they face the future, or they are strongly tempted to make a flight from danger, which takes them away from their place of duty, responsibility, and opportunity. Dr. W. F. Powell, a pastor in Nashville, Tennessee, in the last century, expressed this truth as follows:

*When faith in God goes, Man the Thinker loses his greatest thought.*
*When faith in God goes, Man the Worker loses his greatest motive.*
*When faith in God goes, Man the Sinner loses his strongest help.*
*When faith in God goes, Man the Sufferer loses his securest refuge.*
*When faith in God goes, Man the Lover loses his fairest vision.*
*When faith in God goes, Man the Mortal loses his only home.*

Let us determine to walk by faith with the living God, who has always proven faithful in meeting the deepest needs of those who trust him and obey his loving commandments for their lives.

## I. Faith in faith.

One must have faith in faith to walk the way of faith victoriously.

A. *Many people do not have faith in faith.* The wise man admonishes: "Trust in the Lord with all thine heart; and lean not unto thine own understanding. In all thy ways acknowledge him, and he shall direct thy paths" (Prov. 3:5–6). All of us are tempted to put our confidence in our own human wisdom and understanding. We apply the scientific and logical methods both to the problems of life as well as to the possibilities of the future. If we achieve success by leaning on our own understanding, we become egotistical and conceited. If and when we fail, we experience depression and despair.

B. *Many people lean on the counsel of the ungodly.* The happy man, the successful man, the spiritual man, is one who stays away from the counsel of the ungodly (Ps. 1:1). The ungodly man is he who forgets God, ignores God, or rejects God. He approaches the problems of life as if God did not exist or as if God were unconcerned and unavailable to help.

We live in a day that places tremendous emphasis on the use of the scientific method for solving the problems of life. Not for one moment would I detract from the achievements and the contributions of the use of this method. I would, however, appeal to the reverent use of this method in the spiritual realm (John 7:17). The scientist poses a question, makes an assumption, and performs an experiment to test his or her hypothesis. If people want to find the real meaning of life, they need to try living the life of faith as an experiment to discover if God really does exist. When people put their confidence in the invisible God and seek to live according to the divine plan, they discover in the laboratory of personal experience the reality of him who is invisible to the human eye.

### II. Faith and faithfulness.

A. *Real faith is more than intellectual assent.* Genuine faith, victorious faith in the living God, is not to be equated with mere intellectual assent to the existence of an eternal God. The book of James emphasized this fact by stating, "Thou believest that there is one God; thou doest well: the devils also believe, and tremble" (2:19).

B. *Faith produces faithfulness.* Throughout the Bible and throughout Christian history, people of faith have been people of action. They have been people of moral and spiritual achievement. When people put their full confidence in God, they accept God's way as their way and God's plans as their plans. Hebrews 11, often called Faith's Hall of Fame, presents us with a beautiful display of the fruits of genuine faith. In each instance, faith manifested itself in terms of faithfulness, commitment, and involvement in the will and work of God.

1. Faith caused Abel to worship with his best (Heb. 11:4).
2. Because of his faith, Enoch walked day by day with God (Heb. 11:5).
3. Because of his faith, Noah responded to God's warning (Heb. 11:7).
4. Because of his faith, Abraham walked in obedience to the commandment of God (Heb. 11:8–10).
5. Because of his faith, Joseph resisted the temptations of moral impurity in order to be pleasing to God (Heb. 11:22; Gen. 39:9).
6. Because of his faith, Moses identified himself with the unfortunate in their efforts to achieve freedom and liberty to worship God (Heb. 11:24–27).

### III. The necessity of faith.

The foundation of all spiritual progress is rooted in our faith, while the explanation for most of our failures can be found in our lack of a real faith in the living God.

A. *The undoing sin of ancient Israel was that of no faith or of little faith.* They either refused or neglected to take God at his word and to depend on him to be faithful to his promises. A lack of faith caused their hearts to tremble in fear at the prospect of entering the Promised Land. Because they refused to trust God and to move forward in obedience to his commandments, they were destined to wander in the wilderness for forty years. With the exception of Caleb and Joshua, only those who were too young to be held responsible for their nation's refusal to trust God had the privilege of entering the land that God had promised for them (Num. 14:28–34).

B. *Jesus continuously sought to instill within the hearts of his disciples a great faith in God.*

1. He sought to encourage faith by his Sermon on the Mount (Matt. 5:25–34).
2. He sought to encourage faith by the parables he told.
3. He sought to increase faith by the miracles he performed.
4. No doubt on many occasions he spoke words similar to those recorded by John: "Let not your heart be troubled: ye believe in God, believe also in me" (John 14:1).
5. Jesus repeatedly put forth efforts to make faith in his triumph over death a transforming conviction in the lives of his apostles (Acts 1:3).

C. *Without faith it is impossible to please God (Heb. 11:6).* The refusal to trust God is a denial of either God's ability or willingness to do that which he has promised to do. This is not only an insult to God's integrity; it is an expression of an attitude of human self-sufficiency that cuts people off from the resources God wants to make available to them.

Faith is the human response to God that makes it possible for God both to forgive our sins and to grant us the gift of eternal life (John 3:16; 10:10). Trusting Jesus Christ as the Savior who died for our sins clears the way for God to remove the condemnation that our sin has created (John 3:17–18) and to bestow the gift of everlasting life on us (John 3:36). The absence of this faith or the refusal to believe causes one to die under the penalty of his sin (John 8:24).

Genuine faith in God is essential for the forgiveness of sin and the receiving of eternal life, and also for the victorious walk of life (2 Cor. 5:7; 1 John 5:4).

## IV. The growth of faith.

Faith in God, like faith in a person, is a dynamic thing. It is never static or dormant. This faith is both the gift of God and the work of the individual.

A. *The testimony of Scripture.* "So then faith cometh by hearing, and hearing by the word of God" (Rom. 10:17). Faith has been described as containing three elements: knowledge, mental assent, and trust. As we read the Word of God, we gain information concerning our God (Heb. 11:3) who cares for us (v. 6) to the extent that he has come to us in the person of Jesus Christ (2 Cor. 5:19–20).

B. *The testimony of the saints.* In both the Word of God and in Christian history, we read of those who had personal experiences with the living God. In the biographies of the dead and from the lips of the living, we hear testimonies concerning the trustworthiness of God. These testimonies should contribute toward the growth of our faith.

C. *The testimony of personal experience.* If you will but recall your own personal experiences with God, no doubt your faith in him will deepen, and you will be encouraged to trust him more lovingly and more loyally as you face opportunities, responsibilities, and uncertainties.

You will agree with the poet who said:

*Have faith in God, He's on His throne;*
*Have faith in God, He watches o'er His own;*
*He cannot fail, He must prevail;*
*Have faith in God, have faith in God.*

### Conclusion

If you have not yet responded in faith to Jesus Christ as Savior and Lord, then let me gently but strongly suggest that you receive him into your heart as a guest, as an honored friend, as a physician for the soul. He is the only one who can both meet your deepest needs in the present and make perfect provisions for your future in eternity. Trust him today and determine to trust him through all of your days.

---

## SUNDAY EVENING, SEPTEMBER 6

***Title:*** The Commission to the Witnessing Church

***Text:*** "But ye shall receive power, after that the Holy Ghost is come upon you: and ye shall be witnesses unto me both in Jerusalem, and in all Judea, and in Samaria, and unto the uttermost part of the earth" **(Acts 1:8)**.

### Introduction

Among the terms that the risen Christ used to define the major task of his church was that of witnessing: "Ye are witnesses of these things. And, behold, I send the promise of my Father upon you: but tarry ye in the city of Jerusalem, until ye be endued with power from on high" (Luke 24:48–49). Before his ascension to the Father, the Lord gave his church the divine strategy for world redemption: "Ye shall receive power, after that the Holy Ghost is come upon you; and ye shall be my witnesses both in Jerusalem, and in all Judea, and in Samaria, and unto the uttermost part of the earth" (Acts 1:8).

The activity of the apostles was described in terms of witnessing: "And with great power gave the apostles witness of the resurrection of the Lord Jesus: and great grace was upon them all" (Acts 4:33).

What is the meaning of the term "my witnesses"? What is the nature of a winning witness? How does the modern Christian, who is not an eyewitness of the redemptive acts of the Christ, bear a convincing witness for the Lord Jesus in contemporary society?

**I. Basic assumptions concerning Christian witnessing.**

Certain basic convictions must be kept in mind if the modern Christian is to bear a saving witness. The absence of these convictions eliminates all motivation for witnessing.

A. *Humankind's greatest need is for an experience with God that communicates the forgiveness of sin and imparts the gift of spiritual life.*

B. *God is a God of love and grace and has adequately provided redemption from sin and has given eternal life through Jesus Christ to all who receive him as Lord.*

C. *People are sinners by nature and by choice.* They are lost, separated from God, and do not know the way home. While dead in trespasses and sin, they may be aware that something vital is missing in life, but they most likely will not realize that their deepest need is that of a right relationship with God. Being dead to spiritual reality and being helpless to save themselves, they must have the aid of someone who can tell them the gospel story.

D. *The initiative in all spiritual experiences is with God.* Nonbelievers will not seek God until they are sought by God. It was God who "so loved the world, that he gave his only begotten Son, that whosoever believeth in him should not perish, but have everlasting life" (John 3:16). Salvation is of the Lord in its incipient stages just as much as it is of the Lord in its glorious consummation. It is God who is seeking to save the unsaved, and the personal testimony of a disciple is an instrument used by God to impart faith to nonbelievers.

E. *While the initiative is always with God, the individual believer has an essential part in the divine plan for rescuing people from the waste, tyranny, and wages of sin.* The eternal God, in many and diverse manners, spoke in the past through the prophets. He has spoken his ultimate and final Word in and through his Son. Individual followers can both rejoice and tremble over the privilege and responsibility that they have of being bearers of the good news of what God has done and of that which God wants to do in the lives of all of those who will receive and trust the Savior.

F. *God's will is that all of his children would be communicators of the purpose and power of his love for people.* This divine purpose was revealed in a most gripping manner as Peter interpreted the divine activity on the day of Pentecost: "In the last days, saith God, I will pour out of my Spirit upon all flesh: and your sons and your daughters shall prophesy, and your young men shall see visions, and your old men shall dream dreams: and on my handmaidens

I will pour out in those days of my Spirit; and they shall prophesy" (Acts 2:17–18).

When one keeps in mind that the prophets were primarily spokesmen for God, interpreters of the divine purposes and activities and communicators of the divine truth rather than mere predictors of future events, the privilege and responsibility of being a personal witness takes on additional significance. In the Old Testament economy, only unique individuals were to be spokespersons for God. The Spirit came upon prophets, priests, kings, or military leaders to enable and empower them for some specific task. In the post-Pentecost period, the disciples came to the conviction that every disciple was to witness to what Christ had done in his or her life.

The necessity for a continuing witness by the church is dramatized when one faces the fact that the world is never more than two generations away from being pagan. The matter of witnessing is not an optional matter with the individual follower of Christ. Personal witnessing is imperative. The Great Commission makes such a witness mandatory. Every follower of Christ should be a witness in all places at all times to all persons in all ways. Elton Trueblood has stated this forcefully: "Evangelism is not a professionalized job of a few gifted or trained men but is, instead, the unrelenting responsibility of every person who belongs, even in the most modest way, to the Company of Jesus" (*The Company of the Committed* [New York: Harper and Brothers, 1961], 55).

**II. The meaning of witness.**

Due to the confusion in their minds about their role in the process, many modern disciples of the Lord have never made a direct contribution toward helping another person come into a saving experience with Jesus Christ. While lack of experience, fear of making a tragic mistake, timidity, lack of faith, worldliness, and many other factors may enter the picture, it is highly possible that many hesitate to respond to the Lord's purpose for them to serve as witnesses to his saving grace because they have a false concept of what is expected of them. We need a rediscovery of the basic meaning of the task of witnessing to and for our Lord.

In the book of Acts, the words "witness" and "testify" are used in thirty-five different instances to describe both the task and the mission of the early church. The Greek verb *martyreo,* "to witness," describes "personal testimony to the content, truth, and urgency of the gospel message. The witness is a person who is in a position to know the things of which he speaks and so can attest their truth. He is a person whose testimony is needed by others if they are to know that truth and accept it" (Floyd V. Filson, *Three Crucial Decades* [Richmond: John Knox, 1963], 36).

The witness with which the early church was charged was testimony to the actual occurrence of the redemptive acts of God. The early Christians interpreted this to mean a verbal testimony based on what they had seen with their eyes or handled with their hands or experienced in some indisputable manner. This command carried with it the obligation to interpret what God was doing in these events and to explain the meaning of such to those to whom the testimony was given.

The apostles possessed a witness that was recognized as authoritative in the early church. They were witnesses not only of Christ's teachings, but of the events surrounding his death and resurrection. This was the crowning testimony concerning the action of God in the revelation of Jesus Christ.

That this was the case finds dramatic expression in the description surrounding the potential successor of Judas Iscariot. He must have had firsthand knowledge of the entire ministry of Jesus, but the absolutely essential qualification was that he must be able to "witness with us of his resurrection" (Acts 1:22). The apostles had seen the risen Christ repeatedly. They could testify with complete confidence that he had risen from the dead. As they bore this testimony, adding one bit of evidence to another, there were many who were convinced by the Holy Spirit that indeed Jesus of Nazareth was the promised Messiah, and they responded with faith in him that brought forgiveness of sin and transformation of their lives.

After emphasizing in a most graphic manner the necessity of the church's giving an "incarnate witness" in the form of transformed lives that serve as channels for the grace of God, Dr. Findley B. Edge has pointedly spotlighted the nature of Christian witnessing in a comparison with the modern courtroom witness.

A. *First, "in a court of law the task of the witness is simply to relate the pertinent facts as he saw or experienced them"* (*A Quest for Vitality in Religion* [Nashville: Broadman, 1963], 143). A witness is not allowed to argue or to put pressure on the jury. He or she is to bear testimony to the facts and let the jury arrive at a decision. Edge concludes from this truth that

   > *It would be well if we could replace the term "soul-winner" with the term "witness." Strictly speaking, "soul-winning" is the work of God, not man. Whether the individual to whom we witness comes into a saving relationship depends upon the encounter he has with Christ under the convicting power of the Holy Spirit. The danger is that a person who views himself as a "soul-winner" sometimes invades the sacred arena where God and man face each other for possible encounter and surrender. In his zeal to "win a soul to Christ" through subtle pressures, he induces the individual to "make a profession" which may be only verbal and superficial. The Christian's witness will be as fervent and intelligent as he can make it. But the response the individual makes is his own responsibility.*

B. *Second, the legal witness is permitted to give testimony only to those facts or events that he or she has personally seen or heard.* No witness is expected to know all of the facts in a given case. It is noteworthy that according to Mosaic law, testimony was to be accepted only when it was confirmed by a second witness. While the testimony of one witness for Christ might be adequate to convince an unbeliever that he should forsake the life of sin and unbelief and receive Christ as Lord, it is usually the combined testimony of many witnesses over an extended period of time that finally culminates in the decision of the individual to become a believer and confess and follow Christ. "Each is important because each can add, in some unique and irrevocable act, to the cumulative evidence" (Trueblood, *Company of the Committed*, 67).

C. *Third, Edge is right in saying that "the legal witness has a responsibility to testify; he has no other choice."* In the legal system of our nation, testimony of reputable witnesses can set the innocent free or help convict the guilty of their crimes. The absence of witnesses or the silence of those who have pertinent evidence can mean that the innocent could suffer for crimes of which they are not guilty and the guilty could be set free to prey upon the unsuspecting public.

Christians have no option in the matter of being witnesses. The only choice they have is whether they will be good witnesses or poor witnesses. By the very nature of our salvation and by virtue of the world's great need for Christ, followers of Christ should rejoice at the privilege of bearing an effective witness.

D. *Edge concludes his comparison with the statement that "the legal witness must have some firsthand knowledge of, or contact with, the case under consideration."* Even so, only a person who knows Jesus Christ in an experience that results in the forgiveness of sin and the impartation of the divine life can be a witness for the Lord. If one has no experience with the Lord, he or she has no testimony to give.

### III. Method and motivation.

We should constantly study the New Testament illustrations to improve our methods of witnessing to the saving power of the living Christ. The witnessing of John the Baptist, the personal interviews of Jesus with various persons, the accounts of apostolic witnessing in Acts, and the testimonies of those to whom Christ ministered illustrate the many ways of telling the gospel story. All of these interviews are so interesting and so different that it is difficult to select one as an example.

No one method will work in all cases, for lost people are different and have a great diversity of personal needs. There are many modern Nicodemuses who are religious but are ignorant of essential religious experience. Modern-day Zacchaeuses, rich and self-sufficient, live lonely, miserable, and conscience-striken existences in nearly every city of our land. Modern-day Sauls, zealous for God but blind to the truth of the wonderful Savior, still walk the road toward Damascus. Some people under the burden of a guilty past need someone who can tell them of a Savior who takes the sting out of death and robs the tomb of its power.

Many regard themselves of no value to the kingdom of God and, like lost coins, need to be recovered to usefulness. Others are forlorn, helpless, and afraid like lost sheep and need to be brought home to the fold. Still others are wasted and ruined by sin and are in the grip of despair as they return to the Father. These ones need to be assured of his forgiving grace. Those who would bear a winning witness will, out of their own personal experience with Christ and knowledge of the Scriptures, wrestle to fit the transforming truth to unredeemed souls.

Again, if you want to be a witness to the Christ, you must learn to work with the Holy Spirit. One of the major factors that contributes to an ineffective witness is the lack of sensitivity to the work of the Holy Spirit in human personality. Personal witnesses need to do their very best in the matter of skillful planning, making tactful approaches, using persistent persuasion, and employing the most effective methods in witnessing; but in the final analysis, it is the Holy Spirit alone who can present Christ to the hearts of the unsaved in a convicting and converting manner. Witnesses are human instruments that the Holy Spirit needs, but in the experience of salvation, the last word is always spoken by the Holy Spirit.

### Conclusion

With a message that can save the world morally, physically, intellectually, personally, economically, socially, and eternally, the church needs, not only the best methods for communicating that message, but even more it needs the motivation of a mighty divine thrust out into this world.

Companionship with a living Lord and the power of the Holy Spirit combined with a consciousness of the world's desperate need for Christ provided the early church with a mighty motive that thrust them into their world with a winning witness for Christ. This was the driving force of the first witness. No opposition could deter them. No resistance could discourage them. No persecution could stop their witness.

Jesus Christ is still alive. God is not dead. The Holy Spirit is still present in the hearts of believers. It is time to obey. It is time to bear a witness.

---

## WEDNESDAY EVENING, SEPTEMBER 9

***Title:*** The Deity of the Holy Spirit

***Text:*** John 14:16–18

### Introduction

The Holy Spirit is more than just an influence. Scripture teaches that he is a person and that he possesses all of the essential marks of a personality.

Some of us have difficulty thinking of the Holy Spirit as a person because he is spirit and invisible. It might be helpful for us to ask ourselves, "Will I cease to be a person when I experience physical death?" At death we depart from our physical being, which is our earthly dwelling. We retain the marks of personality—intellect, emotions, and will. The Holy Spirit possesses all of these.

### I. The perfections of divinity are ascribed to the Holy Spirit.

The attributes of God are the attributes of the Holy Spirit.

A. *Eternity.* "How much more shall the blood of Christ, who through the eternal Spirit offered himself without spot to God, purge your conscience from dead works to serve the living God?" (Heb. 9:14).

B. *Omniscience.* "God hath revealed them unto us by his Spirit: for the Spirit searcheth all things, yea, the deep things of God. For what man knoweth the things of a man, save the spirit of man which is in him? even so the things of God knoweth no man, but the Spirit of God" (1 Cor. 2:10–11).

C. *Omnipotence.* "Truly I am full of power by the spirit of the LORD, and of judgment, and of might, to declare unto Jacob his transgression, and to Israel his sin" (Mic. 3:8).

D. *Omnipresence.* "Whither shall I go from thy Spirit? or whither shall I flee from thy presence?" (Ps. 139:7).

## II. The works of divinity are ascribed to the Holy Spirit.

A. *The work of creation is his.* "And the earth was without form, and void; and darkness was upon the face of the deep. And the spirit of God moved upon the face of the waters" (Gen. 1:2).

B. *The work of regeneration is his.* "Except a man be born of water and of the Spirit, he cannot enter into the kingdom of God" (John 3:5).

C. *The work of resurrection is his.* "But if the Spirit of him that raised up Jesus from the dead dwell in you, he that raised up Christ from the dead shall also quicken your mortal bodies by his Spirit that dwelleth in you" (Rom. 8:11).

D. *The Holy Spirit is the source of the miraculous.* "But if I cast out devils by the Spirit of God, then the kingdom of God is come unto you" (Matt. 12:28).

## III. The worship of divinity should be given to the Holy Spirit.

A. *We are baptized in the name of the Holy Spirit (Matt. 28:18–20).*

B. *Seven times in the book of Revelation, obedience to the Spirit's admonition is insisted upon (Rev. 2–3).*

C. *The Holy Spirit aids us in our prayers.* "Likewise the Spirit also helpeth our infirmities: for we know not what we should pray for as we ought: but the Spirit itself maketh intercession for us with groanings which cannot be uttered" (Rom. 8:26).

D. *The Holy Spirit may be sinned against.* "But whosoever speaketh against the Holy Ghost, it shall not be forgiven him, neither in this world, neither in the world to come" (Matt. 12:32).

### Conclusion

With deep reverence we should consider our response to the person and presence of the Holy Spirit of God. He will do his work within us if we will but trust him and cooperate with him.

## SUNDAY MORNING, SEPTEMBER 13

***Title:*** A Dead Man Speaks to the Living

***Text:*** "By faith Abel offered unto God a more excellent sacrifice than Cain, by which he obtained witness that he was righteous, God testifying of his gifts: and by it he being dead yet speaketh" **(Heb. 11:4)**.

***Hymns:*** "O God, Our Help in Ages Past," Watts

"Faith of Our Fathers," Faber

"Give of Your Best to the Master," Grose

***Offertory Prayer:*** Our heavenly Father, we come to you in faith to offer ourselves to you. We bring our very best and dedicate it as a token of our gratitude for your many blessings and as an indication of our interest in the advancement of your kingdom. Out of our abundance we share with the needy. We do so as an act of worship through Jesus Christ our Lord. Amen.

### Introduction

The inspired writer of the book of Hebrews reaches back into the history of Israel and calls into the witness box various heroes who lived by faith (Heb. 12:1–2). Each of these is permitted to speak a word of challenge and cheer to the living. The writer is seeking to encourage the people of his generation to live a life of faith and faithfulness in the midst of trial.

The cloud of witnesses are not spectators who idly view the struggle of God's people: they are testators, heavenly cheerleaders, who would encourage each believer and servant of God to trust in the dependability of God to meet the deepest needs of his or her life.

The saints of God whose achievements are recorded in both sacred and secular history will speak to us today if we will but put forth the effort to listen (Matt. 13:9). Our text speaks of the immortality of influence. It is recorded that though Abel lived at the dawn of history, he lived a life of faith that resulted in faithfulness, and by his life "he being dead yet speaketh." Our text declares that our life is capable of communicating something significant: (1) We speak to those about us, our contemporaries in business and social contacts; (2) we speak to our children and to other members of our family; and (3) we continue to speak after our tongue has grown silent.

What is your life communicating? Does your life impart good news that blesses, or does it communicate that which brings harm into the lives of others?

### I. Abel speaks of a life of faith.

A. *Faith is a response to God and to his will for our lives.* Genuine faith is more than mental assent to the reliability of biblical truths. It is a responsiveness to God's revelation of himself through Jesus Christ and the testimony of those who have known him and lived with him.

B. *Saving faith is a believing response to the gospel (1 Cor. 15:1–4).* The gospel is infinitely more wonderful than good advice; it is the good news of God's love for sinners. It is the good news of how Jesus Christ died on the cross for our sins. It is the good news of how he conquered death and the grave and arose triumphant and is alive for forever. The gospel is the good news of how people can experience spiritual birth and know the eternal God as a loving Father through faith, confidence, and trust in the living Christ.

C. *Faith is the gift of God, and it is also the work of humans.* Genuine faith always presupposes an act in which God reveals himself (Rom. 10:14). The writer declares, "faith cometh by hearing, and hearing by the word of God" (Rom. 10:17). In response to the question, "What shall we do, that we might work the works of God?" Jesus replied, "This is the work of God, that ye believe on him whom he hath sent" (John 6:28–29).

Abel would encourage each of us to respond to the light and to the knowledge of God that we now possess.

## II. Abel speaks of faith and worship.

A. *Genuine faith and real worship are inseparable.* Genuine faith, like genuine love, must find a means of expressing itself. Because of faith in his heart, Abel sought both the presence and pleasure of God through every channel that was available to him.

Genuine worship is something infinitely more than just going to church. Genuine worship is not to be confused with an endless chain of activities, but real faith will express itself in an active manner.

B. *Abel worshiped God.* Worship is the ascription of worth to one who is of supreme worth.

Do you worship the God of Abel, Abraham, and Paul, or have you permitted the god of success to seize first place in your ambitions and activities? Some worship their work and ascribe to it supreme worth. Others worship pleasure and search for one thrill after another. Some worship laziness and are content to live at the expense of others.

## III. Abel speaks of faith, worship, and excellence.

The record in Genesis states, "And Abel, he also brought of the firstlings of his flock and of the fat thereof" (Gen. 4:4). From this text we can assume that Abel brought of the very best that he possessed as an offering unto the Lord. Malachi indicted the people of his day with bringing the very sorriest of their beasts as a sacrifice to their God. With satire and irony, he suggests that they bring the same kind of gifts to their Persian rulers. He seeks to shame them because of the emptiness and cheapness of what they were offering to God.

A. *Abel gave thought to his offering.* With the highest part of his mind and the deepest part of his heart, he came to offer a more excellent sacrifice than did Cain.

B. *He was not thoughtless and careless about that which he offered to God (cf. 2 Cor. 9:7).* Abel's worship was not subject to moods or impulses. He was not seeking a cheap, inexpensive bargain way to gain the favor of God. Like David, he refused to offer to God that which had cost him nothing (2 Sam. 24:24).

C. *Abel's sacrifice was a deliberate and purposeful act of worship.* He brought the very best in faith as a response to God. A poet has suggested that we, like Abel, through faith, give our very best to God.

*Give of your best to the Master,*
*Give of the strength of your youth;*
*Throw your soul's fresh, flowing ardor*
*Into the battle for truth:*
*Jesus has set the example,*
*Dauntless was He, young and brave;*
*Give Him your loyal devotion,*
*Give Him the best that you have.*

*Give of your best to the Master,*
*Naught else is worthy His love;*
*He gave Himself for your ransom,*
*Gave up His glory above;*
*Laid down His life without murmur,*
*You from sin's ruin to save;*
*Give Him your heart's adoration,*
*Give Him the best that you have.*

*—Howard B. Grose*

## IV. Abel speaks of divine approval.

It is wonderful for a believer to know deep within that he or she has God's approval. This assurance came to Abel (Heb. 11:4). Cain speaks to us of divine rejection, but Abel speaks to us of divine approval (Gen. 4:4–5).

A. *Cain did point out the possibility of divine disapproval.* The motive behind Cain's offering was wrong. He did not offer in faith; his sacrifice was not a genuine response to God.

Present-day believers can go through the motions of worship and giving and fail to receive divine approval.

1. Thoughtless and careless worship does not receive divine approval.
2. A gift designed to purchase the approval of God when we are mistreating our fellow human beings will be rejected (Matt. 5:23–24).
3. Ostentatious gifts that are presented out of the desire for the applause of people will not bring the approval of God (Matt. 6:1–3).
4. Gifts that are presented grudgingly or simply out of a feeling of necessity bring no delight to the heart of God (2 Cor. 9:7).
5. Acts of worship or sacrificial gifts not motivated by love bring us nothing (1 Cor. 13:3).

B. *Abel assures us of the possibility of divine approval.*
   1. He offered his gift in faith as a genuine response of his heart.
   2. He offered in humility and love.
   3. He did what he could, and it was acceptable (Col. 3:17).

### Conclusion

In faith let us respond to God. Let us offer up to him, as an act of worship, all that we do and all that we are. The pastor's sermon should be a gift offered up in worship. The special message in song from the choir should be an act of worship. The lesson presented by the teacher should be an act of faith and an experience of worship.

Have you heard what God would say to you through Abel today? Trust God with all that you are and all that you have. Give him your best if you want to experience his best.

## SUNDAY EVENING, SEPTEMBER 13

***Title:*** The Nature of the Witnessing Church

***Text:*** "But ye shall receive power, after that the Holy Ghost is come upon you: and ye shall be witnesses unto me both in Jerusalem, and in all Judea, and in Samaria, and unto the uttermost part of the earth" **(Acts 1:8)**.

### Introduction

The early church bore a magnificent witness to the redemptive acts of the Lord Jesus Christ. This was to be their primary function according to the commission of our living Lord in the words of the text.

In spite of many limitations, the disciples enjoyed fantastic success in Jerusalem, throughout Judea, in Samaria, and unto the ends of the known world of their day.

In this day, in which the church is under severe attack by enemies on both the inside and the outside, it is encouraging for us who love the church to reexamine and rediscover the nature of the witnessing church during the apostolic period. To do so can both rebuke us and encourage us. We need both.

### I. The early church had an incorrect and incomplete understanding of its mission (Acts 1:6).

For some time following the day of Pentecost, the early church was primarily a Jewish institution. They retained their narrow nationalism and the prejudices that went along with such. This is evident by the question that was raised shortly before our Lord's ascension: "Lord, will thou at this time restore again the kingdom to Israel?" (Acts 1:6). At this point in history, even the apostles did not recognize the universal scope of the plan of redemption that had been wrought on the cross and in the empty tomb.

A. *There was much to be learned even by the apostles.* This should remind us that we do not have exhaustive knowledge of the plan and purpose of God for our day. All of our church members need to learn who they are, what they are to do, and how they are to do it.

B. *There is much to be taught to the members of the church.* Complete evangelism calls for the instruction of the new converts in all of the teachings of the Lord. The church is commissioned not only to make disciples and to mark these disciples in baptism, but to lead them toward maturity by a continual program of instruction concerning what it means to be a follower of Christ in this day (Matt. 28:20). The work of the apostles is described as "teaching" no fewer than fifteen times.

**II. The early church was the recipient and the steward of a divine commission (Acts 1:8).**

A. *This commission to make disciples to the ends of the earth was based on love (John 3:16).* God loves sinful people in spite of their sins.

B. *This commission to evangelize is based on the lordship of Jesus Christ because of who he is, what he did, and what he can do if we are willing to respond with loving obedience.* We must cease interpreting the Great Commission as applying primarily to international activity and recognize that the Lord would have us to be constantly at work and making disciples in our own individual world. Someone has said:

> *Some must go.*
> *Some must let go.*
> *Some must help go.*
> *All of us must get going.*

**III. The early church gave itself to united and persistent prayer.**

A. *Acts 1:14: "These all continued with one accord in prayer and supplication, with the women, and Mary the mother of Jesus, and with his brethren."*

B. *Acts 4:24–31: They met opposition and persecution on their knees with their hearts clinging to the promises of God.*

C. *The apostles enlarged the organizational life of the church and by so doing involved more people so that they might not be diverted from prayer and the ministry of the Word.* Acts 6:4: "But we will give ourselves continually to prayer, and to the ministry of the word."

D. *Acts 12:5: "Peter therefore was kept in prison: but prayer was made without ceasing of the church unto God for him."* The early church believed that it was possible for them to communicate with God through believing prayer. As one studies the book of Acts, he or she cannot help but discover that at times their praying was more of a dialogue than a monologue. Not only did they talk to God, but they listened when God was speaking to them.

### IV. The early church witnessed in the energy of the Holy Spirit.

A. *The Holy Spirit promised (Acts 1:8).* John the Baptist said of the Coming One, "He shall baptize you with the Holy Ghost, and with fire" (Matt. 3:11). The Gospel of John records many promises by the Savior concerning the coming of the Holy Spirit (John 14:16–18). The word translated "Comforter" literally means "one called to walk by the side of." The Greek word translated "another" means "another of like kind." This "Comforter," this one called to walk by the side of, was actually to dwell within them, for Jesus said, "for he dwelleth with you, and shall be in you" (v. 17). This is a promise that was to be fulfilled on the day of Pentecost. The Holy Spirit was to be to the church what Jesus Christ had been to the apostles.

B. *The Holy Spirit present (Acts 2:4).* The second chapter of Acts is a dramatic description of what happened on that day when the Holy Spirit entered the church to authenticate it as the instrument of God and to empower it for a ministry of witnessing to an unbelieving world. People who had been ordinary up to this point became the mighty servants of God, for they labored in the energy of God's Spirit.

This divine energy, this power *from* God, this power *of* God, is absolutely essential if a church is to bear a winsome and winning witness in today's world. The Holy Spirit still resides in the church in the heart of each believer. He will manifest himself in a mighty way when his presence is recognized and when the church is responsive to the will of its Lord.

### V. The early church had a program of conservation (Acts 2:41–42).

A. *The new converts were led to accept baptism, and thus they identified themselves as belonging to Jesus Christ.*

B. *They continued steadfastly in the apostles' doctrine and fellowship.* Continuously they were communicating the teachings of Christ and sharing their experiences one with another in a mutually stimulating manner.

C. *"And in breaking of bread."* This can refer to fellowship around the family table, or it can refer to the observance of the Lord's Supper. Most likely it refers to both.

D. *Prayer was continuous.* They discovered in experience the delight and the value of communicating with God through prayer. By having the habit of prayer, they were in constant contact with the Savior.

### Conclusion

Each church can truly be a spiritual organism, the body of Christ, a witnessing community, if its membership will respond to the Great Commission in dependence on the energy of the divine Spirit, and if they will keep the channels of communication open through prayer.

## WEDNESDAY EVENING, SEPTEMBER 16

***Title:*** The Work of the Holy Spirit Relative to the Lost Person

***Text:*** "When he is come, he will reprove the world of sin, and of righteousness, and of judgment" **(John 16:8)**.

### Introduction

Our attention is usually focused on the work of the Holy Spirit in the life of God's children. It would be helpful to recognize that the Holy Spirit also works on the hearts of people who need to be converted to Christ.

There is a work in the hearts of unbelievers that can be performed only by the Holy Spirit. Recognizing this will save believers from the agony of frustration and encourage them to depend on the Holy Spirit to do his gracious work.

### I. The Holy Spirit convicts unsaved people of their need for salvation (John 16:7–11).

Many sincere believers would like to see their unsaved friends become professing Christians, but they hesitate to attempt to bear a witness concerning Christ, for they feel that they must point out their friends' sins and shortcomings. The truth is that only the Holy Spirit can speak to hearts and reveal the need for the holy purity that comes through Jesus Christ. Would-be witnesses must depend on the Holy Spirit to achieve this objective in the hearts of unsaved friends.

A. *The Holy Spirit convicts of sin (John 16:9).*

B. *The Holy Spirit reveals to unbelievers their need for the personal righteousness of Jesus Christ (John 16:10).*

C. *The Holy Spirit reveals to unbelievers that the judgment of God is upon sin and upon sinners who refuse to repent and believe for salvation (John 16:11).*

### II. The Holy Spirit does his convicting work through human instrumentality (John 16:7–8).

### III. The Holy Spirit uses disciples as they use the Word of God (John 14:26; 15:26; 16:13).

### IV. The Holy Spirit invites unsaved people to come to Jesus (Rev. 22:17).

It takes the Holy Spirit to make the invitation real (John 6:44).

### V. It is the Holy Spirit who applies the redemption of Jesus Christ to the hearts of believers and brings about the miracle of the new birth (Titus 3:5).

### Conclusion

If we will trust the Holy Spirit and depend on him to do his work, we will be less fearful and much more effective at bearing witness to those who need Christ as Savior.

## SUNDAY MORNING, SEPTEMBER 20

***Title:*** Enoch: The Walk of Faith

***Text:*** "By faith Enoch was translated that he should not see death; and was not found, because God has translated him: for before his translation he had this testimony, that he pleased God" **(Heb. 11:5)**.

***Scripture Reading:*** Genesis 5:21–24

***Hymns:*** "Walk in the Light," Barton

"Footsteps of Jesus," Slade

"When We Walk with the Lord," Sammis

"Follow On," Cushing

***Offertory Prayer:*** Heavenly Father, we approach your throne of grace this day in faith believing that you are the giver of every good and perfect gift. We believe that you are at work in all things to bring about good to those who love you. With the gratitude of our hearts and with the praise of our lips, we also offer to you the fruits of our labors in tithes and offerings as an act of worship. May your blessings be on these offerings that others may come to worship you in spirit and in truth. Through Jesus Christ our Lord. Amen.

### Introduction

The desire for approval is one of the strongest motives that affects a person's attitudes and actions. In early childhood a child desires the approval of his or her parents. As that child enters school, he or she labors to deserve the approval of teachers.

It is normal for teenagers to desire the approval and the applause of the group to which they belong, and this inward desire for approval explains many of the attitudes and actions that often bring bewilderment to parents. In the process of courtship, both the young man and the young woman eagerly seek to win each other's approval that they might be acceptable as marriage partners.

Inside marriage it is always wise for both partners to work that they might retain and maintain the approval they gained during the courtship process. When a young person enters the business world, he or she seeks to labor so as to have the approval of his or her employer.

This desire for approval is one of the basic drives of human nature. It is of vital importance that we use great wisdom in our choice of those whose approval we desire. If we seek only our inward selfish approval, this will vitally affect our happiness and our actions and attitudes. If we seek the applause of the wicked and not the godly, we will have to do things that are contrary to the will of God to win approval.

The words of our text declare that Enoch lived and labored that he might have the approval of God. It is said that "before his translation he had this testimony, that he pleased God" (Heb. 11:5).

Enoch did not win the approval of God accidentally or incidentally, for it was under the most unfavorable circumstances that Enoch walked with God in such a manner as to hear the words of divine approval. Notice also that Enoch walked with God and enjoyed his approval and praise while walking a common way of life. There is nothing to lead us to believe that Enoch was a professional, vocational servant of God. Very definitely he did not retire from society as a recluse to spend his time in prayer and meditation.

The writer of Hebrews says, as he marshals these great heroes of faith into a position where they can bear their testimony concerning the faithfulness of God, that it was by faith that Enoch had pleased God. Just what does this mean? Is it possible for us to please God today? Is it possible for us to have the inward testimony, like Enoch, that our life and ministry are pleasing to our heavenly Father?

If Enoch could walk with God, then you and I can walk with God. The passage was not written merely that we might have the historical record of what happened in the past. It was written to show us what we can do if by faith we make the same response that these characters who walked through the pages of the Bible made.

### I. Enoch's walk with God.

A. *Enoch was acquainted with God.* To him God was real. Instead of having some information or knowledge about God, he knew God.

1. We can gain information about God by reading the Bible. The Bible is a record of God's activities in which he reveals himself to humankind under all circumstances and conditions.
2. We can learn about God through the testimony of others who know him.
3. We really come to know God through faith in Jesus Christ. There is no way by which a person can come to know God other than through faith in Jesus Christ.

B. *Enoch acknowledged both the person and presence of God.* To him God was something infinitely more than a principle behind the universe. To him God was a personality. The writer of Hebrews states this most forcefully in words that contain one of the best definitions of faith to be found in the New Testament. The writer declares that "God … is" (Heb. 11:6). God not only is, but he is vitally concerned about us and responds to our faith by richly rewarding us.

Enoch did not ignore God. Nor did he forget God. The writer of Proverbs tells us to "trust in the LORD with all thine heart; and lean not on thine own understanding. In all thy ways acknowledge him, and he shall direct thy paths" (Prov. 3:5–6).

Many of us miss the joy of walking with God because we ignore him and forget him. Consequently, we walk in our own way, which often leads to disappointment and disaster.

C. *Enoch was in agreement with God.* "Can two walk together, except they be agreed?" (Amos 3:3). People did not walk across the desert together accidentally. They walked together only when they were in agreement with each other or when they had a definite appointment at some place.

Repentance is the response in which a person pledges to agree with God and accepts his divine viewpoint.

People must be in agreement with God if they want to walk with God. We will never be Christian in our conduct until we accept the mind of Christ and think as he thought. When we agree with our Savior in our habits and attitudes, it will follow like day follows night that our actions will remind others of Jesus Christ.

D. *Enoch appreciated and adored the God with whom he walked.* The Bible does not say that Enoch walked with God because of fear of the consequences if he refused. We are left to infer that he walked with God because he found a deep joy and satisfaction in his presence.

It is in the gospel, the good news of God's love for sinners, that we discover the loving character and gracious Spirit of the God with whom Enoch walked. To know him as Savior is to love him. To know him through continued fellowship is to love him more and more.

**II. The believer's walk with God.**

In the Old Testament we read that "Noah walked with God" (Gen. 6:9). God said to Abraham, "Walk before me" (Gen. 17:1). The psalmist vowed, "I will walk before the Lord in the land of the living" (Ps. 116:9).

In the New Testament the walk of the believer is described in a number of ways. If we are acquainted with God through faith in Jesus, if we will acknowledge his living presence, and if we are in agreement with him, it is possible for us to walk with an abiding awareness of his presence. The characteristics of the believer's walk are described in a number of different ways in the New Testament:

A. *It is a walk of faith.* "For we walk by faith, not by sight" (2 Cor. 5:7). If we want to walk with God, we must believe that Jesus Christ died for our sins and arose victorious over death and the grave, and that he has come into our hearts as Savior and Lord (Rom. 10:9).

B. *It is a walk of newness of life.* The walk of the believer will be different from the walk of the unbeliever. Paul declares that because of the believer's death to a life of sin and the symbolic burial of that old way of life, "like as Christ was raised up from the dead by the glory of the Father, even so we also should walk in newness of life" (Rom. 6:4). This means that the new convert, as well as the older convert, will deliberately "play dead" when he is tempted with evil (Eph. 4:17).

C. *It is a walk in the Spirit (Gal. 5:16).* By walking in the Spirit we are to progress from one stage of life to another and from one place to another consciously led by the Holy Spirit who came to dwell within the heart of each believer at the time of conversion (Titus 3:5; 1 Cor. 3:16). God is a Spirit, and those who would walk with him must have faith to believe in his eternal abiding presence. The Holy Spirit provides counsel and courage as well as wisdom and strength for the task of life if we will but trust him.

D. *It is a walk of love (Eph. 5:2).* To have Christian love toward others is to have a permanent, unbreakable spirit of goodwill toward others. Jesus gave to his disciples a new commandment: "Love one another; as I have loved you, that ye also love one another. By this shall all men know that ye are my disciples, if ye have love one to another" (John 13:34–35). It is this type of Christian love that every church needs to demonstrate, not only within its own fellowship, but among the unbelievers in its total environment.

E. *It is to be a walk in the light (1 John 1:7).* The apostle says, "But if we walk in the light as he is in the light, we have fellowship one with another, and the blood of Jesus Christ his Son cleanseth us from all sin." This is a walk of faith and fellowship, of faithfulness and fruitfulness.

### Conclusion

Have you been neglecting the privilege of walking and talking with God? If so, you would be wise to recognize the joy you have missed. It would be most profitable to you and to others if you would rejoin him in faith and righteousness.

If you have never known the joy of walking with God, then let me suggest that today you invite Jesus Christ to become not just a guest but a permanent dweller in the home of your heart. He will provide you with guidance and help without which you are bound to miss not only heaven at the end of the way but the highest possible happiness here and now.

---

## SUNDAY EVENING, SEPTEMBER 20

***Title:*** The Message of the Witnessing Church

***Text:*** "Therefore let all the house of Israel know assuredly, that God hath made that same Jesus, whom ye have crucified, both Lord and Christ" (**Acts 2:36**).

### Introduction

Dr. James S. Stewart has said, "The first axiom of effective evangelism is that the evangelist must be sure of his message. Any haziness or hesitation there is fatal" (*A Faith to Proclaim* [New York: Scribner, 1953], 12).

The early church was absolutely certain of its message.

### I. The sources of the message of the early church.

A. *The Old Testament Scriptures (Acts 2:25–31).* With his feet firmly planted in the Scriptures, Peter's heart was filled with the Psalms and his mind full of the Prophets, and he preached Jesus Christ as the saving Lord to those who had crucified him.

B. *Personal experiences with the living Christ.* The living Christ had manifested himself "alive after his passion by many infallible proofs, being seen of them forty days, and speaking of the things pertaining to the kingdom of God" (Acts 1:3; cf. 10:41). The early Christians were eyewitnesses as well as verbal witnesses to the fact that Christ Jesus was risen from the dead: "This Jesus hath God raised up, whereof we all are witnesses" (Acts 2:32). They conceived of their task in terms of bearing a verbal testimony of witness that Jesus Christ was alive and able to save. "And we are his witnesses to these things; and so is also the Holy Ghost, whom God hath given to them that obey him" (Acts 5:32).

C. *The inspiration of the Holy Spirit (Acts 2:16–18).* The Holy Spirit came into the church, as had been predicted by the prophet Joel, to enable them to understand both what Jesus had taught as well as the Old Testament Scriptures (John 14:26).

**II. The content of the message of the early church.**

The early church had only one message, and that message was Jesus Christ. Their sermons were saturated with Jesus Christ. Their conversations were permeated with thoughts concerning Jesus Christ. If the church of today would fulfill the purpose of God, both in its community and in the world, it must proclaim Jesus Christ and bear continual witness to his mighty redemptive acts.

A. *Christ was proclaimed as the fulfillment of Old Testament prophecy (Acts 3:13–18; 13:32–33; 26:22–23).* The early church believed that in fulfillment of prophecy the eternal God had clothed himself in a human body and had come to walk in their midst in fulfillment of the hopes and dreams and predictions of the prophets.

B. *They proclaimed that Jesus Christ had died on the cross to deliver humankind from the tyranny and penalty of sin (Acts 2:22–32; 3:14–16; 10:34).* The death of Jesus Christ on the cross was an incomprehensible event to the apostles. For them his death was a public disgrace, a great political tragedy, and a personal disappointment. Following the resurrection and Pentecost, they came to see Christ's death as the supreme exhibition of God's love for sinners. They entered into a full experience of the salvation made possible by the sacrificial substitution of the Lamb of God whom God had sent to take away the sin of the world.

C. *They bore witness to the fact that Jesus Christ had conquered death and the grave (Acts 2:24, 32, 36).* The greatest surprise that the apostles ever experienced was discovering that the tomb was empty and that Jesus Christ had conquered death and the grave. This convinced them beyond any shadow of a doubt that he was in truth the Son of God (John 20:28; Rom. 1:4) and gave wonderful meaning and significance to all that he had said and done. The assurance of his living presence gave reality to worship and made prayer meaningful and sacrificial service a delight. They proclaimed a message with a voice of ten thousand trumpets that death had been defeated and that the grave would no longer be able to retain its victims.

D. *They proclaimed Christ Jesus as the triumphant Lord of their lives (Acts 2:36).* He had conquered sin, death, and the grave. Exalted to the right hand of God, he had been appointed by the heavenly Father to be the Lord over all. These early disciples recognized and responded to his sovereignty. They believed he had the right to lay claims upon them and to issue orders that were binding upon them. In gratitude and love they responded.

E. *The early church assumed that Jesus Christ was present with them in great power (Acts 3:6, 16).* The church of today desperately needs to believe that the triumphant Lord is faithful to the promise that he made to be with us always (Matt. 28:20).

Those who respond to the leading of the Spirit and put forth an effort to bear their testimony, to share their faith, to speak a good word for Jesus Christ, discover that he is present. He always has been. He always will be. We need to pray for faith to trust his promise, and then when we obey we will discover that he is as close to us as our breath.

### III. The communication of the message.

A. *They bore their witness personally (Acts 2:14; 7:2–56; 8:4).*
B. *They bore their witness boldly (Acts. 2:22–23).*
C. *They bore their witness with expectancy (Acts 2:40).*
D. *They bore their witness joyfully (Acts 4:33).*

### Conclusion

Paul was proud of the message he had to proclaim concerning Christ, for Christ had never disappointed him in any way. Jesus never disappoints those who yield their hearts to him. Jesus Christ, because of who he was, what he did, and what he can do, is the only message for the modern church.

## WEDNESDAY EVENING, SEPTEMBER 23

***Title:*** The Work of the Holy Spirit in the Believer

***Text:*** "What? know ye not that your body is the temple of the Holy Ghost which is in you, which ye have of God, and ye are not your own?" **(1 Cor. 6:19)**.

### Introduction

Many modern-day believers are like those in Corinth who were unaware that in the conversion experience the Holy Spirit of God had taken up residence within their hearts. Due to the lack of information concerning this gracious work of God, they neglected to respond to him and cooperate with him.

Paul wrote to the Galatians concerning the gift of the Spirit to every believer (Gal. 4:6–7).

### I. The Holy Spirit dwells in the heart of the believer (1 Cor. 3:16).

The body of the Christian becomes a sanctuary for the Holy Spirit. As such we should recognize its value and its importance to the work of God. As the dwelling place of the Holy Spirit, the body should not be considered evil. The body is the tool the Holy Spirit can use to bring honor and glory to God.

### II. The Holy Spirit gives assurance of salvation to the believer (Rom. 8:16–17).

As the parents of a newborn child speak words of endearment by which they identify themselves and their relationship to the child, even so the Holy Spirit of God comes into the heart of the new convert to speak with a still, small voice concerning the living relationship that has been established with God the Father (Gal. 4:6).

### III. The Holy Spirit dwells within to help us bring our minds and lives into harmony with God's will (Phil. 2:13).

The heavenly Father does not expect us to lift ourselves to spiritual maturity by pulling at our own bootstraps. The Holy Spirit comes into our hearts that he might reproduce within us the mind and character of Jesus Christ (Phil. 2:5; Gal. 5:16).

### IV. The Holy Spirit attempts continually to teach us things concerning Christ and his will for us (John 14:26; 15:26; 16:13).

### V. The Holy Spirit desires to empower us for effective service (Acts 1:8).

### VI. The Holy Spirit will help us to have an effective prayer life if we cooperate with him (Rom. 8:26–27).

### Conclusion

The book of Acts is a dramatic success story of human and divine cooperation. The disciples believed in and responded to the Holy Spirit's leadership and guidance. May God grant us to do likewise.

---

## SUNDAY MORNING, SEPTEMBER 27

***Title:*** Noah: By Faith He Heeded the Warning of God

***Text:*** "By faith Noah, being warned of God of things not seen as yet, moved with fear, prepared an ark to the saving of his house; by the which he condemned the world, and became heir of the righteousness which is by faith" **(Heb. 11:7)**.

***Scripture Reading:*** Genesis 6:5–17, 22

***Hymns:*** "Brethren, We Have Met to Worship," Atkins
"Ye Must Be Born Again," Sleeper
"Yield Not to Temptation," Palmer
"Why Do You Wait?" Root

***Offertory Prayer:*** Heavenly Father, today we offer to you the love of our hearts and the praise of our lips. We bring to you our time, talents, and treasures and recognize all of them as gifts of your grace. As we bring our tithes and offerings, help us to do so as an indication of our desire to place our everything upon the altar in your service. In Jesus' name we pray. Amen.

**Introduction**

We can react to the crises of life in a great variety of ways. We can permit fear to capture the citadel of our soul and react by fleeing from our responsibility and our opportunities, or we can react in faith and stand steady under pressure. Those of us who are Christians should meet every situation with faith in both the goodness of God and in his abiding presence to help us in every time of need.

The recipients of the letter to the Hebrews were in the midst of great trials. They were the victims of persecution and all of the inconveniences and cruelties that accompany being in religious, political, and economic disfavor. The writer of this tremendous book encouraged them to trust in God and to be faithful to his good purpose for them. With inspired selectivity, he calls forth a list of spiritual heroes from the pages of the Old Testament to speak a word of challenge and cheer to those who were now experiencing great difficulty.

The study of history can be a most profitable experience if one reads, not only in order to understand the past, but to gain insight into the present and to what the future most likely holds. Have you ever wondered what George Washington would have to say to our country today if he could address the nation? How would Abraham Lincoln counsel us?

If we would find biblical stories profitable, we must let the characters of the past speak to the present that which they discovered about God in the laboratory of human experience. For while circumstances change, God remains unchanged. What he was, he is. What he did in and through his people, he will do today and tomorrow if we will but respond in faith and cooperate with him.

Today let us listen to the testimony of Noah, who by faith built an ark in obedience to God while all of his countrymen laughed at him. Genuine faith will cause us to be faithful to God and to fear him. Paul says concerning the unbelieving and the ungodly, "There is no fear of God before their eyes" (Rom. 3:18).

Since faith comes by hearing, and hearing by the Word of God, we need to be reminded that the Bible contains many promises from God to his people. These promises are made to those who have faith. Have you discovered these promises and claimed them for your own life? We also need to recognize that the Bible contains many warnings from God. Have you, like Noah, recognized and responded to the warnings of God? How would you respond if you knew that God had spoken a word of warning to you? Like Noah? Or like Noah's neighbors? "Examine yourselves to see whether you are in the faith; test yourselves. Do you not realize that Christ Jesus is in you—unless, of course, you fail the test?" (2 Cor. 13:5 NIV).

### I. God constantly warns us against danger.

A. *The destructive nature of sin.* From the beginning of time, God has warned man against the destructive nature of sin. Some of the first instructions given to Adam in the garden were words of warning. "But of the tree of the knowledge of good and evil, thou shalt not eat of it: for in the day that thou eatest thereof thou shalt surely die" (Gen. 2:17). Adam and Eve did not heed the warning of God. Genesis 3 tells us of their unbelief and of their fall under the destructive power of sin. By their attitudes and actions of unbelief, disobedience, and greed for equality with God, they committed spiritual suicide and polluted the spiritual fountain from which the whole human race was to flow.

The Bible is a record of God's continuing activity to save people from the ravages of sin. If we will respond to God's warnings and accept his gracious invitation with confidence and cooperation, we can be delivered from the awful tyranny of sin.

B. *The peril of self-deception.* God warns us concerning the peril of self-deception: "There is a way which seemeth right unto a man, but the end thereof are the ways of death" (Prov. 14:12), and "The way of a fool is right in his own eyes: but he that hearkeneth unto counsel is wise" (12:15). Repeatedly the Scriptures would say to us, "Be not deceived" (1 Cor. 6:9; Gal. 6:7).

C. *The certainty of God's justice and wrath.* We place so much emphasis on the love and mercy of God that we underemphasize the other side of his nature—his wrath. Because God does love, he cannot tolerate that which violates his own nature and that which destroys humans who are the crown of his creation.

God is a moral God, and our universe is constructed on a moral basis. The universe itself is in opposition to people who flagrantly break the laws of God and the laws of society. Sin by its very nature brings punishment into the lives of sinners. In the Old Testament, we read, "Be sure your sin will find you out" (Num. 32:23). This verse does not teach that all of our sins will be found out by others, but it does declare that our sins will find us out.

Many of the laws of God are what is known as self-executing laws. This means that they carry with them the seed of their own punishment, and that it is impossible for a person to sin and escape suffering. The tragedy is that others suffer also, not *for* our sin but *because of* our sin. The writer of the book of Ecclesiastes observed, "For God shall bring every work unto judgment, with every secret thing, whether it be good, or whether it be evil" (Eccl. 12:14).

### II. Have you recognized the warning of God?

God speaks in a great variety of ways to those who have ears to hear and to those who sincerely desire to escape the way of self-destruction.

A. *Have you let the written Word of God speak to your mind and heart?* The psalmist said, "Thy word have I hid in mine heart, that I might not sin against thee" (Ps. 119:11). The habit of memorizing selected passages of Scripture can be most profitable for both the individual and for the family as a whole. To do so provides the Holy Spirit with a divine channel of communication to our hearts in the time of need that is bound to come for each of us.

B. *God may speak a word of warning to us through the fall of someone else.* Occasionally we see the tragic results of the carelessness of those who ignore traffic signs and signals. At times the traffic offender is the victim, but in many instances others also suffer. Paul had something like this in mind when he said, "Brethren, if a man be overtaken in a fault, ye which are spiritual, restore such an one in the spirit of meekness, considering thyself, lest thou also be tempted" (Gal. 6:1).

There are many wrecks along the highway of life. Each of these could speak a word of caution and warning to us if we but have eyes to see and ears to hear.

C. *God may speak a word of warning to us through some godly, devout person.* It may be in the form of advice or even rebuke. Jesus instructed the members of the early church to be compassionately concerned both for the individual and for the church when one of the members falls into sin (Matt. 18:15–17). The church would be a dynamic moral force in today's world if it was compassionate enough for its own to follow the instructions of its Lord. We miserably fail to obey him and to please him when we resort to harsh criticism instead of exercising compassionate concern for the wayward.

D. *God will speak words of warning to you through the Bible lessons of your teacher and through the sermons of your pastor.*

E. *God has placed the Holy Spirit within your heart, not only to lead and empower you for service, but also to warn you of the presence of spiritual danger.* "Quench not the Spirit" (1 Thess. 5:19). "Walk in the Spirit, and ye shall not fulfill the lust of the flesh" (Gal. 5:16).

## III. Noah's response to the warning of God.

A. *Noah believed God.* He took God at his word. He did not assume that God was speaking just to hear himself talk. He knew that God was not teasing him or merely trying to frighten him.

We need to study the Word of God, not as ancient history, but as God speaking to us in the present.

B. *Having heard God speak a word of warning, Noah was "moved with fear."* This was a godly fear. He was not scared of God in the sense that he wanted to run away from him, but he had a reverent regard for both the truthfulness and the power of God to do what he had said he was going to do. Noah was moved by fear for the welfare of his family, and consequently he prepared the ark in obedience to the instructions of God.

We need to rediscover and reactivate an attitude of wholesome fear of the Lord. The wise man said, "The fear of the LORD is the beginning of knowledge" (Prov. 1:7). He also said, "The fear of the LORD is the beginning of wisdom" (9:10), and "The fear of the LORD is a fountain of life, to depart from the snares of death" (14:27). There is no hope for the person who does not have a wholesome and reverent fear of God.

C. *Noah's faith and fear led to action.* He made decisions that were decisive both for himself and for his family. How have you reacted to the warnings of God?

**IV. God's words of warning.**

A. *The wages of sin is still death (Rom. 6:23).* From the beginning of time, the big lie has been, "You can sin and escape suffering" (cf. Gen. 3:4). People continue to fall for this line of the Evil One and swallow it hook, line, and sinker. Sin not only violates the conscience and deadens the will, but it brings about the death of all that is finest and best within the human soul. Sin separates people from God, from their fellow humans, from their families, and from their better selves.

B. *There is judgment to come.* Without apology or hesitation, the Bible says that one day we all shall stand before God to give an account of our deeds. God would have us meet him on the basis of his mercy rather than on the basis of his justice. We read, "God … now commandeth all men everywhere to repent: Because he hath appointed a day, in the which he will judge the world in righteousness by that man whom he hath ordained; whereof he hath given assurance unto all men, in that he hath raised him from the dead" (Acts 17:30–31).

C. *The law of the harvest is still in force.* "Be not deceived; God is not mocked: for whatsoever a man soweth, that shall he also reap" (Gal. 6:7). It is the law of nature and of God that a person reaps according to the law of kind. We reap what we sow. "He that soweth to his flesh shall of the flesh reap corruption; but he that soweth to the Spirit shall of the Spirit reap life everlasting" (v. 8).

D. *God warns us that there is no escape for those who neglect to repent and believe.* Someone has said, "The shortest road to hell is by the highway of tomorrow." "Boast not thyself of tomorrow; for thou knowest not what a day may bring forth" (Prov. 27:1).

**Conclusion**

Now is the time for all wise and sensible persons to pay attention to the warnings of God and to respond by faith to his invitations and promises. The cross is God's stop sign and red light and barricade on the road to ruin. I urge you to respond to his mercy and love and forgiveness while you have time and opportunity.

## SUNDAY EVENING, SEPTEMBER 27

***Title:*** The Holy Spirit in the Witnessing Church

***Text:*** "But ye shall receive power, after that the Holy Ghost is come upon you: and ye shall be witnesses unto me both in Jerusalem, and in all Judaea, and in Samaria, and unto the uttermost part of the earth" **(Acts 1:8)**.

### Introduction

The book of Acts is a dramatic narrative of divine power and human enterprise. It presents a series of illustrations of what a witnessing congregation can accomplish when empowered by the Holy Spirit.

A study of this book of early Christian history can provide us with the key to the secret of power and progress so that in the providence of God we too may follow in their train in this generation.

### I. The promise of the Holy Spirit.

A. *The promise of the Father (Acts 1:4).* Jesus encouraged his disciples by assuring them that they were to be the recipients of the promised Spirit. Among the messianic promises of the Old Testament were predictions of a time when God would pour out his divine Spirit on all flesh as he had poured it out on individuals in Israel (Joel 2:28–29).

B. *The promise of the Savior (Acts 1:8).* The disciples, selected and called out as the nucleus of his church, were commanded to tarry in the city of Jerusalem until they were endued with power from on high. With an incomplete and inadequate understanding of his purpose for them, Jesus commanded them not to concern themselves with authority but to wait until they should receive the energy of the Spirit of God, which was to come upon them and fill them on the day of Pentecost (Acts 1:7–8).

Peter explained the events that took place on the day of Pentecost as being the fulfillment of this promise and declared the Holy Spirit to be the ascension gift of Christ to his church (Acts 2:33; cf. John 14:16–18).

### II. The presence of the Holy Spirit.

On the day of Pentecost, the Holy Spirit became the dominant reality in the life of the early church and in the individual lives of the disciples. There are more than forty references to the Holy Spirit in the first thirteen chapters of Acts.

A. *"What meaneth this?" (Acts 2:12).* The crowds that thronged Jerusalem had no idea about the nature and significance of that which was happening to the 120 disciples who had been tarrying in obedience to the commandment of the risen and ascended Christ. They heard "a sound from heaven as of a rushing mighty wind." It was not a wind but rather the sound of a wind. They saw upon the disciples "cloven tongues like as of fire." This was indeed an astonishing sight. The crowds were further amazed as they heard these Galileans speak in tongues that were intelligible to so many foreigners who were in Jerusalem at that time. It was only normal that they should ask, "What meaneth this?" and that some would surmise that they had been drinking.

B. *Peter explains and interprets.*

1. "Be this known unto you" (Acts 2:14). By the inspiration of the Holy Spirit, Peter explained the strange phenomenon that they had experienced and witnessed as a fulfillment of Old Testament prophecy.

   A devout Israelite would recognize these cloven tongues of fire as being a visible symbol of the presence of Israel's God, for the Lord had led the children of Israel out of bondage "by day in a pillar of a cloud ... and by night in a pillar of fire, to give them light" (Exod. 13:21).

   When Solomon had dedicated the temple, we read, "The fire came down from heaven, and consumed the burnt offering and the sacrifices; and the glory of the LORD filled the house" (2 Chron. 7:1). This manifestation of the presence of God produced a profound effect on the children of Israel. "When all the children of Israel saw how the fire came down, and the glory of the LORD upon the house, they bowed themselves with their faces to the ground upon the pavement, and worshipped, and praised the LORD saying, For he is good; for his mercy endureth forever" (2 Chron. 7:3).

   When Elijah faced the 450 prophets of Baal on Mount Carmel, the answer to the crucial contest between Baal and God was to be by fire. Elijah challenged, "The God that answereth by fire, let him be God" (1 Kings 18:24). Following the contest, we read, "And when all the people saw it, they fell on their faces: and they said, The LORD, he is the God; the LORD, he is the God" (1 Kings 18:39).

   The events associated with Pentecost were intended by God to make a profound impression on both the early church and their contemporaries from all nations who were assembled in Jerusalem. By these strange and mysterious symbols, God was placing his divine stamp of authentication on that which Jesus had done and taught and the message that the early church was to proclaim, beginning in Jerusalem and going out into the uttermost parts of the earth.

2. "This is that" (Acts 2:16). Peter announced both to his fellow believers and to those who came to see and hear that they were actually experiencing the fulfillment of the Old Testament prophecy spoken through Joel. He declared that the Holy Spirit was to come upon all flesh to equip and empower believers to be witnesses of the mighty works of God. The early church was in the process of doing so at that very moment (Acts 2:11).

   We are to understand in this context that prophecy is not limited to prediction but is primarily to be thought of as "speaking for God." This the early church did with great enthusiasm and effectiveness.

### III. The purpose of the Holy Spirit.

The Holy Spirit came to equip and empower the early church to bear a continuing witness to the truth as Jesus had done during his earthly ministry. Luke, the author of Acts, declares that in writing his gospel he set forth that which "Jesus began both to do and to teach." In Acts he sets forth what the living Christ through the Holy Spirit continues to do in and through his church, which is his body in the world.

A. *Witnessing in Jerusalem (Acts 1–7).* The first seven chapters are a dramatic account of how these early believers, in the power and energy of the Holy Spirit, bore a winsome witness to Christ in Jerusalem.

B. *Witnessing in Judea and Samaria (Acts 8–12).* These four chapters describe how the Holy Spirit led the members of the early church to break across caste and color lines to bear witness to people quite different from those whom they normally would consider the objects of God's love.

C. *Witnessing to Gentiles (Acts 10–11).* In these chapters the Holy Spirit led these early Christians to begin bearing witness to Gentiles, who were normally considered as pagan outcasts outside the circle of God's concern.

D. *Witnessing unto the uttermost part of the earth (Acts 13–28).* The early witnesses moved outside the boundaries of the area known as the Holy Land. They bore a powerful witness to the Jews who were dispersed, and when these Jews refused to continue to hear, they shifted their focus to the Gentiles. The book of Acts tells us how the church changed from a Jewish body to a body that was to become almost completely Gentile.

### IV. The power of the Holy Spirit.

The supreme qualification for bearing a winning witness was and is to be filled with the Spirit of God. "For we wrestle not against flesh and blood, but against principalities, against powers, against the rulers of the darkness of this world, against spiritual wickedness in high places" (Eph. 6:12).

A. *The early believers received a new insight into God's purpose (Acts 2:16–36).* Jesus had said concerning the Holy Spirit, "Howbeit when he, the Spirit of truth, is come, he will guide you into all truth" (John 16:13). This the early church experienced both on the day of Pentecost and in the days that followed.

B. *They were given a new liberty of utterance (Acts 2:4, 11).* They became effective communicators of the wonderful works of God speaking in clear, simple, forceful ways.

C. *They were given a new power of persuasion (Acts 2:37; 4:33; 6:10).* Only the Holy Spirit could have enabled them to speak in the manner that brought conversion to the hearts of the hearers.

D. *They experienced a new boldness in witnessing (Acts 2:22, 36; 4:29, 31).* They had an inner compulsion to bear their personal testimony and to believe in Jesus as Lord. A. T. Pierson says that this "Holy Spirit boldness was due to Holy Spirit fullness." Many of us believe that it is the lack of the power of the Holy Spirit that causes the present-day church to limp when our Lord would have it to be leaping to the task of witnessing to our world.

**V. The path to Holy Spirit power.**

If one reads the New Testament reverently, he cannot help but come to the conclusion that the person and work of the Holy Spirit is something other than a subject for historical research. The Holy Spirit is present today with power to do all that has been done and all that needs to be done to make the church effective in today's world. The big question is, "How?"

A. *Faith.* The Holy Spirit does not work where his presence and purpose are ignored. We do not need to pray for his coming, for he has already arrived. We do need to recognize that he is present in the heart of each believer and present in the congregation when these believers assemble.

If we did more waiting upon the Lord and more worshiping before we attempted to witness, the results would be different. He who does not believe that the Holy Spirit is present to help and guide will never attempt to do anything except that which is humanly possible.

B. *Obedience.* The Holy Spirit came on the day of Pentecost upon a group of disciples who were committed to obeying the command of the living Lord. The Lord had commanded them to tarry, and they responded with trusting obedience. The Holy Spirit's power is declared to be the gift of God to those who will obey (Acts 5:32). The power of God flows in and through hearts and lives that are not grounded by selfishness and disobedience. If we are willing to let the Holy Spirit take over, he will make us over.

C. *United prayer.* The early church witnessed in great power largely because they believed in united prayer. They cooperated in prayer, and when the power of God came upon them, they wielded a mighty spiritual impact upon their generation.

A reverent examination of the prayer life of your church may reveal why the fire does not fall when the pastor preaches.

### Conclusion

If we would labor in something other than the flesh, we must respond to the Holy Spirit in faith and obedience. He will work in us and through us if we are but willing to cooperate.

---

## WEDNESDAY EVENING, SEPTEMBER 30

***Title:*** Walk in the Spirit

***Text:*** "This I say then, Walk in the Spirit, and ye shall not fulfil the lust of the flesh" **(Gal. 5:16)**.

### Introduction

Paul wrote to the Galatian Christians to encourage them to make a proper response to the Holy Spirit that they might not live on the level of their lower nature. He informed them of the struggle that would continue between the Spirit of God, who came into their hearts at the time of conversion, and the lower nature with its sinful appetites (Gal. 5:17–21). It was his earnest desire that they experience the full harvest of the fruit of the Spirit (vv. 22–24). That they might be assured of such, he encouraged them to "walk in the Spirit."

### I. To walk implies progress.

It is not the will of God that we remain as we are or where we are. God would have us to walk forward toward maturity and fruitfulness.

### II. To walk implies direction.

God would not have us to go backward from our task and our opportunities. Neither would he have us to walk in aimless circles. By his Spirit he would lead us in the paths of righteousness and fruitfulness as he led Paul. We read how the Holy Spirit guided his walk: "Now when they had gone throughout Phrygia and the region of Galatia, and were forbidden of the Holy Spirit to preach the word in Asia, after they were come to Mysia, they assayed to go into Bithynia: but the Spirit suffered them not. And they passing by Mysia came down to Troas" (Acts 16:6–8). The Holy Spirit will guide our walk in a similar manner if we are sensitive and responsive to his leadership.

### III. Walking in the Spirit.

There are at least five ways in which we know the Spirit wants us to walk. We can count on him to assist us in every way possible.

A. *The Holy Spirit will help us to walk worthy of our Christian calling (Eph. 4:1).*

B. *The Spirit will help us to walk differently from the unsaved (Eph. 4:17).*

C. *The Spirit will help us to walk in love (Eph. 5:2).*

D. *The Spirit will help us to walk as the children of light (Eph. 5:8).*

E. *The Spirit will help us to walk in wisdom (Eph. 5:15).*

### Conclusion

The Holy Spirit dwells in the heart of the believer. He is as close to you as your breath. By faith recognize his presence. Respond to his leadership, and walk forward into the future with courage and cheer, for God has wonderful things in store for you if you seek to "walk in the Spirit."

Suggested Preaching Program for

# OCTOBER

## ■ Sunday Mornings

Continue the series on the lives of those who occupy Faith's Hall of Fame in Hebrews 11.

## ■ Sunday Evenings

Conclude the series on "The Witnessing Church in the Book of Acts." These messages set forth the manner in which the early church responded to the Master's invitation to discipleship. We can and should follow the example of these victorious disciples.

## ■ Wednesday Evenings

The Epistle of James provides the biblical basis for the Wednesday evening messages.

---

## SUNDAY MORNING, OCTOBER 4

***Title:*** Abraham: The Faith That Obeys

***Text:*** "By faith Abraham, when he was called to go out into a place which he should after receive for an inheritance, obeyed; and he went out, not knowing whither he went" **(Heb. 11:8)**.

***Scripture Reading:*** Genesis 12:1–7

***Hymns:*** "O God, Our Help in Ages Past," Watts

"When We Walk with the Lord," Sammis

"I'll Go Where You Want Me to Go," Brown

***Offertory Prayer:*** Heavenly Father, you are the source of all that is good and worthwhile in our lives. We respond to your goodness with gratitude and with generosity of heart and hand. Today we bring our material substance and offer it to you as an act of worship. Receive these tithes and offerings and add your blessings to them that your kingdom might come and your will be done on earth as it is in heaven. Amen.

### Introduction

Genuine faith is not only something we *believe*, but something we *behave.* True faith is something we do. Genuine faith is more than intellectual assent to a creed or to a system of religious dogma.

"Examine yourselves to see whether you are in the faith; test yourselves. Do you not realize that Christ Jesus is in you—unless, of course, you fail the test?" (2 Cor. 13:5 NIV). Genuine faith involves a positive response to God's plan and purpose for our lives. Is your life pleasing to God? Are you achieving in your own experience the divine destiny chosen for you?

Abraham gave expression to his faith by hearing the call of God and obeying. The call involved a separation from his family and a dedication to God's will: "Get thee out of thy country, and from thy kindred, and from thy father's house, unto a land that I will shew thee" (Gen. 12:1).

Abraham's faith in God expressed itself in loving obedience. He "obeyed; and he went out, not knowing whither he went." Disobedience to the call of God would have placed him in a nameless and forgotten grave. The decision to trust and obey the known will of God was the solid foundation stone for the superstructure of a great life.

At first Abraham's obedience was only partial. He lived at Haran until after the death of his father (Acts 7:4). The best kind of obedience will neither procrastinate nor question the wisdom of God. Ultimately, Abraham's obedience was complete. "And they went forth to go into the land of Canaan; and into the land of Canaan they came" (Gen. 12:5).

Disobedience to the calls and commandments of God is an insult to the truthfulness of God. Close examination reveals that each of God's commandments, being motivated always by love, contains a promise. To disobey is to imply that God is untruthful and untrustworthy.

In the covenant relationship, Israel was to express their faith by obedience (Exod.19:5–6). A study of Israel's history reveals that disobedience was the result of refusing to trust in the goodness of God. Unbelief and disobedience not only endangers the individual but also the welfare of others.

Disobedience to the will of God is an act of self-destruction whether that disobedience be individual or collective, as in the case of a nation or a church.

Abraham had the wisdom of believing that his highest happiness was to be found in loving obedience to God's will even though he was unable to give a rational explanation except on the basis of his faith.

### I. Glad obedience gives assurance of sonship (1 John 2:3–7).

A. *We enter into sonship by faith (Gal. 3:26).* The salvation experience is possible for one and for all under any and all earthly circumstances, for it is by grace through faith rather than by ceremony or ritual.

B. *While it is faith that gives us the privilege of becoming the children of God, loving obedience gives us the inward assurance that we are indeed God's children.* First John was written specifically to believers to impart the assurance of salvation: "These things have I written unto you that believe on the name of the Son of God; that ye may know that ye have eternal life, and that ye may believe on the name of the Son of God" (1 John 5:13). Among the things

John had described as distinguishing characteristics of the children of God was loving obedience.

As Abraham's faith expressed itself in obedience, if our faith is genuine, it will express itself in obedience.

John says, "Hereby know we that we are in him." "Examine yourselves to see whether you are in the faith; test yourselves" (2 Cor. 13:5 NIV).

**II. Glad obedience makes prayer a transforming experience (1 John 3:22–24).**

In the book of Genesis, we find several conversations between God and Abraham. We cannot know exactly how all of this took place, but we can be safe in assuming that these dialogues took place between Abraham and his Creator as a prayer experience, for Abraham was deliberately seeking to obey God's commandments. At times the initiative was with God. Possibly God took the initiative in every instance. Because of Abraham's desire to be obedient to God, he was much more open to hear the divine communications.

A. *Is your prayer life a disappointing experience?* Has God answered your prayers? Have you found prayer to be an enriching experience? Does anything happen when you pray? Have you been disappointed by either God's seeming inability or unwillingness to answer your prayers?

B. *Prayer was designed for the obedient.* There is no basis in either the Scriptures or in experience for one to believe that God intended for us to use prayer as a means of getting that which we would selfishly like to have. Jesus intended and commanded that we pray for the things that are needed for the advancement of God's kingdom work. By prayer we requisition that which is needed not only for the welfare of our own souls but also that which will advance the kingdom of God on earth.

Prayer is like a business credit card. A company will issue a credit card by which an employee can obtain various services or funds for company use. The employee is guilty of a criminal offense if he uses this credit card for personal use. If we are living and serving in obedience to the command of God, we can come before the throne of grace in the name of Jesus and requisition divine resources in a dialogue rather than in a dry and unsatisfying monologue.

Perhaps a part of the emptiness of your prayer life and your failure to receive answers from God is to be traced to a lack of obedience. For to be obedient is to live in communion and to enjoy communicating with the eternal God.

**III. Glad obedience is a proof of our love.**

Jesus appealed to the high motive of love as the basis for obedience on the part of his disciples. This is recognized by all as the highest motivation. He said,

"If ye love me, keep my commandments" (John 14:15). He also said, "Ye are my friends, if ye do whatsoever I command you" (15:14).

A. *By our obedience we prove our love to God.* There is no substitute for obedience. The words of our lips are empty nothings unless with our lives we recognize and obey the commands of our loving Lord. Jesus made this very clear: "He that hath my commandments, and keepeth them, he it is that loveth me: and he that loveth me shall be loved of my Father, and I will love him, and will manifest myself to him" (John 14:21).

B. *By our obedience we prove our love for God to others.* Each child of God is expected to bear a testimony with lip and life concerning the goodness and grace of our wonderful Savior. It is impossible to give voice to a convincing testimony to the unsaved unless they can see the results of glad obedience in our lives.

Continuous glad obedience is a powerful testimony to the unsaved concerning the worthwhileness of the life of faith. Obedience will authenticate and recommend our testimony as we seek to persuade others to become followers of the Lord Jesus Christ. Disobedience will nullify that which we would like to accomplish.

### Conclusion

May God bless you with the faith and wisdom to understand that all of God's commands are motivated by his divine love for us and for others. These commands contain promises either expressed or implied. People with no faith hear the commands of God and consider, hesitate, and refuse to respond. They decide to walk by their own wisdom and to seek their highest well-being in human resources and achievements alone. These people cannot possibly please God.

People of faith hear the commands of God, consider them, and then commit themselves. They consider the character and the nature of God. They consider the loving purposes of God. They commit themselves to a life of trusting obedience.

God is Somebody rather than something. He is worthy of our obedience. Obedience to his will is the highway to a glorious testimony.

## SUNDAY EVENING, OCTOBER 4

***Title:*** Prayer in the Witnessing Church

***Text:*** "Peter therefore was kept in prison: but prayer was made without ceasing of the church unto God for him" (**Acts 12:5**).

### Introduction

To understand the uniqueness of the early church, we must see that church in prayer.

A visitor was once being conducted on a tour through the various facilities of a huge church. The guide said, "We will now visit the power room." The visitor assumed that they were going to see the heating and cooling facilities of the church. Instead, he was led into what appeared to be an assembly room. There were present a number of people in prayer. The tour guide then observed, "This is the room where the power behind the program of this church is generated."

One of the greatest weaknesses in the life of the contemporary church is the neglect of prayer. This explains why we have failed to make a greater impact on today's world evangelistically, morally, and socially.

If either the church or the individual Christian is to make an impact on today's world for Christ, we must rediscover the power that comes through praying, and we must restore prayer to the place that it occupied in the life of our Lord and his apostles. It is interesting to observe the prayer habits of the early church as shown in Acts.

### I. Prayer in the upper room.

A. *They responded to the Lord's command to tarry by giving themselves to prayer and supplication.* "These all continued with one accord in prayer and supplication, with the women, and Mary the mother of Jesus, and with his brethren" (Acts 1:14).

B. *They prayed to God to rule and to overrule in their actions that the will of God might be done (Acts 1:24).*

### II. Prayer and the day of Pentecost.

A. *It was earnest, heart-searching prayer that prepared the hearts of the early disciples for the outpouring of the Holy Spirit on the day of Pentecost (Acts 2:1).* There can be no question that today we are strangers to the divine power that the Holy Spirit makes available to those who genuinely pray (Luke 11:13). It is both futile and disappointing to labor in the energy of the flesh when we could be laboring in the energy of the Spirit of God.

B. *Prayer not only preceded and prepared for Pentecost, but prayer continued to be the regular habit of these early disciples (Acts 2:42).* For them, prayer was not an opportunity to say, "Gimme, Gimme," to God; instead, it was a form of communication in which they not only conversed with God but in which God was able to do his work within their lives.

### III. The hour of prayer.

"Now Peter and John went up together into the temple at the hour of prayer, being the ninth hour" (Acts 3:1). There were set times for going to the temple for prayer.

A. *The church.* The modern church desperately stands in need of having recurring times when the members come together to give themselves to prayer. This would be good for the individual church. Every sincere participant would be greatly blessed, and others would experience the results of this kind of intercessory prayer.

B. *The individual.* Individual Christians need to have a definite time for prayer if they are to deepen their own spiritual lives and permit God to communicate with them on a continuing basis. If we do not have stated times when we appear before the throne of grace, we will most likely discover that we have been neglectful.

### IV. Prayer in the time of difficulty.

The early church found itself facing what appeared to be insurmountable difficulties from time to time. Their problem was not that of an inadequate budget or untrained leadership; their difficulty was that of the malicious opposition of both the religious and political establishments of the day. They were treated as if they were a subversive organization, and they were commanded to refrain from further activities associated with bearing witness to Jesus Christ (Acts 4:1–3). It is interesting to note how they reacted to this opposition (4:23–31). Had they not prayed in the time of difficulty, they would not have had the courage, wisdom, or power to do what they were able to do.

### V. The manner of their praying.

A. *They engaged in united prayer (Acts 1:14; 4:31; 6:6; 12:5).* By so doing they encouraged the faith and devotion of each other. There is power and joy that come through united prayer that are not to be found in private prayer.

B. *They prayed in private (Acts 10:9; 27:22–25).* Each individual must go apart into a private place to have communion with the heavenly Father. Jesus said that we must not only enter the closet, but we must shut the door to be alone with the heavenly Father. We must shut out that which distracts and interferes in order that we might both speak and hear, for real praying is a dialogue rather than a monologue.

C. *They engaged in public prayer (Acts 16:25).* Paul and Silas did not try to conceal their prayers or praises to God from the other prisoners. In the presence of all they prayed, and God heard. They were not only comforted in the jail, but they experienced a joy that made an impact upon the jailer, who later was to say, "Sirs, what must I do to be saved?" (Acts 16:30).

### VI. The results of praying.

A study of the book of Acts reveals some of the fruits of the prayers of the early church. If we examine these, perhaps we likewise will be encouraged to give ourselves to prayer.

A. *Great boldness (Acts 4:31).* Many modern followers of Christ are timid and hesitant about bearing any kind of Christian testimony. This disappoints the Savior and deprives non-Christians of the help they need, namely, faith in the Lord. We need a holy boldness like that of the early church.

B. *Great unity (Acts 4:32).* In our day tremendous emphasis is placed on unity among Christians. The early church, largely because of their prayer life, was said to be of "one heart and one soul."

C. *Great power (Acts 4:33).* The early disciples of our Lord did not have political power, economic power, or social power, but they did have spiritual power. They were "plugged in" to the power of God. They were not dependent on brain power or muscle power. They were effective because they labored in the energy of divine power, which is still available to those who give themselves to prayer.

D. *Great grace (Acts 4:33).* The grace of God was upon them. They responded to God, not on the basis of human merit, but on the basis of God's love and mercy toward sinners. They became the bearers of this grace to the hearts and lives of others. Grace characterized their relationships with each other. They were gracious even toward their enemies.

E. *Great generosity (Acts 4:34–37).* An unparalleled attitude of generosity permeated the life of the early church as they shared with each other according to their needs. This was an uncoerced, voluntary sharing on the part of those who had plenty with those who did not.

While the degree of generosity practiced by the early church is without parallel since those days, the church would be a much more dynamic force in the world if its members were characterized less by selfishness and more by generous giving.

### Conclusion

The church that does not give itself to prayer is already out of contact with its Commanding Officer. Christians who enter the day's work without first talking to their Lord are like soldiers who would go into battle without weapons or carpenters who would go to their job without tools.

May God help each of us to rediscover the importance of prayer and restore it to the place it should have in our lives.

## WEDNESDAY EVENING, OCTOBER 7

***Title:*** James, a Servant of God

***Text:*** "... a servant of God and of the Lord Jesus Christ" (**James 1:1**).

### Introduction

James, the half brother of our Lord, calls himself "a servant of God, and of the Lord Jesus Christ." In the Greek, the word is *doulos*, which means slave. Thus we are in reality slaves of God. Servants have more freedom than slaves do. Servants can quit work if they choose. Servants have definite work and leisure hours. They can bargain for higher wages, and they are free to express displeasure with present income. Servants can quit one place of service and go to another employer. On the other hand, slaves have none of the privileges of a servant. Slaves are purchased possessions of their masters with no will or time of their own. The word *doulos* thus reveals how completely we are to yield ourselves to the Lord.

James is not the only biblical character described as a slave or servant of God.

**I. Abraham was the servant of God.**

A. *God appeared to Isaac and said, "I am the God of Abraham thy father: fear not, for I am with thee, and will bless thee, and multiply thy seed for my servant Abraham's sake" (Gen. 26:24).*

B. *"And he remembered his holy promise, and Abraham his servant" (Ps. 105:42).*

**II. Moses was called the servant of God more times than any other.**

A. *"And Israel saw that great work which the LORD did upon the Egyptians: and the people feared the LORD, and believed the LORD, and his servant Moses" (Exod. 14:31).*

B. *"So Moses the servant of the LORD died there in the land of Moab, according to the word of the LORD" (Deut. 34:5).*

C. *"Now after the death of Moses the servant of the LORD it came to pass, that the LORD spake unto Joshua the son of Nun, Moses' minister, saying, Moses my servant is dead; now therefore arise, go over this Jordan" (Josh. 1:1–2).*

**III. Caleb and Joshua were the servants of God.**

A. *"But my servant Caleb, because he had another spirit with him, and hath followed me fully, him will I bring into the land whereinto he went; and his seed shall possess it" (Num. 14:24).*

B. *Joshua 24:9 and Judges 2:8.*

**IV. David was often called a servant of God.**

A. *"On the eighth day he sent the people away: and they blessed the king, and went unto their tents joyful and glad of heart for all the goodness that the LORD had done for David his servant, and for Israel his people" (1 Kings 8:66).*

B. *"Unto his son will I give one tribe, that David my servant may have a light always before me in Jerusalem, the city which I have chosen me to put my name there" (1 Kings 11:36).*

C. *"I will defend this city, to save it, for mine own sake, and for my servant David's sake" (2 Kings 19:34).*

**V. Elijah was the servant of God (2 Kings 9:36; 10:10).**

**VI. Isaiah was the servant of God (Isa. 20:3).**

**VII. Job was the servant of God (Job 1:8; 42:7).**

### VIII. The prophets were the servants of God (2 Kings 21:10; Amos 3:7).

### IX. The apostles were the servants of God (Rom. 1:1; Phil. 1:1; Titus 1:1; James 1:1; Jude 1).

### X. Epaphras was the servant of God (Col. 4:12).

### XI. All Christians are to be the servants of God.

"Not with eyeservice, as men pleasers; but as the servants of Christ, doing the will of God from the heart" (Col. 3:22).

#### Conclusion

One of the highest honors the Scriptures can bestow on a man is to call him the servant of God. Today each follower of Christ should aspire to the honor of being a true servant of the Lord Jesus Christ. Like Moses the lawgiver, we also can be servants of God. Like David the shepherd boy, the sweet singer of beautiful psalms, later to be king, we can be servants of God. Like Caleb and Joshua, God's soldiers, we can be servants of God. And like the apostles who were faithful witnesses, we can be servants of God.

---

## SUNDAY MORNING, OCTOBER 11

*Title:* Abraham: The Patience of Faith

*Text:* "These all died in faith, not having received the promises, but having seen them afar off, and were persuaded of them, and embraced them, and confessed that they were strangers and pilgrims on the earth" **(Heb. 11:13)**.

*Scripture Reading:* Romans 4:18–25

*Hymns:* "My Faith Looks Up to Thee," Palmer

"Faith Is the Victory," Yates

"He Leadeth Me," Gilmore

*Offertory Prayer:* Holy Father, you have bestowed upon us rich and bountiful blessings in more ways than we can enumerate. You have been gracious and merciful to us. We thank you for every manner of blessing. We come now to give you our tithes and offerings, acknowledging you as the giver of every good and perfect gift. May your blessing be on these offerings for the advancement of your kingdom and for the blessings of the lives of our fellow humans. Amen.

#### Introduction

Abraham is known as the father of the faithful. He became the friend of God because he trusted God not only at the beginning of his life but throughout all of his life; persistently and continuously he trusted God.

In writing to the Roman Christians, Paul paid tribute to the faith of Abraham and called attention to the patient persistence of his faith even when all of the evidence would have indicated that his faith was unjustified. He became a spiritual giant because "he staggered not at the promise of God through unbelief; but was strong in faith, giving glory to God; and being fully persuaded that, what he had promised, he was able also to perform" (Rom. 4:20–21).

By faith, Abraham was initiated into a living relationship with the eternal God. By faith he walked with God and talked with God. He believed even when he could not see and others could not understand. May God grant to each of us not only initial faith but patient faith that keeps on believing and trusting.

### I. Abraham's faith gave him a vision of God.

"By faith he forsook Egypt, not fearing the wrath of the king: for he endured, as seeing him who is invisible" (Heb. 11:27).

If God is—then God is of supreme importance. To Abraham, God was very real; with the eye of his faith, he saw God. With the ear of his faith, he heard the voice of God.

A. *"He went out" (Heb. 11:8).* Because Abraham's faith made God real to him, he obeyed the call of God to leave his home and his country.

B. *"By faith he sojourned in the land of promise" (Heb. 11:9).* Throughout his entire lifetime, Abraham was a stranger and a sojourner in the land of promise. He was unable to possess it though he believed with all of his heart that God had given it to his descendants.

C. *By faith "he looked for a city which hath foundations, whose builder and maker is God" (Heb. 11:10).* Abraham was more concerned about the city of God than he was about the cities of the country in which he lived.

God had taken the initiative and had revealed himself to Abraham. God does this today through the gospel as it is proclaimed both by the church and by individual Christians. By faith Abraham responded with obedience and worship.

As Abraham journeyed, we read, "and there builded he an altar unto the LORD, who appeared unto him" (Gen. 12:7). The altar was a place of prayer, praise, communion, and sacrifice. It was through worship that Abraham nourished his faith. Because he exercised faith, he moved forward. God was able to do mighty things in him and through him.

### II. Abraham's faith included a concept of eternity.

If eternity is, then eternity is all important.

A. *"He looked for a city" other than the cities of the Canaanites (Heb. 11:10).* He sojourned as a stranger in this land of promise with his eyes on God. A lyricist expressed the thought in the following way:

*This world is not my home; I'm just a-passing through,*
*My treasures are laid up somewhere beyond the blue;*

*The angels beckon me from heaven's open door,*
*And I can't feel at home in this world anymore.*
*—Albert E. Brumley*

Students are compelled to live and work in the present with faith in the future. Great expense and effort are involved in securing a college education. Because of their faith in the future, both parents and young people put forth the effort necessary to secure an education. Similarly, Abraham's faith led him to look beyond this life to the future eternal city of God. We would be wise if we lived in time with the issues and values of eternity in mind.

B. *A vision of eternity will encourage a willing detachment from the perishable present.* Each of us lives under the painful pressure of the present. It is exceedingly easy for us to follow the example of Abraham's nephew Lot, who, instead of living for eternal values, decided that immediate material success was of supreme importance. The life of Lot is a dramatic illustration of the fact that one can succeed in time and be a total failure in the things that really matter.

C. *A vision of eternity will encourage an enthusiastic investment in the permanent future.* There is a vast deal of difference between the ant and the grasshopper. The grasshopper lives only for the present. He fills his stomach day by day without any consideration for the future. In contrast, the ant lives in the present with the future in mind. With great industry he engages in cooperative activity to prepare for the future. Instead of living like the grasshopper, people of faith will invest their time, talents, treasure, and testimony in that which is of eternal significance.

Faith is a telescope that brings the distant future into the present. Faith enables one to see things in the future that are hidden from the eyes of those who have no faith. Faith would tell us that our future is wrapped up in the present.

### III. Abraham's faith in the promises of God lifted him into spiritual greatness.

Ours is a day that emphasizes instant services. We are in a tremendous hurry. Most of us are like the proverbial horseman who mounted his steed and rode off in four different directions and arrived nowhere all at the same time.

In this day we are looking for a quick way to get the job done. In this day of instant gratification, some of us are looking for instant success. We are guilty of trying to find easy, convenient, inexpensive ways by which we can achieve spiritual greatness. We need to be reminded that there are no instant giant oaks.

Abraham's patient faith and continuous trusting and obedience made it possible for God to work wonders in him and upon him.

A. *Abraham believed that God is.* "Without faith it is impossible to please him; for he that cometh to God must believe that he is" (Heb. 11:16).

B. *Abraham believed that God was concerned "and that he is a rewarder of them that diligently seek him" (Heb. 11:6).*

C. *Abraham kept on trusting in the God who is trustworthy and dependable.* It was the persistence of his faith that caused him to become the father of the faithful, the friend of God, and the spiritual forefather of each of us who know Jesus Christ as Lord and Savior.

### Conclusion

Abraham went to his death trusting in the promises of God. These promises sustained him and challenged him. He discovered in his own experience that God is trustworthy. May God grant you, not only the faith to begin the Christian life, but also the faith to continue a life of loving and trustful obedience.

---

## SUNDAY EVENING, OCTOBER 11

***Title:*** The Motives of the Witnessing Church

***Text:*** "And daily in the temple, and in every house, they ceased not to teach and preach Jesus Christ" **(Acts 5:42)**.

### Introduction

Jesus warned against the peril of shallow motivation in the Sermon on the Mount. He reminded us that we must not give our gifts in order to receive the glory of people (Matt. 6:1–4). He also warned us against praying to receive the applause of people, for prayer is to be a conversation with God rather than a speech to be heard and admired by people (Matt. 6:5–6). He warned us against displaying our personal piety by revealing our private spiritual disciplines so as to win the approval of people (Matt. 6:16–18). Jesus, in modern terminology, was talking to his disciples about proper motivation. He was declaring that all religious actions and services should be motivated by the single desire to please God.

A motive is that which moves. What the mainspring is to the watch, the motive is to the Christian. What the motor is to the automobile, the motive is to the Christian.

Many motives affect our lives: (1) selfishness—everyone likes to feel important; (2) self-gratification—we like that which pleases us personally, and we like to have our own way; (3) self-interest—it is human nature for each of us to look out for the best interest of self. We find it easy, even if unconsciously, to ask, "What's in it for me?" One does not have to be an expert in motivational research to know that the above motives are inadequate for those who would invest their lives in the service of God and others most effectively.

As we study the book of Acts to discover what it was that made the early church so effective, we find that they did not serve purely out of love. They were human beings like us, and they served out of mingled motives rather than the pure motive of love for God and love for others.

The early church achieved one success after another in what appeared to be an impossible assignment with tremendous handicaps. The book of Acts is a thrilling success story. What were the motives of the early Christians? Can we have the same motives today? Why did the early Christians witness so faithfully?

**I. They discovered the joy of being a bearer of good news (Acts 2:41–47; 5:42; 8:8).**

In obedience to the command of the Lord, they spread by word of mouth the good news of his death and resurrection. They proclaimed God's love for sinners and his desire to forgive sin. They could not conceal the good news that death had been defeated and that the grave had been robbed of its victory. This was such wonderful news that it brought joy to their hearts to bear it. For them, witnessing to the saving acts of Jesus Christ was natural. Not to have done so would have been unnatural, inhuman, and unchristian. They received great inward joy through witnessing.

**II. They recognized and responded to the authority of the crucified but risen and living Lord (Matt. 28:18b; Acts 2:36; 5:29).**

The early Christians believed that God had resurrected Jesus Christ from the dead and had bestowed upon him the authority of lordship. They believed that this gave Jesus the right to issue orders and to command their time, talents, testimony, and treasure.

These early Christians believed that it was right for them to obey Christ even if this obedience brought them into disfavor with both religious and civil authorities. At the risk of being imprisoned and beaten, they chose to obey the Lord.

Many modern Christians consider obedience as being optional. There seems to be little recognition of the present lordship of Jesus Christ. Consequently, disobedience characterizes the modern Christian more so than does obedience.

It was a strong sense of duty, the desire to be obedient, that helped motivate the early church to be a faithful witness to their generation.

**III. They suffered the shock of persecution (Acts 8:3–4).**

It was the shock of persecution that scattered the early Christians. They were very nationalistic and felt that Christianity was a Jewish movement. They were prejudiced against Gentiles to the extent that God put forth special efforts to reveal that the Gentiles were also included in his love and purpose of redemption (Acts 10). Had it not been for the persecution that "stirred up the nest" in Jerusalem, it is highly possible that Christianity never would have gained worldwide significance. The early Christians went everywhere preaching the Word, not because of the compulsion of compassion, but because they were scattered by persecution.

**IV. They were surrendered to the leadership of the Holy Spirit (Acts 8:29; 10:19; 11:12; 13:2; 16:6).**

The Holy Spirit came into the church on the day of Pentecost to equip each believer to be a spokesperson for God (Acts 2:17–18). He came to lead, guide, and teach the disciples as the Lord had taught his apostles (John 14:26). The book of Acts is the dramatic account of divine initiative on the part of the Holy

Spirit and human cooperation on the part of our Lord's disciples. They lived and labored in fellowship with and in the power of the Holy Spirit.

The Holy Spirit is still in the heart of each believer and in the church to carry on the work of the Lord to this day. We need faith to believe that he is present; we need to surrender to him for cooperative endeavors. We need to pray for his power as one of God's best gifts (Luke 11:13).

**V. They believed that all people away from Christ were lost from God and did not know the way home (Acts 4:12).**

Have you ever been lost in a wilderness or desert? Were you ever lost as a child in the park or in a large department store? Can you remember the fright that filled your heart when you recognized that you were separated from loved ones and that you were in a position of danger?

The unbelieving world knows that something is wrong, but many do not know what it is. People have a deep, unsatisfied longing in their hearts that the world with its treasures and pleasures cannot satisfy. The Bible teaches and experience verifies that Jesus Christ provides the clue to the mystery and meaning of life.

The early church believed that people were lost from God and living under the condemnation of sin. They believed that humankind's only hope of forgiveness was through faith in Jesus Christ. They believed that they had been entrusted with the good news that would make it possible for people to be saved from a hell hereafter and to a heaven where the deepest longings of the heart would find full satisfaction in continuing fellowship with God. Because they wanted all people to be saved, they continued to bear their witness.

### Conclusion

It was the natural, normal, and proper thing for a Christian to talk about the joy and satisfaction of knowing Jesus Christ as Savior both in time and for eternity. Consequently, day by day and week by week in the temple, in the synagogues, on the highways and streets—anywhere and everywhere—these early disciples bore their witness. With mingled motives, they loved, they labored, and they lifted men and women toward God. May the same motives command our intellect, our emotions, and our energies in the service of God and of a needy world.

---

## WEDNESDAY EVENING, OCTOBER 14

***Title:*** Are You Short on Wisdom?

***Text:*** "If any of you lack wisdom, let him ask of God, that giveth to all men liberally, and upbraideth not; and it shall be given him" (**James 1:5**).

### Introduction

Life was exceedingly difficult for those to whom James addressed his wonderful epistle. A small Christian minority, even in their places of greatest strength, they were scattered abroad throughout the Roman Empire. They were misunderstood, and in many instances they were the subjects of ridicule and persecution. It was very difficult to know how to be master of circumstances as they faced the trials of life from day to day. Because of these circumstances from which they could not escape, the inspired writer poses a pointed question and makes a practical suggestion.

**I. Do you have a shortage of wisdom?**

James was not seeking to be academic. This question did not arise out of theoretical speculation. He was aware of the difficult situation in which his readers found themselves. By his question and suggestion, he informs them of his awareness of their need for divine insight.

A. *Wisdom is more than the possession of knowledge.* A person can have all the facts and still not know what to do with them.

B. *Wisdom is more than understanding.* One can have all the facts and be sympathetic with the people involved and still not be able to know how to utilize both his knowledge and his sympathy.

C. *Wisdom has been defined as divine insight or divine intelligence.* It has also been defined as sanctified horse sense. James was raising the question concerning whether his readers had a Christian interpretation of the circumstances of life as they faced it.

**II. The source of wisdom.**

"If any of you lack wisdom, let him ask of God" (James 1:5). James declares without any hesitation that God is able and eager to provide people with both an understanding and an interpretation of the problems and possibilities of life. The writer of the book of Proverbs stated it in the following manner: "Trust in the LORD with all thine heart; and lean not unto thine own understanding. In all thy ways acknowledge him, and he shall direct thy paths. Be not wise in thine own eyes: fear the LORD, and depart from evil" (3:5–7). Instead of being proud and conceited, we are to recognize our need for God's guidance. If we will trust him, we are given the promise that he will make our paths straight.

A. *God imparts wisdom to those who, in a prayerful and meditative manner, read his Word with an attitude of expectancy.*

B. *God imparts wisdom through the leadership of his Holy Spirit who dwells within the hearts of believers (1 Cor. 2:10–11).*

C. *God grants us wisdom through experiences of worship.*

D. *God grants us wisdom through the counsel of mature Christian friends.*

E. *God grants us wisdom as we dedicate our mental processes and our intellectual capacity to his leadership.*

**III. The promise of wisdom.**

"Let him ask of God, that giveth to all men liberally" (James 1:5). As God appeared to Solomon and heard his prayer for wisdom, so God will hear our prayer for wisdom (1 Kings 3:5–10).

A. *James was speaking of this promise of wisdom on the basis of his own personal experience.*

B. *The book of Proverbs assures us that wisdom is available to those who desire it (1:2–9).*

### IV. Receiving the wisdom of God.

A. *The wisdom of God comes to those who genuinely pray.* "If any of you lack wisdom, let him ask of God" (James 1:5). God has provided guidance through the ages for those who consult him with a sincere desire to walk in his ways.

Many of us lack wisdom because we have neglected to ask for it. As a service station attendant will not insist that you receive a road map, even so God will not push his thoughts or his ways into a person's thoughts without that person's consent and request.

B. *We must pray in faith.* We must believe sincerely that God is the source of wisdom. We must believe that God is able to give us understanding and insight into the circumstances of life. We must believe that God in his grace is eager to bestow this wisdom upon us. When, in faith, we commit our way to God, we must proceed on the assumption that he will give us guidance through the day and that when tomorrow comes he will be there to continue to guide us even as he guided the children of Israel through the wilderness when they had faith to follow.

### Conclusion

If we hope to live successful lives on this earth, we must humble ourselves and ask for God to fill us with his wisdom. He promises that when we ask, he will provide; but it is up to us to diligently seek his wisdom in his Word and through the filling of his Holy Spirit. When our lives manifest his wisdom in humility, others will see and be drawn to him.

---

## SUNDAY MORNING, OCTOBER 18

***Title:*** The Sermon of an Egyptian Mummy Case

***Text:*** "By faith Joseph, when he died, made mention of the departing of the children of Israel; and gave commandment concerning his bones" **(Heb. 11:22)**.

***Scripture Reading:*** Genesis 50:24–26

***Hymns:*** "Lead On, O King Eternal," Shurtleff

"Faith Is the Victory," Yates

"I Will Sing of My Redeemer," Bliss

***Offertory Prayer:*** Father, once more we thank you for your continued mercies toward us. Morning by morning, new mercies we see. Make us mindful of your greatness, and we will give you the praise. Through Jesus Christ our Lord. Amen.

## Introduction

In faith's Hall of Fame one verse each is given to Isaac, Jacob, and Joseph. William Barclay reminds us that there is one thing in common that links these three heroes of faith together in the mind of the writer of Hebrews. In each of these three cases, the faith that is illustrated and dramatized is the faith of a man to whom death was very near. By faith each of these three was able to face the future with courage and optimism. Genuine faith enables a person to look forward and to see the future as under the government of God and blessed with the presence of God.

Isaac pronounced his blessing upon Jacob shortly after he had said, "Behold now, I am old, I know not the day of my death" (Gen. 27:2). He faced the future with a faith that caused him to pronounce a blessing upon his son.

The blessing of Jacob upon the sons of Joseph is recorded in Genesis 48:9–22. In the conclusion of this blessing, Jacob said to Joseph, "Behold, I die: but God shall be with you, and bring you again unto the land of your fathers" (Gen. 48:21). Because of this faith that enabled him to visualize the future, Jacob blessed Joseph and his sons with the following words:

> God, before whom my fathers Abraham and Isaac did walk, the God which fed me all my life long unto this day, the Angel which redeemed me from all evil, bless the lads; and let my name be named on them, and the name of my fathers Abraham and Isaac; and let them grow into a multitude in the midst of the earth. (Gen. 48:15–16)

His faith was a telescope by which he could look into the future and see the potential of the decisions and actions of the moment.

When Joseph, the prime minister of Egypt, was near death, he required of the Israelites an oath that they would not leave his bones in Egypt. They promised that they would take his bones with them when they returned to the Promised Land. They were faithful to this oath and four hundred years later took his coffin back to the land God had promised (Exod. 13:19).

The record declares that as the children of Israel reached the Promised Land, "the bones of Joseph, which the children of Israel brought up out of Egypt, buried they in Shechem, in a parcel of ground which Jacob bought of the sons of Hamor ... for an hundred pieces of silver" (Josh. 24:32).

All of these men died with their faces toward the future. They trusted God. They walked with God. They talked with God. They obeyed God. Even though they had these blessed experiences, they never fully entered into the inheritance that God had promised, yet their faith kept them looking to the future.

By the oath that Joseph required of the children of Israel and by the presence of his mummy case, he continued to bear witness concerning his optimistic, forward-looking faith. As Abel's life continued to speak after his death, so Joseph continued to speak to the people by means of this mummy case.

## I. Joseph's mummy case reminded them that they were the people of God.

A. *Joseph could have had a splendid monument among the Egyptians.* Like no other people in the ancient world, the Egyptians believed in magnificent monuments and burial chambers for the departed great. Because of the unique contribution that Joseph had made, he could have assumed that he would be enshrined among the greatest in Egypt.

B. *Joseph desired to be identified with the people of God even in his death.* He had no desire for Egypt to be the final resting place of his bones. He wanted to accompany his people in their return to and entrance into the land that was to be their inheritance. By means of this wish he gave expression to his faith in the God of Abraham, Isaac, and Jacob. He deliberately chose to disassociate himself from Egypt, its rules, its gods, and its customs even beyond death.

With all of their faults, the Israelites were the people of God, and Joseph wanted to remind them of this relationship constantly. Joseph believed that as the people of God, they should be different from the Egyptians. For them to become the people that God wanted them to be, they would need to be reminded of their relationship to him and of the obligations that accompanied that privilege.

Today, as in few instances in the past, the church as the people of God is under attack. It is being criticized and maligned. While much of this criticism is deserved, it might be encouraging if we will recognize that God's people have never been perfect. They are always journeying toward becoming God's ideal people. By means of his mummy case, Joseph would not only have his bones returned, but he would remind the people that they were the people of God in a very special way.

## II. Joseph's mummy case was a constant reminder of the promises of God.

A. *God had made some great promises to Abraham and his descendants (Gen. 12:1–3).* These promises had been repeated to Isaac and Jacob. The people of Israel had responded to these promises and walked by faith, though weakly at times, and expected the fulfillment of these promises. As time went by, they discovered the faithfulness of God in the keeping of these promises.

B. *Today the church constitutes the children of Abraham.* The New Testament teaches that those who trust Jesus Christ as Lord are the spiritual descendants of Abraham. As such we are the recipients of the promises, and we also are responsible for assuming the obligations that accompany this position of privilege. "But ye are a chosen generation, a royal priesthood, an holy nation, a peculiar people; that ye should shew forth the praises of him who hath called you out of darkness into his marvellous light: Which in time past were not a people, but are now the people of God: which had not obtained mercy, but now have obtained mercy" (1 Peter 2:9–10).

Our Lord has promised to be with us if we engage in redemptive activity even as God promised to be with Abraham (Matt. 28:20). By faith we need to respond to this promise and obey his commandment to bear a continuing witness.

God has made many precious promises to his children in connection with the privilege of prayer. He has promised his children the divine power they need for accomplishing his work in the world. He has promised us victory over death and an endless fellowship with God and his saints when this life is over.

As Joseph's mummy case reminded the children of Israel of God's precious promises, we should let the Bible, the church, and the transformed life of faithful believers remind us that the promises of God are directed to us. Only as we do so will we be encouraged to work by faith.

**III. Joseph's mummy case was a loud reminder of the presence of God.**

A. *In the house of Potiphar, Joseph had experienced the presence of his Lord.* God had blessed Joseph's efforts, and even Potiphar observed that the blessings of God were upon him. "And his master saw that the LORD was with him, and that the LORD made all that he did to prosper in his hand" (Gen. 39:3).

That Joseph lived in an awareness of the abiding presence of God is dramatically illustrated by his reaction to the wife of Potiphar in her efforts to seduce him into immoral relations. Joseph responded as one who was aware that his life was lived in the presence of God. He was exceedingly eager to please God. In response to the lustful suggestions of this immoral woman, Joseph replied, "There is none greater in this house than I, neither hath [your husband] kept back anything from me but thee, because thou art his wife: how then can I do this great wickedness, and sin against God?" (Gen. 39:9).

B. *God was with Joseph in prison.* Perhaps there is no fury like that of a woman scorned. Joseph found himself falsely accused and unjustly imprisoned. God never forsakes those who trust him and obey him, and the record states, "But the LORD was with Joseph, and shewed him mercy, and gave him favor in the sight of the keeper of the prison" (Gen. 39:21).

C. *God was with Joseph in his first contact with Pharaoh.* Joseph's faith while in prison was what eventually led him by a providential course into the presence of Pharaoh, where he was requested to interpret a dream that was disturbing the ruler. At no time previous was Joseph more aware of God's presence. In response to Pharaoh's request for an interpretation, Joseph said, "It is not in me: God shall give Pharaoh an answer of peace" (Gen. 41:16).

As God had been with Joseph through his varied and exciting career, by the presence of his mummy case, Joseph wanted to bear a witness to the abiding presence of God with Israel. By this symbol he continued to serve as a challenge to their faith.

**IV. Joseph's mummy case was a constant reminder of the purpose of God.**

A. *Salvation for Israel.* God loved the people of ancient Israel and proposed to deliver them from the waste of idolatry and to the joy of a life of worship of the one true and living God.

B. *Salvation for a lost world.* God did not select Abraham and his descendants to be his pets and to be the recipients of his grace for their personal and private enjoyment. From the beginning of redemptive history, God was intending to reach the whole human race.

The Old Testament and much of the New Testament contain a record of how far short the people fell below a proper response to God's gracious purposes for them. In spite of the failures of God's people through the ages, God has not failed, and he continues his efforts to reach and to bless our needy world.

C. *Salvation for you.* Joseph's mummy case and all that it signified concerning God's presence and God's purposes for his people was pointing to the great salvation that some of us have found in Jesus Christ.

### Conclusion

By means of a mummy case, Joseph spoke to the people. By means of a cross and an empty tomb, the gracious God and Father of our Lord Jesus Christ offers to you the gift of forgiveness, the joy of eternal life, and the fruit of a blessed fellowship if you will but trust him and follow him as Joseph did.

---

## SUNDAY EVENING, OCTOBER 18

***Title:*** The Witnessing Church Faces Opposition

***Text:*** "And at that time there was a great persecution against the church..." **(Acts 8:1).**

### Introduction

We live in a day in which the church is being opposed in a number of ways. Christians are persecuted in a number of countries around the world. In the Western world, where Christianity is the dominant faith, the church faces more subtle opposition.

From the very beginning, the church has faced opposition and difficulty. The apostle Paul both encouraged and put the leaders of the church at Ephesus on guard lest they be overly discouraged by the difficulties that the church was to experience after his departure. The church had experienced satanic opposition from its very beginning. Likewise, today the church, the institution Jesus promised to perpetuate, faces satanic assaults from both the outside and the inside (Matt. 16:18).

### I. Difficulties on the outside of the witnessing church.

A. *At the very beginning the Jewish hierarchy sought to crush the witnessing church.*
   1. The Sadducees (Acts 4:1–2).
   2. Saul personified the attitude of the Pharisees (Acts 8:1–2).
   3. The energies of the king were enlisted against the church (Acts 12:1–2). For the modern church to face similar opposition would require the combined ill will of the leading political parties in conjunction with an attitude of disfavor on the part of both the federal and state governments.

B. *Pagan groups with vested interests opposed the witnessing church.*
   1. The owners of the slave girl were violently opposed to the redemptive activities of Paul and Silas (Acts 16:16–23).
   2. Demetrius and the silversmiths were greatly incensed by a new faith that affected their financial interests (Acts 19:24–41).

C. *Jewish bitterness hampered missionary outreach.*
   1. In Iconium the Jews stirred up the Gentiles (Acts 14:2).
   2. This opposition followed Paul to Lystra and Derbe (Acts 14:19).
   3. It was continued in Thessalonica (Acts 17:5).
   4. Paul found opposition in Berea (Acts 17:13).
   5. Opposition was encountered in Corinth (Acts 18:12–18) and in Jerusalem (Acts 21:27) as well.

The apostle Paul was the victim of this bitterness and hostility, and he suffered greatly at the hands of those who thought they were doing a noble service for God (2 Cor. 11:24–28). Some of us must blush when we measure our dedication and determination to do God's will by that of these earlier followers of our Lord. Will we be able to take it if the day comes when the church is persecuted from the outside as it was during the early days of its existence? Persecution has always brought great agony, but it has also purified the church by pruning off superficial, uncommitted followers.

**II. Difficulties on the inside of the witnessing church.**

We live in a day in which the church is being severely criticized by both friend and foe. Friends of the church are often terribly disturbed by the failures and shortcomings of the church. Some experience great depression if they measure the church as it is by what it ought to be.

Without any desire to salve our conscience or to lull ourselves to sleep in complacency, but rather to encourage us to believe that all is not lost, let us examine some of the "inside handicaps" under which the early church bore such a beautiful witness to its world.

A. *Its leadership was immature and selfish and expressed a desire for personal glory in the hoped-for coming kingdom (Acts 1:6–7).* Even the apostles had a shallow concept of all that Jesus intended to accomplish through them. The church is something more than just an organization of fallible human beings. It is an earthen vessel through which the creative Lord would carry on his redemptive work in spite of immaturity and selfishness.

B. *The early church also suffered under the handicap of what appeared to be a very shameful beginning.* We often forget that Christ, the founder of the church, was betrayed by one who was considered to be a part of the inner circle of his closest associates. The organizer of the church had experienced condemnation as a criminal before both the ecclesiastical courts of the Jews and before the legal court of the Roman government. With these handicaps the church lived and labored and established in the hearts and consciences of multiplied thousands of people a faith in the Savior whom they proclaimed as "Conqueror over death and the grave."

C. *Some of the members of this early fellowship were guilty of insincerity and deception (Acts 5:1–11).* The judgment of God fell on Ananias and Sapphira in order to register once and for all the divine opposition to insincerity, deception, hypocrisy, and falsehood. To make a personal application of this passage would cause many modern-day believers to tremble with fear. In spite of this kind of handicap on the inside, the church still moved forward.

D. *The early church was plagued with both racial and religious prejudice that created a division within the fellowship (Acts 6:1–7).* Racial and religious prejudice have been continuous problems in hindering the witness of those who would proclaim Christ as the Savior of all people. In spite of these handicaps, the church has made progress through the centuries.

E. *The witnessing church faced the handicap of financial problems due to a famine (Acts 11:22–30).* One of the greatest handicaps of the modern-day church is the lack of financial resources necessary to render a ministry of mercy and to meet the expenses of missionaries who should be sent to areas of spiritual destitution. These needs could be met if the membership of each church would live by the principle of generosity rather than letting greed dominate their thinking.

F. *Surprising as it may be, one of the problems that the early church faced, at least in some areas, was that of popularity (Acts 14:8–9).* There were some who wanted to jump on the bandwagon without realizing what it really meant to be a Christian. The modern-day church faces the problem of some who join because it is the popular thing to do. They consider themselves to be Christians merely because they have joined the congregation.

In spite of these and many other handicaps on the inside, the early church bore a winning witness that caused thousands of people to receive Jesus Christ as Lord and Savior. Let us face our generation, not in an attitude of defeat because of the weaknesses and failures of people, but with a genuine faith in the dynamic power of the living Christ.

### III. The witnessing church was triumphant.

A. *They realized their indebtedness to a crucified Savior.*

B. *They were obedient to the risen Lord.*

C. *They were gripped by the power of the Holy Spirit.*

D. *They rejoiced in the privilege of suffering for their Savior.*

E. *They had faith in ultimate victory.*

### Conclusion

It would be foolish for us to give up the ship because of handicaps, difficulties, disappointments, and outright opposition. God's family has always been and will always be a human family. Let us thank God and determine to do a better job than we have in the past.

## WEDNESDAY EVENING, OCTOBER 21

***Title:*** The Peril of Self-Deception

***Text:*** "Do not err, my beloved brethren" **(James 1:16)**.

### Introduction

The words of our text can refer to the thoughts presented in the preceding four verses in the first chapter of James, or they can point forward to the challenge of verse 17. For our purpose tonight, let us see them as a warning against the peril of self-deception.

James was dealing with the human tendency to yield to temptation. This is a continuing problem, and we will never in this life find a place of complete immunity from temptation. This should concern us particularly when we face the fact that we can be so easily self-deceived. The wise man said, "The way of a fool is right in his own eyes" (Prov. 12:15). And he also said, "There is a way which seemeth right unto a man, but the end thereof are the ways of death" (14:12).

Most of us rationalize ourselves into believing that everything we do is permissible under the circumstances. Paul warned the Galatians: "Be not deceived; God is not mocked: for whatsoever a man soweth, that shall he also reap" (Gal. 6:7).

Are you aware of the peril of deception in your own life? It is of tremendous importance for you as well as for others that you not be in error at this point.

### I. Some blame God for everything.

As strange as it may seem, some people even blame God for their sins. Adam was guilty of this, for he charged that if it had not been for the woman whom God had given to him, he would not have partaken of the forbidden fruit (Gen. 3:12).

Some people blame God for all tragedies. In blind resignation they say, "It is the will of God." To assume this attitude is to do great harm to one's conception of the character and nature of God.

James makes two statements about temptation.

A. *God tempts no one to sin (James 1:13)*. While God may test people to bring out the good, he never brings about pressure to cause a person to yield to evil.

B. *God cannot be tempted with evil (James 1:13)*. God does not respond to temptation as humans do. There is no way by which God can be lured into evil. No one should ever blame God for the evil that is in his or her own life or in the lives of others. Do not err by blaming God for your yielding to sin.

### II. Some blame others for their failures.

A. *Some blame heredity*. They believe that their father or mother or other ancestors are responsible for the situation in which they find themselves.

B. *Some blame their environment*. They believe that the pressures of an evil society are responsible for their failures.

C. *Some blame evil companions*. It is said that birds of a feather flock together.

D. *Some blame the Devil for their sins and failures.* There can be no question that Satan seeks to tempt and destroy (1 Peter 5:8). To blame either God or others is not to solve the problem that we as individuals face in the matter of dealing with our sins.

### III. Each one is responsible for his own sin.

"When he is drawn away by his own lust, and enticed." (James 1:14)

A. *To listen and to tarry in the time of temptation is to yield.*

B. *Evil desire within leads a person to sin as hunger motivates a fish to swallow the bait on the hook.*

C. *When evil thoughts are permitted to dwell in the mind, they stimulate destructive sinful appetites.*

### Conclusion

If we are to deal adequately with the perennial problem of temptation and with our tendency to yield, we must face up to our personal responsibility. We need to admit our responsibility for past failures and shortcomings. We will never solve the problem as long as we try to place blame on someone else. We can rejoice in the assurance that sincere confession can bring cleansing to the heart and to the conscience. We need to consecrate ourselves continually to God's will. So do not err by failing to recognize who is responsible in the time of temptation.

---

## SUNDAY MORNING, OCTOBER 25

***Title:*** Moses: An Example of Faith and Action

***Text:*** "By faith Moses, when he was come to years, refused to be called the son of Pharaoh's daughter; choosing rather to suffer affliction with the people of God, than to enjoy the pleasures of sin for a season" **(Heb. 11:24–25)**.

***Scripture Reading:*** Hebrews 11:23–29

***Hymns:*** "Trust and Obey," Sammis

"A Mighty Fortress Is Our God," Luther

"How Firm a Foundation," Keith

***Offertory Prayer:*** Our heavenly Father, we acknowledge you as the giver of every good and perfect gift. We thank you for life, for opportunities, for responsibilities, and for the hope that comes to us through faith. Today we come offering ourselves to you. Consecrate these tithes and offerings as visible proofs of our faith and love that others might come to know your Son, Jesus Christ, as Lord and Savior. In his name we pray. Amen.

### Introduction

It is easier to illustrate genuine faith than it is to verbalize a worthy definition. The New International Version translates the Hebrews 11:1 definition like this:

"Now faith is being sure of what we hope for and certain of what we do not see." The inspired writer declares that it is impossible to please God without faith: "Without faith it is impossible to please God, because anyone who comes to him must believe that he exists and that he rewards those who earnestly seek him" (v. 6 NIV).

As members of this congregation, we need to examine ourselves. Are we living the life of faith, or are we just fooling ourselves and attempting to fool others? To examine ourselves seriously can either be very disturbing or very gratifying.

We need the genuine faith that produces faithfulness. The faith that does not produce faithfulness is a faulty faith that needs correcting. We need the genuine faith that produces fruitfulness. It is one thing to hear the Word of God and to respond in a shallow, superficial manner that brings forth no fruit. It is something else to hear the Word and to respond fully and to bring forth fruit "multiplying thirty, sixty, or even a hundred times" (Mark 4:8 NIV).

We need the genuine faith that affects our decisions and choices. Real faith puts God at the center of the universe and at the center of one's individual life. The will of God is permitted to influence our will. Faith causes one to take the long look and brings about a recognition that the future is wrapped up in the dangers and difficulties of the present.

The great heroes of the faith who are marshaled into the witness stand in Hebrews 11 do not seek to define faith so much as they seek to illustrate what faith should mean and what it can mean as one faces the struggles of life. In the inspired testimony concerning Moses, there are five dramatic examples of genuine faith.

### I. The faith of Moses' parents (Exod. 2:1–10).

A. *Faith was stronger than fear.* A devout, God-fearing mother, no doubt with the full cooperation of her husband, found that her faith enabled her to stand steady rather than trembling with fear in the face of the command of Pharaoh to destroy her son. Not only did her maternal instinct inspire her to preserve the life of her son, but it was faith that gave her vision, ingenuity, and a plan.

B. *Faith gave Moses' parents eyes with which to see the future.* These parents recognized that if their people and their faith were to continue, the male child must be preserved. It was the faith of Moses' parents during his infancy that made it possible for the future nation of Israel to have a deliverer and a lawgiver and a leader.

Present-day parents should earnestly pray for the faith to visualize the potential of the children that God grants to their care and custody.

### II. Moses' act of identification with his own people was an expression of genuine faith (Heb. 11:24–25).

A. *Because of faith, Moses refused the popular place of luxury and pleasure.* As the son of Pharaoh's daughter, Moses could have had any pleasure or position of prestige his heart desired. In this day when there is such an emphasis on affluence and delight in luxury, Moses could have been considered the chief among fools to have given up so much. Instead of being foolish, history has declared him to be exceedingly wise because of his act of separation.

B. *Moses chose to suffer affliction with the people of God.* Only a genuine faith could have enabled him to visualize the future significance of this act of identification with a very unpopular cause. It is sad to contemplate how unwilling most of us are to identify ourselves with that which is not popular. Does this not indicate the shallow, superficial nature of our faith?

### III. Moses withdrew from Egypt to wait as an act of faith.

A. *A measure of values (Heb. 11:26).* Because of his faith, Moses was able to visualize the treasures of God. He believed that the treasures of Egypt were counterfeit when compared with the treasures of the spirit that were to be reaped by one who would live a life of trust and obedience.

In a day when success is measured in terms of material values, it would be wise for each of us to take an inventory concerning our investment. The martyred missionary Jim Elliot said, "He is no fool who loses what he cannot keep in order to gain what he cannot lose."

B. *An act of boldness (Heb. 11:27).* It would appear from the historical account of Moses' departure from Egypt that he was moved by fear (Exod. 2:15). The writer of Hebrews understood his action as an expression of boldness and wisdom. It was impossible with his present resources and circumstances to bring about the deliverance of his people, so instead of seeking to lead an abortive rebellion, Moses departed to wait for a more appropriate occasion.

### IV. Moses made arrangements for the Passover feast while still in Egypt (Heb. 11:28).

A. *Blood on the door post (Exod. 12:12–48).* In strict obedience to the command of God, the people were instructed to kill the Passover lamb, to take the blood of that lamb and to strike it on the two side posts and the upper door posts of their houses. Most likely Moses did not realize all that this symbolized, and certainly the people did not fully realize that this was a prophetic picture of the Lamb who was to be slain for the redemption of a lost race (John 1:29; 1 Peter 1:18–20).

B. *The Passover was to be observed annually.* Even though God's people were still in the land of Egypt, Moses gave them instructions that the Passover feast was to be a perpetual observance. He was thus demonstrating his faith in God and his purpose for the people in a distant future. Moses was able to do this because his eye was focused on him who is invisible.

### V. Moses led God's people in crossing the Red Sea (Heb. 11:29).

A. *Israel was delivered.* In obedience to the command of God, Moses led and the people followed. God performed a miracle in nature that enabled them to cross through the Red Sea as on dry ground. Through faith men find themselves doing that which otherwise would be impossible.

B. *Egypt was destroyed.* In attempting to follow where God had led the Israelites, the Egyptian armies were destroyed, and Israel escaped to realize God's appointed destiny for them.

### Conclusion

The life of Moses is a dramatic disclosure of the difference faith can make in one's life. Are you living the life of faith? Are you deciding against that which may be enticing but would lead you away from God's will?

Has your faith caused you to identify with those who are unfortunate and in need of a deliverer as Israel needed Moses? Has your faith led you to attempt that which is physically impossible on the basis of visible resources? Moses succeeded because his eye was on him who is invisible, and he had access to spiritual resources.

Moses knew God. He trusted God, obeyed God, and proved God to be dependable and trustworthy. You can too if you will.

---

## SUNDAY EVENING, OCTOBER 25

***Title:*** Stewardship in the Witnessing Church

***Text:*** "And all that believed were together, and had all things common; and sold their possessions and goods, and parted them to all men, as every man had need" **(Acts 2:44–45)**.

### Introduction

It is impossible for a modern church to duplicate and to reproduce in every respect the early church as it existed in the book of Acts. It would be useless to attempt to do so. The New Testament church that we find in the book of Acts was in many points very different from most modern churches. It possessed no property or buildings. Its leadership consisted, at first, of only the apostles. Its religious life consisted of daily services rather than Sunday services. The people met in homes to share in common meals, to listen to the instructions of the apostles, and to pray.

While we cannot duplicate the early church, there are many things concerning it that we should eagerly seek to imitate. We worship the same Lord. We are empowered by the same Spirit. We are charged with the same mission. We have the same privilege of prayer. The Lord who promised to be with them has promised to be with us.

The stewardship practices of this early church should challenge us to a deeper dedication both to the kingdom of God and to the welfare of our fellow humans.

### I. The early church was characterized by a remarkable generosity.

A. *They had all things in common (Acts 2:44).*

B. *They distributed to each other as they had need (Acts 2:45).*
C. *They contributed to the needs of widows and orphans (Acts 6:2).*
D. *They sold lands and houses to meet common needs (Acts 4:34; 5:1–11).*
E. *The mission church contributed to the relief of the older churches (Acts 11:27–30).*

Two interesting facts should be considered as we measure this spirit of generosity by that which prevails in our modern churches. First, these early disciples were not commanded to practice the generosity to the extent that they did; their generosity was spontaneous.

Second, this generosity was repeated nowhere else during New Testament times, and neither has it been repeated except by very small groups in Christian history.

## II. Is there a logical explanation for the generosity of the early church?

A. *Did they follow the example of the Essenes?* The Dead Sea Scrolls reveal that the Essenes lived together in a communal arrangement in which they shared all things in common.
B. *Was this generosity encouraged by the expectation of the early return of the Savior?* These early disciples eagerly longed for the return of Christ. They were hoping and praying that he would return immediately. This could be a partial explanation for their lavish generosity.
C. *Could it be that they actually believed the teachings of Jesus?*
   1. Jesus had taught, "It is more blessed to give than to receive" (Acts 20:35). Do you suppose that they believed Jesus to the extent that they practiced what he preached and discovered in their own experience that there is a greater thrill that comes through giving than there is through receiving? That it is more blessed to give than to receive cannot be discovered by reading a book. It must be practiced to be proven.
   2. Jesus had cautioned against the peril of making investments that would perish, and he had counseled his disciples to make investments in the kingdom of God, where they would receive dividends of eternal significance: "Lay not up for yourselves treasures upon earth, where moth and rust doth corrupt, and where thieves break through and steal: but lay up for yourselves treasures in heaven, where neither moth nor rust doth corrupt, and where thieves do not break through nor steal" (Matt. 6:19–20).
   3. Jesus had spoken one word of commandment—"Give" (Luke 6:38). The last of that verse is a promise: "Give ... for with the same measure that ye mete withal it shall be measured to you again" (Luke 6:38).

   Many modern-day Christians are overcome with a pocketbook protection instinct to the extent that they have a mental block when they hear the word *give.* Consequently, they miss the promise and the opportunity to discover the radiant joy that comes to the one who lives to give rather than to get.
D. *The royal law of love.* "If ye fulfil the royal law according to the Scripture, you shalt love thy neighbour as thyself, ye do well" (James 2:8).

1. The generosity of the early Christians was voluntary. It was uncoerced. They responded to human need because of love within their hearts.
2. The generosity of the early Christians was spontaneous. Because they had the power to meet human needs, they did so gladly.

### Conclusion

One of our deepest needs is to be givers. Individually, our need to be givers is far greater than the needs of the church for our gifts. May God help each of us to be able to follow the philosophy of Jesus who said, "It is more blessed to give than to receive" (Acts 20:35).

## WEDNESDAY EVENING, OCTOBER 28

***Title:*** The Generosity of God

***Text:*** "Every good gift and every perfect gift is from above, and cometh down from the Father of lights, with whom is no variableness, neither shadow of turning" **(James 1:17)**.

### Introduction

The warning against the peril of self-deception in James 1:16 can refer to that which precedes and to that which follows. Some have deceived themselves into believing that even temptation to evil at times comes from God. James 1:13 would affirm that this is never the case. On the other hand, some may be unaware that all good things are from God.

There are at least four stimulating thoughts in the words of this text.

### I. God is the source of all good things.

We have a tendency to forget this or to ignore it. Some would even deny it. James affirms that God is the origin and the source of all good things.

God uses many different means and methods to bring good into our lives. The eyes of faith will see the grace of God in all that is good. The heart of faith will praise God for all good.

*Back of the loaf is the snowy flour,*
*Back of the flour the mill;*
*Back of the mill the wheat, the show'r,*
*The sun and our Father's will.*

—*M. D. Babcock*

### II. God's gifts are always good.

God's greatest gifts are inward and spiritual. They cannot be weighed on scales or measured with a yardstick. They cannot be evaluated in dollars and cents. Who can place a value on the gift of forgiveness and the assurance of divine sonship? Who can calculate the preciousness of the joy of knowing that heaven is to be our eternal home? Who can evaluate the priceless privilege of the opportunity to serve in the name of Christ?

God has given such a multitude of gifts that many of us do not recognize how generous he is. The psalmist spoke to his own soul and said, "Bless the Lord, O my soul, and forget not all his benefits" (Ps. 103:2).

### III. God's gifts are always purposeful.

God does not bestow his greatest gifts upon us merely for our selfish enjoyment; usually he has a redemptive purpose in mind. To receive and utilize one of God's good gifts causes the individual to drink more fully of the cup of God's salvation. To respond and utilize God's good gifts will have an uplifting and enriching effect upon the lives of the people around us.

Most parents are eager to bestow upon their children gifts that are not only enjoyable but that develop their capacities and abilities for a more complete life. This explains the increasing sales of educational toys. Parents are eager to give that which will be helpful. Similarly, every gift of our heavenly Father is designed and intended to make life fuller for the recipient. Every gift is bestowed to bless not only the recipient but also others through the recipient.

### IV. God is always giving.

The later part of this verse speaks of the nature and character of God as being forever the same. God knows no change of rising or setting like the sun. There is neither shadow nor eclipse of his gracious and loving purpose.

### Conclusion

As the Father of Lights, God is very different from the sun whose benefits we enjoy only during the day. Half of our time is spent in darkness. Unlike the sun, which shines on our part of the world only half of the time, God is ever present to give of his love, his mercy, and his guidance to meet the deepest needs of our lives.

Suggested Preaching Program for

# NOVEMBER

## ■ Sunday Mornings and Evenings

The sermons for the morning and evening services this month carry a dual emphasis. They encourage the church to have compassionate concern for unbelievers, and they encourage unbelievers to make a faith response to our Lord Jesus Christ.

## ■ Wednesday Evenings

Many things are involved in a sincere attempt to respond to our Lord's invitation "Follow Me." The way in which we respond will determine both our success and our joy as the children and servants of God. He will lead us in many ways and to many different places if we follow his guidance.

---

## SUNDAY MORNING, NOVEMBER 1

*Title:* Sleeping in the Harvest Season

*Text:* "He that gathereth in summer is a wise son: but he that sleepeth in harvest is a son that causeth shame" **(Prov. 10:5)**.

*Scripture Reading:* Matthew 9:35–38

*Hymns:* "Praise Him, Praise Him," Crosby

"I'll Go Where You Want Me to Go," Brown

"Bringing in the Sheaves," Shaw

*Offertory Prayer:* Holy Father, today we thank you for all of those whom you used to bring us the knowledge of Jesus Christ our Savior. Today we offer ourselves as communicators of the old, old story that others might come to experience your love and mercy. Accept and bless these tithes and offerings to the furtherance of the telling of the story of Jesus and your love. Amen.

### Introduction

Many parts of the world enjoy a continuous harvest season. One can visit southern Florida, portions of the Rio Grande Valley, Southern California, or other tropical areas and discover a continuous process of sowing and reaping. An orange tree is a case in point. An orange tree may have blossoms that will produce oranges while at the same time it contains small oranges, half-grown oranges, and fully ripe oranges. The orange tree presents a parable of the fact that as Christians we have a continuous harvest season in the spiritual realm. There is never a time when one can say that due to bad weather or to the season of the year it is impossible to labor in the spiritual harvest fields.

While the church should pray and labor and live in anticipation of reaping a spiritual harvest from week to week, it is true also that many churches set aside specific times in the year to concentrate on reaping a harvest of souls for the glory of God. Other churches have abandoned this method for what is called a perennial program of evangelism. It would seem to me that it is not a case of either/or but a matter of both/and. We need to use every legitimate means and method to bring people into a conversion experience with Jesus Christ.

When Jesus saw the multitudes scattered abroad as sheep having no shepherd, he was moved with compassion toward them and said to his disciples, "The harvest truly is plenteous, but the labourers are few; pray ye therefore the Lord of the harvest, that he will send forth labourers into his harvest" (Matt. 9:37–38). When Jesus saw the Samaritans coming out of the city of Sychar, he said to his disciples, "Lift up your eyes, and look on the fields; for they are white already to harvest" (John 4:35). One of the greatest needs of each modern-day church is to recognize that it is located right in the center of a spiritual harvest field where people are threatened with eternal death and separation from the God of grace unless laborers—individual believers, personal followers of Jesus Christ—go out among these people with the story of God's love and of his desire to save.

The words of the text speak words of commendation and words of warning. It declares that he who labors in the time of harvest is indeed a wise son, but he who sleeps in harvest is a son that causeth shame. Are you bringing shame to the heart of your heavenly Father? Are you relating yourself to those about you in a manner that should bring shame to your own heart?

### I. The harvest must be reaped when it is ripe.

A. *Seed time and harvest.* It is a law of nature that before there can be a harvest there must be a time of sowing and cultivation. Farmers will plow up and pulverize the soil. They will then plant the seed. Proper care will be given to the cultivation of the crops in order to reap an abundant harvest in the fall. The church, through each of its members, should be in a continuous process of sowing the seed of divine truth in the hearts and minds of men, women, and children. Careful and continuous efforts need to be put forth to cultivate the confidence and the friendship of these so that in due time, as the Holy Spirit works conviction into the heart, they can be ready for the harvest.

Those who have had experience in attempting to lead people to trust Jesus Christ as Savior have discovered that it takes a long time for some people to become what some have called "ripe prospects" for conversion. To attempt to persuade one of these to make a profession of faith before he or she is prepared in both mind and heart is to experience the same result that a farmer would experience if he tried to harvest his corn while it was still green or to pick his cotton before the bolls opened or to gather peaches while they were still hard and green.

B. *The harvesttime.* While it is true that there is a time to sow and a time to cultivate, there is also a time to reap. To neglect the harvest in the time of reaping is to waste all of the previous effort put forth. It is a law of nature that fruit or grain or vegetables must be harvested when they are ripe or mature. Cotton will lose its weight and color and quality if it is not picked at the proper time. Corn will fall over and rot if it is not harvested before the winter winds and rain come. The golden yellow wheat fields will turn white and will soon rot if not harvested. Peaches, apples, berries, and grapes will fall off from the tree or vine and rot on the ground if they are not harvested. It is also a spiritual law that the souls of men will perish in unbelief unless someone gives to them the message of God's redeeming love and his desire to save.

C. *The harvesttime is now.* We must not be guilty of saying, "There are yet four months, and then cometh the harvest" (John 4:35). While there may be some to whom we have been witnessing that are not yet ready, or ripe, this does not mean that there are not some who are just waiting for someone to encourage them to relate themselves to God in repentance and faith.

A study of the life of Jesus would reveal that he urged upon both himself and his disciples the urgency of the present (John 9:4). Never did Jesus encourage either his followers or those who were considering becoming his followers to wait until tomorrow.

The apostle Paul was ready to preach the gospel at every opportunity, for he recognized that people are lost now and need a Savior (Rom. 1:15). In words that have often been quoted to the unsaved as an encouragement to trust Christ in the present, Paul was actually seeking to persuade the church to engage in redemptive activity. He said, "Behold, now is the accepted time; behold, now is the day of salvation." He is thus declaring that God is ready right now to save those who will come to him through faith in Jesus Christ. These words were actually intended to encourage the Christians at Corinth to get out in the harvest fields and do their work as laborers for the Lord.

### II. Sleeping in the harvesttime results in shame.

The words of the text contain a stinging rebuke for the farmer's son who would idly and carelessly sleep away his day of opportunity during the harvest season. These words contain a stinging rebuke, not only for the average church member, but also for many of us pastors.

A. *Shame to the father.* As good farmers would be ashamed of a son who idled his time away during the harvest season and let the crops waste, so we must bring shame to the heart of our heavenly Father when we spend our days in idleness. Perhaps some of us are like Jonah who slept the sleep of disobedience when he should have been on his way toward Nineveh (Jonah 1:5).

Perhaps some of us are sleeping the sleep of weariness or indifference like Peter and the other apostles on the night before our Lord was crucified (Matt. 26:39–45).

B. *Shame to the son.* The son of a farmer should be ashamed of his conduct if he sleeps through the time of harvest. We as individual church members, the Lord's labor force, should be ashamed of our conduct if we are asleep on the job as far as witnessing to the unsaved is concerned.

A missionary in a South American country entered a city of considerable size with the knowledge that there was no known evangelical congregation in the entire city. As he drove down the street, he was shamed by the signs in the windows advertising American products. He felt pain in his heart as he considered that people selling their products had arrived in the city before missionaries. Someone had been asleep on the job.

## III. How can we know when we are asleep spiritually?

One can be asleep and not know it. There are many different theories as to what sleep is and why we sleep. It is recognized by all as one of the necessities of our continued existence. For one to want to sleep all of the time is unnatural and usually indicates a serious illness. Is it possible that some of us are suffering from spiritual sleeping sickness? Without attempting to explain the theory behind the nature or the necessity of sleep, we would simply affirm that when people are asleep, they do not respond to people around them.

A. *Those who are asleep do not use their eyes.* Are you blind or asleep to the fact of God's great love for all people? Are you blind or asleep to the fact that God wants to use you to communicate the message of his love to a lost and needy world? Are you blind or asleep to the fact that the unsaved about us need to know Jesus Christ more than they need anything else in the world?

B. *Those who are asleep do not use their ears.* While it is true that a loud noise will normally awaken those who are asleep, some have adjusted themselves to going to sleep in the midst of much noise. Are you deaf, or are you asleep so that you cannot hear the distress calls of the unsaved about you?

C. *Those who are asleep are unresponsive to stimuli.* They are in a state of unconsciousness where they are not alert to what is happening. Some of us may be making little response to our personal responsibility to be witnesses. We seem to be unconscious of the dangers to which the unsaved are exposed. We seem to be unconvinced of the power of the gospel. We seem to be unmoved by the greatness of God's love for the unsaved about us. Paul wrote to the Ephesians a message that speaks to us today: "Awake thou that sleepest" (Eph. 5:14).

## Conclusion

There is no question that the church should awaken from its sleep and go to work in the harvest fields that are white unto harvest. All of us must confess that we have been guilty of sleeping on the job. Soldiers have been court-martialed for going to sleep at their post of duty. Ours also has been a serious offense.

We would also say to those among us who continue to neglect to trust Jesus Christ as Savior, "Awake thou that sleepest." You need to awake to your sinful condition and to your need for forgiveness. You need to awake to the certain fact of coming judgment if you continue to neglect to make peace with God. You need to awake to the provisions of God's mercy revealed through the death of Jesus Christ on the cross. You need to awake and recognize that the simple way of salvation is through faith in this Christ who conquered death and the grave and who stands at your heart's door knocking for entrance. He will give you life and light and love if you will let him come into your heart.

## SUNDAY EVENING, NOVEMBER 1

***Title:*** Why Do They Wait?

***Text:*** "How shall we escape, if we neglect so great salvation?" **(Heb. 2:3)**.

### Introduction

Most of us are guilty at least to some degree of putting off until tomorrow the decision or the task that should be taken care of today. Too often tomorrow is next week and next week is next month. This tendency to delay is harmful in every area of life.

The debtor who keeps saying, "I will put forth a serious effort to pay my debts," stands in danger of destroying his credit rating. The sick person who keeps saying, "Tomorrow I will see my physician" may soon find herself in the cemetery. The young person who continues to put off advanced training beyond high school is in danger of finding himself past forty with no skills to secure a good job. The parent who neglects to discipline a child faces the possibility of having her heart broken by a juvenile delinquent.

Both Christians and non-Christians cannot escape the consequences if they develop and follow a policy of delay or postponement. Have you ever wondered why people delay their decision to trust Jesus Christ as Lord and Savior? They offer many excuses, but seldom if ever do they give a reason why they have delayed. It would be profitable for both believer and unbeliever to note the reasons why the unsaved delay their coming to Jesus Christ.

### I. The unsaved are often unaware of their lost condition.

Pride encourages people to refuse to admit that they are sinners in need of the grace, mercy, and forgiveness of God. They look around and see so many people living on a lower level than themselves that they congratulate themselves and reason that they are bound to have a better chance of being accepted by God than others have.

This lack of an awareness of their sinfulness is due largely to the fact that they have measured themselves by others rather than considering themselves in comparison with the holiness and righteousness of God.

Conviction of sin is produced by the Holy Spirit as people hear the gospel and are led to compare their lives with the life and teachings of Jesus Christ.

**II. The unsaved have been blinded by Satan (2 Cor. 4:4).**

Both the saved and unsaved are often unaware of this work of Satan. It is his evil purpose to place a blindfold on the minds of the unsaved to prevent them from responding to the glorious gospel of Jesus Christ (2 Cor. 4:3–4).

A. *The sinfulness of sin.* Satan always presents sin dressed up in pretty colors. Sin always promises profit or pleasure. Few recognize that in addition to being an act of self-destruction, sin is an act of rebellion against God.
B. *The penalty of sin.* From the beginning of human history the Evil One has tried to convince people that they can sin and not suffer. Scripture and history prove that you can no more sin without reaping its penalty than you can run away from your shadow under the noon sun, yet Satan has blinded the minds of the unsaved to believe that they can live a life of sin without reaping its penalty (Rom. 6:23).
C. *The joy of being a Christian.* By every available tool, satanic forces create the impression that God is a "party pooper" and that to become a Christian one must wear a sad, long face and experience no joy in living. This is a lie that has been accepted century after century, particularly by the young.
D. *The way of salvation.* Many substitutes have been offered for the simple way of salvation through faith in Jesus Christ. People have been led to believe that by creed, conduct, or contribution they can gain God's favor.

**III. The lack of concern on the part of the church.**

One of the most painful truths that the Christian should face is that many unsaved people have delayed trusting Jesus Christ because no one has become compassionately concerned for their salvation on an individual basis.

It is one thing to be concerned about the salvation of a lost world. It is infinitely more practical and productive for us to be vitally concerned about the individual with whom we work or with whom we play. Experience and observation reveal that compassionate concern is blessed by God to bring about the salvation of lost people.

Have you been interested in one particular individual, one particular unsaved person, to the extent that you would mention his or her name in prayer before the throne of God's grace each day for a single month? Have you been concerned to the extent that you have given a verbal expression to an unsaved person on as many as three different occasions? Are you deliberately and continually seeking to cultivate the friendship of those who do not know Jesus Christ in order that you might share your faith with them and introduce them to your Savior? Every pastor has observed both in his own experience and in the experience of those in his church that when persistent concern is manifested wisely for the salvation of the unsaved, the overwhelming majority of the individuals involved will eventually become Christians.

### IV. What is your excuse?

A. *Do you love sin with the pleasures that it offers to the extent that you want to live on the level of the sensual?* Do you really want to live on the animal level and never rise up to live on the spiritual level as a child of God? People are made in the image of God. They have the capacity for fellowship with God. To fail to recognize this and respond to it is to deprive oneself of the highest possible manhood or womanhood. To delay coming to Jesus Christ is to degrade yourself and prevent yourself from experiencing the best that life can offer.

B. *Are you afraid of failure?* This can be wholesome rather than destructive. The truth is that you will fail to be genuinely Christian unless you trust Jesus Christ for success even as you would trust him for the salvation of your soul. You must trust him day by day to prevent you from failing and to enable you to achieve success as a child and as a servant of God.

C. *Is your excuse the grip of a degrading habit that you have been unable to cast off?* Then come to Jesus and trust him to come into your life and assist you with breaking this habit. Nowhere does Scripture teach that you must make yourself worthy before you can come to Christ. The Scriptures actually teach that Jesus not only died to save us from the penalty of sin but came to deliver us from the tyranny of sin in this life (Gal. 1:4).

D. *Is your excuse the failure of so many professing Christians?* You should be aware of two things at this point. There is a vast difference between a hypocrite and a failure. A hypocrite is one who deliberately wears a false face with the intention of deceiving. There are few of these in the church. Many in the church do fail to be genuinely Christian just as many students in school fail to make straight A's—but they are still students. The second thing that you should keep in mind is that it is a part of the strategy of Satan to place some of his servants in the church with the deliberate purpose of deceiving and causing some to stumble. The parable of the tares among the wheat illustrates this fact (Matt. 13:24–28).

### Conclusion

We should never arrive at a decision concerning what we should be on the basis of the faults or mistakes of others. We need to use the highest part of our intellect and ask ourselves, "What should I do?" To neglect, delay, or postpone coming to Jesus Christ can be the greatest mistake of your lifetime for both time and eternity.

Today you have both time and opportunity to make the wise decision concerning Christ. With sincere decisiveness come to him now.

*Just as I am, without one plea,*
*But that Thy blood was shed for me,*
*And that Thou bidd'st me come to Thee,*
*O Lamb of God, I come! I come!*
—*Charlotte Elliott*

## WEDNESDAY EVENING, NOVEMBER 4

***Title:*** Follow Me in Personal Spiritual Growth

***Text:*** "And Jesus increased in wisdom and stature, and in favour with God and man" **(Luke 2:52)**.

### Introduction

On at least three different occasions our Lord described discipleship in terms of following. He invited the fishermen to follow him: "Follow me, and I will make you fishers of men" (Matt. 4:19). He said to Matthew the publican, "Follow me" (9:9). Concerning the terms of discipleship, he said, "If any man will come after me, let him deny himself, and take up his cross daily, and follow me" (Luke 9:23).

After his victory over death and the grave, Jesus spoke words to the apostle Peter designed to encourage him to focus his interest and energies on the single task of following. "If I will that he tarry till I come, what is that to thee? follow thou me" (John 21:22). To follow Jesus sincerely is a task that only a believer would attempt. The sincere believer would naturally ask, "What does it really mean to follow Jesus?" To fully answer that question would require a lengthy volume. We shall consider some of the things that following Jesus involves tonight and during future Wednesday evening services. Tonight we will see that if we really want to follow Jesus, we must develop a program for personal spiritual growth.

### I. Luke's gospel speaks repeatedly of the growth toward maturity and effectiveness on the part of the Savior.

A. *Jesus grew as a child.* "The child grew, and waxed strong in spirit, filled with wisdom: and the grace of God was upon him" (Luke 2:40).
   1. Jesus grew physically.
   2. Jesus grew spiritually.
   3. Jesus made progress mentally.

B. *Jesus continued to grow as a man.* "Jesus increased in wisdom and stature, and in favour with God and man" (Luke 2:52).

### II. A spiritual birth produces spiritual infants.

A. *Some have the mistaken idea that children of God are born full grown.*

B. *In an experience of conversion, the new convert receives a twofold blessing: the forgiveness of sin and the gift of spiritual life.* As a recipient of new life from above, as a partaker of the divine nature through the miracle of the new birth, the convert is now in a place where growth toward spiritual maturity is not only a possibility but an obligation.

C. *There are certain defects and imperfections in young children that growth and time alone can remove.* So it is with the child of God.

If both the saved and the unsaved alike could understand this, it would help a great deal to prevent new converts from being overly discouraged and even depressed by their personal failure to practice fully the new faith that they profess. Instead of being overcome with an attitude of defeatism, they would be more determined to succeed in the future. Older brothers and sisters in Christ would be less inclined to be critical of the imperfect steps and ineffective witness on the part of new converts who, in reality, are spiritual infants.

Repeatedly converts are encouraged to put forth the efforts essential for spiritual growth. "Wherefore laying aside all malice, and all guile, and hypocrisies, and envies, and all evil speakings, as newborn babes, desire the sincere milk of the word, that ye may grow thereby" (1 Peter 2:1–2; cf. 2 Peter 3:18).

Both the church, composed of older spiritual brothers and sisters in Christ, and the new convert have an obligation in the matter of spiritual growth.

**III. The necessities for spiritual growth.**

As earthly parents seek to make adequate preparations for the coming of a new baby, and as they seek to make ample provisions for the new baby, even so the heavenly Father has made adequate provisions for the growth of his children.

A. *Food has been provided by the heavenly Father.* One of the first needs of newborns is nourishment, and the same is true for new converts.

The truth of the Word of God is spoken of as both the meat and the milk by which children of God are to nourish the growth of their souls (1 Cor. 3:1–2; Heb. 5:12–14; 1 Peter 5:2).

B. *The opportunity to learn has been provided by the heavenly Father.* Not only does the Word of God provide us with nourishment, but it is also the rule by which we are to receive both profitable instruction and necessary correction in the area of our attitudes, actions, and ambitions (2 Tim. 3:16–17).

The only solid basis on which we can build our lives is to both hear and heed the words of him whom God hath appointed to be our infallible Teacher (Matt. 7:24–29).

C. *Spiritual shelter has been provided by the heavenly Father.* What the home is to children, the fellowship of the church is to be to new converts. New converts must not neglect the privilege of regular public worship if they want to grow (Heb. 10:24–25). It is said concerning Jesus, "And he came to Nazareth, where he had been brought up: and, as his custom was, he went into the synagogue on the sabbath day, and stood up for to read" (Luke

4:16). He did not neglect the opportunities for worship and study and fellowship that the synagogue provided as he grew toward maturity.

**IV. The joys of personal growth.**

A. *The growth of converts brings joy to the heart of the heavenly Father.* As an earthly father delights to see his child grow and develop physically, mentally, socially, and spiritually, even so the heavenly Father rejoices to see us grow.

B. *Spiritual growth makes effective service possible.* An infant can only do the work of an infant. It is a tragedy beyond imagination for a full-grown man to be capable of doing only what a small child can do. It is also tragic for a convert to remain a spiritual infant and never develop vocational competency as a follower of Christ.

C. *Personal growth brings great personal satisfaction to the individual involved.* When we were children, the evidence of growth brought great delight. The same is true concerning spiritual progress.

**Conclusion**

To seriously follow Jesus is to accept and follow a self-imposed discipline that will lead to spiritual maturity and effectiveness in Christian service. Each of us can and should be making progress in that direction.

## SUNDAY MORNING, NOVEMBER 8

***Title:*** Sin—A Fatal Malady in the Heart

***Text:*** "The heart is deceitful above all things, and desperately wicked: who can know it?" (**Jer. 17:9**).

***Scripture Reading:*** Matthew 15:10–12

***Hymns:*** "Great Redeemer, We Adore Thee," Harris

"Blessed Redeemer," Christiansen

"There Is a Fountain," Cowper

***Offertory Prayer:*** Graciously, Father, you have given us your Son. We thank you for all of your blessings to us through him. You have given us your Holy Spirit to dwell within our hearts continuously, and we thank you for his continuing leadership. You have given us your Word to guide our thinking and to encourage us to walk in the way everlasting. You have given us the warmth and love of membership in your family. For these joys we are truly grateful. Today we bring our tithes and offerings and invoke your blessing upon them that they might be used both to spread the glad tidings of your love and to render ministries of mercy to those in need. We do this because we love you and because we want to help others to come to know you through Jesus Christ our Lord. Amen.

## Introduction

What is the matter with our world? All people who think realistically are in agreement that there is something the matter with it—something radically and tremendously wrong—and its condition does not seem to greatly improve. What is the root of our trouble?

Our world has been placed on the examining table, and the doctors have gathered around to examine the patient. These physicians, possessing super knowledge and unexcelled equipment seek to prescribe a corrective treatment for the malady that plagues the world. A flock of nurses attending with chart and pencil jot down the changing symptoms and chronicle every variation in temperature, respiration, and pulse. As each of these social and political, scientific and educational, military and diplomatic physicians makes his or her own independent diagnosis of the illness that plagues our world, the reports that come forth give us an interesting and bewildering story.

## I. Superficial diagnoses.

A. *One physician would say our trouble is commercialism.*

1. The whole world has been commercialized, and this is the source of our degradation.
2. The commercial devil must be cast out of our lives.
3. When we look at Easter and Christmas and Mother's Day, we can understand why some people feel that we are overly commercialized. High pressure advertising has not only made a contribution toward the high standard of living that we know, but it has also made a tremendous increase in anxiety and frustration because of our inability to secure all of the material things that are dangled before us.

B. *Another specialist asserts that our worst malady is sectionalism.*

1. One section of the population is arrayed against another section: the North against the South and the East against the West.
2. One group is clamoring for privilege at the expense of another: blacks against whites, whites against blacks; labor against management, management against labor; rich against poor, poor against rich.

   Human selfishness will manifest itself in every area of life. It is seen in all countries and among all groups. No one is immune.

C. *Some experts declare that the deadly curse of the modern world is nationalism.*

1. On all sides one can notice a bloated, arrogant, exaltation of national honor and prestige.
2. Unless this spirit of extreme nationalism can be controlled, the disasters ahead will be worse than those of the past. All doctors agree that the patient is horribly sick but cannot agree on the nature of the malady. Consequently, we hear of wars and rumors of war.

   It would be profitable for us to turn away from the confusions of the present and sit at the feet of an ancient thinker, the prophet Jeremiah. As a servant of the living Lord, he was a keen observer who saw through to the root cause of the malady that plagues our world. He observed the symptoms. He studied the patient, and after thorough examination, observation, and meditation, he arrived at a diagnosis: "The heart is deceitful above all things and desperately wicked: who can know it?" (Jer. 17:9). It was Jeremiah's deep conviction that the human heart is sick, not slightly or temporarily sick, but dangerously and alarmingly sick. Jesus concurred with this by stating that "not that which goeth into the mouth defileth a man; but that which cometh out of the mouth, this defileth a man" (Matt. 15:11).

**II. The source of human woe is the heart diseased by sin.**

A. *The prophet diagnosed sin as a heart condition.* In its essence, sin is a heart direction away from God.

B. *The Bible reveals to us that this sick heart is a result of humankind's rebellion against their Maker.*

1. People were made in the image and likeness of God (Gen. 1:26–27, 31).
2. People were made for a life of fellowship with God (Gen. 3:8).
3. People were made to engage in cooperative activity with God (Gen. 2:15).
4. People were made to have dominion over the world (Gen. 1:28).

C. *Humans fell from their original state of innocence.* God had given people the power to stand, but at the same time he left them free to fall (Gen. 2:17). The forbidden tree was a symbol. Adam's partaking of the forbidden fruit was motivated by unbelief and doubt, disobedience and rebellion, selfish ambition and greed. This continues to be the attitude of people toward God. Every child of Adam continues to make the same fatal mistake.

Adam by his own deliberate choice and action separated himself from God and in a very real sense shut himself away from God (Gen. 3:22).

Adam lost some of the powers and privileges that belonged to him as he came from the hand of God (Gen. 3:24). Because people have separated themselves from God, their understanding has been darkened, their wills are rebellious, their affections have become corrupt, their souls are polluted, and their bodies have received death wounds.

**III. The consequences of sin.**

Jesus came into a world that was sorely damaged and defaced. Everywhere Jesus went he encountered people whose lives had been wrecked by one disastrous power—sin.

A. *Sin has separated people from God.*

B. *Sin has broken the loving heart of God.* In the parable of the waiting father, usually called the parable of the prodigal son, Jesus revealed the heartbreak of God over human waywardness. God eagerly yearns for the return of his wayward children. People will be saved from waste and ruin only if they return to the home of the heavenly Father through Christ.

C. *Sin has hardened the hearts of people.* It has made them dishonest and untruthful. Sin has produced hypocrisy and sham. Sin has created an unbrotherly spirit and caused one race to be snobbish toward another and one class to be cruel to another. Sin has caused people to be stupid.

### IV. Jesus Christ came to save people from this deadly disease of a sick heart.

The prophet Ezekiel revealed that God wants to give to his people new hearts: "A new heart also will I give you, and a new spirit will I put within you: and I will take away the stony heart out of your flesh, and I will give you an heart of flesh. And I will put my spirit within you, and cause you to walk in my statutes, and ye shall keep my judgments, and do them" (Ezek. 36:26–27).

Jeremiah spoke of this in terms of a new covenant (Jer. 31:33–34). What people need is a new heart with the law of God written on that heart by the Spirit of God.

A. *This new heart, this new nature, this new birth, comes to us through faith in Jesus Christ as Lord and Savior (John 3:5–7).*

B. *This new birth is available to all who will receive Christ (John 3:16).*

1. It offers forgiveness.
2. It offers the gift of eternal life.

### Conclusion

The church should busy itself with the task of publishing the glad tidings of the gospel that people might receive new hearts and new natures. This is the only hope for our world.

As an individual, you need to make a response to Jesus Christ, for he and he alone can cure you from the disease of sin and give you the health of heaven both for now and for the hereafter.

---

## SUNDAY EVENING, NOVEMBER 8

***Title:*** Let Him In

***Text:*** "Behold, I stand at the door, and knock: if any man hear my voice, and open the door, I will come in to him, and will sup with him, and he with me" **(Rev. 3:20)**.

### Introduction

As strange as it may seem, the Christ was speaking these words either to the church of Laodicea or perhaps to all of the seven churches in Asia to whom these letters were addressed. We normally think of these words as picturing the efforts of Christ to enter the heart of the unsaved. Actually, they were spoken to groups of people who considered themselves to be his followers and part of his church.

Are we guilty also? Have we shut out Christ? How long has it been since he has been present in power and love to work his work within the fellowship of our church?

Many of those who consider themselves to be Jesus' disciples are guilty of shutting him out of their lives. What place have you given him in your career? Did you seek his guidance in the choice of a vocation? Do you seek to glorify him in your daily work? Many left him out of their courtship and gave no consideration to him as they made their choice of a marriage partner. Many of these suffer great turmoil of mind and soul today because Christ was shut out. Students are often guilty of shutting Christ out of their classrooms by failing to recognize their opportunity to learn as a stewardship responsibility. Not only is your teacher interested in your academic achievement, but Jesus Christ expects you to study and to develop your full potential.

The tragedy is that many of us shut him out of areas of our lives without even recognizing our guilt. Some of us have restricted him to the Sunday morning Bible study or worship service instead of recognizing that he wants to be our Companion throughout the entire week.

**I. We often shut Jesus out of church.**

The very thought of shutting anyone out of church is contradictory to the Christian conscience. Everyone everywhere should be welcome in the place dedicated to prayer and worship and proclamation of the gospel. It is strange but true that many congregations as a group and individuals in particular shut out the Christ. Do I hear you asking, "How do we shut Jesus out of our church?"

A. *We can shut out Jesus by a careless, nonchalant attitude.* Without intending to be critical, it is easy to recognize that many people come to a worship service with a rather careless, nonchalant attitude, somewhat similar to those who attend an athletic event. They come as spectators without any intention of participating. They drift in and out, more conscious of the people about them than they are of the God whom they should be worshiping.

B. *We can shut out Jesus by a critical spirit toward others.* The very moment that we begin to be critical of others, we lose the attitude of reverent responsiveness that is always associated with worship. To look for and to be critical of the flaws and failures of others always contributes to an attitude of self-righteousness and pride. To be a habitual faultfinder without exception will rob us of the blessed awareness of the presence of the Savior.

C. *We can shut Jesus out of the church by irreverence.* At this point, the average evangelical church could learn much from a typical Catholic worship service. In most evangelical churches, there is a cultivated spirit of friendship that expresses itself in friendly greetings and conversations as the worshipers enter the place of worship. While recognizing warm friendship as an expression of Christian fellowship, we need to beware lest our concentration on greeting our friends and being aware of their presence cause us to miss the presence of him in whose name we meet together.

Even public worship is a private and personal experience in which the individual worshiper enters into the presence of God and lets the living

Christ enter into his heart. This experience is possible only when we concentrate reverently so as to let God become real to us.

D. *We can shut out Jesus by our lack of faith.* Jesus promised, "Where two or three are gathered together in my name, there am I in the midst of them" (Matt. 18:20). It would greatly assist us in our worship if we would come expecting the living Lord to be present in the service. He is eternally present to meet the deepest needs in the lives of those who trust him and are willing to listen when he speaks through songs, Scripture, sermons, and fellowship.

As a young person, one of my prime motives for regular church attendance was to have fellowship with my friends. I must confess that there were times when I went to church primarily because of my desire to be with a girlfriend. With this same attitude of expectancy and delight, we should go to church out of a sincere desire to experience the presence of the living Lord.

**II. We can open the door and let Jesus in.**

If we will let the living Christ come into our worship services and be the guiding Light in our lives, he will have a profound and benevolent effect in many areas of our lives.

A. *Jesus will guide us in our choices with infallible leadership.* He will guide us as we make the choices that largely determine our destiny. He will help the young in their choice of a career and in their choice of a marriage partner. He will assist the mature person with the decisions that must be made from week to week.

B. *Jesus will influence our conversations.* At times all of us need a bridle on our tongues. The inspired writer tells us that we cannot domesticate the tongue so as to tame it and prevent it from doing harm (James 3:7–10). While we cannot tame the tongue, we can control it. One of the most effective ways of accomplishing this desired objective is to recognize that the living Lord is a listener to every conversation. To do this continuously will eliminate slander, gossip, and unkind words.

C. *Jesus will transform our conduct.* A consciousness of the abiding presence of the living Lord will encourage us to think his thoughts and imitate his actions. We will never become Christian in our conduct until we become aware of his abiding presence. Paul explained the change that had taken place in his life as being the result of the presence of the living Christ in his heart: "I am crucified with Christ: nevertheless I live; yet not I, but Christ liveth in me: and the life which I now live in the flesh I live by the faith of the Son of God, who loved me, and gave himself for me" (Gal. 2:20).

D. *Jesus will sensitize our conscience.* There is much misunderstanding about the conscience. Some say that if people will follow their consciences, they will never go far wrong. This is a half-truth. The conscience does nothing more than say, "Do right." The content of our consciences tells us what is right. The customs of the community, the teachings of parents, and in some instances the teachings of the church provide the content of the conscience. The only way we can trust our conscience is to let the Christ so dwell in our hearts and minds that he provides the content for our conscience. When we let him in to perform this function, a great change takes place.

E. *Jesus will enlarge our compassion.* To associate with the living Christ is to discover his love for others and his desire to minister to their needs. To follow him is to discover the joy of giving and serving and meeting the needs of others. To allow Christ fully into one's heart always enlarges the horizons of that person's concern for his or her fellow humans.

**III. Jesus wants to come in.**

A. *Jesus wants to come into your church.* Every worship service can be a time in which you receive the counsel of the living Lord. In tenderness and love, he will complain concerning that which is destructive and hurtful to you and to others. He will offer correction in a manner that will encourage you if you will but listen and heed. He can speak words of forgiveness that can bring the joy of cleansing and relief from the burden and pain of guilt.

B. *Jesus wants to come into your heart.* He does not want to stand on the outside and merely talk through the screen. Nor does he want to hurt or condemn you. He wants to bring the blessings of a loving Father into your life. He can do this only if you let him in as Savior and Lord, Teacher and Friend.

### Conclusion

Let Jesus fully come into your heart. Give him the key to every area of life. Let him in eagerly, for to neglect or refuse to let him in is to impoverish your life. Let him in immediately, for you have waited too long already. You have missed too much of what he has for you.

---

## WEDNESDAY EVENING, NOVEMBER 11

***Title:*** Follow Me in Genuine Worship

***Text:*** "And he came to Nazareth, where he had been brought up: and, as his custom was, he went into the synagogue on the sabbath day, and stood up for to read" **(Luke 4:16)**.

### Introduction

In one of B. B. McKinney's famous hymns, the chorus takes the form of a pledge:

> *Wherever He leads I'll go,*
> *Wherever He leads I'll go,*
> *I'll follow my Christ who loves me so,*
> *Wherever He leads I'll go.*

Many sing this chorus without giving much thought to what they are saying. Others hesitate to sing these words because of their fear of where God might lead. There are some who sing these words without ever recognizing that God may want to lead them somewhere. Some would be surprised to learn that if they would really follow Jesus, one of the places to which he would lead them repeatedly would be the place of worship. The text states that "as his custom was, he went into the synagogue on the sabbath day." By this we can assume that during all the years before our Lord began his public ministry, he was very consistent in his habits of both public and private worship.

## I. What is worship?

Jesus insisted that worship was something infinitely more than being physically present in a place dedicated to God (John 4:21–24). One can be physically present in the temple and engage in ritual and forms of worship without having a true experience with God (Luke 18:10–12).

A. *Genuine worship is both an attitude and an activity.* It is an attitude of reverent awe felt in the presence of the Holy God.

B. *Genuine worship is the adoration and appreciation of God as one contemplates and experiences his love, mercy, and grace.*

C. *Genuine worship is an experience of communion in which the soul is in dialogue with the Eternal.*

D. *Genuine worship is an experience in which the worshiper gives self to God and at the same time receives all that God has for him or her.*

## II. Benefits of worship.

A. *The believer who sincerely follows Jesus in worship will discover an increasing harmony between his or her will and the will of God.* Harmony is what produces peace of mind and heart. When there is discord between one's will and the will of God, a tempest will rage continuously in the soul.

B. *The believer who sincerely follows Jesus in worship will be blessed with a sense of security.* As God becomes more real through repeated experiences of worship, fear will be dispelled and a calm serenity will possess the soul. An attitude of optimism will be more likely in the midst of the difficulties of the present and the uncertainties of the future.

C. *The believer who sincerely follows Jesus in worship will be delivered from the tyranny of the material.* Through worship the believer will become convinced that the main purpose for living is not to accumulate material goods but that true security comes through faith in the goodness of God.

D. *The believer who sincerely follows Jesus in worship will discover solutions to his or her problems.* It is interesting to note that our Savior resorted to prayer as he faced the selection of his apostles (Luke 6:12–13). When people misunderstood the spiritual nature of the kingdom, Jesus found it necessary to go apart for a worship experience in prayer (Matt. 14:23).

As Jesus faced the awful prospect of setting his face toward Jerusalem and the burden of the cross, we read that he went up into a mountain to pray (Luke 9:28). Jesus prayed in Gethsemane as he faced the prospect of the cross on the following day. Luke tells us, "There appeared an angel unto him from heaven, strengthening him" (Luke 22:43). Apart from following him in genuine worship, there is no solution to be found for the problems that are going to trouble us.

**III. Aids to worship.**

A. *The synagogue services aided Jesus in worship.* The worship services of your church can greatly aid you in your efforts to have continuing experiences with the living God.

B. *The study of the Scriptures can greatly aid you in your efforts to worship if you will study them reverently and responsively, trusting the Holy Spirit to reveal to you the truth that your heart stands in need of from day to day (John 14:26; 16:13).* Jesus was a diligent student of the Scriptures and stored away the great truths of God in his mind and heart. These verses of Scripture aided him immeasurably. His quotations of the Scriptures during his temptation experiences and while he suffered on the cross are cases in point.

C. *Listening to or singing the great hymns can aid your worship.* It is said concerning our Lord that following the Passover feast and the institution of the Lord's Supper, "when they had sung an hymn, they went out into the mount of Olives" (Matt. 26:30). From this we can assume that the singing of hymns was a vital part of the worship experience of our Lord and his disciples.

D. *Private worship had a prominent place in the habits of Jesus.* Several passages tell of Jesus' private prayer time. For example: "In the morning, rising up a great while before day, he went out, and departed into a solitary place, and there prayed" (Mark 1:35). "And he withdrew himself into the wilderness, and prayed" (Luke 5:16). "And it came to pass in those days, that he went out into a mountain to pray, and continued all night in prayer to God" (6:12). The best preparation for effective public worship is private worship.

**Conclusion**

Before we can work effectively in the vineyard of our Lord, we must wait before him in worship. The responsibility of our work should compel us to worship. And our worship will motivate us and enable us to work and serve effectively.

## SUNDAY MORNING, NOVEMBER 15

***Title:*** "Repent Ye, and Believe the Gospel"

***Text:*** "And saying, The time is fulfilled, and the kingdom of God is at hand: repent ye, and believe the gospel" **(Mark 1:15)**.

***Scripture Reading:*** Mark 1:1–15

***Hymns:*** "O Worship the King," Grant
"I Will Arise and Go to Jesus," Hart
"I Am Resolved," Hartsough

***Offertory Prayer:*** Today, our Father, we sit at the feet of Jesus and hear him say, "It is more blessed to give than to receive." We believe that our highest happiness and greatest joy and usefulness are to be found through the unselfish giving of ourselves to you and to others and in our giving of money to you. Help us also to remember to be givers in every area of life. Bless these tithes and offerings to the glory of your name and to the advancement of your kingdom. Amen.

### Introduction

Jesus came into our world, which in reality is his world, to change both the minds and the ways of people. In his opening message, he announced the emphasis of his mission: "Repent ye, and believe the gospel" (Mark 1:15).

If we are to understand the mind and mission of Jesus, we must discover the meaning of this primary command, this initial invitation. To misunderstand at this point is to arrive at the wrong conclusion. It is very possible that the church has failed to be the dynamic force morally, socially, politically, and spiritually that our Lord intended it to be because of a colossal misunderstanding concerning repentance, which is the primary demand of the Christian faith. William Douglas Chamberlain contends that the church has not understood the words "Repent ye" in their profound, far-reaching, revolutionary significance. He declares that if the church is really to be the church, we must reexamine the New Testament and discover the revolutionary significance of this primary demand of our faith. Repentance is positive rather than negative. The call to repentance and faith is not primarily a threat. The demand for repentance is not a plea for remorseful thinking concerning sins and shortcomings committed in the past; instead, it is positive and forward looking and calls for an inward change of attitude that prepares one to participate in the wonderful work of God. While a godly sorrow for sin is involved, it is not primary.

### I. The emphasis on repentance.

The word *repent* occurs fifty-six times in the New Testament. In thirty-four instances it occurs as a verb, and in twenty-two instances it occurs as a noun.

A. *The New Testament opens with a trumpet blast as we hear John the Baptist say, "Repent ye: for the kingdom of heaven is at hand" (Matt. 3:2).* John, the forerunner of the Lord, was calling for a change of attitude on the part of the people toward God and toward life.

B. *Jesus began and concluded his ministry emphasizing repentance.* "Repent ye, and believe the gospel" are the first words Mark records as falling from the lips of the Savior. In the conclusion of Jesus' earthly ministry, Luke verbalizes the Great Commission in terms of the call for repentance and an offer of forgiveness: "[Jesus] said unto them, Thus it is written, and thus it behooved Christ to suffer, and to rise from the dead the third day: and that repentance and remission of sins should be preached in his name among all nations, beginning at Jerusalem. And ye are witnesses of these things" (Luke 24:46–48).

C. *Jesus sent out the twelve apostles, and they went throughout the countryside "and preached that men should repent" (Mark 6:12).*

D. *After Peter had explained the miraculous events taking place on the day of Pentecost and what God had done in and through Jesus, many were convinced that he was indeed the Christ.* They cried out, "Men and brethren, what shall we do?" (Acts 2:37). The first word of Peter's response was "repent." This is the primary demand of genuine faith. It is a gracious invitation rather than a threat.

E. *In the seven letters of the risen Christ to the churches of Asia Minor there is a recurring call for repentance.* Genuine repentance is not only the initial experience of the Christian life, it is to be a progressive and continuing experience as one discovers the mind of Jesus Christ and the will of God.

## II. The implications of repentance.

By making repentance the primary demand of the Christian faith, Christ was calling for something other than a fear of punishment for sin. He was calling for something other than an emotional crisis involving remorse, shame, and sorrow because of sin. We all feel remorse when we experience the consequences of sin. But this remorse was not the thing Jesus considered important.

Jesus was calling for something more than acts of penance in which an individual would put forth an effort to make restitution for wrongs done either to God or one's fellow man. Jesus was calling for something more than good resolutions and reformation. One can reform and be a good Pharisee.

In calling for repentance, Jesus was inviting people to reverse their thoughts. He was challenging them to make a complete change of their mental outlook and life design. The Lord was calling for an inward transformation of their basic ideas and objectives for life. In modern terminology he was saying, "You must change your attitude and outlook." He was inviting them to bring their minds into harmony with the mind of God. The change in the thoughts toward God is primary. A change in conduct or behavior is the consequence of repentance. These will follow as day follows night once there has been an inward acceptance of the thoughts and ideas of God.

Isaiah the prophet said that the wicked ways of humans are the result of their unrighteous thoughts:

> Let the wicked forsake his way, and the unrighteous man his thoughts: and let him return unto the LORD, and he will have mercy upon him; and to our God, for he will abundantly pardon. For my thoughts are not your thoughts, neither are your ways my ways, saith the LORD. For as the heavens are higher than the earth, so are my ways higher than your ways, my thoughts than your thoughts. (Isa. 55:7–9)

A study of this invitation to repentance reveals that the only way people can come to God is by a change of attitude in which, with the help of God, they rise to where they seek to think the thoughts of God. Only as we think his thoughts can we live as he would have us.

Real repentance involves an inward change of attitude toward God, toward sin, toward self, and toward others.

A. *Repentance is a change of attitude toward God.* It is possible as the unbeliever hears the good news about God that comes through Jesus Christ. Through Jesus Christ God reveals himself as the unselfish God who seeks the fleeing and self-destructive sinner. Through Jesus Christ God offers the cleansing of forgiveness and the gift of eternal life.

Through Jesus Christ, God reveals his love for us individually and personally. He reveals that he wants to be our loving Father. If people will respond to this good news about God in Jesus Christ with a change of attitude from distrust to trust, from rebellion to cooperation, from resentment to welcome, from hate to love, a tremendous transformation is sure to follow in their conduct.

B. *Repentance is a change of attitude about sin.* Even God cannot save a person from sin without that person's cooperation. The call to repentance is a challenge to recognize the evil, deadly, destructive nature of sin and to change the attitude concerning it from one of love to hate, from the practice of clinging to it to the practice of fleeing from it.

What makes a thing sinful? Are the pleasures of sin something a capricious God would deny us because of divine selfishness? Many think this is the case. A study of that which God forbids will reveal in all instances that behind the divine prohibition there is a desire to prevent us from suffering the consequences of either an action or an attitude that is destructive by its very nature.

C. *Repentance involves a change of attitude toward self.* People by nature consider themselves to be independent and self-sufficient. In pride and self-confidence they seek their own futures in their own ways without regard to God or to their fellow humans.

In genuine repentance people accept the concept that they are made in the image and likeness of God; and in redemption they no longer belong to themselves. They accept the idea that they belong to God and that their lives should be lived so as to glorify God (1 Cor. 6:19–20).

D. *Repentance will reveal itself by a change of attitude toward others.* Each individual will be recognized as one for whom Christ died, an object of God's loving concern.

Genuine repentance, the primary demand of our faith, cannot be limited to the initial experience of becoming a Christian. It must be a continuing experience in which we journey from the mind of the flesh to the mind of God as revealed in Jesus Christ. Paul wrote to the Romans of the necessity of the continuing renewal of the mind (Rom. 12:2). He also wrote to the Philippian Christians challenging them to let the mind of Jesus Christ be the objective of their heart's desire (Phil. 2:5).

### III. The invitation to repent.

A. *John the Baptist, speaking for God, invited people to repent.* His words were not just a command; they were a gracious invitation.

B. *Jesus began and concluded his earthly ministry both commanding and inviting people to repent.* His command to repent was not a threat so much as it was a gracious, loving invitation for people to change their attitude toward God.

C. *Jesus commissioned his church to occupy itself continually with the task of extending this gracious invitation to people to repent and believe the gospel.*

In obedience to this command, this worship service is being conducted and this sermon is being proclaimed.

### Conclusion

Jesus Christ, the sinless, stainless, spotless Son of God, died with his arms extended and hands nailed to a cross. Someone has rightfully surmised that the manner of his death was a symbol of the earnest appeal of God to the hearts of people to repent and believe the gospel. The appeal is to your heart today.

## SUNDAY EVENING, NOVEMBER 15

***Title:*** The Gospel of God's Presence

***Text:*** "For it is God which worketh in you both to will and to do of his good pleasure" **(Phil. 2:13)**.

***Scripture Reading:*** Philippians 2:5–16

### Introduction

The Bible is full of the gospel! Many of us have accepted only a part of the gospel as the whole gospel, thus impoverishing our souls. We need to discover more and more of the gospel as time goes by. Paul stated the heart of the gospel in his epistle to the Corinthians (1 Cor. 15:1–4). While the gospel centers in the mighty redemptive acts of Jesus Christ in which he died for our sins and arose triumphant over death, we must not limit the gospel to these two mighty events, for the gospel is the good news about God and his purpose for people through faith in Jesus Christ. There are many facets to the good news concerning God's provisions for people. We need to study the Bible continually to discover more and more of the good news of God's plan for our lives. Today let us discover "the gospel of God's presence."

Our text is located between two inspired words of exhortation and encouragement. Paul challenges the Philippian Christians to give God their undivided love and cooperation that they might fully experience his great salvation for them (Phil. 2:12). He follows our text with a challenge to avoid complaining and disputing among themselves. Between these two words of instruction, he makes an exciting statement about God.

**I. God is introduced: "For it is God."**

A. *Paul had discovered in his own personal experience that God is love (Rom. 5:6–8).*

B. *Paul had discovered that God deals with sinful people in terms of his own grace and mercy rather than in terms of people's worth and merit (1 Tim. 1:11–15).* Paul believed with all his heart that the Creator, on the basis of his grace, was vitally concerned, not only with the well-being of humanity as a whole, but with individuals in particular. He reminds the Philippian Christians of this interest of their God.

**II. God's presence within: "For it is God ... in you."**

Paul reminds the followers of Christ in Philippi that the eternal God has entered into the heart to work his work of redemption.

A. *Immanuel—God with us.* The prophet Isaiah spoke of the day when the eternal God would clothe himself in human flesh and dwell in the midst of people (Isa. 7:14).

John, the apostle, based his gospel on the belief that the eternal God had visited the earth in the person of Jesus of Nazareth: "The Word was made flesh, and dwelt among us, (and we beheld his glory, the glory as of the only begotten of the Father), full of grace and truth" (John 1:14). John believed, as devout believers believe today, that in Jesus Christ people beheld the eternal God with a human face and in human form.

B. *The temple of God.* Jesus spoke to his disciples of the coming of the Holy Spirit in terms that were beyond their power to comprehend at the time (John 14:16–18). He was describing that which God had planned for them following the day of Pentecost when the Holy Spirit was to come in mighty power to carry forward that which Jesus had begun. Later Paul explained this to the Corinthians by telling them that the Holy Spirit had taken up residence in the heart of each believer. He asked them, "Know ye not that ye are the temple of God, and that the Spirit of God dwelleth in you?" (1 Cor. 3:16).

Paul was encouraging the Philippian Christians to recognize that their God was not an absentee God who dwelled in the distant somewhere.

Actually, the eternal God was as close to them as their breath. In the person of Jesus Christ, he had dwelt with humans, but in the Holy Spirit he had come to dwell within the heart of believers.

### III. God's gracious activity: "For it is God which worketh."

Paul had expressed the belief at the very beginning of his epistle that God was at work in the hearts of people with a gracious purpose. "Being confident of this very thing, that he which hath begun a good work in you will perform it until the day of Jesus Christ" (Phil. 1:6). Paul informs them that God has not completed his work in their lives when he forgives their sin and adopts them as his children.

A. *God is at work upon us.* The loving Father is not satisfied with us as we are. He has noble plans for us and works to accomplish that plan.

On one occasion Jesus said, "My Father worketh hitherto, and I work" (John 5:17). From this we can assume that the Christ who served as a carpenter before he began his public ministry is concerned about building something significant with our lives.

B. *God is at work in the world about us.* Sometimes we forget this, and sometimes we may find it difficult to believe, but the truth is that God works in many ways to accomplish his purpose within our lives.

### IV. God's method of work: "It is God which worketh in you, both to will and to do."

The divine method of working his work within our heart and life is inward rather than external. It is designed to secure our voluntary cooperation, for God does not desire that we feel like slaves driven before a master.

A. *God works on the inside by filling us with a holy discontent with ourselves as we are.* God reveals himself to us in one way or another that helps us to see our moral imperfections (Isa. 6:5; Luke 5:8).

B. *God works on the inside by giving us a deep hunger and thirst for righteousness (Ps. 42:1–2; Matt. 5:6).* Deep within the soul of every person there is a hunger for God that nothing else can satisfy. This hunger has been described as "a God-shaped vacuum" that only God can fill.

C. *God works on the inside to assure us of the possibility of significant achievement.* Paul believed that it is possible for the Christian to do anything and everything that God wants him to do. "I can do all things through Christ which strengthened me" (Phil. 4:13).

D. *God would encourage us to walk in the paths of righteousness, which not only bring inward satisfaction but also lead to significant service to others.*

### V. God's good purpose: "Both to will and to do his good pleasure."

A. *Jesus lived his life utterly devoted to the will of God.* Repeatedly, he was given indications of the divine approval. Particularly, this happened at the time of his baptism, at the time of his transfiguration, and again shortly before his crucifixion. His resurrection from the dead was the stamp of God's approval on all that he ever achieved.

B. *In the parable of the talents Jesus taught that it was possible for each person to conduct himself or herself so as to receive the commendation of God (Matt. 25:21–23).*

C. *Paul faced the end of his earthly journey in the confidence that he had cooperated with the God who had been at work within his heart, and consequently a reward awaited him (2 Tim. 4:6–8).*

### Conclusion

God has not left us to live our Christian lives by our own ingenuity and effort. He has come to dwell within our hearts, and our task is to cooperate continuously with him as he works within us from day to day. He is not an absentee Savior who gives us instructions once a year. He dwells within our hearts continuously and has promised never to leave us or forsake us. May each of us respond to this gracious truth and take courage as we face the future.

---

## WEDNESDAY EVENING, NOVEMBER 18

***Title:*** Follow Me to the Mountainside for Study

***Text:*** "Seeing the multitudes, he went up into a mountain: and when he was set, his disciples came unto him: And he opened his mouth, and taught them, saying…" **(Matt. 5:1–2)**.

### Introduction

Nicodemus the Pharisee had an interview with Jesus one night in which he said, "Rabbi, we know that thou art a teacher come from God: for no man can do these miracles that thou doest, except God be with him" (John 3:2). Even Jesus' enemies recognized him as a teacher who taught the way of God in truth without partiality (Matt. 22:16). One of the greatest needs of present-day Christianity is to recognize and respond to his authoritative message.

### I. The lecture on the mountainside.

We commonly speak of the "Sermon on the Mount." Actually, it was not a sermon; it was the lecture of an authoritative teacher who had come from heaven with a message for people.

In this lecture on the mountainside, the Master Teacher set forth the nature and characteristics of the citizens of the kingdom he had come to establish (Matt. 5:1–9). He described the influence of these subjects on the kingdom of God (vv. 10–19). He set forth in vivid detail illustrations of the conduct expected of those who became his followers, learners, students, or disciples (5:20–7:23).

In graphic terms he declared that one's relationship or attitude to these teachings on the mountainside determined his destiny (Matt. 7:24–27). He described the destiny of the man who not only heard but heeded these authoritative teachings as like a wise man who built his house on the rock (vv. 24–25). The destiny of the hearer who sits on the mountainside and listens to his teachings but refuses or neglects to heed is likened to a foolish man who built his house on sand (vv. 26–27).

**II. Truths to be learned.**

This lecture on a mountainside contains dynamic truths that are relevant for life today. They must be learned with the mind if we are to be true followers of Jesus Christ.

A. *It was not a sermon to be enjoyed.* Often a pastor will have members of the congregation say, "Pastor, I sure enjoyed the sermon." The pastor never really knows what his members are saying when they speak in this manner. It could be that they were entertained. It could be that they were comforted. It could be that they felt complimented.

B. *Lessons to be learned.* For students to become effective readers or writers, they must learn, not only the words of a vocabulary, but also the laws of grammar. For students to become effective accountants, they must learn not only the ten basic numerals, but also the laws of addition, division, multiplication, and subtraction, not to mention bookkeeping skills. For students to become accomplished pianists, they must recognize, not only a piano keyboard, but they must also learn musical scales, key signatures, sharps and flats, and a multiplicity of musical terminology. And at the same time, they must put in enough practice utilizing this information to produce a beautiful harmony.

Even so, to be true followers of Jesus Christ, people must do more than just profess their faith and mouth pious platitudes and sentimental generalities about being religious. The word *disciple* and the word *discipline* are built on the same root. The word *discipline* does not mean to punish; it means to follow a course of instruction and training that "corrects, molds, strengthens, or perfects." To be disciples of Jesus means that we must sit at his feet and learn what he taught and determine to practice in our own experience that which God would have us to do.

**III. He opened his mouth and taught them.**

William Barclay sought to describe Jesus as the Master Teacher. He said that the words that fell from Jesus' lips were immediately arresting, universal in appeal, immediately intelligible, and permanently memorable. In his teaching methods, Jesus used the unforgettable epigram, the thought-provoking paradox, the vivid hyperbole, and penetrating humor, as well as parables (*The Mind of Jesus* [London: SCM, 1960], 96–102).

Jesus never presented his truths in an overbearing, dogmatic manner. He challenged people to think for themselves concerning the eternal verities. Perhaps the most important teaching method Jesus used was the influence of his own personality, for in infinite love he was a personification of his own teachings.

### IV. How do you respond?

A. *You can let your mind be like the wayside upon which the seed fell and the birds came and devoured them (Matt. 13:4).*

B. *You can make a shallow, superficial response to the teachings of Jesus and let them perish and die like the seeds that were sown in the shallow soil that covered underlying stones (Matt. 13:5, 20–21).*

C. *You can let the truths be crowded out and choked by the cares of the world and by the deceitfulness of riches (Matt. 13:7, 22).*

D. *You can respond to the teachings of Jesus reverently, responsively, and regularly, and be like the seed that fell into the good ground that brought forth "some an hundredfold, some sixtyfold, some thirtyfold" (Matt. 13:8, 23).*

### Conclusion

Follow Jesus to the mountainside classroom, sit at his feet, recognize his unique person, respond to his truths with a hungry heart, and be a diligent student. Then others will recognize you as a true disciple.

---

## SUNDAY MORNING, NOVEMBER 22

***Title:*** The Faith That Saves

***Text:*** "I kept back nothing that was profitable unto you, but have shewed you, and have taught you publicly, and from house to house, testifying both to the Jews, and also to the Greeks, repentance toward God, and faith toward our Lord Jesus Christ" (**Acts 20:20–21**).

***Scripture Reading:*** James 2:14–20

***Hymns:*** "The Solid Rock," Mote

"O for a Faith That Will Not Shrink," Bathurst

"A Mighty Fortress Is Our God," Luther

***Offertory Prayer:*** Heavenly Father, the greatest need of our world is its need for you. There are areas of our world where the light of the miraculous gospel of Christ has never shone. Multitudes have never heard of your love and of your desire both to forgive and deliver from the tyranny of sin. Today we bring our offerings as an indication of our desire to support the work of missionaries. We dedicate ourselves afresh to being good witnesses for you in our own community. In Jesus' name we pray. Amen.

### Introduction

As Paul made his way toward Jerusalem, he enjoyed a conference with the leaders from the church at Ephesus. Among a number of things he did was to condense into capsule form the message he had preached, focusing particular attention on the human response that should be made to the gospel. He declared that he had not hesitated at the point of declaring to both Jews and Greeks the need for "repentance toward God, and faith toward our Lord Jesus Christ." In these terms he described the heart response that is necessary for a person to receive the forgiveness of sin and the gift of eternal life.

In speaking of the need for people to repent, Paul was affirming the necessity of there being an inward change of the mind and will toward God, toward sin, toward self, and toward others.

Let us face the question of what kind of faith a person must have to experience salvation. Repeatedly the Bible speaks of the place that a person's faith has in receiving salvation through Jesus Christ. For example:

> But as many as received him, to them gave he power to become the sons of God, even to them that believe on his name (John 1:12).
>
> For God so loved the world, that he gave his only begotten Son, that whosoever believeth in him should not perish, but have everlasting life. For God sent not his Son into the world to condemn the world; but that the world through him might be saved (John 3:16–17).
>
> To him give all the prophets witness, that through his name whosoever believeth in him shall receive remission of sins (Acts 10:43).
>
> Therefore we conclude that a man is justified by faith without the deeds of the law (Rom. 3:28).
>
> Therefore being justified by faith, we have peace with God through our Lord Jesus Christ (Rom. 5:1).
>
> Knowing that a man is not justified by the works of the law, but by the faith of Jesus Christ, that we might be justified by the faith of Christ, and not by the works of the law: for by the works of the law shall no flesh be justified (Gal. 2:16).

The faith that is referred to in these verses is more than intellectual assent to the existence of God, for James 2:19 says, "Thou believest that there is one God; thou doest well: the devils also believe, and tremble." One can believe everything the Bible teaches and still be outside of the family of God. We read in the book of Acts about Simon the sorcerer. He believed and was baptized (Acts 8:13), yet later he tried to purchase the power of the Holy Spirit, and Peter said to him, "Thou hast neither part nor lot in this matter: for thy heart is not right in the sight of God.... For I perceive that thou are in the gall of bitterness, and in the bond of iniquity" (Acts 8:21, 23). James inquires rhetorically concerning the value of a faith that produces no fruits: "What good is it, my brothers, if a man claims to have faith but has no deeds? Can such faith save him?" (James 2:14 NIV). Do you have the faith that saves?

**I. The faith that saves is the faith that responds to the gospel (1 Cor. 15:1–4).**

The gospel is something infinitely more than good advice. Primarily, it is good news concerning God that is communicated to us through Jesus Christ.

A. *Christ died on the cross for our sins (1 Cor. 15:3).* He came to die. He lived to die.

B. *Christ rose again the third day (1 Cor. 5:4).* Christ conquered death and the grave. He arose triumphant, revealing the reality of immortality. He is a living Savior who has walked down through the corridors of time to this present day. He confronts the heart of each person with God's love as dramatically disclosed in his death on the cross. He offers people not only forgiveness for the past but also for the present and the future.

The faith that saves is a faith that receives this news about God's love for sinners and receives Jesus Christ as Lord and Savior.

### II. The faith that saves is the faith that surrenders to the will of God.

When Paul was confronted on the road to Damascus by the vision of the living Christ, he asked, "Who art thou, Lord?" When he discovered that it was the living Christ, there arose from his heart the question, "Lord, what wilt thou have me to do?" (Acts 9:5–6). In this question he implied a surrender of his personal sovereignty to the sovereignty of Jesus Christ. He was making Jesus Christ the Lord of his life. In his epistle to the Roman Christians, Paul says that salvation comes to those who in their hearts believe and respond to the gospel to the extent that with their mouths they confess Jesus Christ as their Lord (Rom. 10:9).

### III. The faith that saves causes one to stop sinful habits.

Sin is destructive and deadly. Even God himself cannot save people from their sin unless they decide to forsake evil and cry out to God for assistance to live the separated life.

A. *When Matthew the publican responded to the call to conversion, "he left all, rose up, and followed him" (Luke 5:28).*

B. *Paul commended the Thessalonian Christians because they "turned to God from idols to serve the living and true God."* A primary implication of baptism is that the new convert is now both disposed toward and determined to "walk in newness of life" (Rom. 6:4).

### IV. The faith that saves is a faith that serves.

Our Scripture reading from James emphasizes that genuine faith will manifest itself in ministries of helpfulness and mercy toward the unfortunate (2:14–17). Jesus said that you would be able to tell the true from the false by their fruits (Matt. 7:16–20). Paul told the Ephesian Christians that the children of God have been created by God unto a life of good works (Eph. 2:10). This is true, for when people respond to the gospel with a genuine trusting faith, the miracle of the new birth takes place within their souls and they become a child of God with love and compassion and a desire to help others. It is said that Jesus "gave himself for us, that he might redeem us from all iniquity, and purify unto himself a peculiar people, zealous of good works" (Titus 2:14). If you have a faith that does not motivate you to service in the name of your Lord, then you need to reexamine the genuineness of that faith.

**V. The faith that saves is a faith that satisfies.**

To know Jesus Christ as a personal Savior, as life's most wonderful Friend, and as heaven's infallible Teacher is to enjoy a peace that passes all human understanding.

To be a Christian is much more than just believing that there is a God. To be a Christian is more than having a high code of ethical rules by which you conduct your life. To be a Christian is to be in a living relationship with Jesus Christ himself.

**Conclusion**

Do you have faith that saves? If you don't, you can. The Bible does not speak about the quantity of the faith you must have to be saved. Rather, it focuses on the object of your faith. Are you willing to accept Jesus Christ to be all that the New Testament claims him to be? Can you give mental assent to the truth of what the New Testament declares concerning him? If so, then commit your life to him by faith, depending on him to do for you that which he has promised to do, and you will discover his presence and power at work in your own heart and life.

---

## SUNDAY EVENING, NOVEMBER 22

***Title:*** What Is Your Life?

***Text:*** "What is your life? It is even a vapour, that appeareth for a little time, and then vanisheth away" **(James 4:14)**.

**Introduction**

For many years *This Is Your Life* was a popular television program. Celebrities were chosen as guests, and interesting events and achievements out of the life of the person being spotlighted were dramatized. You and I will probably never be spotlighted on a television program, but we would be wise to face the question, "What is your life?" There probably would be as many answers as there are persons, because each life is unique.

James asked his readers, "What is your life?" to emphasize the brevity of life and the urgent need for the guidance and help of God if we are to make our lives meaningful and productive.

**I. "What is your life?"**

It is a vapor.

A. *It is a vapor that appears for a little time.* A vapor can be seen only briefly, for it evaporates and disappears.

B. *It vanishes away.* The psalmist was grieved as he considered the brevity of the human life, but he rejoiced in the eternal nature of God's mercy (Ps. 103:15–18).

### II. "What is your life?"

It is a mystery.

A. *Life has been defined as the absence of death.*

B. *Death has been defined as the absence of life. People stood in awe before the mystery of life.*

### III. "What is your life?"

It is the breath of God (Gen. 2:7). Apart from the breath of God, a human is but a pile of dust. Life is God's gift to us. God is the Author and Giver of life.

### IV. "What is your life?"

It is a trust from God. We must all give an account of our stewardship of the gift of life (Rom. 14:12).

The writer of Ecclesiastes, speaking from the viewpoint of common sense rather than from a heart filled with great faith, declared, "God shall bring every work into judgment, with every secret thing, whether it be good, or whether it be evil" (Eccl. 12:14).

### V. "What is your life?"

It is an opportunity to serve. Our Lord understood and defined life in terms of an opportunity to minister to the needs of others: "Even the Son of man came not to be ministered unto, but to minister, and to give his life a ransom for many" (Mark 10:45). Those who would follow Jesus must accept his attitude and his ambition concerning the purpose of being.

### Conclusion

What is your life? If you have not trusted Jesus Christ as your Savior, you do not have life (John 3:36). You have the capacity to receive the gift of everlasting life if you will but receive him. He is eager to bestow on you this gift if you will trust him as Savior and Lord: "I am come that they might have life, and that they might have it more abundantly" (John 10:10; 20:31).

---

## WEDNESDAY EVENING, NOVEMBER 25

***Title:*** Follow Me to the Secret Place of Prayer

***Text:*** "In the morning, rising up a great while before day, he went out, and departed into a solitary place, and there prayed" **(Mark 1:35)**.

**Introduction**

If we want to be true followers of Jesus Christ, we must follow him regularly to the secret place of private prayer and communion with God. Repeatedly the Scriptures tell us that he went apart, away from the crowd, to be alone with God: "It came to pass in those days, that he went out to a mountain to pray, and continued all night in prayer to God" (Luke 6:12); "When he had sent the multitudes away, he went up into a mountain apart to pray: and when the evening was come, he was there alone" (Matt. 14:23); "He was withdrawn from them about a stone's cast, and kneeled down, and prayed" (Luke 22:41).

If our Lord found it both necessary and profitable to enter the secret place of prayer, it would seem absolutely essential that we, his followers, would need to follow his example and want to imitate his actions.

**I. Jesus sought the secret place for prayer.**

A. *Jesus prayed during his baptism (Luke 3:21).* For Jesus, prayer was more of a dialogue with God than a monologue in which he expressed his own personal wishes (cf. Luke 3:21–22; 9:28–31).

B. *Jesus went apart for prayer when people wanted him to set up an earthly kingdom rather than a spiritual kingdom (Matt. 14:21–23).* Evidently he needed divine strength and wisdom and assistance during a difficult time in his ministry.

C. *Jesus went to the secret place of prayer when he faced major decisions.* He spent an entire night in prayer before choosing his apostles (Luke 6:12–13).

D. *From the loneliness of the cross the Savior prayed that his crucifiers might be forgiven (Luke 23:34).* Although there were many in the vicinity at this time, he had entered the sanctuary of God's presence in prayer to intercede for those who had nailed him to the cross.

Shortly after praying this prayer for his crucifiers, Jesus prayed a prayer of committal for his own soul (Luke 23:46).

**II. Jesus encourages us to find the secret place for prayer.**

"Thou, when thou prayest, enter into thy closet, and when thou hast shut thy door, pray to thy Father which is in secret; and thy Father which seeth in secret shall reward thee openly" (Matt. 6:6).

A. *Jesus assumed that the children of God would want to pray.* The words of this verse are not phrased as a command. They are the expression of an assumption. Jesus assumed that we would hunger for fellowship and communion with our heavenly Father. He assumed that our desire for victory over sin and temptation and Satan would motivate us to seek the presence and power of our God. He assumed that our need for wisdom and grace to help in every time of need would pull us again and again into the throne room of our God and heavenly Father.

B. *Jesus suggested that we enter the closet and close the door.* Did you take this verse very literally? Did you find it difficult to get in the closet in the first place? After entering the closet, did you find it difficult to close the door? If so, your interpretation of this verse was not as far from the truth that Jesus was seeking to impart as you might think.

1. It is difficult to withdraw completely into a private place where you can enter into an unhindered experience of communion with God.
2. It is difficult to close the door and shut out everything that would distract one's concentration on God. Getting the door closed refers to the removal of all attitudes that are contradictory to the will of God and to the confessing and forsaking of all sins that are contrary to the will of God.

   For some of us it has been a long time since we have had an experience in the place of prayer in which God was very, very real and in which the divine will was made known, divine wisdom was bestowed, and divine power was imparted. The lack of these good gifts from the hand of the heavenly Father explains our ineffectiveness as modern Christians.

### Conclusion

Do you have a secret place of prayer? Have you erected an altar where you regularly seek to enter into communion with the heavenly Father? One does not have to visit a mountaintop or a forest to find a secret place for prayer. The primary requisite is to have a deep desire for such a place and a determination to follow the example and the suggestion of Jesus as found in the words of our text.

Your private place of secret prayer can be any place where you seek to enter into the throne room of the heavenly Father. It could be the bedroom, the living room, the basement, or the attic. It could be in a majestic cathedral or in a simple chapel. It could even be in the very center of a large congregation of worshipers on Sunday morning if you would but bring your soul into tune with God's will and listen with hearing ears, look with seeing eyes, and respond with a believing heart.

---

## SUNDAY MORNING, NOVEMBER 29

***Title:*** How Can We Face Death?

***Text:*** "O death, where is thy victory? O death, where is thy sting?" **(1 Cor. 15:55 RSV).**

***Scripture Reading:*** 1 Corinthians 15:47–56

***Hymns:*** "Great Is Thy Faithfulness," Chisholm

"It Is Well with My Soul," Stafford

"What a Friend We Have in Jesus," Scriven

***Offertory Prayer:*** Father God, we thank you for the bounty of your grace toward us. We thank you for blessings in the material realm. We thank you for blessings in the family. We thank you for your blessings on the work of our heads and hearts and hands. Accept our tithes and offerings as indications of our love and of our desire to share your love with a needy world. In Jesus' name we pray. Amen.

## Introduction

The British Museum in London contains an exhibit of a body that has been preserved in a remarkable way. It is the body of a man dehydrated by the hot sands of Egypt in which he was buried. The body is in a crouching position, shaped like a question mark. It seems to me that this is a parable of death. Death is an enigma though it is common to all. It is as much a part of natural life as birth. Whether great or small, high or low, powerful or powerless, we all will die.

## I. The Greek concept of death.

A. *The ancient Greeks examined the mystery of death and came up with an answer.* They decided that humans are kin to the gods. Therefore, every person has a spark of divinity and is immortal.

B. *The Greeks believed that a human lives in a body, the body is matter, and all matter is evil; inside that evil body there lives a human soul and spirit that is good.* Therefore, they saw humanity as a soul shut up in the cage of a body. They viewed death as liberation: when a person died, his soul was emancipated from his body and returned to the deity from which it came. The soul was then absorbed into that deity, like a drop of water returning to the ocean by evaporation.

C. *But the Greeks had no concept of resurrection.* They had no belief in a bodily resurrection; that would have been a contradiction in terms to them, for they thought the body was evil. They had no concept of personal survival or personal identity beyond death.

## II. The Hebrew concept of death.

A. *The Hebrews' understanding of death was very different from that of the Greeks.* The Hebrews believed in a place of existence after death that they called Sheol, the place of shades. The earth was the abode of humans and animals, and heaven was the abode of God and the angels. They had no concept of humans going to heaven where God was, but they knew that humans did not remain on earth. Therefore, they spoke and wrote of Sheol as the grave or the pit. It was the place of shadowy existence after death. There was no personal identity there.

B. *The psalmist saw Sheol as a contradiction because the shades could not glorify God.* He wrote in Psalm 6:5 (RSV): "In death there is no remembrance of thee; in Sheol, who can give thee praise?"

The Greeks saw death as escape for the immortal soul. The Hebrews saw death as a shadowy existence in nothingness.

### III. The New Testament concept of death.

A. *Immortality is the gift of God to those who believe.* "To all who received him, who believed in his name, he gave power to become children of God" (John 1:12 RSV). Jesus said that if we believe in him, we have eternal life, beginning now.

The Christian view of death centers on the resurrection of Jesus Christ. We have an insight and understanding of death and life after death that is not characteristic of other groups.

B. *Christians, because of Jesus' resurrection and postresurrection appearances, are no longer left with blind guesses about life after death.* We have been given an authentic glimpse of glory. Therefore, we can have certainty about life after death.

C. *Death wears two faces.* It is like the Roman god Janus, for whom the month of January is named. Janus had two faces, facing opposite directions. Death is like that. Death from the human point of view looks like defeat and tragedy. But from God's point of view, death is victory and triumph: "Precious in the sight of the LORD is the death of his saints" (Ps. 116:15).

D. *"Death is like blowing out a candle, because the dawn has come."* This quote aptly describes the reality of death. Death can be terribly tragic, but it is not the worst phenomenon. While the prospect of dying can be very bleak, there is no reason to have an ultimate fear of it. The resurrection of Christ means that death has died.

Lift up your hearts! Christ is risen from the dead, and every person who places faith and trust in him will rise and be clothed with immortality and live forever in the presence of the Lord.

*It will be worth it all when we see Jesus,*
*One glimpse of his dear face,*
*All sorrow will erase.*
*So bravely run the race, till we see Christ.*
—*Alton H. McEachern*

### Conclusion

Let me dare for just a moment to be intensely personal, to probe a bit, and to perhaps plant a question in your mind that will set you thinking. The hope I have talked about belongs to every born-again believer. If today should be the day of your death, do you have the kind of faith relationship with God that would mean eternal life?

You can have this hope of glory. If you have never received Christ as your own Lord and Savior, I invite you to turn from sin and self right now and receive him as your personal Lord. If you will do that, God's Holy Spirit will work a miracle in your life.

## SUNDAY EVENING, NOVEMBER 29

***Title:*** "The Sin Which Doth So Easily Beset Us"

***Text:*** "Let us lay aside every weight, and the sin which doth so easily beset us" **(Heb. 12:1)**.

### Introduction

Most of us have what we call "a besetting sin." By a besetting sin we refer to some personal weakness or shortcoming. Usually we justify or explain our reason for tolerating this sin to the extent that our conscience does not hurt us too much.

What is your besetting sin? Is it a vile temper? Is it a critical spirit? Is it a sharp tongue? Is it profanity? Could it be spiritual idleness?

Instead of a different sin for each person, the writer of the book of Hebrews is referring to a sin that is common to us all—the sin of unbelief. The sin of unbelief is the sin that God's people have been guilty of through the ages. Failure to exercise faith was the undoing sin of the Israelites. Weak faith plagued the early church. Our failure to trust God robs the modern church and individual Christians of spiritual power and achievement.

The sin of unbelief causes unbelievers to remain lost and under the wrath of God. It causes the children of God to remain in spiritual infancy.

### I. Our unbelief and the Savior.

A. *It is a source of grief to him.*

B. *Lack of confidence disappoints his love.*

C. *Little faith is an insult to his truthfulness.*

D. *Failing to trust him hinders his purposes for us.*

### II. The results of this besetting sin.

A. *Imaginary dangers darken the pathway ahead when we do not face the future with faith in the living Lord (James 4:2).*

B. *Without faith the resources of God that come in response to believing prayer are undiscovered (James 4:2).*

C. *Without faith the fear of failure captures the heart of the one who would be the servant of Christ, and he or she will attempt only that which is humanly possible (Phil. 4:13).*

D. *Without faith we place limitations on both the power and the activity of God (Ps. 78:41).*

E. *Refusal to trust God dishonors and displeases him (Heb. 11:6).*

### III. The cause of little faith.

A. *We have a natural inclination to see obstacles and difficulties and to form opinions on the basis of mere appearances.* We depend too much on human agency alone.

B. *We forget and ignore the presence of God (Zech. 4:6; John 14:12).*
C. *We fail to recognize that faith is both the gift of God and something that we develop as we discover that God is faithful in keeping his promises (Mark 9:23–24).*

**IV. The cure for little faith.**

How can we put aside the besetting sin of unbelief and grow faith?

A. *Put faith in faith.* Instead of trusting alone in human ability and common sense, recognize that the presence and power of God comes into human life through the channel of faith.
B. *Interpret the Bible, not only as a history of what happened in the past, but also as a revelation of what can happen in the present.* Identify with biblical characters and recognize that we can depend on God to respond toward us as he did to them in ages gone by. This is the whole purpose of the challenge in Hebrews 12:1 and the list of witnesses that are marched on to the witness stand of Hebrews 11. Each of these would tell us that God can be depended on and that we can trust him implicitly.
C. *Pray for the gift of an increasing faith (Luke 17:5).*
D. *Place your confidence in the promises of God to the very limit of your ability and capacity (Heb. 11:23).*

**Conclusion**

We trust God for the salvation of our souls through the death of Jesus Christ on the cross. Let us also trust him with the daily decisions and responsibilities we face.

## Suggested Preaching Program for

# DECEMBER

### ■ Sunday Mornings

"The Coming of Christ" is the theme for the first three morning services. The last Sunday morning makes a suggestion concerning necessary preparation for facing the New Year.

### ■ Sunday Evenings

"Perils to Avoid" is the theme for the Sunday evening services.

### ■ Wednesday Evenings

Continue the messages based on our Lord's invitation "Follow me."

---

## WEDNESDAY EVENING, DECEMBER 2

***Title:*** Follow Me to the Valley to Serve

***Text:*** "He saith unto them, Follow me, and I will make you fishers of men" **(Matt. 4:19)**.

***Scripture Reading:*** Luke 9:37–42

### Introduction

Preceding this incident at the foot of the mountain, the three apostles had experienced a unique revelation of the deity of Jesus. For a short time, the glory of God shone forth through the veil of human flesh. In attempting to describe this experience, John recorded, "and the Word was made flesh, and dwelt among us, (and we beheld his glory, the glory as of the only begotten of the Father), full of grace and truth" (John 1:14).

This was both a terrifying and an awe-inspiring experience that brought a strange delight to the heart to the extent that Peter suggested, "Master, it is good for us to be here: and let us make three tabernacles; one for thee, and one for Moses, and one for Elias" (Luke 9:33). Peter, and perhaps the other two apostles also, had a desire to continue this heavenly experience and converse.

Many of us can sympathize with Peter, for we have had moments of high inspiration and spiritual ecstasy that we have wished to prolong indefinitely. Perhaps it was during a time of evangelistic services or at a youth camp. Some have been rather distressed because of the inability to perpetuate this high state of spiritual awareness and joy. While it is normal for us to desire such a state, it is both interesting and profitable to note that if we truly follow Jesus, he will also lead us down from the top of the mountain into the valley where human need and human suffering are so prevalent.

Jesus the Savior would have us know that the inward satisfaction and delight that come as a result of communion with God is not to be considered as an end in itself. These moments of communion and conversation with God in prayer are to equip us to go out where human need cries out (Luke 9:38–39).

**I. Jesus came to serve: "For even the Son of man came not to be ministered unto, but to minister, and to give his life a ransom for many" (Mark 10:45).**

Jesus had defined his mission in terms of ministering to the needs of others. In his daily activities, he went about this task of ministering to the needs of others with a sense of urgency. He said, "I must work the works of him that sent me, while it is day: the night cometh, when no man can work" (John 9:4). He ministered throughout the day and even until after nightfall. The needy and the suffering continued to come to have their needs met by Jesus. He gave himself unreservedly in service to others. It has been suggested that the best biography of the Savior ever written is found in Acts 10:38, where he is described as one "who went about doing good, and healing all that were oppressed of the devil."

**II. Christ would lead us to serve.**

Human nature has not changed. People still desire to be great. They hunger for status and position and recognition. The apostles were guilty of desiring positions of prestige and prominence. In recognition of this desire, Jesus said to the Twelve, "If any man desire to be first, the same shall be last of all and servant of all." On the night before he was to be crucified, he demonstrated dramatically his desire that his disciples follow him in unselfish service. He assumed the role of a servant and washed the feet of his disciples. Then he said, "I have given you an example, that ye should do as I have done to you. Verily, verily, I say unto you. The servant is not greater than his Lord; neither he that is sent greater than he that sent him" (John 13:15–16).

A. *We can follow the example of Jesus in ministering to the sick (Mark 1:34).*
B. *We can follow the example of Jesus in feeding the hungry (John 6:8–13; cf. James 2:14–17).*
C. *We can follow the example of Jesus in a ministry to the sorrowing (Mark 5:36–43).*

**III. Created unto good works.**

"For we are his workmanship, created in Christ Jesus unto good works, which God hath before ordained that we should walk in them" (Eph. 2:10).

By inspiration the apostle declared unto the Ephesian Christians that they had been created in Christ Jesus for the purpose of performing or producing good works. People who have been born of the Spirit of God have a greater capacity for compassion. With the coming of the Holy Spirit into the heart, there is a desire not only to share the good news of God's grace, but also a desire to be of help to others.

A. *Jesus loved people.* As Christians it is possible for us to love even the unlovable. We need to let God's love fill our hearts and flow through us in ministries of mercy to those in need.
B. *Love seeks to express itself.* Christian love within the heart must demonstrate itself or dwindle and die.

### Conclusion

To be a true follower of Jesus Christ is to invest time and talents and treasure and testimony in deeds of service to others.

---

## SUNDAY MORNING, DECEMBER 6

***Title:*** The Uniqueness of the Christian Religion

***Text:*** "Jesus saith unto him, I am the way, the truth, and the life: no man cometh unto the Father, but by me" **(John 14:6)**.

***Scripture Reading:*** John 14:1–12

***Hymns:*** "Crown Him with Many Crowns," Bridges

"Jesus Is All the World to Me," Thompson

"Tell Me the Story of Jesus," Crosby

***Offertory Prayer:*** Today, holy Father, we bring the gold, frankincense, and myrrh of our tithes and offerings and present them to him who was born to be our King. We ask your blessings on these contributions to the end that all people everywhere might hear the message of your grace and the gospel of your dear Son, Jesus Christ. Help us to give after the pattern by which our Savior gave himself for us. Amen.

### Introduction

Some people look upon Christianity as an uninteresting negativism, and others look upon it as nothing more than pious, ethical behavior. Some others equate a vague belief in God in combination with a mild humanitarian benevolence as Christianity. Yet others consider any religious emotionalism as a demonstration of genuine Christianity. It should be recognized that these shallow, superficial concepts are not synonymous with the faith that first awakened the world like a thousand trumpet blasts.

Genuine Christianity was and is a dynamic force of immeasurable power for good because of the living presence and power of Jesus Christ. Christianity is more than a creed; it is Christ living, working, and ministering in and through those who have committed themselves to him as Lord as well as Savior.

As we approach the Christmas season, it can be very profitable for us to recognize that genuine Christianity is unique because of the uniqueness of Jesus Christ.

**I. In Jesus Christ we have an adequate and accurate revelation of the nature, character, and purpose of God.**

A. *Jesus Christ came into the world that he might reveal God.* "No man hath seen God at any time; the only begotten Son, which is in the bosom of the Father, he hath declared him" (John 1:18).

B. *Jesus claimed to be an accurate revelation of God.* "Jesus saith unto him, Have I been so long time with you, and yet hast thou not known me, Philip? he that hath seen me hath seen the Father; and how sayest thou then, Shew us the Father?" (John 14:9; cf. John 14:2, 6–7, 9–12).

An agnostic professor of comparative religion approached a convert from Hinduism to Christianity with the question, "Which of the teachings of Christ changed you?" The new convert to Christianity replied, "None. It was Christ who changed me." Humans are religious creatures. Because of the God-shaped vacuum in our hearts, we are always seeking. We find the fulfillment of our deepest needs when we discover Jesus Christ.

**II. In Jesus Christ we have dramatic demonstration of the divine estimate of humans.**

A. *Humans are the crown of God's creativity.*
B. *Humans are of supreme value to God.*
C. *Humans have fallen short of the divine design.*
D. *Humans are the objects of divine redemptive activity.*
E. *Humans were made for fellowship with God.*

**III. In Jesus Christ we have the highest moral ideal ever conceived.**

A. *Some consider the Sermon on the Mount impractical.*
B. *The Sermon on the Mount assumes regeneration.*
   1. Repentance.
   2. Faith.
C. *The Sermon on the Mount is based on ethical absolutes, for God is personal.*

**IV. In Jesus Christ we discover a divine dynamic for moral and spiritual progress.**

A. *Jesus Christ personifies the highest possible manhood.* He demonstrates the ideal both in his attitudes and in his actions.

B. *By Jesus' divine power, he enables us to become that which would have been impossible by human strength alone (Phil. 4:13).*

**V. The distinguishing characteristic of a Christian is the practice of love.**

A. *Jesus commanded his disciples to live by the principle of love (John 13:34–35).*

B. *The love of which Jesus speaks is to be defined in terms of a persistent, unbreakable spirit of goodwill (John 4:19; Rom. 5:51).*

## Conclusion

Christianity is a living, vital relationship to a divine person, and that person is Jesus Christ. Christianity is the only religion that involves an intrinsic relationship between its founder and his followers. Jesus Christ is a living Savior, and Christianity is a fellowship with him, rather than a mere creed concerning him or a code of conduct announced by him.

# SUNDAY EVENING, DECEMBER 6

***Title:*** The Danger of Drifting

***Text:*** "Therefore we ought to give the most earnest heed to the things which we have heard, lest at any time we should let them slip" **(Heb. 2:1)**.

***Scripture Reading:*** Genesis 13:7–13

## Introduction

What is the greatest danger we face today? Some people fear a biological or chemical terrorist attack. Many dread cancer or some other disease. Some fear a fatal plane or automobile accident. These are things that can destroy the body. What we should be more concerned about is endangering our souls by drifting away from the path of spiritual progress. The words of our text warn us strongly about the danger of drifting.

## I. The warning is for all of us.

A. *A pastor can drift, and some have.*
B. *A deacon can drift, and some have.*
C. *A Sunday school teacher can drift, and some have.*
D. *A husband and wife can drift apart, and some have.*
E. *Young people can drift along through life, and some have.*
F. *A church can drift along in comfortable complacency without a compassion that compels it to engage in a crusade of concerned witnessing to the unsaved in the community.* Some have.
G. *A nation can drift away from the moral foundations and values that have made it great.* Ours has.

## II. It is easy to drift.

An unknown poet wrote a poem called "A Real Man." A mother copied it and hung it on her son's bedroom wall. It warns against the peril of drifting.

*It is easy to drift with the current swift*
*Just lie in your boat and dream.*
*But in nature's plan, it takes a real man*
*To paddle the boat upstream.*

A. *We have a natural tendency to follow the path of ease.*
B. *On all sides we are encouraged to avoid the difficult.*
C. *We like to follow the path that is natural and normal.*
D. *Most of us like to follow the crowd, and we are pressured by the crowd.* We fail to recognize that the crowd is usually wrong on most of the vital issues that affect life.
E. *We have a natural tendency to look for the least expensive, easiest, most convenient way to do that which is important.* We fail to realize that there are no shortcuts to success.

The world, the flesh, and the Devil continue to lead us astray. They would continue to encourage us to drift. Any dead fish can drift downstream, as the poem says.

## III. Why do we drift?

One could answer this question by saying, "The world, the flesh, and the Devil" and be correct. Let's consider it from a more practical standpoint.

A. *A built-in tendency to sin.* Even the born-again Christian sometimes has a tendency to do that which is contrary to the will of God (Gal. 5:17). Satan continues to tempt us through promises of profit or pleasure, so we need to recognize that we can be duped by him. Unless we take steps to prevent our falling into sin, it is certain we will do so.

A fear of falling into sin that could nullify our Christian witness and disqualify us as the spokespeople of our Lord is wholesome and necessary if we are to achieve success as the servants of God (1 Cor. 9:25–27).

B. *Ignoring the presence and the work of the Holy Spirit.* Many who have trusted Jesus Christ as Lord and Savior are uninformed that God has bestowed within them the gift of the Holy Spirit (Gal. 4:6). In the conversion experience, the Holy Spirit enters the heart of the believer to reproduce in his mind and character the mind and character of Jesus Christ: "For it is God which worketh in you both to will and to do of his good pleasure" (Phil. 2:13).

The Holy Spirit cannot do his greatest work when his presence is ignored and there is no cooperation on the part of the believer. Not to respond eagerly and continuously to the inward promptings of the Spirit is to follow a course of drifting away from God's will and way.

C. *Neglecting the means of growth.* Some have failed to recognize that the conversion experience produces a spiritual infant rather than one who is spiritually mature. To neglect the means of spiritual growth can be detrimental to the spiritual well-being of the new convert.

1. A devotional study of the Word of God is the milk and the meat by which the child of God is to grow (1 Cor. 3:1–3; 1 Peter 2:2).
2. Communion with God through prayer is as necessary for the health of the soul as sunlight is for the health of the body.

3. Fellowship with God's people in the church is as necessary fo growth of the soul as is the love of a family for the development of a child (Heb. 10:24–25).

D. *Clinging to some known and secret sin.* Only a fool will treat sin lightly (Prov. 14:9), for sin will destroy a person. Sin is to the soul what infection is to the body. For a believer to tolerate known sin in his life is to encourage spiritual bad health. Unless there is a forsaking of this sin, whether it be in the realm of omission, commission, or disposition, the sinner is sure to drift.

Why do you drift? Are you letting the poor example of some older brother or sister in Christ cause you to drift away from the Lord who gave his life for you on the cross?

Have you let some trouble or sorrow or disappointment cause you to drift away from the Christ who said, "Come unto me all ye that labor and are heavy laden and I will give you rest"? One can sympathize with the young widow and mother who felt bitter because of the sudden death of her husband, but for her to quit praying and to quit trusting God is as irrational as it would be for a desert traveler to throw away his water jug.

Is it possible that you have drifted along in mediocrity because no one has created within you a burning desire to be an extraordinary Christian? The absence of desire to be something above the ordinary will encourage goalless drifting. [Repeat poem.]

## IV. It is time to quit drifting.

A. *Drifting is dangerous.* It is dangerous for the Christian, for a lost world waits to hear the message of salvation, and those who are drifting along will not communicate that message.

B. *Drifting is deadly.* Some fishermen were "drift" fishing below a dam in Kentucky several years ago. While concentrating on catching fish, they failed to recognize that the currents were pulling them into a place of great danger. An official of the dam sounded a warning with a horn. The men in the boat began frantically attempting to get their motor started, but the motor died, and those above the current saw an overloaded boat containing five persons go down. All perished. Drifting in the spiritual realm can be even more deadly. The unsaved can drift over the precipice of death into eternity unprepared to meet God.

C. *The crucified and risen Christ would confront us in the midst of our drifting and challenge us to cease our aimless and meaningless way of life.* By his death on the cross and by the challenge of an exciting partnership, he calls each of us to the upward life.

## Conclusion

If you are a drifting disciple, you would be exceedingly wise to rededicate your life and to begin again doing the things that not only please the Savior but that bring delight to soul. If you are among the great host drifting along and delaying the decision to come to Jesus Christ, then you should be warned today that drifting is both dangerous and deadly. Today as you have heard the good news of God's love for you, you have had the opportunity to respond to that love with the confidence of your heart and with the cooperation of your will. Make that decision now.

## WEDNESDAY EVENING, DECEMBER 9

***Title:*** Follow Me into the World to Witness

***Text:*** "Thou sayest that I am a king. To this end was I born, and for this cause came I into the world, that I should bear witness unto the truth. Every one that is of the truth heareth my voice" **(John 18:37)**.

### Introduction

The angel described the mission of the Christ child to Joseph in terms of his being the Savior: "And she shall bring forth a son, and thou shalt call his name Jesus: for he shall save his people from their sins" (Matt. 1:21). John the Baptist directed the attention of his followers to Jesus by saying, "Behold the lamb of God, which taketh away the sin of the world" (John 1:29).

Jesus said many things concerning his mission from God to humans. "Think not that I am come to destroy the law, or the prophets: I am not come to destroy, but to fulfil" (Matt. 5:17). "For even the Son of man came not to be ministered unto, but to minister, and to give his life a ransom for many" (Mark 10:45). "For the Son of man is come to seek and to save that which was lost" (Luke 19:10). "I am come that they might have life, and that they might have it more abundantly" (John 10:10).

Tonight we will focus our attention on our text, John 18:37, which describes Jesus' mission in terms of bearing a witness to the truth. The word "witness" in this verse is to be thought of, not in terms of an eyewitness who sees, but as a speaker who verifies with his testimony that which he knows to be the truth.

### I. Jesus was a witness.

"What he hath seen and heard, that he testifieth; and no man receiveth his testimony. He that hath received his testimony hath set to his seal that God is true" (John 3:32–33).

A. *Jesus was a witness concerning the nature and character of God.* Because he was God and because he came from God to humans, Jesus had firsthand knowledge concerning the nature and character of God. His life and ministry were efforts to reveal God. By precept and parable he sought to communicate truths about God.

By the life that he lived and by the death that he suffered and by the triumph that he experienced over the tomb, Jesus bore witness concerning God.

B. *Jesus was a witness to people.*
   1. Jesus gave a testimony about God to the woman at the well (John 4).
   2. Jesus gave a testimony about God to a tax collector (Luke 19:1–10).
   3. Jesus gave a testimony about God to publicans and sinners (Luke 15:1).
   4. Jesus gave a testimony about God to the proud Pharisees and scribes (Luke 15:2–32).
   5. Jesus gave a testimony concerning the declaration of God's love for sinners by suffering on the cross.

**II. You are witnesses.**

Following the victorious conquest over death, Jesus taught his disciples many things that he had been unable to teach them before his crucifixion. He helped them to understand that his death on the cross had been a demonstration of God's great love for sinners rather than some tragic accident that brought to a disappointing end their dreams for a messianic kingdom. He helped them to see that if people would recognize God's love and respond with faith and repentance, they would receive the remission of sins and the gift of new life.

The climax of this instruction was Jesus' commission to them in which he described their continuing function in terms of bearing a testimony concerning God's great love: "Ye are witnesses of these things" (Luke 24:48). He was not merely asserting that they were eyewitnesses to these redemptive events; rather, he was declaring that they were to be audible, articulate, verbal communicators of what God has done to deliver people from the tyranny of sin.

By the very nature of the case, a witness can only relate pertinent facts that he or she has personally experienced or observed. The apostles had a unique testimony because they had seen him with their eyes, they had heard him with their ears, and they had handled him with their hands. We cannot give their personal testimony, for we have not had their experience.

If we are to be true followers of Jesus Christ today, he would lead us to give our own personal testimony or witness concerning both our conversion experience and the goodness of God to us along the road of life. By the giving of our testimony, we become the means by which others are encouraged to have faith. Through the testimony of many witnesses and the work of the Holy Spirit, unbelievers are convinced and respond to the gospel message with faith that saves.

A. *The witness of our life.* The life that we live authenticates or makes void the testimony of our lips. If we truly follow Jesus in a life dedicated to God and to the service of our fellow humans, our influence will verify the testimony of our lips.

B. *The witness of our labor.* Jesus said, "By their fruits ye shall know them" (Matt. 7:20). Others should be able to see the evidence in our conduct of the presence of Christ within our heart. Christ within our heart should encourage us to be humble before God and merciful and kind toward people.

C. *The witness of our lips.* It is not enough just to live a good life, as important as that is. The lack of a good reputation can discredit the testimony of a witness.

It is not enough to express Christianity in generous deeds of mercy; we must also give a verbal testimony if people are to hear the gospel.

### Conclusion

If we are to be true followers of Jesus Christ, we must recognize and respond to our opportunities to bear a witness concerning him and for him to others.

---

## SUNDAY MORNING, DECEMBER 13

***Title:*** Christ the Lord

***Text:*** "For unto you is born this day in the city of David a Savior, which is Christ the Lord" **(Luke 2:11)**.

***Scripture Reading:*** Isaiah 9:6–7

***Hymns:*** "Hark! The Herald Angels Sing," Wesley
"Joy to the World! The Lord Is Come," Watts
"Ye Servants of God," Wesley

***Offertory Prayer:*** Gracious and loving Father, during this time of year we are reminded over and over of the lavishness of your gift to us in your Son, Jesus Christ. Today we bow with the wise men and present to him the gift of our love, the gift of reverent worship, the gift of grateful hearts, and the gift of dedicated lives in his service. Bless the bringing of these tithes and offerings that his name might be made known to the ends of the earth. Amen.

### Introduction

The mysterious wise men came from the East in search of the one whose birth was to usher in a new era. They came saying, "Where is he that is born King of the Jews? for we have seen his star in the east, and are come to worship him" (Matt. 2:2). The mention of an unborn babe who was to be a king aroused the jealousy and fear of Herod. The possibility of a rival king stimulated his fear to the extent that he commanded that all male children in the city of Bethlehem below two years of age were to be slain to eliminate this suspected future rival for the throne.

The title "king" in those days had a significance that is almost forgotten in our day. A king exercised authority over a nation of individuals, and according to his wishes, people perished or prospered. Today we give little thought to the title "king," because there are very few kings who exercise any authority over their subjects.

During this Christmas season it would be profitable if each of us would listen to the angelic announcement of the birth of the Christ and make a positive response to the title of King, or Lord, that was bestowed upon him at the time of his birth. In our sentimental consideration of the babe who was born in Bethlehem to be our Savior, we might miss the title that provides us with a clue to understanding the means by which he is to be the Savior of people.

Few words in our religious vocabulary have suffered a greater loss of original meaning than the word "Lord." In modern usage this word has been robbed of its original content. We let this title glide across our tongue rather glibly, as if it were nothing more than a given name. In reality it is not a name; it is a title. To use it as a name is to misrepresent its significance.

We need to understand the meaning of "Lord" that we might properly respond to the person whose birth we celebrate at this season of the year. To neglect or to refuse to respond to the implications of this title of the Savior is to deny ourselves of that which he came to accomplish in the lives of people.

The Greek word *kurios* is a word with a wide variety of meanings, each of which has significance for understanding the person and ministry of Jesus Christ.

**I. *Kurios*—"lord"—was the normal address of respect in everyday Greek.**

The modern term is *sir* in English; *herr* in German; *monsieur* in French; and *senor* in Spanish.

**II. *Kurios*—"lord"—was a title of authority.**

A. *By this title a distinction was indicated between the master and a slave.* In the ancient world, slavery was a universal practice. The population was divided into freemen and slaves. The slave's owner was a *kurios*—a master. As such, he could command the energies and efforts of his slaves. He could buy a man as a slave, and he could sell a slave that he owned to someone else. The slave was at the disposal of his *kurios*—his master.

B. *Jesus used this word to distinguish the slave from his master.* "No servant can serve two masters: for either he will hate the one, and love the other; or else he will hold to the one, and despise the other. Ye cannot serve God and mammon" (Luke 16:13).

C. *This title* Kurios— *"Lord," which the angels ascribed to the babe who was born in Bethlehem, indicated that he was one who would have the right to command.* Many of us have failed to recognize and respond to this fact.

The captain of a ship has the right of command. He is the executive officer over all that transpires on the ship. At his command the ship departs from port, and at his command the ship follows a course to his chosen destiny. The captain is lord.

The commanding officer of a military base is a lord. His authority is respected by both the officers and the enlisted personnel. He has the right of command. The people on the base pattern their lives according to his orders.

The angels said, "Unto you is born this day in the city of David, a Saviour, which is Christ the Lord." Are we guilty of anarchy and rebellion against him whom God ordained to be our Lord and Master?

**III. *Kurios*—"lord"—was used to describe absolute possession or ownership.**

He who owned a house, a field, an animal, or a slave was a lord. The word that Jesus used in describing the owner of a vineyard is this word *kurios* (Luke 20:13). This word is also used to describe the owner of the colt upon which Jesus made his triumphal entry into Jerusalem (Luke 19:33).

In announcing that Jesus Christ is Lord, the angels were actually introducing him to us as the owner of all things.

In John's gospel we read, "He came unto his own, and his own received him not" (John 1:11). He came to his own people, and they refused to recognize or respond to him. Israel's tragic response to him has been repeated over and over through the centuries. When the Lord is rejected and people are left to their own resources, they lose proper perspective.

**IV. *Kurios*—"lord"—was used to denote one who served as a guardian.**

In the ancient world, legal rights were denied to women as individuals. To engage in any business or contract or to hold possession of property, a woman had to have a guardian. This guardian could be the husband, a brother, or possibly a more distant relative. By means of a guardian, the rights of the unfortunate were protected.

There is substance for an entire sermon on the thought of Jesus Christ serving as our Guardian, Savior, and Redeemer. He protects us not only from ourselves but also from satanic forces. He is a guardian who has promised to be with us throughout all of our days in all of our ways.

**V. *Kurios*—"lord"—was the standard title of the Roman emperors. To be lord implied sovereignty, power, and authority.**

A. *By means of this title, the emperor issued orders and decrees.* Often when a pastor writes to his people he will affix his signature over his title or office as pastor. When a Roman emperor issued an edict, proclamation, or order, he would sign it with his signature and the title "*Kurios.*"

B. *This title summed up his authority in the same way that a president serves by virtue of his office and a police officer serves by virtue of his oath and uniform.* The emperor exercised his authority in more instances and far more extensively than that of any present ruler.

The angelic announcement of the Christ child's birth contained the idea that Christ was to exercise this kind of authority over the souls of people. For us to recognize this may help us to understand why Herod was concerned to the extent that he eliminated the male children in the vicinity of Bethlehem.

**VI. In the Greek translation of the Hebrew Bible, *Kurios*—"Lord"—was regularly used as the name of Israel's God.**

In the ascending scale of the various meanings of the word *kurios,* this is the highest. It is used of him whom the Hebrews considered to be their God. We are not reading too much into the angelic announcement when we declare that they were announcing that the eternal God had chosen to enter the realm of human activity through the womb of a virgin. God had chosen to clothe himself in human flesh and dwell among people to disclose the divine love, mercy, grace, power, and purpose for people.

### Conclusion

From your heart are you able to say to Jesus, "You are my Master, and I will be obedient to you as a devoted slave"? Can you honestly say, "You are my Owner, and I will let you occupy every portion and position of my life?" Can you say, "You are my Guardian upon whom I depend for protection and guidance?" Are you willing to say to him, "You are my Emperor, and because you loved me enough to die for me, I want to be faithful to you in living a life dedicated to the growth of your kingdom"?

Can you with Thomas say to Jesus, "My Lord and my God" (John 20:28)? When we make Jesus the Lord of our lives, he becomes our Savior. He brings us an inward assurance of peace and helps us to relate to others in a manner that produces peace among people.

If we are to observe this Christmas in a proper manner, we must yield the sovereignty of our lives to him who alone is Lord.

## SUNDAY EVENING, DECEMBER 13

***Title:*** The Peril of Forgetting God

***Text:*** "Beware that thou forget not the LORD thy God, in not keeping his commandments, and his judgments, and his statutes, which I command thee this day" **(Deut. 8:11)**.

***Scripture Reading:*** Deuteronomy 8:1–20

### Introduction

Most of us are forgetful at times. Sometimes it can be embarrassing or upsetting, but at other times it can be tragic. On one occasion a prospective groom forgot his marriage license. On another occasion a husband forgot that his wife had gone to town with him and discovered her absence only after he had arrived back home. Did you ever hear a parent say to a child, "You would forget your head if it were not connected to your body"?

Moses, the servant of God, warned the people against the peril of forgetting God.

### I. The warning against forgetting God.

A. *Moses warned, "Beware that thou forget not the LORD thy God" (Deut. 8:11).*

B. *The Passover feast was inaugurated that the people might be reminded annually of the great deliverance from slavery that God accomplished for Israel (Exod. 12:43).*

C. *Jesus instituted baptism and the Lord's Supper as symbolic ordinances, reminders of the mighty redemptive acts by which we are delivered from the penalty and power of sin.*

The psalmist declared that the heavens are a constant proclaimer of God's presence and power. "The heavens declare the glory of God; and the firmament sheweth his handiwork" (Ps. 19:1).

**II. Have you forgotten God?**

A. *Some people forget God in the time of peace.* When there is peace in the heart, peace in the home, and peace in the country, some are inclined to forget their need for God.

If peace has prevailed in your life, have you let this provide an occasion for you to forget him who is the source of peace?

B. *Some people forget God in the time of prosperity.*
1. They forget that it is God who gives them the power to get wealth (Deut. 8:18).
2. They ascribe their success in the material realm to their own personal ability and effort (Deut. 8:17).
3. As people become successful, they assume an attitude of self-sufficiency. Their preoccupation with material values crowds out thoughts of God.

C. *Some people forget God in the time of adversity.* Instead of rushing into the presence of God for help, some rebel and become cynical and deliberately shut God out. They forget his goodness and his promises.

D. *Some people forget God when decisions are made.* It is sad that the very source of the streams that are to vitally affect our future are forgotten. We forget to consult God. Many people will consult their relatives, their physician, their banker, and their lawyer but never think to consult God. Many of us go contrary to the suggestion of the wise man (Prov. 3:5). We lean on everything and everyone except God for guidance.
1. God should not be forgotten in the choice of a career.
2. God should not be forgotten in the choice of a companion.
3. God should not be forgotten as we seek to develop character.

**III. The fearful results of forgetting God.**

A. *People are left to their own limited human resources.*
B. *Life becomes a bitter, hopeless struggle.*
C. *Life drifts off its true course.*
D. *Life falls below its highest potential.*
E. *Life becomes confused, and fear and fatalism reign within the heart.*
F. *Life is spent in the service of lesser gods.*

**Conclusion**

God promised Israel that he would never forget them: "Can a woman forget her sucking child, that she should not have compassion on the son of her womb?

yea, they may forget, yet will I not forget thee" (Isa. 49:15). God reminds us of his presence in a multiplicity of ways. May God give us eyes that see the reminders of his presence, and may he grant us the wisdom to be responsive that we might ever remember his goodness and mercy toward us.

## WEDNESDAY EVENING, DECEMBER 16

***Title:*** Follow Me to the Cross to Suffer

***Text:*** "He said to them all, If any man will come after me, let him deny himself, and take up his cross daily, and follow me" **(Luke 9:23)**.

### Introduction

At the age of twelve, Jesus expressed an awareness of his unique relationship to God and of a divine purpose for his being in the world (Luke 2:49). Shortly before his prayer of committal from the cross, Christ cried out in joyful triumph, "It is finished" (John 19:30). The crucifixion was no accident to meet an emergency in the plan of God. Jesus spoke repeatedly of it following Peter's great confession (Matt. 16:21). Jesus left Galilee for Jerusalem and the cross against the advice of his disciples (John 11:8).

If we are to be true followers of Jesus Christ, we must face the fact that a cross is involved. During the days of Jesus, the cross was not a beautiful emblem to be worn on a chain about the neck or on a lapel. It was a thing of cruelty and a symbol of sin.

Because of the love that carried Christ to the cross, this symbol of shame has been transformed into a symbol of glory. The cross, which was a thing of cruelty, is now a symbol of mercy. Instead of being a symbol of fear, it is now a symbol of courage and inspiration.

Thomas Shepherd wrote a beautiful poem in which he asked the question, "Must Jesus bear the cross alone, and all the world go free?" He then answered that question by saying, "No, there is a cross for everyone, and there is a cross for me."

### I. Must Jesus bear the cross alone? Yes.

In a very real sense, Jesus was the only one who could bear the cross. In the hymn "There Is a Green Hill Far Away," Cecil Alexander has explained why Jesus Christ alone must bear the cross and die on it for us.

*There was no other good enough*
*To pay the price of sin.*
*He only could unlock the gate*
*Of heaven and let us in.*
*Oh, dearly, dearly has He loved,*
*And we must love Him, too.*
*And trust in His redeeming blood,*
*And try His works to do.*

Charles H. Gabriel has penned the words:

*He took my sins and my sorrows,*
*He made them His very own;*
*He bore the burden to Calv'ry,*
*And suffered, and died alone.*
*How marvelous! how wonderful!*
*And my song shall ever be;*
*How marvelous! how wonderful!*
*Is my Savior's love for me!*

Why would the sinless, spotless Son of God have to die on the cross? While he was suspended between the heavens and the earth, the wicked rulers derided him, saying, "He saved others; let him save himself, if he be Christ, the chosen of God" (Luke 23:35). The soldiers also mocked him saying, "If thou be the king of the Jews, save thyself" (Luke 23:37). And one of the malefactors railed on him saying, "If thou be the Christ, save thyself and us."

A. *Why did Jesus not come down from the cross?*
   1. It was not because he was a fake.
   2. It was not for the lack of power.
   3. It was not for the lack of assistance.

B. *Jesus bore the cross alone:*
   1. Because of God's love for a lost world.
   2. Because of the world's desperate need for a Savior.
   3. Because Jesus was the only one who could save. "For he hath made him to be sin for us, who knew no sin; that we might be made the righteousness of God in him" (2 Cor. 5:21). "For Christ also hath once suffered for sins, the just for the unjust, that he might bring us to God, being put to death in the flesh, but quickened by the Spirit" (1 Peter 3:18).

## II. Must Jesus bear the cross alone? No.

In Thomas Shepherd's beautiful hymn the answer comes: "No, there is a cross for everyone, and there is a cross for me." A multitude of people in this day have confused the burdens of life with the cross of Christ. There is a vast difference between a burden and a cross. A burden is something we have to bear, sometimes out of necessity, sometimes out of choice. Not all burdens are crosses, but every cross is a burden, which is voluntarily taken out of love for God or out of love for others and borne for the glory of God and for the good of humankind.

The cross was an instrument of death. To bear a cross was to die. For the Christian to bear his or her cross is to die to self and selfish interests and ambitions. To follow Jesus in bearing a cross is to do something more than just denying certain things to ourselves. Truly to bear a cross is to deny self. It is to say no to self and yes to the will of God.

A. *To follow Jesus in bearing the cross is to put the will of God before family relationships.* "If any man come to me, and hate not his father, and mother, and wife, and children, and brethren, and sisters, yea, and his own life also, he cannot be my disciple" (Luke 14:26).

B. *To follow Jesus in bearing the cross is to give the will of God priority over earthly possessions (Luke 14:28–33).*

C. *To follow Jesus in bearing the cross is to voluntarily assume a burden for the glory of God and for the good of needy people.*

### Conclusion

Paul wrote to the Philippian Christians, "It has been granted to you on behalf of Christ not only to believe on him, but also to suffer for him" (Phil. 1:29 NIV). These are strange words to the ears of the modern believer. Because of our instinctive desire to avoid suffering and to evade hardship, many of us have deprived ourselves of the joy of cross-bearing. It was because of the joy that was set before him that Christ endured his cross. His was to be the joy of making God's love known, of saving people from sin, and of having the approval of the heavenly Father.

If we do not follow Christ in bearing a cross, we will have no crown at the end of the road.

## SUNDAY MORNING, DECEMBER 20

***Title:*** God's Greatest Gift

***Text:*** "For unto us a child is born, unto us a son is given" **(Isa. 9:6)**.

***Hymns:*** "Jesus Shall Reign Where'er the Sun," Watts

"Angels from the Realms of Glory," Montgomery

"Glory to His Name," Hoffman

***Offertory Prayer:*** Our Father and our God, you who are the Author and Giver of every good and precious gift, to you we give thanks for your unspeakable gift to us, Jesus Christ, your Son and our Savior. Today we give ourselves and our substance in grateful worship to you. Bless these gifts to the honor and glory of your name. Amen.

### Introduction

God's greatest gift to people is often overlooked at Christmastime. Today we concentrate our attention on that gift foretold by the prophets: God's only begotten Son (Isa. 9:6).

It is the tragedy of tragedies that so few have properly related themselves to the Christ who was born in Bethlehem and laid in a manger. The wise men came asking, "Where is he that is born King of the Jews?" (Matt. 2:2). We should be asking: "Who is he?" and "What do you think of the Christ?"

Is Jesus Christ merely a mythical or legendary figure? Is he simply the most notable figure on the pages of history? His birthday gave the world a new era, dividing the past from the future at a focal point. His majesty has given the world its most immortal paintings. His love has inspired the world's masterpieces of art, sculpture, and music. His influence has inspired earth's greatest philanthropies. More books have been written about him than have been written about all of the kings who have ruled from earthly thrones.

Who is this Son whom God has given?

**I. God has given unto us a supernatural Son.**

A. *Jesus was supernaturally conceived and born of the Virgin Mary.*

B. *Christianity is built and based on a supernatural Christ.* Christianity is more than a creed or code; it is a fellowship with a risen and living Christ. Those who reject the virgin birth and explain away Christ's miracles and deny his resurrection have only a pale, weak, anemic human Christ who has no power with which to save a sinful race.

**II. God has given unto us a sinless Son.**

Christ was "in all points tempted like as we are, yet without sin" (Heb. 4:15).

A. *Christ refrained from all willful transgression.*

B. *Christ was the very essence of personal purity.*

C. *The verdict of Pilate, the Roman governor, was "I, having examined him before you, have found no fault in this man touching those things whereof ye accuse him" (Luke 23:14).*

At Jesus' baptism, God spoke from heaven, expressing the divine approval of Christ (Matt. 3:17). He made a second expression of approval at the transfiguration (Matt. 17:5). The resurrection of Christ was a public demonstration of the divine acceptance of his substitutionary death on the cross.

**III. God has given us a Son who suffered as our substitute.**

A. *The prophet Isaiah foretold the substitutionary death of the Suffering Servant of God (Isa. 53:5–6).*

B. *The angel told Joseph that Mary's unborn child was divine and that he would be the Savior of his people (Matt. 1:21).*

C. *When John the Baptist introduced Jesus to his disciples, he called him the one who would bear the sin of the world (John 1:29).*

D. *Jesus defined his objective for coming into the world in terms of giving his life as a ransom for many (Mark 10:45).*

E. *Jesus described himself as the Good Shepherd who lays down his life voluntarily for his sheep (John 10:11).*

F. *Paul declared that while we were still rebel sinners against God, God loved us and gave his Son to die for us (Rom. 5:6).*

G. *The Sinless One, by a divine decree, was made to be sin for us that he might suffer in our place, saving us from the penalty of sin (2 Cor. 5:21).*

H. *He who was rich beyond imagination became a pauper that we, through his poverty, might be made indescribably rich (2 Cor. 8:9).*

I. *God's greatest gift, his sinless Son, suffered for us sinners that he might return us to God (1 Peter 3:18).*

**IV. God has given us a Son who is an all-sufficient Savior.**

A. *He takes care of the past by the pardon of every sin and the forgiveness of every transgression.*

B. *He takes care of the present by his abiding presence.*

1. He is the mind of God speaking out to people.
2. He is the voice of God calling out to people.
3. He is the heart of God throbbing out to people.
4. He is the hand of God reaching out to people.
5. He is the Savior who can meet the deepest needs of the soul.

C. *He takes care of the future by providing a home at the end of the journey.*

### Conclusion

Have you received the royal Guest into your heart? It is time to let him in. Do not ignore him or shut him out. Accept God's greatest gift by receiving his Son as the Lord of your heart and life.

---

## SUNDAY EVENING, DECEMBER 20

***Title:*** The Peril of Shutting Out Jesus

***Text:*** "And she brought forth her firstborn son, and wrapped him in swaddling clothes, and laid him in a manager; because there was no room for them in the inn" **(Luke 2:7)**.

***Scripture Reading:*** John 1:11–12

### Introduction

Some have been critical of the innkeeper in Bethlehem because he turned away the holy family, and they were compelled to find shelter in a stable. Some have been sympathetic toward the innkeeper because he was deprived of the privilege of providing a place for the birth of the Christ child because all of the space available had already been occupied when Joseph and Mary arrived. Many sermons have been preached on the text, "There was no room for them in the inn."

Have you ever considered the possibility that we are guiltier of shutting out the Christ than was the innkeeper in Bethlehem?

John's gospel declares that Christ came to his own, and his own received him not (John 1:11). The Jewish nation rejected him as the Messiah, and in so doing they excluded themselves from the great redemptive activity of God in the world.

Thus the church became the chosen instrument by which God would make his ways known to the world.

The last written message of the living Christ to his churches is found in Revelation 2–3. These seven letters are concluded with a rather pathetic picture of the Christ on the outside standing at the door knocking and requesting entrance.

Have you shut Christ out of your life? Have you shut Christ out of your church? Many of us do so without realizing it.

### I. Have you shut Jesus out by a lack of faith in his promises?

Jesus promised his disciples, "Lo, I am with you always, even unto the end of the world" (Matt. 28:20). He also declared, "For where two or three are gathered together in my name, there am I in the midst of them" (Matt. 18:20). When you come to the house of God for prayer, praise, and proclamation, do you come expecting to experience and to respond to the living Christ? If you do not come expecting him, most likely you will miss him. By your preoccupation with your own affairs, you will miss an experience with him who conquered death and the grave.

### II. Have you shut out Jesus by cultivating a critical spirit toward others?

Fellowship with Christian friends is invaluable. Many people declare that they prefer to worship in a small church where it is possible to know and be known by all who are present. This is a legitimate desire, but if our primary emphasis is on knowing people, we may miss the presence of God. While knowing everyone present can cause us to feel comfortable, if we permit a critical spirit toward the frailties and shortcomings of others to capture our minds, our worship experience will be short-circuited. The moment we begin to exercise a critical attitude, we cease to worship and we isolate ourselves from the Christ who wishes to commune with us.

### III. Have you shut Jesus out by irreverence?

Concentration of the mind and heart on God and his will for our lives is essential for worship. It is impossible for us to chat with others and at the same time hear what the living Lord would say to our hearts. Worship, while it might take place in the midst of a huge congregation, is a very personal and private thing. Only as we have a reverent, trusting, responsive heart can we enter the throne room of God or can we let the Christ come into our hearts in all of his fullness.

### Conclusion

During this Christmas season each of us should be very certain that we have allowed the Christ to occupy the place that rightfully belongs to him in our lives. We need to avoid the possibility of following in the footsteps of the innkeeper.

## WEDNESDAY EVENING, DECEMBER 23

***Title:*** Follow Me: An Invitation to High Adventure

***Scripture Reading:*** Matthew 4:18–22

### Introduction

All of us are seeking adventure and excitement in some way or another. Many hear the call of the sea and interpret this as a command, and consequently they sail the high seas from one country to another. Others have heard the call of the wild and have spent their lives on the frontiers of human activity and progress.

Some have heard the call of the field and have spent their lives out in the open among living things. Others have heard the call of gold and find themselves chasing dollars. From time to time, some of us hear the call of the water, and we find ourselves sitting on the bank of a stream or in a boat on a lake.

If we would want the deepest satisfaction that the heart can experience, with the ear of the soul we need to hear the call of God and respond with faith and faithfulness to his love and grace for our lives. The greatest pleasure and the highest sense of self-satisfaction that one can know is to have the assurance that he knows the eternal God and that he is living his life in cooperation with God's purpose.

### I. The promise of this invitation.

"Follow me, and I will make you fishers of men" (Matt. 4:19). This invitation from our Lord is a command. Jesus was saying to these men, "I will take your techniques and your methods, and I will give you the thrill of bringing into a person's life the greatest possible joy that can come to him."

A. *The call of the sea promises excitement.*

B. *The call of the wild promises game.*

C. *The call of the field promises fruit.*

D. *The call of the water promises fish.*

E. *The call of gold promises profit.* Usually there are those among us who have responded to the call of gold with all of their minds, hearts, souls, and energy. Some of us have reaped a part of the promise of plenty, but some of us have not. A false god always promises plenty, but it never completely satisfies. It always disappoints.

F. *The call of the Lord promises souls for our rewards.* The joy and delight of helping someone experience the love, mercy, and grace of God are excelled by no other thrill and excitement. Jesus said, "If you will come and follow me, I will take you with your experience, skills, and talents and teach you and train you to become the means by which others will be saved." There is no greater service you can render an individual than to lead him to Jesus Christ as Savior.

## II. The invitation explained and applied.

Jesus is extending an invitation for people to invest their lives in that which is of present and eternal significance. Being a genuine Christian means more than attending church.

A. *If we want to follow Jesus, we must accept his attitudes.* We must accept his attitudes as our attitudes, his ideas as our ideas, his concepts as our concepts, and his values as our values. Paul said to the Philippians, "Let this mind be in you, which was also in Christ Jesus" (Phil. 2:5). Accepting the mind of Jesus Christ as our viewpoint is repentance in positive terms.

B. *If we want to follow Jesus, we must identify with his ambitions.*
   1. To do the will of God in all things. What was deep within the mind of Jesus Christ that caused him to be willing to go to the cross and die for us? He came to the world to do the will of God in all things. This was his supreme objective (Luke 22:42; John 4:34).
   2. To serve the needs of others (Mark 10:45).
   3. To make known the good news of God's love to others. For this Jesus lived, died, and arose.

C. *If we want to follow Jesus today, we must adopt his affections.* What did Jesus love?
   1. He loved God supremely.
   2. He loved people sacrificially to the extent of dying for us.

D. *If we want to follow Jesus, we must imitate his actions.* People will begin to see Jesus in us only after we think as he thought, love as he loved, and redirect our lives according to his purpose.

## III. The gracious invitation is extended.

A. *To Philip, the spiritual leader.* "The next day Jesus decided to leave for Galilee. Finding Philip, he said to him, 'Follow me'" (John 1:43 NIV).

B. *To Peter, Andrew, James, and John who were professional fishermen.* They heard and heeded the invitation of Jesus (Matt. 4:19).

C. *To Matthew the tax collector.* "As Jesus passed forth from thence, he saw a man, named Matthew, sitting at the receipt of custom: and he saith unto him, Follow me. And he arose, and followed him" (Matt. 9:9).
   1. Matthew gave up a comfortable job, but he found a destiny.
   2. Matthew lost a good income but found honor.
   3. Matthew lost a comfortable security, but he found an adventure he never could have imagined.

## Conclusion

"And they straightway left their nets and followed him." Do you suppose that Jesus' disciples ever regretted following him, accepting his attitudes, identifying with his ambitions, imitating and accepting his affections, and letting their actions become such that even their enemies took knowledge of the fact that they had been with him?

Have you ever known one man who regretted that he said yes to Christ? Have you ever known any man who wished that he could go back and go through life without Christ? Jesus satisfies the deepest hunger of the heart. Once we have received him as Lord and Savior, he will continue to lead us in personal spiritual growth and genuine worship. He will lead us to the mountainside for study and to the secret place for prayer that we might be equipped to go out into the valley of human need bearing a winning witness and bearing our cross triumphantly. And finally he will lead us into heaven to rule and reign forever.

---

## SUNDAY MORNING, DECEMBER 27

***Title:*** The Necessity of Forgetfulness

***Text:*** "Brethren, I count not myself to have apprehended: but this one thing I do, forgetting those things which are behind, and reaching forth unto those things which are before" **(Phil. 3:13)**.

***Scripture Reading:*** Philippians 3:7–14

***Hymns:*** "O for a Thousand Tongues," Wesley

"My Jesus, I Love Thee," Anonymous

"Higher Ground," Oatman

***Offertory Prayer:*** Holy Father, on this last day of the year, we thank you for the abundance of your blessings on us. We pray for more grace that we might be more worthy of your goodness toward us. We acknowledge you as the Giver of every good and perfect gift that has come to us. We bring these tithes and offerings as indications of our gratitude for present blessings and as an indication of our faith in the sufficiency of your provisions for us in the future. We thank you for the opportunity and for the ability to be givers. Through Jesus Christ our Lord. Amen.

### Introduction

Often we hear people complain about their inability to remember. Particularly is this the case concerning names. If we are to remember vividly, we must concentrate with our undivided attention.

We are told by those who have studied the human mind that nothing is ever completely forgotten. The things that we have done, said, heard, or seen are stored away in the computer of our unconsciousness. Sometimes without any deliberate effort on our part, something will happen that will provoke the computer to lift up into our conscious thought something that happened decades ago. We need to give careful attention to that which we feed into our minds and memories.

Memory is one of the most valuable faculties we possess. To be a victim of amnesia in which the past with all of its relationships is forgotten is a tragedy of indescribable proportions. One of the greatest sources of joy we possess is that of memory.

There are two sides to the coin we call memory. Memory can be a great blessing to us. There are many things we should remember, such as the goodness and faithfulness of God (Ps. 103:2), the kindness of others, the truths that make life worth living, the warnings of both God and humankind's highest wisdom (Ps. 9:17), and the high resolves that have lifted our lives closer to God.

There is also an evil side to the coin we call memory. Memory can be a devil to defeat and destroy us both in the present and in the future. In view of this, the text "forgetting the things which are behind" is most appropriate. On this last Sunday of the year, there are some things that it would be wise and profitable for us to forget.

**I. Some need to forget past success.**

A. *People have a natural tendency to want to rest on their laurels.* Consider the Pharisee (Luke 18:11–12).

B. *We should be grateful for past blessings and achievements, but we must beware lest we find ourselves looking backward rather than forward.*

C. *Paul had many achievements for which he could have been proud.* He had been a great pastor, he was a famous evangelist, he was an outstanding missionary, and he was perhaps the most influential author the world has ever known, yet he still did not count himself as having perfectly and completely achieved his destiny: "I count not myself to have apprehended."

**II. Some need to forget past failures.**

A. *Not all of us have been successful.*

B. *Some of us have had miserable failures.*

1. Personal life.
2. Family life.
3. Business life.
4. Spiritual service.

Peter disappointed his Lord. He was terribly disappointed in himself, yet he experienced the forgiveness of his Lord and then forgave himself of his failure. This enabled him to preach the great sermon on the day of Pentecost.

Jonah was a great disappointment to God, yet God gave him another chance, and Nineveh repented because of his preaching.

**III. All of us need to forget past grievances.**

A. *Do you keep a list of resentments?*

B. *Do you plan to lug all of your old grudges into the new year?*

C. *Do you continue to cultivate a quarrel with your relatives?*

D. *Are you and your spouse carrying on a running battle?*

E. *Do you have some gripe with your parents?*

F. *Are you angry with God because your life is not all that you had hoped it would be?*

Jesus pointed out the necessity of our refusing to harbor grudges in his words to Peter about forgiveness. "Then came Peter to him, and said, Lord, how oft shall my brother sin against me, and I forgive him? till seven times? Jesus saith unto him, I say not unto thee, Until seven times: but, Until seventy times seven" (Matt. 18:21–22).

Jesus' attention was focused on the well-being of the victim of the offenses. He was aware that hatred was like poison and would eat out the heart like acid.

If we are to face the new year with hope for success, we must forgive and forget past grievances.

**IV. All of us need to forget our handicaps.**

A. *Everyone has some type of handicap.* If we major on our handicaps, we will never get the job done. We must refuse to look for an alibi.

B. *A handicap can be a real blessing.* Even the apostle Paul speaks of his having a thorn in the flesh (2 Cor. 12:7). Instead of majoring on his handicap, Paul trusted more in God and found the strength that he needed for a victorious life.

**V. All of us need to forget our fears.**

A. *Do you fear tomorrow?*

B. *Do you fear failure?*

C. *Do you fear death and eternity?*

### Conclusion

The way to forgetfulness is by the pathway of forgiveness. To forgive means to refuse to retaliate and at the same time to restore warm feelings. We need to forgive others. We need to forgive ourselves, and by so doing we will have made greater progress toward forgetting things that would hinder and drag us down as we try to walk into an unknown tomorrow with God.

*It is better to walk in the dark with God,*
*Than walk alone in the light.*
*It is better to walk with Him by faith,*
*Than walk alone by sight.*

—*Lucy A. Bennett*

## SUNDAY EVENING, DECEMBER 27

***Title:*** The Peril of Being Shortsighted

***Text:*** "Ponder the path of thy feet, and let all thy ways be established" **(Prov. 4:26)**.

### Introduction

Most of us are afflicted with eye trouble. We are shortsighted. We refuse to look ahead and see the destination to which our pathway inevitably leads. We labor under the impression that we can choose a way of life that is detrimental yet think that we can escape the destination to which that way of life leads.

Most of us would like to arrive at a successful destiny in life. We know that to achieve this goal we must follow the path of self-discipline and self-denial of things that would distract us and prevent us from achieving that which is most important.

Most of us are like the child who prefers a quarter in preference to the promise of fifty cents tomorrow. We are like the student who chooses an easy course that requires little effort to the more profitable course that requires rigid self-discipline for mastery. Many young people make a tragic mistake in selecting a companion in marriage when they follow the romantic impulse of the moment instead of taking the long look concerning what marriage really involves.

Many of us have made the same mistake that the young couple made who yielded to the appeals of high-pressured advertising and purchased an abundance of things that were really not essential and found themselves on a financial precipice. Life would be much different if each of us would ponder the path of our feet, giving consideration to the ultimate outcome of our present-day attitudes, ambitions, and actions.

Moses prayed for Israel, "O that they were wise, that they understood this, that they would consider their latter end!" (Deut. 32:29). The psalmist prayed, "LORD, make me to know mine end, and the measures of my days, what it is; that I may know how frail I am" (Ps. 39:4) All of us could profitably join with the psalmist in praying, "So teach us to number our days, that we may apply our hearts unto wisdom" (90:12). An awareness of the beauty of life could impress us with the preciousness of life and with the urgency of the present, for our destiny tomorrow is wrapped up in the decisions of today.

Repeatedly Haggai urged the people of his day to "consider your ways" (Hag. 1:5, 7). Are they wise? Are they profitable? Will your ways lead to the right destination?

**I. Ponder the path of thy feet.**

A. *It is not enough to desire the right destination.* Balaam prayed, "Let me die the death of the righteous, and let my last end be like his!" (Num. 23:10). While Balaam prayed this prayer, he failed to achieve his desired destiny.

B. *We can all be self-deceived.* The wise man said, "All the ways of a man are clean in his own eyes; but the LORD weigheth the spirits. Commit thy works unto the LORD, and thy thoughts shall be established" (Prov. 16:2–3). While recognizing the peril of self-deception, he advises us that the only way by which we can escape this peril is deliberately to commit our ways unto God to let him establish the thoughts by which we decide the course of our lives.

C. *The Word of God is a safe guide for our feet.* "He that refuseth instruction despiseth his own soul: but he that heareth reproof getteth understanding" (Prov. 15:32). The Word of God will speak both words of criticism and words of commendation to those who read it reverently with a desire to do God's will in all of their lives.

### II. Ask for the old paths.

When Jeremiah served as God's spokesman to his nation, he counseled both the nation and the individuals, "Stand at the crossroads and look; ask for the ancient paths, ask where the good way is, and walk in it, and you will find rest for your souls" (Jer. 6:16 NIV). The prophet would speak to each of us and say, "Stop, look and listen. Take the long look."

A. *Every road leads to a destination.*
   1. The heavily traveled road may lead to the wrong destination.
   2. The novel, adventuresome road could lead to certain death.

B. *Where is the good way?*
   1. All old roads are not good roads.
   2. The good road is always an old road because it has been tested and proven to lead to the right destination.

### III. And walk therein.

A. *It is not sufficient just to have a thorough knowledge of the good road.*

B. *It is not enough to have great admiration for the good road and for those who walk therein.*

C. *It is not worthy of commendation merely to make plans to get on the good road.*

D. *One must make the decision to sever all hindering connections and get on the good road with an attitude of dedication and determination to follow the road that leads to the life abundant through faith in God and faithfulness to God.*

### Conclusion

Jesus said, "I am the way, the truth, and the life: no man cometh unto the Father, but by me" (John 14:6). He is the way out of the wilderness of sin. He is the way through an uncertain tomorrow. He is the way into the family of God. He is the way up to the highest possible manhood and womanhood in this life and to the home of the heavenly Father in the life beyond. Accept Christ as your Savior, and you are on your way. Accept Christ as your Savior, and you will have the truth. Let Jesus Christ become your Savior and Lord, and you will live.

---

## WEDNESDAY EVENING, DECEMBER 30

***Title:*** What Is Your Prayer?

***Text:*** "We must all appear before the judgment seat of Christ, that each one may receive what is due him for the things done while in the body, whether good or bad" (**2 Corinthians 5:10 NIV**).

### Introduction

Our text declares that one day each of our Lord's disciples will appear before his judgment seat to give an account of his stewardship. Our Lord, who has saved us by his grace, and who has given us the gift of eternal life, wishes to bestow upon us rewards for faithful service. It is wonderful to think that our God loves us and saves us by grace and assures us of an eternal home, and that in addition he wants to reward us for the service we render. It is sad to contemplate that there are some who could suffer the loss of rewards by their failure to achieve the potential God has planned for them. What does God's record say concerning your achievements, services, and ministries? The record that you have made is now history. You cannot go back and change yesterday, but you can plan to move ahead today.

### I. Your record.

If you could write a record of your achievements, what would it say?

### II. Achievements are never accidental.

Have you ever known a concert pianist who achieved that position accidentally? Have you ever known anyone to secure a college degree without having made plans to do so? Have you ever known anyone to accumulate a significant amount of money in a savings account without making plans and following through on those plans with regular deposits? Significant achievement, materially or spiritually, is the result of both decisions and determination to carry through to a successful conclusion.

### III. What do you pray that you might accomplish?

As you contemplate reporting to the Lord concerning your ministry for him, do you have any burdens of concern for which you are praying and for which you would like this congregation to join you in prayer? Individual Christians cannot achieve all that they want to achieve without the encouragement and assistance of the other members of the body of Christ with whom they associate, worship, witness, and minister. In the remaining part of this service and time of prayer, let each of you who will, share with the congregation the one great prayer of your heart as you contemplate your individual responsibility toward God and your responsibility to your church as a servant of God.

If you will, please stand and give voice to the concern of your heart about which you will be praying and for which you would like to request the prayers of the other members of this congregation.

***Closing Prayer:*** Heavenly Father, you have heard these sincere expressions of deep desire from the hearts of your people. We believe that these burdens of concern have been bestowed upon us by your Holy Spirit. We want to follow in the footsteps of our living Lord by responding to every impulse of your Holy Spirit. Help us to think with the mind of Christ. Help us to love with the heart of Christ. Help us to let our feet take us to where he would have us to go. We yield our wills to him for the rendering of ministries of mercy. Amen.

# *Miscellaneous Helps*

## MESSAGES ON THE LORD'S SUPPER

***Title:*** Looking at the Lord's Supper

***Scripture Reading:*** Matthew 26:26–30

### Introduction

On the night before his crucifixion, our Lord Jesus observed the Passover with his disciples in the upper room. Following the departure of Judas Iscariot, he instituted the ordinance that we know as the Lord's Supper. This significant ordinance crystallizes the gist of the gospel. It symbolizes the substitutionary and redemptive death of the Son of God. With reverent awe let us look at this ordinance in several different ways as we prepare to participate in a worthy manner.

### I. We should look backward.

In deep meditation and in complete consecration, we should look backward to the atoning Christ whose body was slain and whose blood was shed for our redemption from sin (Heb. 9:22–26; 1 Peter 1:18–19; 1 John 1:7).

### II. We should look upward.

With an attitude of reverent submission, we should look upward to the Christ who has been exalted to a position of lordship over all things (Phil. 2:5–11). The Christ who died on the cross now sits on the throne. He has been appointed by God to occupy the throne of the heart of each of us. He alone is worthy to have complete sovereignty over our will. If we would properly partake of the elements of the Lord's Supper, we should earnestly seek to make him the Lord of our lives.

### III. We should look inward.

With the purest motives possible, we should look into our own hearts and request divine help to purge out every attitude or ambition that is contrary to the mind and spirit of our Lord. In sincere repentance, with genuine love, and with deep gratitude, we should recall how Jesus Christ died that we might live. He became poor that we might be rich. He gave his all that we might have all of the grace and goodness of God.

### IV. We should look forward.

"For as often as ye eat this bread, and drink this cup, ye do show the Lord's death till he come" (1 Cor. 11:26).

Our Savior came first as a peasant. He will come the second time as the Prince of God. He came the first time in great humility. He will come the second time in great glory and power. He came the first time to occupy a cross. He will come the second time to occupy a throne before which every knee shall bow and every tongue shall confess that he is Lord of Lords.

### Conclusion

We look backward, we look inward, we look upward, and we look forward in faith and love and gratitude and hope. With all of our minds, hearts, and souls, let us concentrate on what our Lord did for us on the cross as we partake of the elements that symbolize the giving of his body and his life for our salvation.

---

***Title:*** Why Did Jesus Die?

***Text:*** "For as often as ye eat this bread, and drink this cup, ye do show the Lord's death till he come" **(1 Cor. 11:26)**.

### Introduction

The day that Christ was crucified was the darkest day the world has ever witnessed. On that day humankind revolted against the love of God, refused to accept Christ as God's Son, and slew him by nailing him to a cross.

In spite of the awfulness of humankind's terrible sin of crucifying the Savior, the disciples came to understand that, in the death of their Lord, God had done his kindest work for humankind. It would be appropriate for us to raise the question, "Why would the sinless, stainless, spotless Son of God have to die? Why did he institute a meal in which the elements were given great symbolic significance with a design of perpetuating the memory of his death on the cross?" To have the correct answer is to have the key to the Christian religion. To understand Christ's death is to discover the essence of Christianity. To grasp the significance of his sacrificial death is to understand the heart of God's revelation of his love and mercy.

### I. Jesus Christ died on the cross to reveal the evil nature of sin.

Not only in our age, but in every age, people have been inclined to minimize and excuse sin. There are many who deny that there is any such thing as sin. There are others who joke about sin and treat it lightly. Others tolerate and coddle sin in their own hearts and lives.

Jesus died on the cross because of our sin. Had humans not been sinners, it would not have been necessary for him to die. If sin were not something terrible, dark, and destructive, Calvary would not have been necessary.

If there had been no dread malady in the heart that causes people to depart from God and live a life of waste and ruin, then Jesus Christ died as an unrealistic idealist.

It is the testimony of the Scripture that Christ died for our sins (1 Cor. 15:3; 1 Peter 2:24; 3:18).

We should let the elements of the Lord's Supper speak to us concerning the deadly, destructive, evil nature of our sin that required the death of Jesus Christ for our deliverance and forgiveness.

### II. Jesus Christ died on the cross to redeem and save us (Mark 10:45).

A. *Jesus was the perfect substitute.* He died to ransom us from sin (Mark 10:45).
B. *He is the Good Shepherd who gave his life for his sheep.*
C. *The Sinless One assumed the burden of our sin and suffered in our place that we might obtain his perfect righteousness (1 Cor. 5:21).*

### III. Jesus Christ died on the cross to enlist and inspire our service.

A. *Because Christ died for our sins, we should be inspired to die to sin and to devote our lives to a life of righteousness, both in relationship to God and in our conduct toward our fellow humans (1 Peter 2:24).*
B. *Next to our salvation, the privilege of service is the greatest gift of God to humankind (Phil. 1:29; Rom. 12:1).*
C. *Gratitude for God's unspeakable gifts, through the Savior who was willing to die and who triumphantly lives again, should cause us to dedicate ourselves in service to him.*

### Conclusion

As we partake of the bread, which symbolizes Christ's body, and the wine, which symbolizes his blood, let us dedicate our lives and bodies to the Savior.

---

## THEMES FOR WEDDING CEREMONIES

***Title:*** In All Thy Ways

***Text:*** Proverbs 3:5–6

### Introduction

The words of the wise man are applicable for all persons in all seasons and under all circumstances. At no time are his suggestions better than when a man and woman leave their separate ways of life and join together to begin a new way of life.

On this occasion we should trust in the Lord and recognize that marriage is part of his benevolent plan and purpose for us. Marriage is more than a human arrangement; it is a divine provision for the welfare of the race and for the fulfillment and happiness of the individuals involved.

A wedding is a significant time for the couple involved, for their families, for their church, and for the community as a whole. We come together to hear a young couple solemnly pledge before God and witnesses their firm and steadfast decision to assume not only the rights but the responsibilities that are associated with marriage.

The writer of Proverbs declares that if we will but recognize and acknowledge the Lord in all of our ways, he will make our paths straight and lead us in a manner that will help us achieve the happiness and success for which our hearts hunger. Give him first place in your love and loyalty. Give your companion a love and loyalty second only to your Lord. Place your own wishes and well-being in a position subordinate to the will of God and to the happiness of your companion. If each of you will determine to love God supremely and serve him steadfastly, if you will determine to give your companion the happiness that genuine love always wishes, you will discover that you are achieving both happiness and success as time goes by.

## The Ceremony

If you, then, _____and _____, have freely and deliberately chosen each other as partners in this holy estate and know of no just cause why you should not be so united, in token thereof you will please join your right hands.

*Groom's Vow:* _____, in taking the woman you hold by the right hand to be your lawful and wedded wife, before God and the witnesses present you must promise to love her; to honor and cherish her in that relation; and leaving all others, cleave only unto her and be to her in all things a true and faithful husband so long as you both shall live. Do you so promise? (*Answer:* "I do.")

*Bride's Vow:* _____, in taking the man you hold by the right hand to be your lawful and wedded husband, before God and the witnesses present you must promise to love him; to honor and cherish him in that relation; and leaving all others, cleave only unto him and be to him in all things a true and faithful wife so long as you both shall live. Do you so promise? (*Answer:* "I do.")

*Pastor's Response:* Then are you each given to the other in advances or reverses, in poverty or in riches, in sickness and in health, to love and to cherish, until death shall part you.

*The Ring(s):* For unnumbered centuries the ring has been used on important occasions. It has reached its loftiest prestige in the symbolic significance it vouches at the marriage altar. It is a perfect circle having no end. It symbolizes your desire, our desire, and God's desire, that there be no end to the happiness and success for which your heart hungers. It is thus a symbol of the unending plan and purpose of God for your happiness and well-being.

*Pastor's Question:* Do you give these rings to each other as a token of your love for each other? (*Answer:* "We do.")

*Pastor's Question:* Will each of you receive this ring as a token of your companion's love for you, and will you wear it as a token of your love for your companion? (*Answer:* "We will.")

*Closing Proclamation:* Here in the presence of your parents, your relatives, and your friends; here in the presence of the living God, you have made vows. These vows are binding upon you by the laws of this state. They are binding upon you by the law of God. And they are binding upon you by the law of your own love for each other. You have sealed these vows by the giving and receiving of rings. Acting in the authority vested in me as a minister of the gospel by this state, and looking to heaven for divine sanction, I now pronounce you husband and wife. What therefore God hath joined together do not let anything put asunder. Amen.

---

***Title:*** Walk in Love

***Text:*** "Be ye therefore followers of God, as dear children; and walk in love, as Christ also hath loved us, and hath given himself for us an offering and a sacrifice to God for a sweet-smelling savour" **(Eph. 5:1–2)**.

**Introduction**

Paul encouraged the disciples of our Lord at Ephesus to walk in love. Jesus had commanded his disciples to live by the principle of love (John 13:34–35). Unselfish, sacrificial love was to be the badge of identification by which the world would recognize his disciples as his followers.

Human beings need love more than anything else in the world. A famous physician has said, "We must learn to practice love or we will perish." The human spirit was made for love. Without love a personality withers and dies like a water lily transplanted in a desert. In no relationship is the practice of Christlike love more necessary or more productive of happiness than in the marriage relationship.

In Paul's great hymn of love recorded in 1 Corinthians 13, he declares that love is more important than any other gift or ability or activity. He sets forth some of the characteristics of Christian love.

**I. Christian love is very patient (v. 4).**

**II. Christian love is very kind (v. 4).**

**III. Christian love never boils with jealousy (v. 4).**

**IV. Christian love is never envious (v. 4).**

**V. Christian love does not cherish inflated ideas of its own importance (v. 4).**

**VI. Christian love is never rude, unmannerly, or indecent (v. 5).**

**VII. Christian love is never self-seeking, nor does it pursue selfish aims (v. 5).**

**VIII. Christian love is never quick to take offense and keeps no score of wrongs (v. 5).**

**IX. Christian love is never glad when others go wrong (v. 6).**

**X. Christian love always rejoices when truth prevails (v. 6).**

**XI. Christian love can overlook faults and is always hopeful for the best (v. 7).**

**XII. Christian love keeps on loving in spite of some things that are unlovable (v. 8).**

(The actual ceremony should follow this brief study of the nature of Christian love as set forth in 1 Cor. 13:4–8).

**The Ceremony**

Dearly beloved, we are assembled here in the presence of God to join this man and this woman in holy marriage, which is instituted of God, regulated by his commandments, blessed by our Lord Jesus Christ, and to be held in honor among all people. Let us therefore reverently remember that God has established and sanctified marriage for the welfare and happiness of humankind. Our Savior has declared that a man shall leave his father and mother and cleave unto his wife.

By his apostles God has instructed those who enter into this relationship to cherish a mutual esteem and love; to bear with each other's infirmities and weaknesses; to comfort each other in sickness, trouble, and sorrow; in honesty and industry to provide for each other and for their household in temporal things; to pray for and encourage each other in the things that pertain to God; and to live together as heirs of the grace of life.

*Question addressed to Bride's Father:* Who gives this woman to be married to this man? (*Answer:* "I do" or "Her mother and I.")

*The Pastor Speaks to the Couple:* If it is your sincere and steadfast desire to assume the rights and responsibilities of holy marriage, you will so indicate by joining your right hands.

*Groom's Vow:* ____, wilt thou have this woman to be thy wife, and wilt thou pledge thy troth to her, in all love and honor, in all duty and service, in all faith and tenderness, to live with her and cherish her, according to the ordinance of God, in the holy bond of marriage? (*Answer:* "I do.")

*Bride's Vow:* _____, wilt thou have this man to be thy husband, and wilt thou pledge thy troth to him, in all love and honor, in all duty and service, in all faith and tenderness, to live with him and cherish him, according to the ordinance of God, in the holy bond of marriage? (*Answer:* "I do.")

*Vows:* (The bride and the groom shall each repeat the following vows.) I, _____, take thee _____, to be my wedded wife [husband]; and I do promise and covenant, before God and these witnesses, to be thy loving and faithful husband [wife] in plenty and in want, in joy and in sorrow, in sickness and in health, as long as we both shall live.

*The Ring(s):* (Groom) This ring I give thee in token and pledge of our constant faith and abiding love. (If it is a double ring ceremony, the bride should repeat this also as she places the ring on the finger of her groom.)

*After offering a prayer for the blessings of God upon the couple, the pastor will say the following:* By the authority vested in me as a minister of the gospel, I now declare that you are husband and wife according to the ordinance of God and the law of this state in the name of the Father, and of the Son, and of the Holy Spirit. What God hath joined together, let no man put asunder.

## MEDITATIONS FOR FUNERAL SERVICES

***Title:*** Comfort Concerning Those Who Are Asleep

***Scripture Reading:*** 1 Thessalonians 4:13–18

### Introduction

Comfort is needed when death invades our presence and takes from our midst one who was near and dear to us. Comfort is needed as we think of the departed. Comfort is needed because of our loss. Comfort is needed as we face the future.

In times like this, we can rejoice in the comfort that is available to us through faith in Jesus Christ. In 2 Corinthians Paul emphasizes this great truth concerning the comfort that comes from God to those who suffer: "Grace be to you and peace from God our Father, and from the Lord Jesus Christ. Blessed be God, even the Father of our Lord Jesus Christ, the Father of mercies, and the God of all comfort; who comforteth us in all our tribulation, that we may be able to comfort them which are in any trouble, by the comfort wherewith we ourselves are comforted of God" (vv. 2–4).

### I. God does not want us to be overly concerned about those who die in the Lord (1 Thess. 4:13).

Paul wrote so that the Thessalonians might be informed. He was eager to dispel their doubts and their fears. While recognizing that it was normal and proper for them to know sorrow, he declared that the sorrow of the Christian should be different from the sorrow of "others which have no hope."

### II. The dead in Christ are with the Lord.

As Paul anticipates the visible and victorious return of the Lord Jesus Christ, he declares that those who have died in the faith will come with the Lord when he returns (1 Thess. 4:14).

Paul sought to encourage the saints in Corinth by saying, "If our earthly house of this tabernacle were dissolved, we have a building of God, an house not made with hands, eternal in the heavens" (2 Cor. 5:1).

Paul declares that while we remain at home in our physical body, in a very real sense we are absent from the Lord (2 Cor. 5:6). He saw death as the experience by which the believer moved out of his physical body to "be present with the Lord" (v. 8).

### III. Victory over death and the grave is promised to those who know Jesus Christ (I Thess. 4:15–16).

The resurrection of Jesus Christ from the dead was the firstfruits of the final resurrection of all of those who respond to God through faith (1 Cor. 15:23). The term *firstfruits* is a technical term that referred to the first of all ripe fruits that were to be offered in God's house as an act of recognition and allegiance to God who was the giver of all good things. By using this term in reference to the resurrection of Christ, the apostle was seeking to communicate the truth that "for as in Adam all die, even so in Christ shall all be made alive" (v. 22). This is to take place when Christ returns to the earth (v. 23).

### IV. Separation will be a thing of the past in eternity: "So shall we ever be with the Lord" (I Thess. 4:17).

There are many causes for sorrow and grief in this life. Perhaps among these is separation from those we love. This is true when husband and wife are separated. This is true when parents are separated from children. This is true when friends are separated. One of the wonderful things about heaven is that there will be no more separation from God and from those whom we love as his children.

John described the conditions that will prevail in heaven: "God shall wipe away all tears from their eyes; and there shall be no more death, neither sorrow, nor crying, neither shall there be any more pain: for the former things are passed away" (Rev. 21:4).

### Conclusion

Paul encouraged the Thessalonian Christians to find comfort in these precious promises. The comfort he speaks of is more than the result of recalling pleasant memories of the past. He is challenging them to face the future with faith, courage, and good cheer in the assurance that death has achieved no final victory and that the grave must one day surrender its victim.

Let us be still and know that God is real. He is concerned with our heartaches and our heartbreaks. He has sent his Son Jesus Christ to taste death for us. He raised Christ back to life that he might deliver us from the fear of death (Heb. 2:14–15). In the midst of our sorrow, let us rejoice in the grace and goodness of God and take courage for the living of these days.

---

***Title:*** Memorial Service for a Christian Who Died in the Service of His Country

***Scripture Reading:*** Psalms 23; 46; John 14:1–6

### I. Biographical sketch.

A. *Vital information concerning birth and family.*

B. *Information concerning conversion, baptism, and church membership.*

C. *Information concerning military career, achievements, honors.*

### II. Sober thoughts for us all.

A. *We memorialize one who has stood between us and the enemy.*

B. *We memorialize one who dedicated his life, like millions of others, to preserve our freedom.*

C. *We memorialize one who has made the supreme sacrifice for his country.*

1. His wife has also made a great sacrifice.
2. His children have made a great sacrifice.
3. His parents have made a sacrifice.

D. *We memorialize one who has died that we might be free.*

1. We are not free to forget.
2. We are not free to waste.
3. We are not free to lose what he died to preserve.

### Conclusion

Because of his sacrifice and the sacrifice of many others, we remain free. We are free to live, love, worship, and serve. We are free to preserve and to perpetuate those values for which he gave his life. Let each of us dedicate ourselves to our God and to the ideals for which our country stands that his death might not be in vain.

For both our comfort and our strength as we face the future, let us look by faith to our final home where there will be no more suffering and separation or sadness. Through faith in Jesus Christ, we can be a part of that heavenly family (Rev. 21:1–4).

---

Title: Graveside Service for an Infant

### Introduction

For comfort, for mercy, for help in this time of need, let us allow God to speak to us from the Scriptures.

### I. Matthew 18:1–5.

### II. Matthew 19:13–15.

### III. Matthew 18:10–14.

### IV. Isaiah 40:11.

In this passage the Good Shepherd is pictured as having a special concern for the lambs. He gently carries them in his bosom. This picture of our wonderful Savior can bring glad comfort to our hearts in this time of need.

### V. Second Samuel 12:22–23.

A. *While David's child was alive, David did all that could possibly be done for him.*

B. *When the child died, David faced and accepted the fact that the child could not be brought back.*
C. *David was comforted by the faith that he would someday go to be where his infant child had gone in death.*

### Conclusion

We cannot bring the child back to us, but through faith in our wonderful Lord, we can have the assurance that we can go to be with this little one. Because we know that God loves us and because we know that our God is the God who never makes a mistake, let each of us face the future with faith in his goodness. He will be present to help us. By his grace he will meet the deepest needs of our lives.

## MESSAGES FOR CHILDREN AND YOUNG PEOPLE

***Title:*** "Honor Your Father and Mother"

***Text:*** "Honor your father and mother"—which is the first commandment with a promise" (Eph. 6:2 NIV).

### Introduction

When Paul wrote to the children and young people of Ephesus urging them to honor their parents, he was actually quoting from the Ten Commandments that God had given to Israel through Moses.

How can you honor your father and mother? Was the apostle Paul encouraging children and young people to build a monument in honor of their parents? Was he suggesting that they write a biography to eulogize their parents? Most likely he was suggesting that they conduct themselves in a manner so as to bring both satisfaction and delight to their parents.

Children usually are on the receiving end in the parent-child relationship. The parents provide the home, food, clothing, and most of the other things that are enjoyed in childhood. Parents themselves think more in terms of what they can give to their children than they do in terms of what they can receive from their children.

Have you ever stopped to think about how you might be able to bring the greatest possible joy to your parents? There are great limitations placed on what you can give to your parents by virtue of the fact that you have very little money to spend for gifts. Paul would probably make some very practical suggestions to you such as the following.

### I. You can honor your parents and bring great delight to them by an attitude and habit of obedience (Eph. 6:1).

A. *One of the Ten Commandments requires that children be obedient to their parents (Exod. 20:12).* If you do not learn to practice obedience at home toward your parents, you will not know how to obey the rules of your classroom at school, the laws of your country, or the laws of God. Every parent will take pride in and be delighted by an obedient child.

B. *The love that you have in your heart toward your parents can best express itself by an attitude of obedience.* There is no substitute for obedience. To be disobedient is not only to upset your parents, but such an attitude will bring you trouble throughout life.

**II. You can honor your parents and bring great delight to them by expressing gratitude.**

How long has it been since you sincerely thanked your parents for the many things that they do for you? Your parents gave you life. They have loved you and cared for you when you were unable to care for yourself. They have spent vast sums of money for your well-being. Most likely they are providing, at personal sacrifice, for your future well-being. The best way to express gratitude is with a gift from time to time as you become aware of what your parents have done and are doing for your welfare. An attitude of gratitude is not only a mark of courtesy, it is a practice that brings real delight into the hearts of others.

**III. You can honor your parents and bring great delight to their hearts by making your contribution to the well-being of the family.**

Did it ever occur to you that as a child you have a contribution to make toward the happiness and success of the family unit? Are you as regular in fulfilling your duties, such as keeping your room clean, discharging various chores, doing your homework, etc., as you would like for your father to be in the matter of providing you with money for an allowance or other things that you would like to have? Do you try to make your mother and father happy as you would like for them to make you happy? What is your contribution toward the happiness of your father and mother? What can you do to help the home operate more smoothly?

**IV. You can honor your parents and bring great delight to their hearts by doing your best in your work.**

By work we are not thinking in terms of your securing a job and earning a living. A part of the responsibility of parents is that of providing the material resources needed until you reach maturity and independence. Even though you do not have a job that pays a salary, you still have work to do. Have you ever thought of your schoolwork in terms of your job as your parents think of their professions? Even at an early age you should recognize that you have a mission in life and that adequate preparation is necessary. Your Lord wants you to do your best, and your own heart hungers for the best.

**V. You can honor your parents and bring great delight to their hearts by deciding for Christian conduct on all occasions.**

In some respects it is much more difficult for a person to be genuinely Christian in this day and time than it was several decades ago. There are many voices that would invite you to walk in paths of pleasure that can produce nothing but pain and disappointment. The demands of the crowd will be with us as long as we live. Instead of letting the pressure of the crowd or the whim of the moment be the determining factor of your conduct, make Jesus Christ your Leader, Guide, and Helper in every circumstance.

## Conclusion

These five practical suggestions have been offered for your consideration as you seek from day to day to be what God would have you to be. Your following these suggestions will cause your parents to rejoice, and you will accomplish far more in life than you would have if you had you made no firm decision concerning your responsibilities and opportunities within the home.

---

Title: The Experience of Zacchaeus

***Scripture Reading:*** Luke 19:1–10

## Introduction

Zacchaeus was a publican, which meant that he collected taxes for the Romans in a certain area of his country. His cooperation with the Roman army and his profiteering at the expense of his fellow countrymen made him, like all the other publicans, hated by the people of his community.

One day it became known that Jesus was going to pass through Jericho on his way to Jerusalem. Since he was the most famous person in all of the country, everyone wanted to see him as he passed through. Zacchaeus heard that Jesus was coming, and like the others, he wanted to see this famous teacher and miracle worker who was considered by some to be the Son of God.

The crowds surrounding Jesus as he passed through Jericho were so great that Zacchaeus was at a great disadvantage, for he was a short man. He needed to think of a way to see Jesus.

Suddenly it occurred to Zacchaeus that if he were to climb up in a sycamore tree along the way by which Jesus was to come, he would be able to see Jesus without being harmed by the press of the crowd. Little did he realize what was in store for him.

Jesus was the Friend of sinners. His eyes were constantly open to see the needs of those about him. His ears were open to hear the heart cry of those who were lonely and distressed. His ministry was intended to be a blessing, not only to the good and innocent, but also to the guilty and the outcast. As Jesus approached the sycamore tree, he looked up and saw the rich publican perched on a limb looking down. Let us try to imagine some of the thoughts that passed through the mind of Zacchaeus.

## I. Zacchaeus thought, "He sees me."

Never had Zacchaeus felt so conspicuous as he did when Jesus lifted his loving eyes with penetrating insight and looked up to see Zacchaeus sitting on a limb. Zacchaeus was shocked and embarrassed and wished that he could disappear.

Did it ever occur to you that Jesus also sees you? He sees you right now. He saw you yesterday. His loving eye was upon you a year ago. He sees the secret unspoken thoughts of your mind. He sees the emotions that surge through your heart.

## II. Zacchaeus thought, "He knows me."

As Jesus looked up and saw Zacchaeus, he called him by name and said, "Zacchaeus, make haste, and come down; for today I must abide at thy house" (Luke 19:5). It could be that they had met before. It could be that Zacchaeus had attended the banquet that Matthew had had following his conversion (Luke 5:29). It is possible that Zacchaeus had been present on some occasions when Jesus had spoken and someone had informed Jesus concerning who he was. Zacchaeus was overwhelmed with the thought, "He knows me." Jesus knew his name.

Did it ever occur to you that Jesus knows you? He knows your birthday. He knows the grades that you make at school. He knows your middle name. He knows your nickname. He knows everything about you.

## III. Zacchaeus thought, "He loves me."

Most of the people in Jericho hated Zacchaeus. They would not walk down the street with him or invite him into their homes. They treated him as a traitor to his country. He could see hate in their eyes and on their faces.

There was something in Jesus' face and in his tone of voice that warmed the heart of Zacchaeus. He rejoiced in the assurance of God's love for him.

Are you aware that Jesus loves you in spite of the fact that in many ways you are unlovely and unlovable? He loves you to the extent that he was willing to die on the cross for your sins. He loves you and wants you to let him come into your heart so that he can bestow upon you the blessings of God. He will always love you, not because of your loveliness, but because God is love.

## IV. Zacchaeus thought, "He wants me."

Zacchaeus rushed to get down from the limb of the sycamore tree. With great haste and joy he led Jesus to his home. During their conversation Zacchaeus was overwhelmed with the thought that despite the fact that he sees me and knows all about me, he still loves me and wants me. He found this difficult to believe.

Are you aware that Jesus not only sees you and knows you but that he also loves you and wants you?

## V. Zacchaeus decided, "He can have me."

Zacchaeus was fortunate that he was short, for this led him to climb the sycamore tree to see Jesus. Jesus saw Zacchaeus, knew him, loved him, and wanted him.

Zacchaeus made the wisest decision of his life when he decided to turn his heart, home, life, and business over to the will of God. He made Jesus his Lord, and Jesus said to him, "This day is salvation come to this house." Zacchaeus determined to live a life of honesty and kindness and charity toward others (Luke 19:9).

You would be wise to follow the example of Zacchaeus in his decision to let Jesus Christ have first place in his heart and life. You can be certain that Zacchaeus never regretted his decision. And you can be certain that you will never regret your decision to let Jesus Christ be your Lord and Leader in your life.

---

***Title:*** "Speak, Lord, for Thy Servant Heareth"

***Scripture Reading:*** 1 Samuel 3:1–10

## Introduction

God's dealings with us are always wonderful. There is something both mysterious and miraculous about the way in which God speaks to the hearts of people.

The Scripture that we have read describes how God communicated with a boy who was eventually to become a great prophet and a great leader of his people. There are several interesting things in this story that are profitable for your consideration.

## I. Samuel was living away from his parents (1 Sam. 2:11, 18, 26; 3:1).

Samuel had been given to his parents in response to his mother's prayer for a child. His mother, above all things, had desired the privilege of being a mother. She prayed earnestly for a child, and God heard her prayer. In gratitude she dedicated Samuel to the service of God. He began his training at a very early age in the temple service.

God may speak to you in your home. He can also speak to you when you are away from home, at church, or while you are at school or camp.

## II. God spoke to Samuel while he was just a child (1 Sam. 3:1).

We cannot know exactly what Samuel's age was when the voice of God came to him. He could have been ten or fifteen or possibly eighteen. The significant thing is that God spoke to him while he was still a child. Some think that God speaks only to those who are mature. Others insist that God speaks only through the aged. If God spoke to Samuel while he was but a youth, it follows that God will speak to boys and girls and young men and young women today.

## III. The voice of God came to Samuel in the silence of the night (1 Sam. 3:3).

Perhaps Samuel heard God speak to him in the silence of the night because he was too busy during the day to hear God's voice. The psalmist said, "Be still, and know that I am God" (Ps. 46:10)

A. *God always speaks softly.* He never raises his voice. He never shouts or screams at us. He speaks with a still, small voice that can be heard only by those who seek the nearness and the silence of communion with him in prayer and meditation.

B. *God always speaks personally.* His messages to us are directed to our individual needs.

### IV. Samuel did not recognize the voice of God immediately.

A. *The first time God spoke (1 Sam. 3:4).*
B. *The second time God spoke (1 Sam. 3:6).*
C. *The third time God spoke (1 Sam. 3:8).*
D. *The fourth time God spoke (1 Sam. 3:10).*

Did it ever occur to you that God has been seeking to speak to your heart? Is it possible that you have not heard him?

### V. Samuel needed help to recognize and understand the voice of God.

All of us do.

A. *Many times parents can help you recognize and understand the voice of God as he speaks to you.*
B. *Your Bible teacher who seeks to lead you in a study of the Bible can help you to understand God's message to your heart.*
C. *Your pastor would help you to understand and to respond to God's message for your heart.*
D. *Most of us have friends whom God can use to help us understand his message.*

### VI. God continues to speak to those who will listen.

A. *God speaks to those who study the Bible.*
B. *God speaks through the message of your pastor as he preaches.*
C. *God speaks to you through the singing of hymns and songs and choruses.*
D. *God speaks to you with a still small voice by the Holy Spirit.*

### Conclusion

You would be very wise to respond as did Samuel to the voice of God. He responded by saying, "Speak; for thy servant heareth." God will speak of his love, God will speak of his plan for your life. God will speak of the help that he wants to provide you. God will speak of his hopes of what can be accomplished through your life if you will hear and heed his Word and cooperate with his purpose for you.

---

Title: "The Lord Will Do Wonders among You"

*Text:* Joshua 3:5

### Introduction

Joshua was Moses' chief assistant. When it came time for a new leader to take over following the death of Moses, Joshua was the man charged with that responsibility. In his first message to the people, he made a statement to which every young person could listen with great profit. As his people faced the difficulties of the future, he challenged them by saying, "Sanctify yourselves: for tomorrow the LORD will do wonders among you" (Josh. 3:5). Joshua believed that God wanted to accomplish wonderful things through the people with whom he lived and worked. We can make the same assumption today.

### I. The mystery of tomorrow.

No one knows what tomorrow holds. Someone has calculated that if you could correctly predict the future for five minutes, you could soon make a fortune by investing in the stock market. If you knew the future for five minutes, you could buy stocks before they went up in price and sell them immediately before they decreased. No one can predict accurately the future even for five minutes.

A. *Tomorrow can be exciting.*
B. *Tomorrow can be challenging.*
C. *Tomorrow can be sad and tragic.*
D. *Tomorrow can be filled with achievements and honors.*
E. *Tomorrow can be filled with fears and frustrations.*
F. *Tomorrow can be filled with failure and disgrace.*

### II. The meaning for today.

"Sanctify yourselves." Joshua challenged the people to recognize that their tomorrow was wrapped up in the decisions of today. The word *sanctify* means to dedicate oneself to a purpose and then voluntarily discipline oneself in order to achieve that purpose. Joshua was challenging them to dedicate themselves to their God and to his will for their lives.

A. *Have you dedicated yourself to Jesus Christ and to his will for your life?*
B. *Have you dedicated yourself to a life of purity, honesty, and truthfulness in all relationships?*
C. *Have you dedicated yourself to a program of study that will prepare you for academic achievement in the future?* You have not lived long enough yet to witness the tragedy of one being forced to drop out of college because he had neglected to apply himself while in junior high or high school.
D. *Your tomorrow is wrapped up in the decisions of today.* Your destiny tomorrow will be determined by the fork of the road you choose today.

### III. The Lord can do wonders in and through you.

A. *God will give to each one (who decides to live the life of faith and faithfulness) the gift of spiritual life.*
B. *David faced Goliath the giant with faith and courage because he had dedicated himself to God (1 Sam. 17:37).* Both his mind and his muscle were dedicated to his God.
C. *John's gospel (6:1–14) tells us of the boy who shared his lunch of five barley loaves and two small fish with Jesus so that he could multiply it to feed the multitudes.* History is filled with illustrations of those who presented their loaves and fish to Jesus Christ. He blessed them and multiplied them and accomplished great wonders through them.

### Conclusion

God is a wonder worker. He will do wonders in your life tomorrow if you dedicate yourself to him today honestly and sincerely. Dedicate yourself to doing your best today, and with God's help, wonderful things will happen in your life and through your life tomorrow.

## SENTENCE SERMONETTES

The reading of the Scriptures is preventive medicine.
The Bible is God's love letter to us.
Following every Calvary, there is an Easter Sunday.
Faith is like a muscle that grows stronger as it is exercised.
"Expect great things from God! Attempt great things for God!" (William Carey)
Gratitude is the memory of the heart.
Happiness is not a destiny but a way of life.
You cannot kill time without injuring eternity.
Nothing good is easy.
The sun never rises in hell.
Time is the womb of eternity.
Human goodness is no substitute for divine righteousness.
Destruction is more rapid than construction.
Hell is an eternal lament.
God does not want your service out of fear but out of love.
The grace of God runs faster than human transgression.
The God who made the heavens will stoop and dry our tears.
Idleness destroys happiness and corrodes the moral nature.
Our first great duty is to find the work in which we can be the most.
Atheism breeds anarchy as like begets like.
A seeking soul can never be hid from Jesus.
Christless marriages lead to godless homes and often to lawless divorces.
No man can do Christ's work except in Christ's way.
The wages of soul winners are sure, and they are paid in the coinage of eternal life.
A clean heart will clarify the mind.
Perfect love casts out selfishness.
Christ, the Timeless One, had no time to waste.
An ounce of experience is worth a ton of theory.
What people think of Christ reveals what they are themselves.
A life that has no Christian roots cannot yield Christian fruits.

# SUBJECT INDEX

# INDEX OF SCRIPTURE TEXTS

Leadership Network Innovation Series

## Sticky Church

*Larry Osborne*

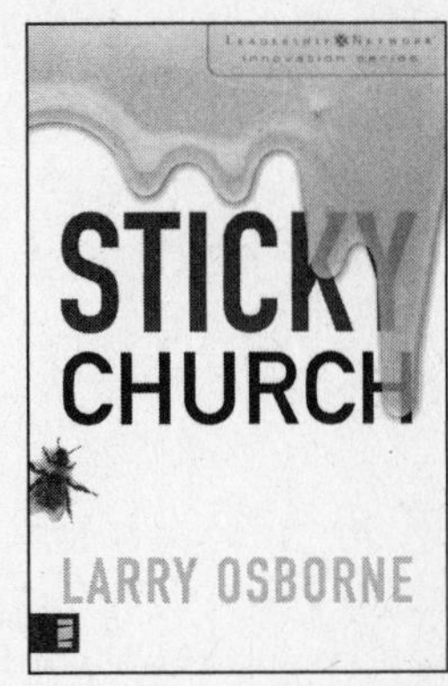


In *Sticky Church,* author and pastor Larry Osborne makes the case that closing the back door of your church is even more important than opening the front door wider. He offers a time-tested strategy for doing so: sermon-based small groups that dig deeper into the weekend message and tightly Velcro members to the ministry. It's a strategy that enabled Osborne's congregation to grow from a handful of people to one of the larger churches in the nation—without any marketing or special programming.

*Sticky Church* tells the inspiring story of North Coast Church in Oceanside, California, and offers practical tips for launching your own sermon-based small-group ministry. Topics include:

- Why stickiness is so important
- Why most of our discipleship models don't work very well
- Why small groups always make a church more honest and transparent
- What makes groups grow deeper and stickier over time

*Sticky Church* is an ideal book for church leaders who want to start or retool their small-group ministry—and Velcro their congregation to the Bible and each other.

Softcover: 978-0-310-28508-3

# It

## How Churches and Leaders Can Get It and Keep It

*Craig Groeschel*

When Craig Groeschel founded LifeChurch.tv, the congregation met in a borrowed two-car garage, with ratty furnishings and faulty audiovisual equipment. But people were drawn there, sensing a powerful, life-changing force Groeschel calls "It."

What is It, and how can you and your ministry get—and keep—It? Combining in-your-face honesty with off-the-wall humor, this book tells how any believer can obtain It, get It back, and guard It.

One of today's most innovative church leaders, Groeschel provides profile interviews with Mark Driscoll, Perry Noble, Tim Stevens, Mark Batterson, Jud Wilhite, and Dino Rizzo.

This lively book will challenge churches and their leaders to maintain the spiritual balance that results in experiencing It in their lives.

Hardcover, Printed: 978-0-310-28682-0

*Pick up a copy today at your favorite bookstore!*

# Mounce's Complete Expository Dictionary of Old and New Testament Words

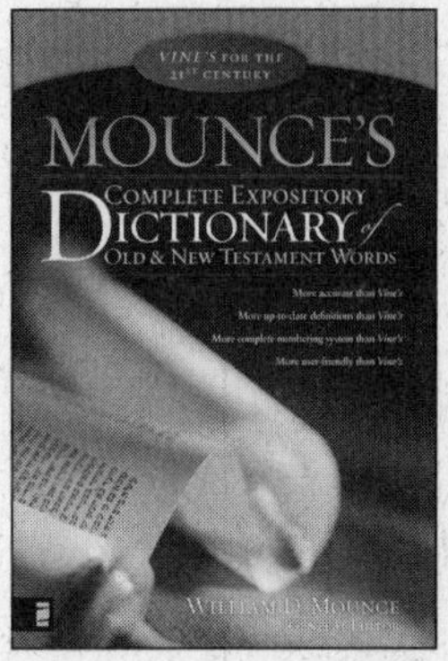


*William D. Mounce*

For years, *Vine's Expository Dictionary* has been the standard word study tool for pastors and laypeople, selling millions of copies. But sixty-plus years of scholarship have shed extensive new light on the use of biblical Greek and Hebrew, creating the need for a new, more accurate, more thorough dictionary of Bible words. William Mounce, whose Greek grammar has been used by more than 100,000 college and seminary students, is the editor of this new dictionary, which will become the layperson's gold standard for biblical word studies.

Mounce's is ideal for the reader with limited or no knowledge of Greek or Hebrew who wants greater insight into the meanings of biblical words to enhance Bible study. It is also the perfect reference for busy pastors needing to quickly get at the heart of a word's meaning without wading through more technical studies.

What makes Mounce's superior to Vine's?

- It has the most accurate, in-depth definitions based on the best of modern evangelical scholarship
- Both Greek and Hebrew words are found under each English entry, whereas Vine's separates them
- It employs both Strong's and G/K numbering systems, whereas Vine's only uses Strong's
- Mounce's accuracy is endorsed by leading scholars

Hardcover, Jacketed: 978-0-310-24878-1

*Pick up a copy today at your favorite bookstore!*

# The Promise-Plan of God

## A Biblical Theology of the Old and New Testaments

*Walter C. Kaiser Jr.*

What is the central theme of the Bible?

Given the diversity of authorship, genre, and context of the Bible's various books, is it even possible to answer such a question? Or in trying to do so, is an external grid being unnaturally superimposed on the biblical text?

These are difficult questions that the discipline of biblical theology has struggled to answer.

In this revised and expanded edition of his classic work *Toward an Old Testament Theology,* Walter Kaiser offers a solution to these unresolved issues. He proposes that there is indeed a unifying center to the theology and message of the Bible that is indicated and affirmed by Scripture itself. That center is the promise of God. It is one all-encompassing promise of life through the Messiah that winds itself throughout salvation history in both the Old and New Testaments, giving cohesiveness and unity to the various parts of Scripture.

Hardcover, Printed: 978-0-310-27586-2

*Pick up a copy today at your favorite bookstore!*

## Share Your Thoughts

**With the Author:** Your comments will be forwarded to the author when you send them to *zauthor@zondervan.com.*

**With Zondervan:** Submit your review of this book by writing to *zreview@zondervan.com.*

## Free Online Resources at www.zondervan.com/hello

**Zondervan AuthorTracker:** Be notified whenever your favorite authors publish new books, go on tour, or post an update about what's happening in their lives.

**Daily Bible Verses and Devotions:** Enrich your life with daily Bible verses or devotions that help you start every morning focused on God.

**Free Email Publications:** Sign up for newsletters on fiction, Christian living, church ministry, parenting, and more.

**Zondervan Bible Search:** Find and compare Bible passages in a variety of translations at www.zondervanbiblesearch.com.

**Other Benefits:** Register yourself to receive online benefits like coupons and special offers, or to participate in research.